Whole Child/Whole Parent

Harper's
MAGAZINE PRESS

POLLY BERRIEN BERENDS

Whole Child Whole Parent

HARPER'S MAGAZINE PRESS

PUBLISHED IN ASSOCIATION WITH HARPER & ROW, NEW YORK

Library of Congress Cataloging in Publication Data
Berends, Polly Berrien.
  Whole child, whole parent.

  Includes bibliographies.
  *1. Children—Management. 2. Children—
Care and hygiene. 3. Parent and child. 4.
Children's literature—Bibliography. I. Title.*
HQ769.B515   649'.1   73-18654
ISBN 0-06-120356-4 (pbk.)

75 76 77 78 79 10 9 8 7 6 5 4 3 2 1

Grateful acknowledgement is made for permission to reprint the following:

"Child Moon" and "Baby Toes" from *The Sandburg Range* by Carl Sandburg. Copyright 1930 by Harcourt Brace Jovanovich, Inc. Copyright 1958 by Carl Sandburg. Reprinted by permission of Harcourt Brace Jovanovich, Inc.

"i am so glad" from *Complete Poems 1913–1962* by E. E. Cummings. Copyright 1940 by E. E. Cummings. Copyright 1968 by Marion Morehouse Cummings. Reprinted by permission of Harcourt Brace Jovanovich, Inc.

"i thank you god" from *Complete Poems 1913–1962* by E. E. Cummings. Copyright 1950 by E. E. Cummings. Reprinted by permission of Harcourt Brace Jovanovich, Inc.

Passages from *The Dhammapada* translated from the Pali by P. Lal. Copyright © 1967 by P. Lal. Reprinted by permission of Farrar, Straus & Giroux, Inc.

Passages from *The Religions of Man* by Huston Smith. Copyright © 1958 by Huston Smith. Reprinted by permission of Harper & Row, Publishers, Inc.

Passages from *The Sailor Dog* by Margaret Wise Brown. Copyright 1953 by Western Publishing Company, Inc. Reprinted by permission of the publishers.

"Star Wish" from *Lullabies and Night Songs* arranged by Alec Wilder, edited by William Engvick. Copyright © 1965 by Alec Wilder and William Engvick. Reprinted by permission of Harper & Row, Publishers, Inc.

Lines from *The Way of Life: According to Laotzu*, translated by Witter Bynner. Copyright © 1944 (renewed 1972) by Witter Bynner. Reprinted by permission of John Day Company, Publisher.

Passages from *Toybook* by Steven Caney. Copyright © 1972 by Steven Caney. Reprinted by permission of Workman Publishing Co.

Contents

with unlimited gratitude to
the unreasonably faithful at Harper's
the friends wherever
the teacher who is "not even here"
the family in love
and to above all without whom
all ways now here
no thing

"Why do elephants paint their toes red?"
"I don't know, Why?"
"So they can hide in cherry trees."
"I never saw an elephant in a cherry tree."
"See, it works!"

"How are you?"
"Perfect, thank you. I'm just traveling incognito."
"Oh? As what are you disguised?"
"I am disguised as my self."
"Don't be silly. That's no disguise. It's what you are."
"On the contrary it must be a very good disguise,
    for I see that it has fooled you completely."

Beginning

What he saw as One was One, and what he saw as not One was also One. In that he saw the unity, he was of God; in that he saw the distinctions, he was of man.

–The Wisdom of Lao tse, *trans. by Lin Yutang*

Wholeness and Oneness

ABOUT THE BOOK

The word *whole* in the title of this book does not apply to the book. It refers to the children and the parents, their essential wholeness. The book is partial. It is partial to parents and children; it *aspires* to be partial to truth. The book is also not whole in the sense that it is not complete but rather only a beginning. Chronologically this book does not go much beyond the first three or four years of parenthood and childhood—and even here the surface is barely scratched. Whole also means one. This book is concerned with the idea that there is ONE and that the substance of this one is spirit rather than matter. This is not a new idea. It is older than old. Ages ago there were already a few people who said it was true. They said knowing this was the answer to everything. They were notably tranquil and beneficial people in a troubled and hostile world.

The idea of parent and child is traditionally an idea of two, of relationship between one and the other. We know having a child is a good idea and that we should be happy, yet it is so often a "mixed blessing." We wait and wait for this baby to happen to us and right away we start wondering when he will ever grow up. So he grows up and immediately we are yearning for the days when he was just a little baby. Along the way we keep letting each other down. We seem to hurt and mess up the lives of those we love most. Yet we keep knowing that the days of parent- and childhood are good. We keep wanting to have children and to become parents, and we are never quite satisfied with the idea that unhappiness is "just a fact of life." Even if we get used to it for ourselves, we cannot accept it for our children.

This book is an attempt to take the idea of *one* and to see how it is expressed in and how it might ease this circumstance we have always called two. It is either true or it isn't. It either works or it doesn't. It doesn't have to be argued or defended. First it must simply be understood. When we understand it we will be able to tell if it is true and works, or false and doesn't. So there is no effort in this book to persuade or convince, but only to find out and understand.

HOW TO USE THIS BOOK

From the most practical and mundane to the idealistic and lofty, on every level some effort has been made to discover the underlying principle at issue. Truth is either supremely practical or it isn't truth. It is only when we see how truth is relevant, how it applies to or is revealed in our most mundane experiences that any kind of realization can be said to have taken place. Sometimes it is our practical problems that drive us toward truth—when all else fails. Sometimes (less often) we start with a principle, understand it, and then see unproblematically how it is expressed in the ordinary. This book operates in both ways and needs to be read both ways. If part of it seems too philosophical or religious, it will soon turn to the concrete; if it seems too trivial, it will soon turn again to the more significant.

Where specific products or techniques are recommended, the most useful thing about the recommendation should be the principles on which the choice has been made. Products will keep changing, children will always surprise us, and we will forever be called upon to respond in new ways. But whether or not we discover them, the underlying principles must remain the same. When we don't know these principles we are only guessing—what to buy, what to say, how to act, and even what our objectives ought to be. We worry a lot or rely heavily on the opinions of others; or we try to become calloused, indifferent, or fatalistic. But it's difficult to be calloused or indifferent toward these little ones who have never meant any harm and who deserve what they expect: the best. If we can discover the principles involved, life becomes easy. Sometimes it happens—we shop successfully, guide our children harmoniously, and find ourselves momentarily able to perceive what is really happening and what is called for. Then we don't need books or techniques or strategies or assurances; we know. So that's what to look for in this book or, for that matter, in any situation—the underlying principle, something to go on.

In keeping with these ideas, the book has not been organized according to any of the usual approaches. Although it begins at a beginning (conception) and more or less ends at an end (fledgling), it is not otherwise in chronological order; in fact, it was not even written in chronological order. Neither is it organized according to types of things or kinds of activities or situations. In all of our chronological development we hope we are growing toward something, and in every activity and in every situation we are hoping to find something. Both for ourselves and for our children the real objective is happiness, which we vaguely know is not a matter of having something, doing something, going somewhere, or even becoming something. Happiness, we suspect, is a matter of certain existential qualities—spirit, fulfillment, unity, freedom, beauty, truth, and love. So this book is organized according to these existential issues or objectives, what our children might do and what we as parents might know that could lead to our finding these qualities of happiness.

ABOUT THE AUTHOR

If there is only One—one Lord, one Intelligence, one Divine Mind—an author is just someone in the audience interested enough to take notes, a spigot through which the water passes. Actually a spigot is that part of a tap which must be withdrawn in order that the liquid may flow through. That's how it is, at least, that's how it should be with an author. It's not what he knows, but how interested he is in finding out—how willing to set himself aside. It is probably error (and the suffering that accompanies it) more than anything that forces us to become interested in truth. So the author is just someone sufficiently acquainted with error to be concerned with seeking truth instead of just carrying on or getting by.

A RAFT FOR CROSSING: QUOTATIONS

Quotations here and there in this book are intended to show the relevance of the great mystical teachings to the practical experience of child-rearing and, at the same time, to bring to light the far-reaching spiritual significance of even the meanest momentary details of our experience as parents. In the introduction to his translation of the *Tao te Ching*, R. B. Blakney writes:

The remarkable unanimity of the great mystics of China, India, Persia, the Holy Lands and Europe is one of the truly impressive facts of the spiritual history of the human race.

–Blakney, *The Way of Life, Lao Tzu*

It *is* remarkable and worthy of investigation that so many wise men independently of each other saw life in so much the same way and in such radical contrast to the views of those around them. One thing they all insisted on is that freedom from preconceptions is an absolute prerequisite to any realization of spiritual understanding. Another thing they have all maintained absolutely is the importance of not confusing the teacher as a redemptive person with the redemptive teaching. To be loving parents, to be wise, to be happy—it is all the same; everything clung to has to be let go.

Pai-chang asked: "What is the ultimate end of Buddhism?"
Ma-tsu said: "This is just where you give up your life."

–D. T. Suzuki, *Zen Buddhism*

Jesus said "If any man would come after me, let him deny himself and take up his cross and follow me. For whoever would save his life will lose it, and whoever loses his life for my sake will find it.

–Matthew 10:39

Buddha said: "Only he crosses the stream of life who wishes to know what is known as unknowable."

–*The Dhammapada*, trans. by P. Lal

He also said: "Monks listen to the parable of the raft. A man going on a journey sees ahead of him a vast stretch of water. There is no boat within sight, and no bridge. To escape from the dangers of this side of the bank, he builds a raft for himself out of grass, sticks, and branches. When he crosses over, he realizes how useful the raft has been to him and wonders if he should not lift it on his shoulders and take it away with him. If he did this, would he be doing what he should do?"
"No."
"Or, when he has crossed over to safety, should he keep it back for someone else to use, and leave it, therefore, on dry and high ground? This is the way I have taught Dhamma [teachings], for crossing, not for keeping. Cast aside even right states of mind, monks, let alone wrong ones, and remember to leave the raft behind."

–*The Dhammapada*, trans. by P. Lal

Many of the quotations in this book are from the Bible (King James and Revised Standard Versions) and from the teachings of Buddhism and Taoism. They are but the sticks, branches, and grass which may be useful to some as a raft for crossing over. But remember to leave the raft behind. Do not get caught up on either bank of the stream with the raft itself and with questions about whether it is better to be a Taoist or Christian or Buddhist. On the near bank it is easier to build a raft using everything buoyant that we can get our hands on. There is no advantage to using only maple or only pine, especially if one is in a hurry to cross over. On the far bank the raft is no longer necessary and will in fact impede our progress if we linger over it or try to take it with us.

Booknotes

Nearly 500 books are annotated and recommended in the following pages. Some are listed by topic in each chapter and a great many language-building and storybooks appear in the chapter called "Truth," which is almost entirely devoted to books.

With the exception of a few fall 1974 titles, the bibliographies in this book include books published through spring 1974. All prices quoted were updated in January 1975 and are subject to change. See the Book Title Index at the back of the book for prices.

In preparing the bibliography of children's books between 3,000 and 5,000 books had to be read and considered. And perhaps here is the best place to extend profound thanks to the many publishers who responded so generously by simply sending their books for consideration—boxes and boxes of books! Though it seemed a hopelessly large undertaking, there was no other way to make a selection since most publishers do not list books for preschoolers separately. The youngest age level in most catalogs is kindergarten or preschool–

3rd grade, lumping together the spoon-feds with the lunch-pailers, the nontalkers with the readers.

Not much has been published with the preschooler specifically in mind. Some of the best materials are to be found among the easy-to-read books for older children which are carefully and concretely written with clear communication in mind. Among the least appropriate are the super-sophisticated picture books that appeal to many adults but mean very little to preschoolers. Also of little value to purchase for the home are some expensive hardcover concept books which have been prepared especially for preschoolers but which have no value after the child acquires the minimal amount of basic information included in them. Many of these would be worth buying in paperback but as $4 and $5 and $6 hardcovers are better borrowed from the library.

Best are the real storybooks—the few around that can be boiled down to terms understandable by the preschooler and used first as a picture book, then as a word book, then as a concept book, and finally as a story book.

For the most part paperbacks are the only purchases that make sense, especially on the preschool level. Instead of one hardcover at $5 (which may or may not be on target and which in any case will probably be outgrown in a month or two), it is possible to buy five paperbacks among which several are likely to be useful and one may even become a long-time favorite. Paperbacks are relatively inexpensive and so far they tend to be the cream of the crop, the tried and true titles publishers know will sell. Publishers would put more titles into paperback if they could sell more paperbacks. So the possibility of offering parents fully annotated lists of carefully chosen *inexpensive* books seemed ideal, good for every one. It had to be attempted.

We had hoped to list specific worthwhile titles from among the very inexpensive (19–39¢) mass-market lists. However, because of their vast number (approximately 500 per publisher) and the fact that they are in print only on a fluctuating basis, it was not possible to do this with the exception of the Little Golden Books. But do be on the lookout for the wonderful bargains among the Elf, Wonder, and Tell-a-Tale books. Just be sure to read through them before you buy them. And remember that, like everything else, the prices of books are constantly changing.

Another nearly categorical omission in this bibliography are some pleasant and well-illustrated expensive hardcover books that are worth borrowing from the library but not necessary to own. It is a good idea to borrow these from the library, which is the best place to shop for hardcover children's books anyway. Take one out. If you and your child have read it five or ten times and it's overdue and still going strong, maybe you should consider buying a copy. In any case, owning books is no substitute for trips to the library, which are always a treat. Let the preschoolers choose their own books, attend story hours if there are any for their age group, and listen to records. As good as the zoo and more edifying.

Book selection criteria

In selecting children's books these priorities (not necessarily in order of importance) were adhered to as carefully as possible.

Price—Preschoolers, perhaps almost more than children of any other age, should *have* as many books as possible. We asked: Is this inexpensive book worth reading, say, 10 times? Is this more expensive book worth so much that it should be owned rather than simply taken out of the library? Except for the big books (anthologies, songbooks, wordbooks) titles over $2 were included only on grounds of all-around superiority, extreme interest to preschoolers (classics by juvenile acclaim), or their ability to make a special contribution to the child's life or world view.

Effectiveness—Is the book inviting, entertaining, relevant, and understandable by the child? If it isn't interesting, it is worthless and most books that are dull really lack authenticity. Partly interest is a matter of timing, but some books are a bore regardless. To determine which books were effective with preschoolers we tried them out on a variety of children under 4 years old. The main virtues all the books that "worked" with the children had in common were concreteness and a good dramatic structure.

Informative value—Does this book provide the child with some useful information? The main concern of the preschool child is what to expect in the wide world and how he should behave in it. More strictly factual books are listed elsewhere in this book according to topic.

Beauty—In both art and text does it foster the child's appreciation of beauty by being well crafted and designed, graceful, original, beautiful? On the preschool level some especially important qualities of beauty are efficiency (clarity and simplicity of expression), vitality, brightness, and joy.

Truth—Is it, on some level, expressive of existential meaning? On the preschool level this means mostly does it foster the child's positive expectancy of life in general and his growth as an enthusiastic, friendly, and confident *individual*. On a deeper level it is also desirable for a book to express significant philosophical or spiritual understanding for the child who will remember the book in years to come, and for the parent of the present who must read it aloud so many times.

The ideal read-aloud book inspires the parent now and the child when grown while in the meantime offering the child of the present appreciable values, good models, exposure to beauty, useful information, and good entertainment. This was the best we sought. Minimally we tried to rule out books that were totally contrary to the values expressed in this book and those that seemed merely inane.

Book specifications

It is easier to anticipate what a book will be like and thus to choose effectively titles that are what you want if you read the physical descriptions of them as well as the notations about content. Here is how to interpret the specifications given in this book:

Measurements—Width is given first, then height; for example, 7″ x 4½″. It is the page size that is measured not the cover. All measurements are rounded off to the nearest ¼″.

Binding—What is really important in a binding is the sewing rather than the material of the cover. Except for paperbacks, almost all books are covered with cardboard wrapped in either paper or cloth. *Hardcover* is used to describe the really sturdily bound books,

strongly sewn and glued. *Board* refers to books with cardboard covers (with or without dust jackets) whose binding is adequate but less secure. Paperbacks obviously are books covered with stiff paper or flexible cardboard.

Color—The term 1 color means that the art is the same color as the type (this includes black-and-white photographs). The term 4 colors includes "full" color (though actually more than 4 colors may be required to produce a really brilliant picture) plus certain less full techniques employing 4 flat colors or screens. Where two color terms are given, the use of color usually alternates: two pages may have black-and-white illustrations while the next two may be in three colors. If no color descriptive is given, there is no artwork.

Length—Publishers start counting pages in a variety of places, depending on the production procedures they are following. To simplify matters in this book all pages, including the pasted-down sides of the endpapers, have been reckoned into the total page count.

Author and Artist—All the children's books listed are illustrated. Where no illustrator is mentioned the illustrations have been done by the author.

Level—The recommended children's books have been roughly broken down into levels (1–4) of sophistication, interest, and difficulty for the preschooler. It is very important that these numbers not be misconstrued as signifying age. Though many of these books were originally intended (and may indeed be worthwhile) for older children, every one has been appreciated by a number of children 3 years old and younger. Whether a book is appropriate for a child depends less on the child's age than on his interest and previous book

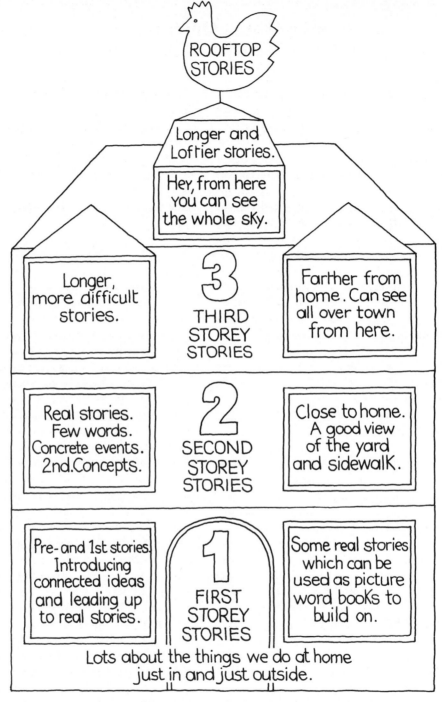

ROOFTOP STORIES

Longer and Loftier stories.

Hey, from here you can see the whole sky.

3
THIRD STOREY STORIES

Longer, more difficult stories.

Farther from home. Can see all over town from here.

2
SECOND STOREY STORIES

Real stories. Few words. Concrete events. 2nd. Concepts.

Close to home. A good view of the yard and sidewalk.

1
FIRST STOREY STORIES

Pre- and 1st stories. Introducing connected ideas and leading up to real stories.

Some real stories which can be used as picture word books to build on.

Lots about the things we do at home just in and just outside.

MY BOOK HOUSE

and life experience; and, of course, some of the best books make different contributions at different levels. The opposite diagram summarizes the distinctions between levels as they have been applied in this book. Except for the storybooks, which are grouped according to level in the chapter entitled "Truth," these levels are indicated by a parenthesized number at the end of each book description.

Stars—Books preceded by a star (*) are titles that seem superior to us. We think a home library containing all starred titles would be well equipped for a preschooler.

Love and Knowledge: The Ideal as the Real

Throughout this century there have been many theories of child-rearing, all emphasizing parental love or authority or the striking of a proper balance between the two as the secret to raising whole, happy children. Each theory has offered some people some assistance with their children. But where they all fall short is in endowing parents with the love we need to be loving and the knowledge we need to be authoritative. No matter how much we agree that love and authority are desirable and necessary, we still struggle to locate and tap the resource that will make us loving and assured. Where love is called for we find ourselves short-tempered or apathetic; where authority is called for we find ourselves frustrated or uncertain. So the question is where do we get the love to be loving? where the understanding on which to speak with authority?

A premise of this book is that love and knowing have to come together. Authority must be based on knowledge of truth and the knowledge on which authority must be based is love. Likewise love must be based on knowledge, on knowing authoritatively that love, lovingness, lovability (goodness) are the truth about us, our children, and life itself. In other words love is not primarily sentimental or physical or psychological; it is idea(l). Therefore it must be known before it can be genuinely expressed. No matter how hard we try, it is not possible to be loving at the same time that we perceive ourselves or our children as even momentarily unlovable or in any essential way bad. We can only be loving when we are aware of goodness.

Everybody agrees that love is ideal, but by ideal most of us mean unreal—desirable maybe, but more than can be expected. In this book, however, the idea(l) is assumed to be real. Where the ideal is not what we experience in our lives, it is only unknown, unrealized. The content of knowledge is never something you can hold in your hand; it is always idea. Logically then the only true knowledge we can ever have is ideal. The ideal is not unreal; it is the real unrealized. Ideal man is only unrealized man, that is, man who has not realized the truth about himself. The same is true of the ideal loving parent and child. The quest to realize love (the love that is knowledge, the knowledge that is love) is the heart's desire and the lifelong task of both parent and child. It is the only valid purpose of our being together and the only workable way.

To show the practicality of this perspective, much attention is given in this book to such things as books, equipment and play activities. Yet our main concern is not with attitudes or techniques of child-rearing, but with the quest for an understanding that can bring love into our lives and the lives of our children as realization. Even where products and activities are discussed, the concern must not be simply with having or doing or saying the right (or even the effective) parental thing, but with perceiving and realizing the truth of ideal reality. It is the only practical way. No technique or toy or statement can ever be anything more than a stopgap measure unless it is based upon an awareness of truth, a truly realistic perception of reality. Wherever such perception exists, everything we need to have or do or say follows as spontaneous byproduct and love becomes effortless.

Each chapter in this book has an idea as its title, a quality or aspect of idea(1) reality which all of us are seeking. These titles are not so much descriptions of the chapter contents as they are goals *in the light of which* everything in the chapters should be considered. The first chapter deals a little bit with the initial issues of parenthood: conception, pregnancy, preparation, delivery, and such fundamental concerns of the early days and years as eating and sleeping. It is suggested that these subjects be considered in the light of *spirit*. The substance of an idea is spirit. If we wish to be parents in the spirit of love, we must first know love. We will have to understand that the spirit of love is, in fact, the substance of our being.

It seems to be a given in the human condition that we do not already understand what we need to understand. So there is no shame to be entertained in connection with our failures as parents or our struggles with our children. Problems are inevitable, but having admitted that, we can take joy from the fact that they are not necessary. We do not have to settle for them or allow them to last.

The ideal never begins and never ends. In any situation look for that which is eternally so. Try to distinguish it from the passing. What will pass or what wasn't before is nothing more than a negative sign of the eternally true we do not yet know. Everything we need to know (and, hence, have, do, or say) follows from our simply letting go of the passing, and acknowledging the eternal. In this way the needed love and authority can be immediately released to us and through us.

There is so much to look forward to when a baby is on the way. Parenthood is surely among the most beautiful of all phases of human existence. But it is valuable to know just what it is that we are looking forward to, and to make sure that our anticipation is valid. Otherwise we are in for a shock. While it is obviously a mistake to have children because of not having anything better to do, if we are to be happy with this blessing it is important for us to know *at the very least* that we haven't anything better to do at the time. It is easy enough to feature ourselves charmed by the gurgling, smiling baby or the so earnest child bursting with sincerity and sweet questions—and certainly this is all part of the wonderful way it is. But how many times a day do you picture yourself vaulting the table and saying evenly, "Oh no, darling, you'll have to *drink* your milk before you can get the macaroni out of the bottom of the glass." At how many ten-minute intervals in how many nocturnal hours will you get up cheerfully when your not-quite-housebroken toddler crawls into bed with you, pulls off his disposable diaper and announces brightly, "I have to pee!"?

A sense of humor helps a lot, but there is only one way to look forward to all this with realistically happy anticipation, and that is to have a pretty clear idea of what's in it for us. Realistically speaking, realization of ideal reality is the whole point. Parenthood is just the world's most intensive course in love. Yet we are not becoming parents merely to give or to get love. Rather we are to discover love as a fact of life and the truth of our being, and so bring it into expression as the fact it is rather than the impossible dream it has always seemed. When we know that love is who we are, to be authoritatively loving toward our children will be a glorious matter of course.

Jesus said: "Before Abraham was, I am."
–John 8:58

Hui-Neng said, "If you come for the faith, stop all thy hankerings. Think not of good, think not of evil, but see what at this moment thy own original face doth look like, which thou hast even prior to thy own birth."
—D. T. Suzuki, *Zen Buddhism*

Buddha said, "Be a lamp to your self, be like an island. Struggle hard, be wise. Cleansed of weakness, you will find freedom from birth and old age."
–*The Dhammapada*, trans. by P. Lal

Jesus said, "You must be born again."
–John 3:7

John said, "In the beginning was the word."
–John 1:1

Spirit

Meister Eckhart said, "The seed of God is in us. Given an intelligent and hard-working farmer and a diligent field hand, it will thrive and grow up to God, whose seed it is; and accordingly its fruits will be God-nature. Pear seeds grow into pear trees, nut seeds into nut trees, and God seed into God."

—*Meister Eckhart,* trans. by R. B. Blakney

In the beginning was the word.

—John 1:1

Getting the Idea

CONCEPTION

Mostly it is said that we *get* pregnant, *give* birth, and *have* babies. But if getting, giving, and having are all we understand of this process, both we and our children are likely to be quite miserable. The important thing, to us and to our children, is that we become parents. Having children doesn't turn us into parents, it just makes us busy. It takes becoming fatherly, motherly, parently to make us parents. Conception begins when we first conceive the idea of becoming parents. Now we are responsible for learning what this means and for redefining ourselves accordingly. For this we can use at least nine months. A good question to start with is: What's so great about a baby coming, what's so great about becoming a parent? A lot of us have children before we ever consider these things. But it's better to give the idea a little thought as soon as it occurs to us, as soon as we conceive.

THE PARENTING IS TO THE PARENT

It is seeming clearer and clearer that the parent/child relationship exists as much for the parents' growth as for the child's. While the physical maintenance of the child may be a full-time job for the parents, the child's growth seems more or less to take care of itself until adolescence when he becomes responsible for consciously seeking maturity. In the meantime his dependency on us, though total, is actually fairly superficial. We say the child in the womb is completely dependent on his mother, but he is not depending on her to be his mother—she is merely his environment. As long as this environment is adequate his unfoldment toward birth goes on, regardless of whether the mother knows much about motherhood or children.

After birth, things are only slightly different (although our experience is vastly different). Childhood, too, seems to be a temporary condition to be outgrown, and it is given to the child himself to hunger and thirst after whatever he needs to help him do this. The mother is still only the environment—though now a more obviously mental and spiritual one than a physical one—and the caretaker of this environment.

In short, we do not mold, make, raise, bring up, the child at all. We can help or hinder, but our basic responsibility is mostly custodial.

So who needs whom? Of course the child needs the parent, and we are all too aware of the damage that can be wrought by ignorant, irresponsible, or overzealous parenting. But a less obvious and yet existentially vital fact is that most of us need our children. There are a few people walking this earth who learn the arts of motherliness and fatherliness without children, and they are very wise. But most of us benefit from the big push our children give us toward the discovery of these qualities—qualities which are absolutely necessary to our fulfillment and of more lasting value than most of the lessons of childhood. We learn them for the sake of our children, but they benefit us most of all. Once we have learned to be truly motherly and fatherly (we need, of course, to become both) we will always be much happier. The gain is not the having of children; it is the discovery of love and how to be loving. The foundation of love is the knowledge of goodness. The qualities of this love are receptivity, patience, innocence, humility, trust, gratitude, generosity, understanding, and the desire to be good for goodness' sake. Interestingly enough all these qualities are perceivable in the purity of infancy. The child is thus among the finest proofs and teachers of love. And there is no discordant experience that cannot be harmonized by the realization of love.

It is not anachronistic to be singing the praises of motherhood at a time when women are concerned with women's liberation. Of course every woman should be liberated from all the absurd prejudicial ignorance that confines and defines her as some sort of living household appliance and sex resource. But there are levels of liberation to be had, and once we know we aren't first-class sex objects and second-class citizens (it is only important that *we* know it) we will find ourselves yearning for yet higher levels of freedom.

Wherever men have been left out in this book, it is where they have not yet opted in. Women's lib, men's lib; it is all the same. All anyone can do to help anybody in this world, including the children, is to find the way himself.

Each man to himself, and each woman to herself, such is the word of the past and present, and the word of immortality;
No one can acquire for another—not one!
No one can grow for another—not one!

The song is to the singer, and comes back most to him;
The teaching is to the teacher, and comes back most to him;
The murder is to the murderer, and comes back most to him;
The theft is to the thief, and comes back most to him;
The love is to the lover, and comes back most to him;
The gift is to the giver, and comes back most to him —it cannot fail;
The oration is to the orator, the acting is to the actor and actress, not to the audience;
And no man understands any greatness or goodness but his own, or the indication of his own.

—Walt Whitman, *A Song of the Rolling Earth (A Carol of Words*

If Tao (the Way) could be made a present, everybody would have presented it to his parents. If Tao could be told about, everybody would have spoken to his brothers about it. If Tao could be inherited, everybody would have bequeathed it to his children and grandchildren. But no one could do it.

While Pregnant: Meditations and Preparations

Unto us a child IS BORN
Unto us a son IS GIVEN
Not OUT OF us
    BY us
    FROM us
Not we are going to MAKE
    we are going to HAVE
    we are going to GET
But UNTO US A CHILD IS,
    IS BORN!

• Don't go overboard on the study of pregnancy, obstetrics, pediatrics, or child psychology. Study parenthood. What is the ideal mother? What is the ideal father?
• Don't go overboard on maternity clothes either. Like any other clothes, maternity clothes are mostly a matter of individual taste. The only valid guidelines are practical ones. A great variety of unnecessary maternity accessories is available. For example, while you may need underpants and bras a size or two bigger than usual by the end of your pregnancy, you do not need special maternity bras or pants or corsets at higher prices than normal ones.

As for outer garments, it is a good idea to buy them when you need them, but no sooner. If you buy maternity clothes too early in your pregnancy, you may outgrow them before the end. It is just as important to look nice while pregnant as when not pregnant, but this does not depend upon having a large wardrobe. A few well-chosen outfits which fit loosely and are drip-dry will do nicely. If elastic waistbands are uncomfortably tight or too loose, sever them and sew tapes to the ends and tie them according to your comfort. In some stores panels can be bought for temporarily converting slacks and skirts to accommodate your greatness. Knee-length dresses are more comfortable if worn slightly longer than usual. Pants suits with tunic tops are totally satisfactory. And be grateful for any opportunities to borrow that may come your way, especially expensive items such as winter coats. Most people are happy to share their stock of maternity clothes which are, after all, worn for only a few months.

If necessary, maternity clothes can be purchased by direct mail through the catalogs of most large department stores. For $1, Mothercare, Ltd. (Cherry Tree Road, Watford WD2 5SH, England) offers a superb 196-page, 4-color catalog of maternity and baby clothes and supplies. But start early if you wish to deal with Mothercare as it takes time to get the catalog and then to order and receive what you want. Remember pregnancy is only 9 months and the real pregnant part is only about half of that.
• Learn some lullabies.
• Make some toys.
• Practice being motherly while brushing your teeth, grocery shopping, and riding the bus, where hugging and gushing and being a soft bosom or lap have no relevance. Learn to regard and pay respect silently to the perfection of everyone and everything in every situation, especially when it is not at all apparent.

Disassociate all seeming imperfection from the reality of the person (yourself included), situation, or activity with which you are confronted. *Let* perfection reveal itself.

• Tie-dye or embroider some crib sheets. The easiest way to "tie" is to place rubber bands around bunches of the fabric. Use already prepared liquid dyes, at double strength.

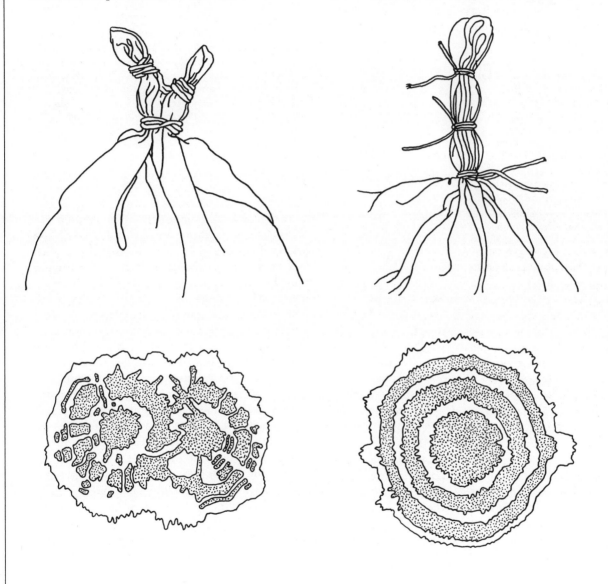

- Fix up the baby's corner or room.
- Meditate on the idea of *letting*. Letting to be born. Letting sleep. Letting be. Letting mature. Also *fostering* and *encouraging*.
- When your belly is as big as a bushel basket, sing the old slave spiritual "This Little Tiny Light of Mine."

This little tiny light of mine,
I'm gonna let it shine.
This little tiny light of mine,
I'm gonna let it shine.
This little tiny light of mine,
I'm gonna let it shine.
Let it shine, let it shine, let it shine.

Hide it under a bushel? No!
I'm gonna let it shine.
Hide it under a bushel? No!
I'm gonna let it shine.
Hide it under a bushel? No!
I'm gonna let it shine.
Let it shine, let it shine, let it shine.

- Hang a hook for a mobile over the crib.
- Make a mobile to hang from it.
- Get rid of all the old clothes in your closet —the ones you've been saving in case they might come back into style. Do the same thing with worthless, old-fashioned ideas you have closeted in your head. Also get rid of the things and thoughts you still wear that are not becoming.
- Meditate on the word *carry* and try to distinguish between its spiritual and its material meanings. Carrying high. Carrying low. Stop carrying on and carry on. Don't get carried away. Let yourself be carried along.

Hearken to me . . . all . . . which are borne by me
from the belly, which are carried from the womb;

and even to your old age I am he; and even to hoar hairs will I carry you: I have made, and I will bear; even I will carry and will deliver you.

–Isaiah 46:3–4

And the dragon stood before the woman which was ready to be delivered, for to devour her child as soon as it was born. And she brought forth a man child who was to rule all nations with a rod of iron; and her child was caught up unto God, and to his throne. And the woman fled into the wilderness where she hath a place prepared of God in which to be nourished for a thousand, two hundred, and threescore days.

–Revelation 12:4–6

Things

Baby seat—This is a sort of bookstand for babies to eat, sleep, be awake, and travel in—a place where the baby can see what's going on and be a part of things without straining to hold her head up or being held. These are a fairly recent development, and it's hard to imagine what parents ever did (with us!) without them. Dinner is ready and your baby won't sleep? Put her on the table in her baby seat. You'll have a more peaceful hot dinner and she'll soon be lulled to sleep by the conversation. For the wide-awake 2- to 5-month-old who wants to use his hands, the baby seat has one drawback: dropped toys fall out of sight and reach. But put the whole seat into a highchair with some interesting things on the tray to look at and learn to pick up. Or turn a cardboard carton the right size on its side as a desk as shown. □

[*Note:* See Additional Information at the back of this book regarding specific products.]

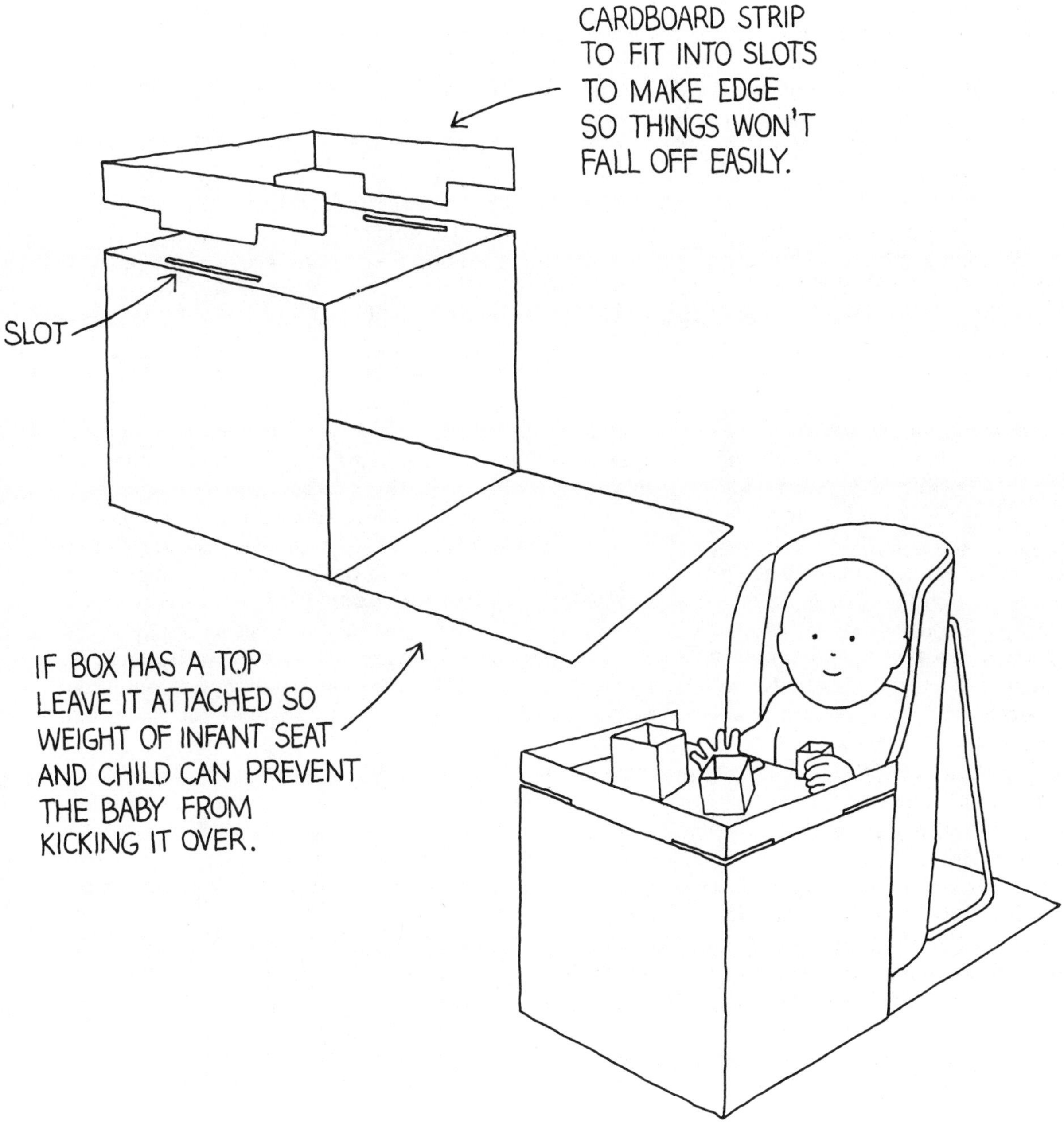

CARDBOARD STRIP
TO FIT INTO SLOTS
TO MAKE EDGE
SO THINGS WON'T
FALL OFF EASILY.

SLOT

IF BOX HAS A TOP
LEAVE IT ATTACHED SO
WEIGHT OF INFANT SEAT
AND CHILD CAN PREVENT
THE BABY FROM
KICKING IT OVER.

Comfortable chair—A rocking chair with armrests *is* all it's cracked up to be for nursing and lulling a baby in. But whether it rocks or not, be sure to have some sort of very comfortable place to sit down on in the baby's room.

All the better to see, hear, and feel with, my dear—A mobile over the crib, a music box or a bell, a soft and smooth (latex) or furry toy, and a soft light for looking at are all that's needed in the toy department at first. See the chapters called "Unity," and "Beauty" for specific suggestions regarding small toys, mobiles, and music boxes.

Rug—A really cheerful patchwork rug can be inexpensively made from carpet samples available in carpet stores. Sometimes you have to pay for them and sometimes you can get them for free. A nice pattern can be achieved by cutting the samples into modular pieces. For example, use only two shapes—a square and a rectangle exactly half as big as the square. This gives a nice random effect, and it's easy to make the edges come out even. Cut from the back with an X-acto knife or single-edged razor blade. To attach the pieces you can either use iron-on rug binding or glue the pieces to a large sheet of canvas or burlap. The former is easier and adequate; the latter is sturdier.

Baby bath—Tubs are cumbersome and generally not worth the trouble. While it's easier to bathe the baby in a tub on the table than in a regular tub, it is not easier to carry the whole thing to and from the sink. Very heavy and very sloshy. Also very temporary. As soon as the baby can sit up by herself, she will have the most fun in the big tub anyway. Unless you have a counter beside your sink where the baby tub can be filled, used, and emptied, skip this purchase. □

There are various other ways of coping. A good-sized kitchen sink makes a fine tub for a baby. And the regular bath tub is perfectly good as long as you don't object to getting down on your knees. Just put an inch or two of water on the bottom and let her lie on her back, splashing and kicking to her heart's content. Another nice idea, though not practical on a day-in day-out basis, is to take the baby into the bath with you. After all, she's used to floating around.

Changing table—Buy one that suits you or improvise. In the beginning you can use one end of the crib. If you have an auxiliary portable crib for trips, use it for your changing table. With the mattress in the high, infant position, it is ideal—spacious and safe.

Changing mat—In the early days you may find it handy to have an extra changing station near the kitchen or in the living room. Just a good-sized rubber sheet will do, or from Mothercare, Ltd., you can buy an excellent pad for this purpose—vinyl-covered foam with raised edges to prevent the baby from rolling off. □

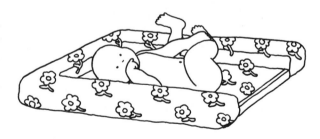

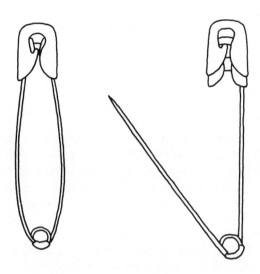

Safety pins—The plastic-headed safety pins which are most readily available are not safe. Sooner or later the plastic cracks and the pin-point fairly shoots out. Regular metal safety pins (heavy ones) are preferable. Even better are those with an extra sliding metal cap which actually locks the pin closed. Try the old cake of soap trick if you have difficulty pushing pins through diapers. Just keep the pins stuck in a cake of soap by the changing table. Or forget the whole thing and use disposable diapers with tapes. More expensive but so easy it's funny. □

Indispensable dispenser—Mount a toilet paper dispenser on the wall beside the place where you will be changing diapers, and forget about tissues, tidy wipes, cotton balls, cozy cleans, and supersorbants for clean-ups. They are expensive and no better in the end (on the end? for the end? between the ends?) than the most obvious but last-to-be-thought-

of toilet paper. Install the dispenser out of reach of your child who, remember, will be standing, reaching, and unrolling before he's out of diapers.

OINTMENT: A MEDITATION

You may wish to buy a good-sized jar of some sort of all-purpose ointment in the preparation for the coming baby. But at the same time it is important to reject the notion that the baby will have to have diaper rash because all babies do. The worst kind of pollution is mental pollution and among the most prevalent pollutants are the many little worries in circulation concerning our babies' physiological and psychological ill-being. The list includes colic, diaper rash, cradle cap, gas, teething, reactions to injections, the need to suck, getting buckteeth from sucking, spoiling, food allergies, attachment to bottle, attachment to security blanket, and later on the "terrible twos," sibling rivalry, Oedipus complex, and Electra complex, *ad infinitum*.

The big trouble with these ideas begins when we as parents accept them into our consciousness. Once established as belief they tend to become self-fulfilling prophecies. Some of these ideas we accepted so long ago that we do not even recognize them as beliefs. We have come to rely on them as excuses ("So *that's* what's the matter with him!" she sighed thankfully). We even refer to them resignedly as "facts of life." Moreover we are constantly being bombarded with new ideas for distress and an infinite variety of embellishments on the old ones. They are presented in various insidious ways. An advertisement for a skin preparation begins, "When your baby gets diaper rash . . ." *When,* it says. Not *if,* but *when!*

And when the dragon saw that he was cast unto the earth, he persecuted the woman which brought forth the man child. And to the woman were given two wings of a great eagle, that she might fly into the wilderness, into her place where she is to be nourished for a time, and times, and half a time, from the face of the serpent.
–Revelation 12:13–14

Now the fact is that, while almost nobody escapes all these problems, hardly anyone is afflicted with them all either. And there isn't anything on the list that everyone experiences. It's amazing if you stop to think about it. Evidently, while the experience of some discomforts is more or less inevitable, not one is an absolute necessity of life. So it is possible that our babies can grow up without suffering all the discomforts we have always taken for granted. The early years of child- and parenthood can be free of many of these problems and the rigamarole and anguish that accompany them. It is equally useless to blame ourselves or fear such little difficulties when they occur, but there is no point in insisting on or clinging to them either.

Oil has been employed by man as a symbol for both good and evil. It is *the* environmental pollutant, heedlessly dumped into the waterways, damaging and destroying and sliming up life and beauty. The water becomes unpotable and the ducks upon it so encumbered that they drown. Right there in its most suitable environment the healthy duck designed for floating drowns! There is just as much water in the river and just as much health in the duck, but the polluting oil interferes with their effectively being what they truly are. The rapport between the duck and the river is blocked; they can no longer jointly manifest the principle of buoyancy.

It is important to note that such pollution can occur only as the essential purity and worth of the river and the life it supports are not perceived and appreciated in the first place. The real pollution, therefore, is mental.

In parenthood the water is love and the river is the individual consciousness of the parent. The duck is, of course, the child—fully equipped, paddling somewhere through the parent's sphere of consciousness. The love is there—abundant and sustaining. The child is whole. The parent is whole. Love will flow through us to support the child entirely as long as there are no interfering pollutants in our stream of consciousness.

As with any other form of pollution, purification is what is needed. Like the waterways, the rivers of our minds are already polluted; indeed it seems that we cannot come to an appreciation of purity until we have suffered the consequences of pollution. So purification means first of all a clean-up operation, recognizing and ridding our thoughts of certain old unquestioned beliefs and concerns. To some extent this is a simple matter of affirming that "it ain't necessarily so." But this purification is one of the most important tasks of pregnancy.

Purification also means exercising discrimination over the new ideas we admit into consciousness regarding life itself, ourselves as pregnant, and, above all, our children as living beings.

But no purification is possible apart from

an appreciation of purity. Unless the essential purity and sufficiency of both love and the child as an expression of love are perceived and valued it is not possible to become pure. Everything material reflects or is symbolic of some idea. As a symbol, diaper rash can be seen as expressing the idea of friction. All the discomforts listed at the outset are in some sense frictional. As an idea, friction is an expression of dualism—the belief in two powers, positive and negative, good and bad. It is the same as saying that love is not enough—something else is stronger or something else is needed or something else *is*. But insofar as we are able to perceive the sufficiency of love as the only and abundant power, both the idea and the experience of friction can be minimized, allowing instead the realization of buoyancy, flow, at-onement.

So it is important, both during the preparatory period of pregnancy and in all our days, that we constantly seek awareness of the sufficiency of love and the essential perfection of our children. Despite all appearances and suggestions to the contrary, we must constantly hold in the forefront of our thoughts the perfect, whole, unmarrable essential nature of the child and the power of love to bear him up. This is not simply the power of positive or wishful or magical thinking. We do not cause or influence anything to be good any more than we make the river pure by not dumping garbage into it. If we don't dump garbage into the river, the purity of the river remains apparent. Wholeness, goodness, perfection are the truth of being. By not entertaining negative thoughts, we are simply allowing this wholeness the best opportunity to become evident. Such purifica-tion is one of the most basic aspects of man's role in love. Love is not done; it is allowed.

Thou who art of purer eyes than to behold evil and canst not look on iniquity.
—Habakkuk 1:13

Beloved, we are God's children now; it doth not yet appear what we shall be, but we know that when he shall appear we shall be like him, for we shall see him as he is. And every man that hath this hope in him purifieth himself even as he is pure.
I John 3:2–3

The other historical use of oil as a symbol is for anointment. First there is purification and then the anointing or acknowledging and honoring of essential wholeness, perfection, goodness. It is an act of hallowing that really occurs in the mind of the one doing the anointing. The little jars of ointment we buy for our babies should be this kind of oil. We bathe our children, washing away impurities with pure water, and then we oil them with fine ointment that no friction or chafing may occur. At the same time we must purify our thoughts, washing away the belief in two powers—the fears that our children are not quite perfect, that love is not enough protection for them. Then through the acknowledgment of the reality of only one power we can allow real ointment, the oil of love to soothe and bless us and our children. Perhaps ultimately the ointment itself is not really necessary (who provides the duck with the protective feather oil that keeps him afloat on the water?), but we can use it gratefully as we try to purify our thoughts.

More and more doctors are suspecting more and more diseases and afflictions of being psychosomatic in nature, and a few of these doctors venture to suggest that thought may be the underlying factor in all matters of health and sickness. But, by themselves, such ideas may not be truly helpful. In fact, without additional understanding they may awaken exacerbating self-justificatory and self-blaming anxieties in those already afflicted. If illness is psychosomatic, then for healing to take place it is necessary for the underlying unhealthy or false ideas to be replaced by healthy, true ones. Beliefs have to be dispelled by understanding, not by contrary beliefs. In the meantime it is, of course, often necessary to treat symptoms medically. Even to know *about* the healthy true ideas is not sufficient One cannot arbitrarily cease from taking medicine or giving it to one's child simply on the basis of a theoretical knowledge that a disease is mental any more than you can step out on a tightrope or, even worse, allow your child to do so, on the basis that you know it is possible. It *is* possible, but you have to have a keen immediate rapport with the law of gravity first. Anyone who needs it should not simply refrain from using medicine. Medicine should not be taken casually; it should even be taken rarely. But it is not to be feared any more than it should be worshiped. It is simply not the ultimate answer any more than a peacekeeping force is the answer to war. As we do whatever we have to do to cope with and cure our difficulties and diseases, the important thing is that we be continually concerned with the possibility of transcending them.

Hui-Neng said: "From the first not a thing is."
—D. T. Suzuki, *Zen Buddhism*

Lao Tsu said: "The nameless is the origin of heaven and earth; Naming is the mother of the ten thousand things."
—A. Watts, *The Way of Zen*

Clothing

Considerations in buying clothing

• Ease in putting on and taking off.
• Ease for changing diapers in (should have snap or zipper crotch or be open at the bottom).
• Ease of care (should be no-iron, machine-washable, machine-dryable, or drip-dry).
• Length of usefulness.
• Season of birth (warm or cold, and take your home temperature into account, too).
• Size of infant. A great big baby of 8 to 11 pounds at birth will wear newborn or small-size things for only a short while, if at all. Even smaller babies grow fast. So don't overdo on the initial wardrobe.
• Effectiveness as clothing. Basically this means comfort and freedom for the baby (warm enough; cool enough; doesn't ride up, fall off, come undone, bunch or lump up, stop circulation below the waist, fall over face).
• Looks—as you like.

Layette clothing sets—These include a variety of knitted cotton kimonos, nighties, pants, and tops and are generally not useful. The problem is partly a matter of too many alternatives. Within a few days of the baby's birth you have found which of these is easiest to put on and does the best job. Everything else is either a drag to put on or doesn't fit comfortably, and you are still stuck with the matter of folding and storing all these diverse articles of clothing in some kind of neat way. A lot of extra decisions you don't need for a start.

Stretch suits—Probably the best buy all around for the early days, provided the weather isn't excruciatingly hot. If you have enough stretch suits, you don't really need anything else. They meet all the criteria for baby clothing superbly, and they can adequately replace nighties, booties, sweaters, and undershirts. Long-sleeved, footed, snap-crotch stretch suits are the most useful throughout the year and good for twenty-four hours a day. Short-sleeved, leg-less, romper and sunsuit versions are also made for the hottest summer days.

Nylon tricot infant suits—These come in the same style as the terry stretch suits, though they are less stretchy and tend to be a bit dressier. They cost more and are outgrown sooner than stretch suits, but they dry in no time at all—2 minutes in the dryer or about 30 minutes in the bathroom (squeeze out in a towel first). So besides being cute for dress-up, one or two of these can be a boon for those clumsy, early days when everything may be supersaturated before breakfast.

Cotton knit nighties—Another useful substitute for or general supplement to stretch suits (especially at nighttime). Because they ride up and do not cover the feet, they are not as all-purpose as stretch suits—nor as dressy. But they are less expensive, easier to change diapers in, and of course they can be washed and dried at the hottest temperatures. They are quite warm, however, and not much good for the hottest weather in unairconditioned or unbreezy homes. Some people get extra mileage out of these gowns by resurrecting them as nightwear when their children learn to walk. Crawling children cannot wear them because they crawl into the chest of the gown. But the nighties certainly look adorable on beginning walkers, when nonskid bare feet are an asset for toddling without toppling.

Wee Willie Winkie runs through the town,
Upstairs and downstairs in his nightgown,
Rapping at the windows, crying through the lock,
"Are the children all in bed?
Now it's eight o'clock."
–Mother Goose

Undershirts—You may want to keep your newborn baby in undershirts, but, generally speaking, they are an unnecessary extra effort. Since you are constantly picking up the baby under the arms, any undershirt that is not pinned to the diaper rides up and becomes a constricting wad across the chest and under the arms. Undershirts mean double laundry and extra dressing. For extra warmth a sweater, jacket, or blanket that can be easily donned or removed as you go in and out of heated and air-conditioned buildings is a better answer than an undershirt. By far the most prevalent tendency in dressing babies is overdressing. Babies do not need to be baked after they come out of the oven.

Bunting—In winter a bunting of some sort is a good idea. The most useful ones are those with hoods, mittened sleeves, and no legs. The sack-type bottom makes it easier for changing diapers and allows the baby plenty of freedom for kicking without kicking off the carriage blanket. It is also a good place for transporting an extra diaper or tissue. The sleeved kind is better than the straight sack kind because it allows the baby to move her arms without becoming uncovered. Get a machine-washable bunting, and if possible buy one with a hood that ties snugly under the chin and does not brush constantly against the baby's cheek. Such brushing makes some infants want to nurse at inconvenient moments.

Boy and girl clothes for babies—As you like, but don't be in a hurry. The growing up happens very quickly. Little boy suits with separate tops and bottoms always result in bare midriffs with pants below and tops above the belly. So select one-piecers or those two-piecers that snap or button together. Little girl dresses are irresistibly adorable and now come in all the drip-dry fabrics. Never fall for one that needs ironing or she will very likely outgrow it between the first washing and the time you get around to ironing it.

Don't raise boys to be boys and girls to be girls. Raise whole, individually unique children. The ideal man/woman is as gentle as a woman and as strong as a man. The differences between boys and girls can be acknowledged and appreciated, but they do not have to be taught. Group or sex membership is less a means of identifying uniqueness than of stereotyping sameness. Positive and negative group identifications dull the child's sense of his inborn individual uniqueness and worth.

Knitted muk-luks—When the time comes for standing and walking, bare feet are the best nonskid base. But if it happens to be wintertime and cold, you may want some kind of footgear for toddling on bare floors. Footed stretch suits are slippery. Booties continue to fall off as fast as you put them on and are slippery. Leather moccasins are a good idea, but most fall off (they tie too high—on or above the ankle bone instead of below). Shoes seem premature and awkward. Here's a good pattern for some knitted muk-luk-type booties. Elastic in the ankles keeps them on and their leather soles are nonskid.

Size 5 needles
2 oz. knitting worsted or equivalent
1' hat elastic
1 leather elbow patch (optional)

Sole. Cast on 22 stitches (sts) for outside edge of sole. Work garter stitch, increase 1 st. each side every other row 6 times (34 sts.). Decrease 1 st. each side every other row 6 times (22 sts.). Bind off.

Body. Cast on 54 sts. for lower edge of body. Work garter st. for 8 rows. (4 ridges will be on outside of bootie). Next row work 10 sts and slip to holder. Bind off next 14 sts. Knit 6 sts. instep. Do not break off yarn—tie on another piece of yarn (from outside of package of same wool) to the next st. and bind off next 14 sts. Knit to end of row, then slip remaining 10 sts. to another holder. Break off yarn. Work garter stitch on 6 sts. of the instep until piece is the same length as bound-off sts. Slip these 6 sts. to a holder. Break off yarn. Next row slip first 10 sts. to needle, add 6 sts. of instep and add 10 sts. on 2nd holder (26 sts.). Attach yarn and work in ribbing of K 1, P 1 for 8 rows. Then add 1 st. each side every 4th row until 40 sts. Work 2 more rows and then bind off. (Keep ribbing in pattern as you add sts.)

Sewing up. (1) Sew instep pieces to body on right (out) side. (2) Turn inside out and sew back seam of body piece. (3) Pin body piece to sole, lining up the front and back edges of the sole with the outer edges of body piece. Ease in pointed ends at front and back. (4) Run hat elastic around second row of ribbing loosely on inside. Adjust for tightness.

Leather sole. From a prepackaged leather elbow patch, cut and sew on soles to fit booties. This is optional, for protection against slipping on bare floors. Not necessary for carpeted floors or non-walking babies.

Wireworks—Handy for keeping booties and mittens on. Cut pieces of coated electric wire (bellwire) and weave them through booties and mittens at the narrowest point of the child's ankle (just below the ankle bone) or wrist (just below the wrist bone). Bend and tape the ends of the wires over so that there's no danger of scratching. Once the booties or mittens are well on, simply twist the ends of the wire once. There's a period between 1 and 2 years when children *will* shake their mittens off to touch the snow, then cry for you to put the mittens on, then immediately shake them off again. At such times this idea is a tremendous help. It also works on slipper socks.

Beds

The main factors to be considered in buying a bed for a baby are budget, space, safety, appearance, quality, and durability. Your life style will come into play here, too—whether you travel much, whether or not you plan to have more children. No one can say what's best for you but here are some issues to consider.

Bassinet, cradle, basket, car bed

The most attractive thing about these is that babies look so totally adorable and cozy in them, but for the most part they are not necessary and they are outgrown very quickly, often in a few months. Nevertheless, if you have the space and the money or a lending or giving friend, you may be very happy to have one of these small beds as a temporary or auxiliary sleeping place. In the very early days of night feedings, it may be handy to have the baby next to your bed at night in-stead of in a separate room. Small beds are also useful for the traveling baby, although the baby young enough to be in a basket can also be safely bedded down on a normal adult bed with a bolster on either side. Just don't make the mistake of thinking that any of these things will do for a bed for very long. And don't forget that the separable baskets of many carriages (look for one with carrying handles) are good for small-bed purposes.

Cribs

There are three basic types of cribs: portable inexpensive, standard moderately priced to expensive, and unusual and expensive. There is something to be said for each. Regarding the material quality of standard models, the October, 1971, issue of *Consumer Reports* says it all. But before buying a standard crib, here are a few other things to consider.

If you can avoid or transcend the bedtime power struggle most people have with their children, it will not be necessary to keep your child in a crib much longer than a year and a half. After that, the sides of a crib are really not needed for safety. Using them as restraints to keep the child in bed doesn't have to be harmful, but it is desirable for both the parent and the child if a better reason for staying in bed than not being able to get out can be discovered by this time. Then it becomes possible for the child to lie down at will or to get up in the morning and play quietly alone without disturbing anyone. And, of course, what is implied here is a harmony for both parent and child with the ideas of sleeping and waking that many people never attain in their entire lives.

In any case, unless you plan to keep the child in a crib for longer than two years, the standard cribs are really larger than necessary. Smaller cribs are perfectly adequate and leave more room for play space.

Whatever crib you buy, look for simplicity and openness as well as sturdiness, safety, and convenience. Check *Consumer Reports* for recent evaluations of major models. Remember that you are buying a bed, not a safe deposit box or a learning center. If there is anything to be learned in bed, it is the fine art of grateful retirement, peaceful sleeping, and cheerful waking.

Small collapsible cribs—such as the Porta-Crib, are perfectly adequate, quite inexpensive, and attractive beds for babies up to at least 2 years. Of course their main claim to fame is collapsibility for traveling or storage, but they are also nice on a permanent basis. The foam-filled, vinyl-covered mattress can be placed in two positions, and the top of one side is hinged for opening outward. Mattresses are available in two thicknesses. The thicker one is firmer and stays made up better and is preferable if the crib is to be used on a permanent basis. The fitted knitted sheets of most manufacturers come in Porta-Crib as well as standard crib size.

Standard cribs—Most have solid headboards and footboards that make them seem unnecessarily dark and confining. So, if you decide to buy a standard crib, you may want to look for one with simple spindles on the ends. Don't buy a double drop-sided crib—they are more expensive, less sturdy, and, even if you have the crib in the middle of the room, you will probably fall into a routine of picking up the baby from only one side. □

Unusual, expensive cribs—These include a variety of the worst and the best. Among the worst are some highly elaborate, extraordinarily ugly contraptions that are supposed to expedite early learning. They are all cluttered with built-in toys for stimulating the baby in bed! Entirely overlooked is the idea that bed is a place to sleep.

Some perfectly lovely expensive cribs convert to junior beds. The only difficulty here is the concept of a junior bed. A junior bed is not a necessary purchase (see "Junior Beds" below); therefore, a combination crib/junior bed is not much of a bargain. One crib combination that does seem worthwhile is the Crib/Settee from New York's Children's Workbench, a smaller than standard crib that converts to a settee or small sofa for a child's room. □

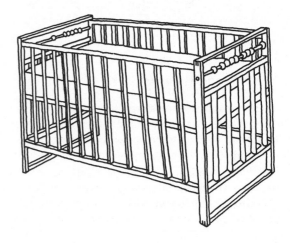

After speaking so enthusiastically about a crib that costs more than $100, it seems necessary to mention that, of course, no bedstead is really necessary. Around the world undoubtedly more people are sleeping on the floor on simple mats than in beds as we know them. This same procedure can be followed with mattresses if you prefer. Then, of course, there is never any danger of falling.

Junior bed—Do not make the mistake of believing that you need a transitional bed, that is, something with guard rails and between a crib and a twin bed in size. Guard rails are not necessary, and if you do use them it will be only for a week or so. Sooner or later you will have to buy a normal-size bed for your child. If you have the space buy a twin bed whenever you think he is ready to leave his crib.

How to move from crib to bed—This is easy. Place a chair or small table of the same height as the mattress beside the bed at the child's head. If he rolls off the bed onto the chair, his feet will land on the floor. By the time this has happened, he will be awake enough to climb back into bed. Within a week or two this will probably stop occurring altogether as he will now have a built-in awareness of the limits of the bed. Also by now you will have discovered how nice it is to sit beside the open bed at bedtime for a song or story, so you will probably leave the chair there anyway. At first, as an extra precaution, you may want to put some pillows or a quilt on the floor by the bed. If you're superprecautious, simply place the mattress on the floor until the child becomes used to sleeping without sides. But this seems a little melodramatic, and most children make the move without ever falling.

Bedding

On their first day home from the hospital one family ran through all their bedding before noon—two crib sheets, four receiving blankets, three rubber pads, and about four layette nightgowns. They sent out for more receiving blankets and did hand laundry until the humidity verged on rain. But after the first day they never got to the bottom of the pile again. The four extra receiving blankets became dustcloths.

The determining factors in deciding how much bedding is needed for these early days are laundry facilities and the parents' savoir faire. If it's a first baby and you're a rank beginner at diapering, you may need a few extras for leakage, especially if you don't have very easy access to a washer and dryer.

But even if you are a beginner with no skills, a few tricks can help to keep the laundry level low:

• Never wake up a sleeping baby for a change.

• Until the baby learns to move around in bed, it isn't necessary to change the whole bed just because there is a damp spot in one corner of it. Move the baby instead.

• Let the baby sleep on a baby-size pad of cottonized rubber on top of the sheet. If small spit-ups or wetnesses occur, just change the pad.

Knitted, fitted crib sheets—You'll keep using these as long as the baby stays in a crib so, if in doubt, buy more rather than fewer—you'll use them eventually—but three to six should be enough. These are soft to sleep on, and a breeze to launder. If you like to tie dye, try a crib sheet. One family made a beautiful blue sheet with white patches that their two children variously saw as clouds, moons, and owls.

Receiving blankets—Four will do. These blankets are used for swaddling in the hospital, where babies are generally dressed in no more than an undershirt and diaper. Once the baby is home and in stretch suits, this swaddling is not as necessary, except as a way to keep covers on during the first couple of weeks. To swaddle, fold one corner of the blanket toward the middle. Place the baby on the blanket with his head just above the fold. Pull one of the side points of the blanket across the baby's chest, under his arm, and tuck it behind him. Pull the bottom point up toward his chest. Wrap the other side point across the front of the baby, under his arm, and tuck it in behind. What a wad! A swaddle of baby!

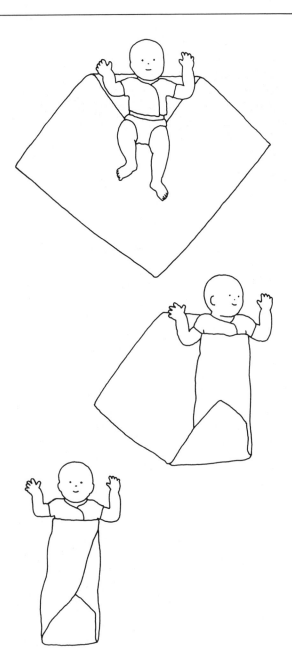

Cottonized rubber sheets—Two crib-sized ones should be sufficient. If the mattress is vinyl-covered you don't have to have any, but you will still probably want them to soften the mattress surface beneath the sheet and to avoid always having to wash off the mattress.

Four to six so-called puddle pads will be handy for sleeping on (see tips above) and as lap pads and places for changing. They can be bought precut in almost any infant supply department or variety store. In some good-sized fabric and department stores this material can be less expensively bought off the bolt and cut with pinking shears to the desired size. Don't put in a very hot drier.

Mattress pads—These are optional. Some people like to use them to soften the mattress surface or instead of a rubber sheet. But a rubber sheet is really more practical and all that's necessary between the cotton sheet and the mattress.

Bed-making—Once the baby begins to move around (about a month), the bed-making arrangements have to be revised a bit. There are two approaches. One is to make the baby, to dress him in warm enough clothing so that it doesn't matter whether he stays covered or not. The other is to make up the bed like a real bed, with tucked-in top sheet and blanket.

If you follow the baby-making approach, you will want thermal or acrylic, blanket-weight sleep suits for cold nights. The disadvantages of this approach are that the suits are expensive, a bit cumbersome for diaper changing, somehow a bigger project to launder, and often too warm for running around in before bed.

If you follow the bed-making approach, you can use season-weight pajamas and just toss

on or take off extra blankets as the temperature changes. The bed-making approach seems easier all the way around except for one thing. Most of the ready-made top sheets and blankets for cribs are too narrow. It is crucial that the top sheet and blanket be wide enough to tuck in well under the mattress on both sides without being stretched tightly across the child. Otherwise the child becomes uncovered and tangled up. About the only solution is to cut down larger sheets and blankets. Ideal dimensions for a 5-inch thick standard crib mattress are $5\frac{1}{2}$ feet long by $4\frac{1}{2}$ feet wide for top sheets and 5 feet long by $4\frac{1}{2}$ feet wide for blankets. Extra blankets may be smaller, of course.

Fake-a-quilt—A good washable quilt is unbeatable. One family received one that had been made by covering a ready-made, synthetic baby blanket with drip-dry cotton. The top layer of cotton was a quiltlike print. The bottom was covered with a plain, bright yellow. The whole thing was stitched together on a sewing machine, and the top was dec-

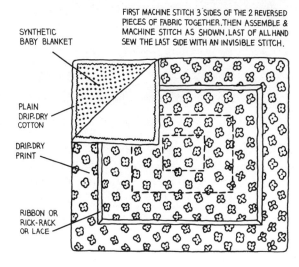

orated approximately 3 inches from the edge of the quilt with a strip of grosgrain ribbon to match the bottom. There was something almost magically right about the thickness, stiffness, and weight of this quilt. As a cover, it was stiff enough so that the child could turn over without becoming tangled up, and it was light enough to stay across his shoulders when he inched his way toward the head of the crib. As a floor pad, it was the closest this family ever came to using a play pen. It provided a soft cushion under the baby and yet was stiff enough not to crumple up under him.

An even easier way to make a quilt is to buy some washable prequilted material. If it is one-sided, sew two pieces together for a thick quilt, or line it with a piece of drip-dry fabric. Some material comes already lined or quilted on both sides and only needs to be cut and trimmed.

Make-a-quilt—Real patchwork quilting is a lovely art. Many books on the subject are available. Two are:

The Standard Book of Quilt Making and Collecting
by Marguerite Ickis
The whole story of quilt making, including patterns, stitches, construction, and history. Very good on pattern cutting and assembly, but no discussion of the use of wooden quilting frames.
Dover Publications, Inc.; paperback, 1 color, 6¾" x 9½", 286 pp.

How to Make Whirl-I-Gigs and Whimmy Diddles
by Florence Pettit
A wonderfully detailed book on the execution of a variety of American folk crafts. It gives excellent, illustrated instructions on quilting, including frame construction, pattern design, assembly, and stitching. See page 72 for a complete description of this book.

Blanket—Fake fur or fake lamb's wool or scraps of cotton can be appliquéd to a cut-down blanket or blanket-size piece of washable suit fabric (buy 5 feet from a 58-inch wide bolt). Make a happy-faced clown from old scraps of cotton, a fake fur teddy bear with print-bottomed paws and button eyes and a soft velvet or kid-glove nose, a fake fur kangaroo with a print-lined pouch that holds a removable baby kangaroo stuffed with a thin layer of alpaca or polyurethane foam. It is best to machine-stitch around the edge of each piece to be appliquéd, to prevent raveling. Then fold and iron along the stitching, baste or pin, and sew to blanket. Fancy appliqué stitches may be learned from sewing books, or you can make the stitches invisible. An even easier approach might be the new "Stitch Witchery"—sheets of adhesive that are supposed to turn almost any sewing endeavor into an iron-on affair. Ready-made blanket trim can be bought in any sewing or notions department.

DWELLING PLACE

*. . . In his ship Scuppers had a little room. In his
room Scuppers had a hook for his hat and a hook for
his rope and a hook for his spyglass and a place for
his shoes and a bunk for a bed to put himself in.*

*At night Scuppers threw the anchor into the sea
and he went down to his little room.*

*He put his hat on the hook for his hat, and his
rope on the hook for his rope, and his spyglass on
the hook for his spyglass, and he put his shoes under
the bed, and got into his bed, which was a bunk, and
went to sleep."*

–Margaret Wise Brown, *The Sailor Dog*

Lots of people spend time and effort decorating their children's rooms in ways that
quickly prove to be inefficient, unsafe, inconvenient, monotonous in appearance, and impossible to keep orderly. Covered with cute,
busy things, the walls, crowd in; the floors are
dangerously cluttered with educational toys
and toy parts; and the bed is a sort of padded
cell, littered with things that are used by the
child only for pitching over the side. The
child's bedroom, which should be where he
finds peace enough to sleep, becomes a restless
place were he does not like to be.

As long as we are pregnant, our children
live within the confines of our physical bodies.
We are never more intimately connected with
each other than at this time, yet scarcely ever
again will we have so little knowledge of each
other. At the birth of our child, suddenly and
at long last, we confront each other, an overwhelming experience that defies description.
Only two other transitions in human experience are as enormous as these moments in
which, materially at least, we become parents.
The other two monumental human experiences
are our own birth and death; and, from the
standpoint of human lifetime, in both of these
experiences we are aware of only one side of
the transition.

Yet no matter how dramatic the experience
of child-bearing seems, from the child's side
the move from womb to room is not so tremendous as we are inclined to think. The
ideal child/man/woman remains what it has
always been, a perfect, complete idea—spiritually whole, unending, unbeginning. On a
material plane where it lives as an immature
being seeking maturity or the realization of
this ideal selfhood, the move from the mother's belly to her lap is not so huge either.

*Keizan said: "Birth cannot alter the mind,
embodiment cannot transmute Original Nature.
Though the essential and the physical bodies have
changed, mind is as it has always been."*

–*Zen Poems, Prayers, Sermons, Anecdotes,
Interviews,* trans. and ed. by Stryk and Ikemoto

In the womb or out, the very young child lives almost entirely within the limits of the parent's consciousness. He is capable of realizing very little as yet; he has not yet become conscious of his ideal nature. As his parents we are only just approaching the possibility of this realization ourselves. For the most part, the very young child is subject only to *experiences,* and his experience is almost totally governed by the ignorant beliefs or enlightened awareness of his parents. He lives as much in us after he is born as he did while still in the womb. We are his environment as long as he is a child.

Therefore, as we prepare a room or corner for the coming baby, it is appropriate to seek the highest possible awareness of idea(l) man and his idea(l) dwelling place and then to consider how the qualities of ideal dwelling place might be translated into terms the child can experience. What are the ideal qualities that we might wish to bring into his experience as an environment? What will best serve him on his path toward realizing his ideal selfhood? Disregarding the apparent weakness and limitation of the newborn babe and considering only his ideal, intelligent, whole selfhood (call it potential if you prefer), it is obvious that the proper environment should include peace, beauty, order, simplicity, joy, and love.

It is not necessary to give specific suggestions on how to fix up the baby's room. If we cultivate an awareness of these qualities in consciousness, they will be reflected in the decoration, furniture, and arrangement of the child's nook or room. The important thing is to address everything in the child's room to the ideal child, not to the material one; and the room will thus be a lovely dwelling place. In preparing the room, it may be helpful to consider the spiritual or existential issue behind each aspect of the room and its furnishings:

• Floor: security, ground of being, freedom. Make sure it remains unhazardous, uncluttered, and spacious in appearance.
• Walls: security, protection, privacy, but again also freedom. Do not let them become confining, oppressive, or overly cluttered.
• Light fixtures, windows, curtains: light, illumination. Choose things that lend themselves to envisioning or seeing beyond, not to entertaining or occupying the eyes.
• Toys: fulfillment, unfolding consciousness. As with lights and windows, it is the function of toys to lead children beyond themselves, not merely to entertain.
• Bed: peace, stillness, letting go. It is not a cage or a playpen or a learning or achievement center.
• Arrangement: simplicity, order, efficiency, unity.
• Decor: beauty—again, toward seeing beyond.

Such a room will be joyful but not exciting (and therefore not eventually boring); it is, after all, a place of privacy and rest. It will be cheerful, and appreciable but not stimulating or startling. It will emphasize becoming rather than having, seeing rather than sights, understanding rather than doing. And love— how does a room reflect love? It cannot be pinpointed. It is the overall result of the consciousness of true goodness—the goodness of the child and the goodness of life as they are met in thee, the parent, tonight.

In the end, of course, the room is nowhere;

the child is not brought peace or love or security or beauty or vision by the room at all. It is in our consciousness where he meets these realities. Once we achieve the kind of awareness that can reflect itself in the preparation of a lovely room, the room is no longer necessary. It never really was, except as an exercise for us. You can go anywhere, sleep on anything, do with nothing, and the child will still be happy and grow beautifully if his earthly dwelling place, the mind of the parent, is love-filled.

My people will abide in a peaceful habitation,
in secure dwellings, and in quiet resting places.
–Isaiah 32:18

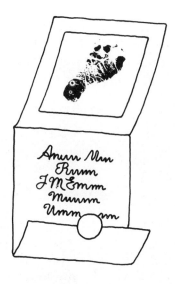

Birth Announcements

In all hospitals babies are automatically footprinted on arrival. If you remember to ask in advance or at the time (but not later), it is usually possible to have an extra print made for a keepsake. For less than $10 this can be duplicated a hundred or more times by photo-offset (look under "Printing" in your telephone classified directory) to be used as birth announcements. You can either have the announcement printed along with the footprint, or you can cut the footprint out and glue it to the top third of a strip of colored construction paper that you have cut and folded in advance. Write your announcement on the middle third. Fold up the bottom third, fold down the top third, and seal with a stick-on label from a stationery supply store. Turn over, address, and mail.

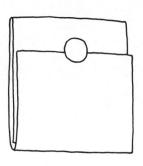

Special Delivery: Birth of the Mother

Traditionally childbirth has been thought to be a more or less painful experience that the mother endured with more or less grace depending on the degree to which she was fearful, brave, or lucky. With anesthetics came the possibility of doing away with the experience of pain altogether. For several decades nearly every woman in this country who could afford it slept through the event of childbirth, waking only in time to be introduced to her baby by a doctor or nurse.

Recently the idea of staying awake throughout labor and delivery has been gaining favor, partly on the ground that it is better for the child and partly because of a growing desire not to miss the truly wonderful event. With this change in attitude numerous techniques have been developed for avoiding pain while staying awake, for dealing with pain if it occurs, and for being an effectively cooperative participant in the delivery of the baby. For some people pain-accompanied tensions based on fear of the childbirth process are alleviated simply by being told what's going on or by having their husbands present. Breathing and relaxing skills seem to help others pass more tranquilly and comfortably through labor and delivery.

Regardless of delivery techniques there are (and have always been) some for whom the moments of childbirth pass harmoniously and with surprising ease, and many for whom they are difficult and dreadful. For some women the moment of delivery comes so quietly and so painlessly that the first sign of labor is in fact the birth of the child. No time to go to the hospital, no breathing techniques, no labor, no pain.

By and large it is believed that the explanation for these differences is ultimately to be found in medical science. Theories are accordingly advanced but nothing has turned up yet that applies consistently enough to be counted true. Many advocates of conscious childbirth techniques believe that the answer lies in the mother's skill in executing these techniques (both mentally and bodily). But again, the results are spotty when it comes to the record of difficult versus easy births. Some of the best-prepared and seemingly "with it" mothers have the worst labors, whereas some of the least prepared and most inept breeze through with no complications at all.

There seems to be little question but that choosing to be alert and awake during the moments of childbirth is a positive step. And it is certainly better to view birth as a healthy and happy event rather than a sort of hazardous emergency sapping the strength of the mother just before the demands of motherhood are placed upon her. But the possibility of even more revolutionary changes in viewpoint must never be ruled out as long as any disharmony remains.

The minutest nearest subatomic particles and the farthest stars have been observed to behave so unreasonably as to bewilder scientists. Most believe that further objective data will eventually dispel the confusion. But there are a few individuals who suspect that the greatest variable in scientific observation is the scientist himself, the personal and universal preconceptions he brings being reflected in the phenomena he perceives. The Copernican revolution is a partial example. Before Copernicus all stellar and solar observations were reviewed from the preconceived standpoint that the earth was at the center. Data that did not jibe seemed irrational and inconsistent (and was indeed attributed to an irrational God) until Copernicus exposed the fact that the only inconsistent, irrational element was the scientists' premise that the earth was the center of our universe. Once that premise was relinquished it was an easy step to perceive all the available data as orderly and rational. Physicist Werner Heisenberg's "Principle of Uncertainty" hypothesizes that "the very act of observing disturbs the system." And at the very least science in general concedes that there is no such thing as truly objective scientific observation. This in turn leaves open to question the issue of whether or not matter is the true substance of reality at all. If it isn't then it becomes clearly important to seek knowledge of ideal or spiritual reality.

In this light it is conceivable that technique may be of little importance or relevance. If the perceivable behavior of the stars simply reflects what the scientist believes, then a bigger or more powerful telescope may only augment his experience of that belief. If the basic belief is erroneous, then further understanding can occur only after the belief is relinquished.

If you wish to go out of your house, the first thing you do is to head for the door. But suppose as you near the door you become more concerned with the door than with going out. Perhaps you fear that the door will not open or that you will be unable to open it. In no time at all you find yourself struggling with the lock or trying to bash down the door or calling for help to open the supposedly troublesome door. Or perhaps you simply become interested in, distracted by, the door itself, stopping to examine its frame, latch, hinges, carvings, or the grain of the wood. Either way, as long as you remain fascinated with the door, it will not be possible to pass through the doorway. Your thought precedes your progress, and if thought does not pass beyond the doorway, neither will you—not unless someone forcibly gets you through.

This is analogous to the experience of many women and their children at the time of birth. After a healthy pregnancy and seemingly happy anticipation of the arrival of a child, many mothers (prepared and unprepared) experience long or painful labor in which both they and their children seem to be stuck in the doorway.

For both the scientist and the mother then, perhaps the primary issue is the relinquishing of false beliefs or concerns. This seems reasonable, since it is only in letting go of one idea that it becomes possible for another one to occur; and since, if there is such a thing as truth, the only possibility of conflict or disharmony is through belief in or devotion to something else. The object is to realign one's thought with what really is, or with the harmonizing ideal (principle) rather than the material symptom of belief.

One belief common to all of the childbirth approaches described above is that childbirth is the bodily separation of the mother and child from each other. This is similar to the traditional belief of observing astronomers that the only event was taking place on the observable star. But on an ideal plane—that is, in the realm of idea or thought—the moment of childbirth is, or could be, something else entirely, or at least something more.

Once we had the idea that there might come into the world a child who would be our son or daughter and for whom we would care as parents. Unrealized, but written into this idea, is all the potential of ideal man/womanhood, which includes the possibility of the baby, too, one day becoming a parent. Likewise before we were born—that is, always—has the idea of our becoming parently been a part of our idea nature. So the true event that from the side of the child is called childbirth is from the side of the parent, parent-birth. Perhaps then delivery is not a matter of expulsion but of revelation, since ideally what is happening for both the child and the mother is the further coming to light of some aspect of what they already truly are. So rather than pushing the child from the womb, perhaps it is as the mother reaches for the idea of motherhood that the child is released or revealed.

The moments of birth are as significant in the unfoldment of the mother and child as passing through a doorway is in any journey outside. It is a matter of moments, a mere transition, and yet the whole focus of many parents during pregnancy is on labor and delivery.

From the standpoint of investment of time and thought, it seems unbalanced to spend the days of pregnancy preparing for childbirth when it is parenthood with which we will be largely concerned from the moment of delivery on. Ideologically, perhaps it is even impossible for a child to be born to a woman who still thinks of herself as a pregnant woman, just as it is impossible to pass through a doorway while giving one's full attention to the door.

Technically, as long as a woman is pregnant the offspring is a fetus. Perhaps the *child* can be born only to a *mother,* or at least to a woman who has surrendered her claim to pregnancy or obstetrical knowledge or fear of pain in favor of a receptivity to some further revelation of truth and power. Of course, it is equally impossible for the child not to be born once the time has come. The question is no longer birth or no birth, but smooth or difficult birth. The child's unfoldment cannot easily be stopped at this point. Either the mother can participate harmoniously or else the child must be forcibly extricated from her.

This might explain the seemingly irrational divergence of the labor and delivery experiences of women, regardless of their chosen approach to childbirth. It makes little difference what technique is employed in the pursuit of truth as long as the basic premise or belief is erroneous. Any technique employed by the mother during childbirth may serve only to augment her experience of what she unconsciously or secretly believes. To the extent that belief is in accord with reality, the experience will be harmonious; to the extent that belief is in error, the experience will be disharmonious.

Theoretically at least, childbirth could occur effortlessly to anyone whose thought is fully aligned with a valid idea of motherliness, since understanding of the motherly role—the fostering of the child's becoming his true self —is part of the definition of motherliness. In other words, the proper response of the mother in childbirth would be revealed to her from moment to moment, either directly in consciousness or through the doctor as obstetrician.

If we discern the principle that the true event of childbirth takes place in consciousness, we will prepare for childbirth during pregnancy, not by preparing for events of childbirth or studying embryology, but by heightening our consciousness of what motherliness and fatherliness really are, by becoming parently in thought and mode of being. Many will still inevitably choose to follow a method, since, after all, we will live where we are, doing the best we understand until we know something better. Even so it will be helpful to maintain an emphasis on the preparation for motherhood.

Likewise in labor it is well to keep one's thoughts on these qualities of parentliness and on the substantial nature of the event. These considerations can help to hold the event in perspective and keep us from becoming disproportionately involved with the door, instead of the vista before us. This will be helpful in overcoming the experience of pain (both physiological and psychological, both during and after birth), and it will help to foster an atmosphere of peace and gratitude in which to greet the child. A child is being born! We are here to welcome him. He is bringing new love, light, wisdom, and purpose into our lives. We are witnessing vitality and intelligence and power for good in operation in our lives! We are becoming parents. We are about to begin to learn to love and give as we have never been motivated to love and give before!

Besides the fact that this may be the best way to expedite the birth process, it is obviously best for the well-being of the arriving child. Whether or not the labor goes smoothly or with a little distress is of small consequence. For most families the result will be healthy and harmonious, regardless. But in the life of the child it is clearly more important to be welcomed into the arms of a consciously motherly individual than someone skillful at pushing babies out into the world. And the distinction between the value of these two orientations is no greater for the newborn child than for the newborn mother. To be happy we must become what we are.

Before she was in labor she gave birth; before her pain came upon her she was delivered of a son. Who has heard of such a thing? Who has seen such things? . . . Shall I bring to birth and not cause to bring forth? says the Lord; Shall I, who cause to bring forth shut the womb? says your God.

–Isaiah 66:7–9

i am so glad and very
merely my fourth will cure
the laziest self of weary
the hugest sea of shore

so far your nearness reaches
a lucky fifth of you
turns people into eachs
and cowards into grow

our can'ts were born to happen
our mosts have died in more
our twentieth will open
wide a wide open door

we are so both and oneful
night cannot be so sky
sky cannot be so sunful
i am through you so i

–e.e.cummings, *i am so glad and very,*
Poems: 1923–1954

Getting Used to and Sustaining the Idea

Eating and sleeping are likely to become suddenly heightened concerns in any home with a new baby. *Struggle* is the word that describes what goes on in most families. Eating and sleeping are both aspects of nourishment, and the following pages are loosely concerned with these issues and their significance. While considering these matters, some good questions to ask are: Just who is being nourished and with what and by whom? What is the sustenance that truly sustains and nourishes this idea that has become our child, this idea that we are? What is the nourishment that helps us and our children to become more fully what we truly, ideally, are?

A MOUNTAIN IS A MOUNTAIN

Ch'ing-yuan said: *"Before I had studied Zen for thirty years, I saw mountains as mountains, and waters as waters. When I arrived at a more intimate knowledge, I came to the point where I saw that mountains are not mountains, and waters are not waters. But now that I have got its very substance I am at rest. For it's just that I see mountains once again as mountains, and waters once again as waters."*

–A. Watts, *The Way of Zen*

It seems that almost everything we encounter in life has two meanings: its apparent meaning, which is what we first experience, and its deeper meaning, which we can come to understand. The experiences that go along with the apparent meaning tend to be discordant, forcing us slowly toward consideration of the deeper meaning.

From a material standpoint, we may see a rock as a stubborn obstacle—dangerous, harsh, and slippery when wet. But if we look on through the rock to see what enduring qualities of life are revealed there, we see steadfastness, reliability, security, protection, immutability—exactly the reverse of the material perception. The difference lies in the point of view. In the material perspective, the self and the rock are viewed as separate things encountering each other. Mastery, control, personal autonomy, dominance are deemed the issues. In the other perspective, both the rock and the self are assumed to be reflections of one life that is infinite. Here understanding is seen to be the key. Which point of view is truthful? The answer is to be found through sincere testing. If one point of view produces conflict, injury, or frustration, it is false; if one results in peace and harmony, it is true. But we do not really choose between these two points of view. Rather we evolve from one to the other. Most of us are inclined to hit our heads against the rock a painfully long time first.

Now let's substitute the new baby for the rock. For the first time we hold her in our arms. She is so tiny, so cute, so weak and helpless. We can hardly wait to cuddle and feed and teach and take care of her. Then, all aglow, we take her home, and the crying starts and the sleepless nights begin. And she isn't cuddly, she's struggly. Instead of expressing beautiful parental love we seem to be engaged in some sort of marathon power struggle in which she is winning the no-sleep event hands down. Within a week we are either so worried about the mess we are making of this baby's life or so furious over the mess she is making of ours that we can only remember how cute she is when she is asleep.

But how would it be if we looked at her that other way? Suppose instead of tininess we saw the vastness of life: instead of weakness, vitality; instead of helplessness, wholeness; instead of ignorance, intelligence and alertness and purity? And then suppose we could know that these same qualities which are the baby's true nature are the truth about us and life, too?

When I was pregnant I thought, "A baby is a baby and a mother is a mother." But when we came home from the hospital I found a baby is not a baby and a mother is not a mother. And ever since I have been learning.

Twinkle, twinkle, little star,
How I wonder what you are,
Up above the world so high
Like a diamond in the sky.
Twinkle, twinkle, little star,
How I wonder what you are.

–Traditional nursery rhyme

At night when I sing "Twinkle Star" for them, I always wonder what our children are. Tiny guiding lights, shining in our lives, forcing us to look up—raising our point of view from the earthly to the heavenly. The babe of Bethlehem, the star that led the wise men! And didn't someone once say that it can all be seen, it can all come calmly clear, we can all be changed in the twinkling of an eye?

WHAT HAVE I DONE TO MY LIFE?

For the many of us for whom the early days with the new baby are fraught with one trial or another, here are some assurances:

• For some people it's incredibly easy. This does not mean you are terrible or ungifted parents or that you got a dirty deal. It means that the difficulties *can* fall away.

• The really dependent days are so few that you could almost miss the whole thing. Suppose you live 90 years (why not more?) and your child, who is born when you are about 30, strongly depends on you for $3\frac{1}{2}$ years at most. If you wish away those $3\frac{1}{2}$ years, you may spend $56\frac{1}{2}$ being nostalgic over what you missed. *That's* unhappiness!

• The baby needs peace more than sleep. Believe it or not, so do you. So don't struggle over sleep. Just learn to be peaceful together.

• The baby needs love more than food. So don't struggle over eating. Learn to be loving together.

• Give yourself over for the time being. Learn what is to be learned. Enjoy what is to be enjoyed. What could be more important to our long-range happiness than learning true peace, love, beauty, harmony. Money? A career? Time to play tennis? Certainly there is nothing wrong with keeping up with these things. It's fine if it works out. But if it doesn't, remember we have $56\frac{1}{2}$ more years for them.

• So look for peace, love, beauty, harmony *unconditionally*. Find them in the baby and in yourself. Enjoy being together.

• The baby does not want to die, and he does not depend on you to do his living for him. We are servants, suppliers, and helpers, and having loving parents can make all the difference in the happiness and smooth unfoldment of the baby's life. But don't exaggerate your own importance with illusions of either self-blame or pride. While children certainly need mothering and fathering, they do not specifically need *us* as their mothers and fathers. The best reason for being with our children is not simply that they need us, but that we need to become what we are, motherly and fatherly. Hardly any experience could change our lives more beneficially or faster than a correct appreciation of the significance of this one called parenthood.

• If you have to go to work, you have to go to work. It's no big deal. Find someone loving to care for the baby; and when you leave, do not think that you are abandoning her. She lives in your consciousness. Guard her in your thoughts; know her to be in perfect health and in perfect love and care. The biggest task of parenthood is in thought. Parental consciousness can be maintained anywhere. This does not mean worrying and fretting and calling home every five minutes. As a parent, seek simply to be aware of parentliness.

• Do not worry about what you don't yet know. If life is a process of understanding, then, of course, we don't already know. New experiences such as this overwhelming one of parenthood do not exist so that we can put what we already know to the test or on display, but rather so that we can learn what we need to know. The new situation that demands new understanding of us is also the channel through which that understanding may come. What we need to know is always a given in the situation that requires this knowledge. Prior experience is not necessary. Urgencies are provided and all that is needed is sincere receptivity.

BEDTIME

A distinguished teacher was once asked, "Do you ever make any effort to get disciplined in the truth?"
"Yes I do."
"How do you exercise yourself?"
"When I am hungry I eat; when tired I sleep."
"This is what everybody does; can they be said to be exercising themselves in the same way as you do?"
"No."
"Why not?"
"Because when they eat they do not eat, but are thinking of various other things, thereby allowing themselves to be disturbed; when they sleep they do not sleep, but dream of a thousand things. This is why they are not like myself."
–D. T. Suzuki, *Introduction to Zen Buddhism*

A lot of people have trouble going to sleep at night or waking up in the morning. It is said that both difficulties are a reflection of the belief that man is the author of his own existence. Sleep is not something we can do. It is not authored. It is allowed. If we think we are the authors of our own existence we may be reluctant to wake up—it is so dangerous and so tiring to be alive. By the same token we may be reluctant to sleep—even while yearning to rest we may harbor the secret fear that if we stop thinking and doing we shall cease existing.

Likewise if we have an exaggerated sense of responsibility for our children, we may keep them awake in the busyness of our minds. If we believe we author their lives, we may also be unconsciously involved in the process of trying to author their sleep. This is impossible, since sleeping is a process of letting go, something that is allowed. If a baby is busy, restless, struggling at bedtime and yet you can see that he is yearning to rest, see if you are not busy, too—with ten thousand thoughts. The thoughts can be anything—he's got to sleep, he needs it, he's got to sleep, I need it, I have to get some time to myself, maybe if I do this, maybe he wants that, why won't he sleep? Is it so? Then try to acknowledge that, at least for the moment, neither you nor the child has any needs beyond the awareness of love. Corny? Well, just try it.

Turn your child over to love. Turn yourself over to the idea that love and peace simply *are*. For just a few minutes do not *think* of what you have to do or what must be done or what the baby needs. Whether or not you remain in the room with the child for a brief time before and after bedtime, simply give some quiet thought to the possibility that love is. Behold the child not as a burden or a body in need or a responsibility too great or a cherished possession, but as an expression of love. Behold yourself the same way, acknowledging that love is bearing you up and flowing through you unendingly. Then no matter what has to be done, allow yourself to be peaceful. Hold or don't hold the child, whichever seems most harmonious. But be very honest.

It is not easy to be peaceful. You are not being peaceful if your mind is racing. Cultivate peaceful consciousness; rely on the idea that love is sufficient. And then in the silence it

may happen that love, the only discovery of ultimate importance, breaks in upon you as a reality, as the truth of being. If this happens, the baby will surely be sleeping peacefully and you will surely be refreshed for any task, but it will not matter.

This learning to be even momentarily, truly peaceful, still of mind as well as body, is not easy for most people. It takes much practice. It tends to be especially difficult in the early days of parenthood, when our lives are so suddenly different and we are worried about our ignorance as parents. We are constantly fretting mentally, so the child may continue to be restless and his sleeping habits unpredictable and brief. It will be suggested to you that the baby is manipulating you and that you are spoiling him. Don't believe it. If you start to believe a power struggle is going on, lose. He doesn't know anything about power struggles. If you start a power struggle with him, even if you win, you lose. Especially if you win, you lose. Because in the process he will have learned that power struggle is. So just hang in there and seek a still and loving consciousness, this stillness of mind into which love pours itself. Let the problems fall away, let sleep, let be.

Unless the Lord builds the house
those who build it labor in vain.
Unless the Lord watches over the city,
the watchman stays awake in vain.
It is in vain that you rise up early
and go late to rest,
eating the bread of anxious toil;
for he gives to his beloved sleep.

Lo, sons are a heritage from the Lord,
the fruit of the womb a reward . . .

–Psalms 127:1–3

Lullabies and parting thoughts

SEAL LULLABY

WORDS BY RUDYARD KIPLING

TUNE BY ALEC WILDER

REASSURINGLY

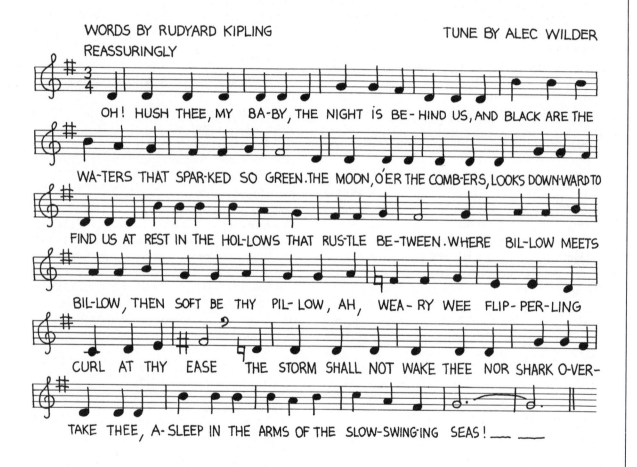

OH! HUSH THEE, MY BA-BY, THE NIGHT IS BE-HIND US, AND BLACK ARE THE

WA-TERS THAT SPAR-KED SO GREEN. THE MOON, O'ER THE COMB-ERS, LOOKS DOWN-WARD TO

FIND US AT REST IN THE HOL-LOWS THAT RUS-TLE BE-TWEEN. WHERE BIL-LOW MEETS

BIL-LOW, THEN SOFT BE THY PIL-LOW, AH, WEA-RY WEE FLIP-PER-LING

CURL AT THY EASE THE STORM SHALL NOT WAKE THEE NOR SHARK O-VER-

TAKE THEE, A-SLEEP IN THE ARMS OF THE SLOW-SWING-ING SEAS! __ __

Wynken, Blynken, and Nod one night
   Sailed off in a wooden shoe—
Sailed on a river of crystal light,
   Into a sea of dew.
"Where are you going, and what do you wish?"
   The old moon asked the three.
"We have come to fish for the herring fish
   That live in this beautiful sea;
   Nets of silver and gold have we!"
     Said Wynken,
     Blynken,
     And Nod.

The old moon laughed and sang a song,
   As they rocked in the wooden shoe,
And the wind that sped them all night long
   Ruffled the waves of dew.
The little stars were the herring fish
   That lived in that beautiful sea—
"Now cast your nets wherever you wish—
   Never afeared are we";
   So cried the stars to the fishermen three:
     Wynken,
     Blynken,
     And Nod.

All night long their nets they threw
   To the stars in the twinkling foam—
Then down from the skies came the wooden shoe,
   Bringing the fishermen home;
'Twas all so pretty a sail it seemed
   As if it could not be,
And some folks thought 'twas a dream they'd
     dreamed
   Of sailing that beautiful sea—
   But I shall name you the fishermen three:
     Wynken,
     Blynken,
     And Nod.

Wynken and Blynken are two little eyes,
   And Nod is a little head,
And the wooden shoe that sailed the skies
   Is a wee one's trundle-bed.
So shut your eyes while mother sings
   Of wonderful sights that be,
And you shall see the beautiful things
   As you rock in the misty sea,
   Where the old shoe rocked the fishermen three:
     Wynken,
     Blynken,
     And Nod.

—Eugene Field, *Wynken, Blynken, and Nod*

STAR WISH

TRADITIONAL
NOT TOO SLOWLY
TUNE BY ALEC WILDER

STAR LIGHT, STAR BRIGHT, FIRST STAR I SEE TO-NIGHT.

WISH I MAY, WISH I MIGHT HAVE THE WISH I WISH TO-NIGHT.

I see the moon, the moon sees me—
over the mountain, over the sea.
Please let the light that shines on me,
shine on the one I love.

As far as I know, all children are moon-struck. Even in the city where the lights blink and blaze insistingly, where the sky is often only a straight-up chimney patch, even in the daytime, if the moon is out—just a pale, pale sliver moon—the child will find it at once. "Oh look, there's the moon!" Is the friendship between this round, clear wonder whose hand holds mine and the one in the sky (both with their whispers of faces) founded on a deep, inborn awareness of true calling? Does he already know, can he still remember, that the beauty and happiness of his whole life are to reflect a greater light? Does he already suspect that the darkness lies only in the shadow of turning away from the light in whom there is no shadow of turning? Does he already guess that in standing under (understanding) the light there is no shadow to be cast? See how he already casts about in the darkness for the light! This moonchild of mine keeps on reminding me that I must be moon for him as he is one to me.

Every good endowment and every perfect gift is
from above, and cometh down from the Father
of lights, with whom there is no variableness
neither shadow of turning.

—James 1:17

The child's wonder
At the old moon
Comes back nightly.
She points her finger

To the far yellow thing
Shining through the branches
Filtering on the leaves a golden sand,
Crying with her little tongue, "See the moon!"
And in her bed fading to sleep
With babblings of the moon on her little mouth.

—Carl Sandburg, *Child Moon*

There is a blue star, Janet,
Fifteen years' ride from us,
If we ride a hundred miles an hour.

There is a white star, Janet,
Forty years' ride from us,
If we ride a hundred miles an hour.
Shall we ride
To the blue star
Or the white star?

—Carl Sandburg, *Baby Toes*

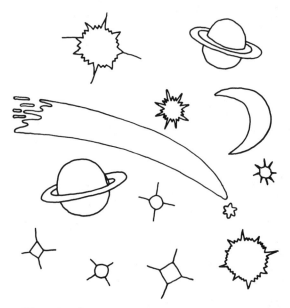

Glow-in-the-dark stars and moon—It is possible to purchase luminous paper stars, comets, and moons that self-adhere to the ceiling

LORD, BLOW THE MOON OUT, PLEASE — UNKNOWN

BED IS TOO SMALL FOR MY TIR-ED-NESS GIVE ME A HILL SOFT WITH

TREES TUCK A CLOUD UP UN-DER MY CHIN LORD

BLOW THE MOON OUT PLEASE. ROCK ME TO SLEEP IN A CRA-DLE OF

DREAMS SING ME A LULL-A-BYE OF LEAVES. TUCK A CLOUD UP

UN-DER MY CHIN LORD BLOW THE MOON OUT, PLEASE

WEE BABY MOON — UNKNOWN

THERE'S A WEE BABY MOON JUST A LY-IN ON HIS

BACK* WITH HIS LITTLE TI-NY TOES IN THE AIR;

AND HE'S ALL BY HIM-SELF IN THE DEEP BLUE

SKY, BUT THE FUNNY LITTLE MOON DOES'NT CARE

* For a long time someone we know thought this meant that the moon had a lion on his back.

over a child's bed. They are mysterious and pleasant to see in the dark—and small enough to give the impression of being real stars in a real sky. Expose to bright light for a minute or so and the stars will glow for an hour. □

Bedtime books about bedtime

A lot of books for bedtime are listed here because there are a lot of bedtimes (alas, sometimes several per night) and because this is an ideal time for books. It is a time to be still together and a time to leave the day behind. A time to let go. But books are wonderful for the morning, too. Children wait so long for us in the morning. Take five minutes before breakfast to read just one story and see what a difference it makes in the start of a day.

[*Note:* Numbers in parentheses indicate comprehension levels (not age) as outlined on pp. 7–9, 195, 197, 201, 207. Starred titles are those deemed superior for a preschoolers' home library. See pp. 6–7, 193–94 for additional information regarding book notations and selection.]

A Child's Good Night Book
by Margaret Wise Brown, illus. by Jean Chalot
Where everyone and everything goes when night falls. Ends with, "Dear Father hear and bless thy beasts and singing birds, And guard with tenderness small things that have no words." The rather crude art is strangely beautiful.
Young Scott, hardcover, 4 colors, 8¼" x 9½", 40 pp., (1–4).

The Golden Sleepy Book
by Margaret Wise Brown, illus. by Garth Williams
7 stories and poems about going to sleep. Charming illustrations.
A Little Golden Book. Golden, board, 4 colors, 6½" x 8", 24 pp., (3–4).

* Goodnight Moon
by Margaret Wise Brown, illus. by Clement Hurd
Just the best, coziest kind of good night ever.
Harper & Row, board, 4 colors, 8" x 6¾", 40 pp., (1–4).

Hush, Hush, It's Sleepytime
by Peggy Parish, illus. by Mel Crawford
All the farm animals, and finally the children, draw close to their mothers and become ready for sleep. Nice art and atmosphere.
A Little Golden Book. Golden, board, 4 colors, 6½" x 8", (1–2).

I Wonder What's Under
by Doris Herold Lund, illus. by Janet McCaffery
Instead of rehearsing what isn't under the child's bed (no ghosts, monsters, or bears), the father in this book tells exactly what's under the bed (rug, dust, floor, kitchen ceiling . . . earth, world). A sensible approach whether you buy the book or not.
Parents Magazine Press, hardcover, 4 colors, 10" x 7¼", 48 pp., (3–4).

Little People of the Night
by Laura Bannon
A little boy stays up and goes out at night to see who all the creatures are that he's been hearing from his bed.
Houghton Mifflin, paperback, 1 color, 6½" x 7¾", 32 pp., (3).

Lullabies and Night Songs
music by Alec Wilder, illus. by Maurice Sendak
A very beautiful book to look at that includes a number of very lovely songs. Some of Sendak's finest illustrations.
Harper & Row, hardcover, 4 colors, 9" x 12½", 88 pp.

* Nite-Lite Library
by Robert Kraus and N. M. Bodecker
Includes three small books: *Good Night Little ABC, Good Night Little One,* and *Good Night Richard Rabbit.* All have covers that glow in the dark after being held under a light. It sounds gimmicky, but children love them, and the text and art inside are charmingly simple.
Springfellow and Dutton, board, 4 colors, 32 pp. 4½" x 5½", (3).

Poems and Prayers for the Very Young
selected and illus. by Martha Alexander
A book of perfectly lovely prayers and prayerful
poems for very young children. Includes a number
of nonreligious poems that simply inspire
wonderment and awareness. And the prayers are
not sentimental or patronizing.
Random House, paperback, 4 colors, 8″ x 8″, 32 pp.,
(3).

NOURISHMENT

Almost invariably the arrival of the new baby
seems to bring about some sort of tremendous
involvement with food and feeding. Whether
we are breast- or bottle-feeding, our entire
lives are suddenly wrapped up in bodily proc-
esses. Is it time for a feeding? Is the baby getting enough? Has she eaten too much? Hungry again or just tired? I've been feeding her
the whole afternoon so I haven't even started
to fix supper.

What happened to motherhood? Is there
nothing to it but maintenance? Somebody told
us that babies are nothing but little eating
and pooping machines. We didn't think that
was a nice joke at the time—now we don't
think it is a joke at all.

So after a few months the digestive difficulties abate. The breast/bottle struggle has
worked itself out. The baby didn't die and
neither did we. Enter solid food—tidbits
everywhere and little jars of this and that.
Now on top of the concern with eating enough,
you add the worry of whether or not he's eating the right things. Next he begins to feed
himself—and his hair and his eyes and the
highchair and the floor. Oddly enough he's a
little shy of messing up his clean hands with
the fingerpaints you bought for him. He likes

squash and beans and creamed chicken better.
One mother used to toy with the idea of plac-
ing her son in a different room for each meal—
that way she was sure that the house would be
thoroughly washed once every twenty-four
hours.

And all this time the shopping, cooking,
and cleaning up connected with your own
meals goes on, getting more and more complicated as the baby becomes mobile and wants
to play an active role in the kitchen. Somewhere along the way you've translated your
lunch into all-day snacking, and though you
feel you're eating nothing you are putting on
weight. Your hungry baby woke you at 5:00
A.M.; here it is 10:30 P.M. and you're just
starting to wash the dinner dishes.

But all the time we sort of know, and we
even say from time to time, that there just
must be an easier way. We can't quite believe
that it has to be so hard or so unpleasant. Yet
many of us never find the way—we simply endure. As with everything else, the answer
seems to lie in a right understanding of who
we really are and what it is that we are really
about.

Our difficulties reflect a strictly material
view of ourselves, the baby, and the process of
nutrition. It is always the idea that precedes
the experience. Quite unconsciously we tend
to think of our offspring in material terms.
We "made" a baby, "gave" it birth, and now
we have to feed it so that it can become big
and strong.

Did we make the baby? *How* did we do
that? Did the baby make the baby? When we
hold the brown seed of the sweet pea in our
hands or when we plant it in the soil, where is
the colorful blossom? Is it in the seed? Will

we put it into the seed? Can we say that it doesn't exist? No, we can only say that it is not material. We and the seed are participating in the materializing of an idea. What is the substance of an idea? Spirit. And what or where is the beginning or the end of an idea? No beginning. No end.

So here we are with this baby on our hands, and we are acting as if stuffing it full of food will make it into something more or other. It's as if we tried to make a sweet pea blossom out of a seed by stuffing it with soil.

The baby, like the seed, is but a partial manifestation in material terms of a whole idea. Anyone's business on this earth is to unfold or blossom, expressing what one truly is —one's idea- or ideal self—to the fullest possible extent. In material terms the baby is a sort of promise, and its growth should be the coming true of that promise. This is the same process we are going through; we are but at a different stage.

What is needed for this growth to take place? As we have begun to see, the answer is not simply material food; it is nourishment. As mothers and fathers, our job is not to create but to nourish. In nutrition the concern is with maintaining life . . . strengthening, building up, and promoting health. And what is health? Its root is the Old English word *hale* or *whole*. It is the same as the word *holy*. *Holy* is the sacred version of the word *whole*, *healthy* is the profane version. The difference between the words *healthy* and *holy* is only the distinction that has been made historically between the physical and the spiritual.

In the light of the above, however, it can be seen that a strictly physical concept of health has nothing at all to do with wholeness. The body can never be whole—it is at best a partial representation of a spiritual ideal. Doctors correctly refer to the baby's breathing and the beating of his heart as vital signs. They *are* not vitality, they *have* not vitality, but they express or signify vitality. It is the unfolding of the whole idea(l) self of the child with which we are concerned. Since the substance of an idea is not material but spiritual, it is obvious that spiritual nourishment is what the child needs.

So the answer to all those difficulties is holiness—or if that is too churchy or irrelevant in connotation we could say *wholiness*. We need a whole concept of the child, a whole concept of ourselves, and a whole concept of nutrition. In a terrible experiment, a number of infants were once raised without any demonstrations of love. They were meticulously fed, changed, and bathed, but never fondled or talked to. They all died. They were fed nothing of their true selves, so they had nothing to manifest.

The ideal food for fostering the ideal growth of the ideal child must be love, since, after all, the ideal man is above all loving man. There is a sense in which we can say that food makes the man. If we want our children to become peaceful, assured, grateful, and loving adults we must nourish them with peace, assurance, gratitude and love.

So what have we been feeding our baby? Probably mostly milk and worry—also discouragement, guilt, resentment, despair, and general uptightness. No wonder things have been going so badly. Fortunately the baby is not yet conscious enough to learn these things from us or even to experience them on an emotional plane. He is so largely a material translation of his ideal self that most of the mental nutrition (or malnutrition) we pass on to him is translated into temporary physical terms. He is not at all conscious of our worry or nervousness—he merely experiences them and reveals them to us in terms of physical discomfort, struggling, spitting up, etc. However, if we can feed him on love—the true stuff of his true self—we will see this translated into a physical state of peaceful well-being.

But we can only feed him what we have, and we can only have what we know. Once we reach physical maturity, our nourishment is more and more a matter of pure idea. As ideal selves, our fulfillment ultimately depends upon our consciousness of the truth about ourselves. This means knowing and expressing love, peace, gratitude, assurance, generosity, and joy.

At this point we can begin to see how the baby is as much an instrument of nourishment for us as we are for him. We can foster his growth as a peaceful and loving individual only if we nourish him with love and peace. We can express love and peace only if we know love and peace. And we can know love and peace only if this is what we hunger for and feed upon in consciousness. Though we do not quite know why, most of us would do more for our babies than we have ever been willing to do for anyone, even ourselves. In this way the wee child (seemingly so helpless) awakens in us a tremendous appetite for understanding and so brings us to the table of love.

Practically speaking what does this mean? To the extent we genuinely understand and appreciate that love is the central issue, our lives can be transformed. Instead of feeling secretly resentful about the sacrifices we are making (of, say, sleep, time, and our college education) to feed the child, we can now be appreciatively aware that we are feasting with him on the milk of love. In such an atmosphere all the former problems disappear altogether, diminish in number and intensity, or cease to be problems.

In breast-feeding, now that we are no longer uptight the milk flows freely and does not sour the stomach. The baby, no longer surrounded by worry, becomes his peaceful, comfortable self. Now, though we enjoy them more, we may have fewer feedings, also fewer diapers and spit-ups (less digestive difficulty), less laundry, and—though we need it less—more sleep. We are suddenly struck by the fact that the milk (which we did nothing to make) *is there.* Likewise the love we wish to express is also simply there whenever, like children turning to their mother's breasts, we sincerely turn our attention to it.

The work of food preparation, spoon-feeding, and cleaning up is also decreased to a large extent. Having greater faith in the wholeness of the child, we don't manufacture seven-course trial menus anymore and we don't spend hours trying to "get him to eat." One mother used so many pots and pans fixing supper for her baby that she had to wash dishes before she could cook dinner for herself and her husband. Best of all, we enjoy all these proceedings more, because it is pleasanter to be concerned with fellowship and generosity and love at mealtimes and because we understand that this expression of goodness is as important to our fulfillment as to the child's.

Now the counter where the meals are prepared is the altar at which the mundane becomes the sublime. The material self is sacrificed for the discovery of the ideal self. The kitchen is the holy of holies, the joyful of joyfuls of the home. Here the work of consecration is carried out, the translating of our lives and the lives of those we love from material into spiritual terms.

Breast-feeding

Like newborn babes, long for the pure spiritual milk, that by it you may grow up to salvation; for you have tasted the kindness of the Lord.

–I Peter 2:2–3

But I have calmed and quieted my soul, like a child quieted at its mother's breast, like a child that is quieted is my soul.

–Psalms 131:2

It is good that so many women are again seeking to breast-feed their babies. It is beautiful, really, the way the child turns to the mother and the mother bends to the child and what each needs just comes. But breast-feeding shouldn't become cultic. It isn't a necessity. It should be valued for what it signifies about ideal reality. Some of the biggest advantages of breast-feeding are for the mother. It is an almost unbeatable exercise in love and faith which can enrich us with important new layers of understanding. If it goes well, it can also spare us many messy feeding days. Many mothers feed their children nothing but breast milk until around 5 months. Then food is gradually introduced (by this time the babies can eat without slobbering everything all over the place). And by 8 or 9 months the babies are proficient with training cups and largely able to feed themselves. No bottles ever! In general if you want to breast-feed it seems well to (1) imagine that you are a cave woman with no other alternative; (2) situate yourself in the most peaceful circumstances possible for each feeding; (3) seek a profound awareness of love; (4) affirm that there isn't anything in the world more important for you to do at the moment.

Feeding

Almost as soon as he starts receiving solid food (assuming it isn't introduced for a few months), the baby begins to want to feed himself. Now he will eat the soft foods you prepare for him more happily if you also give him something to be busy with. He has important problems to solve. At last the whole, loaded fist arrives inside the mouth. But it cannot be opened there. How to remove the hand without dropping the food into the lap? It's not easy, and it's not neat. But it's very funny and quite beautiful if beheld in the right light. He will like to pick up and feed himself pieces of canned, peeled fruit, of bananas, cheese, macaroni (it dissolves even if swallowed whole), small meatballs made of puréed cooked meat, a slice of toast, five or six peas, soft sandwich cubes, and all kinds of omelets. □

Don't forget that a full set of teeth is not necessary for chewing—all of the above can be managed without any teeth at all. Also don't forget that the baby does not have to be made to eat, and don't worry that he will like only what's bad for him. The most important thing about the meal is the friendly, appreciative, peaceful coming together.

Training cups—Lidded cups are indispensable for helping the very young child learn to drink from a cup by himself. Transparent ones are handy because you can see at a glance if there is anything left in the cup, but they are more breakable than some of the opaque ones. □

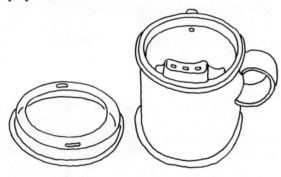

Pyrex pie plates—In the 8-inch size, these make good plates for preschoolers who have outgrown the "cereal" dishes designed for babies, but who still need sides to help them load their forks and spoons.

Clothes pins—To convert anything—dish towels, cloth diapers, table napkins—into bibs use small, plastic clothes pins (the kind with a spring). Use two clothes pins and you can fashion yourself an apron out of any hand towel.

Cookbooks

It's very easy these days to go overboard on the subject of nutrition. It is possible to make a religion out of vitamins and eating, and specimens out of our children. Health is important, but it must be viewed as wholeness, not just physical well-being. In fact, it's *unhealthy* to lose perspective and become overly concerned with diet and health. There are quite a few "healthy" cookbooks available— some specifically concerned with the diets of babies and children. They can indeed be helpful, but it is well to use them less as references on nutrition than as stores of menu ideas. Read for inspiration regarding what you might fix for your young child and how you might prepare it.

Highchairs

We couldn't possibly do a survey of all the highchairs in existence or recommend a best one. But a little can be said about the concerns involved. The biggest is the clean-up. Be sure to buy a highchair with a detachable tray (for washing in the kitchen sink) and with a space between the back and seat (for easily sponging off squashed food). The bigger the tray the better since there are so many other nice things to do in highchairs besides eating. Some trays extend back a little under the arms which prevents a few of the inevitable spills. It should be possible to set the tray in several positions (nearer or farther from the child). You may also want an adjustable footrest though this seems a less important concern. Try taking the tray off and putting it on once or twice to see if it goes easily. Make sure that, when mounted, the surface of the tray is level. This seems so obvious, but we once used one with slanted arms. Everything slid toward the child and ulti-

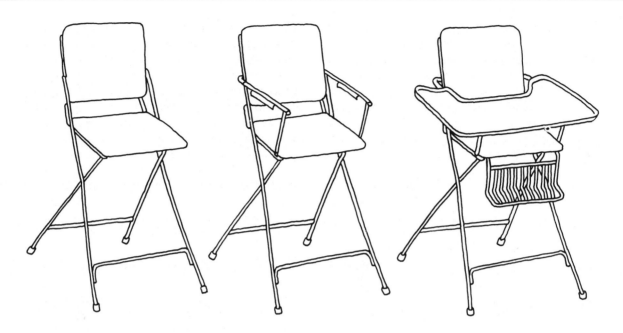

mately wound up in his lap! Chrome and vinyl are easier to clean than wood. □

Old-fashioned Highchairs—We bought an old-fashioned, wooden highchair, partly because we were ignorant, partly because in our small apartment the highchair had to live in the living room, and partly because we found an irresistibly lovely one in a thrift shop for $9. But it was a trial! The tray was not detachable and had nasty little corners that were almost impossible to clean. There wasn't much to do about the cleaning problem although a coat of bartop varnish helped to make the surface more readily washable. But worst of all, because the tray was not adjustable, our son kept standing up on the seat and turning around to gnaw (with his mouth full of pudding) on the back posts. It wasn't until our second child was doing his standing thing (as

maddening as it is dangerous) that someone who once worked in a children's hospital told us what to do. The answer was run an apron or dish towel across his chest, under his arms, and tie it behind the chair. Even he was relieved by this end to a long wrestling match. You can also use a harness for this purpose.

The highchair is not only an eating place. It can also be used as a place of quiet refuge, heightened concentration, and change of pace and perspective. At the end of the day when she may be a little restless and tired and you are fixing her supper, let your child sit beside you in her highchair. She will like to watch what you are doing, to help, or to play with some kitchen tools. And at the end of a family meal when she would like to get down but you would like to finish eating first, give her a simple puzzle to work in the highchair. Finally, the highchair is a wonderful place for creative projects that might otherwise be hazardous to your decor. A small pad of paper and some watercolors, crayons, or felt-tip markers (water-based ones), play dough—the very young child will enjoy all these activities with greater concentration and less mess in the gentle confinement of the highchair.

Someone's in the Kitchen

After you get through the feeding fuss, you enter the under-foot phase. It would take you five minutes alone to fix supper but someone you know wants to be held. Ever try to operate an eggbeater with one hand? Once again, it is helpful to understand that the time he spends with us in the kitchen may be as nourishing for him as what he eats. It is even more helpful if we can see that there is something for us in all this as well.

There are two reasons for including our children in our kitchen activities. One is that we can't keep them out and get anything done at the same time. The other is that this is the best place in the house for both of us to learn more of what we most need to know. We each have certain material and certain spiritual work that can best be done in the kitchen. The preschooler's biggest task is to explore the material properties of his world and how to deal with them. For this there is no finer or better-equipped learning laboratory than the average kitchen. Our own material work in the kitchen is all too obvious and endless to need detailing here. But above all, here in the kitchen is where the spiritual nutrients of, for example, love, humility, abundance, steadfastness, and appreciation are most concretely expressible. Here especially we can discover for ourselves and demonstrate for our children what these qualities mean. By consecrating our work and ourselves into these terms, both we and our children will be well nourished before we get to the table. Here are a few practical ideas to be filed under nourishment.

Best kitchen toys

For children under a year, the *potato and onion bin* is delightful and, relatively speaking, creates an easy mess to clean up. The onions are fascinating to peel, and washed potatoes are great rumblers and rollers.

The *coffee pot* (nonelectric, metal percolator, or drip pot) is the world's best first puzzle and stack toy.

Have some low *cupboards* and *drawers* that are all clear for the baby. Putting in and taking out *pots and pans, colanders, strainers, plastic containers,* or just opening and closing the doors themselves—are all absorbing and edifying activities for tiny hands.

Until label-peeling is discovered, *canned goods* can be used for blocks and are especially fun if you happen to store them on a *turntable.*

From the kitchen drawer come endless delights of *smaller utensils:* spoons, spatulas, pinchers, an old egg beater, measuring cups, whisks (we never really needed to buy a rattle). Egg and apple slicers, cookie cutters, potato ricer, and butter knife make a fine modeling set when play-dough age is reached.

A set of *cookie cutters* is nice to have when there are children around, it isn't always easy to find good ones. Besides cookie-making, these are good for cutting sandwiches (an effortless way to teach shapes—eat a semicircle!), play dough, and even watermelon.

The *kitchen sink* with a little water and some ladles, cups, sieves, and the wonderful coffee pot or some boats will last for hours. Almost all educators agree that this water play is important for children, and the children's own, deep interest in it seems proof.

A *cannister of rice* is *the* indoor substitute for sand and water play. It is good for pouring, piling, stirring, scooping, and shoveling. It is clean, not sticky, and okay to eat. If you insist, it can even be washed and cooked later. We found that this rice play was so absorbing that we built a special table for the purpose —called "rice table" after the Indonesian, twenty-one dish, smorgasbord-type meal. At our rice table twenty-one dishes may be used, but of course only one recipe is followed. To make a rice table that can nicely double as a sand and water table, simply build a table approximately 24 inches in height and with a small saber saw cut a hole into which a basin can fit. If you don't have a saber saw, buy a rectangular basin and design the table top with a space for it.

Magnetic letters, numbers, and shapes—The word has gotten around that the refrigerator door is a useful place for these. And it's true. At first the shapes are nicest, but the numbers and letters become useful quickly. Don't keep quantities on the door for they quickly wind up on the floor and are a nuisance to collect. Just a few at a time will do. And buy only the letters, shapes, and numbers; don't bother with the magnetic boards, unless you decide on the magnetic chalkboard which serves two purposes. These magnetic things also work on most bathtubs.

Foods for thought

Fresh green peas in the pod—A bowlful is a miracle of abundance and beauty and mystery any two-year-old can appreciate. A whole afternoon of package-opening and healthy (unsticky) nibbling, and perhaps talking a bit about growth and how the peas got there.

Corn on the cob—Give her one ear as a present. Let her husk it leaf by leaf (help only when she finds it too difficult), discovering the silk and, at last, the amazing hundreds of row-by-row kernels. She will like it raw as well as cooked. Introduce her to both ways.

Popcorn on the cob—Even more amazing, if you can find it. For best protection of your house, don't butter.

A pumpkin—On Halloween a 1½-year-old and his mother made a jack-o'-lantern. The process filled nearly a whole day of waking time. The child mostly sat and watched in his highchair, delighting first in the revelation of the seeds ("What do you suppose we will find?" he was asked) inside the huge, round, orange ball. While the mother carved the face, the child helped with the sorting of the seeds from the meat. They roasted the seeds for a snack and cooked the pumpkin meat (with brown sugar and butter) for a vegetable to be eaten that evening by the glow of the smiling, candlelit jack-o'-lantern. The second year he was too busy to sit so long, but enjoyed choosing a face, did a little scooping, and still appreciated it a lot.

Pomegranate—Astonishing!

Apple—If you slice an *apple* in half horizontally, you can see that the seeds are positioned in the form of a five-pointed star. If you've ever tried to draw such a star, you will marvel at the perfection of this one which got there without your help. Try the same thing with a *pear*. "Hey! How did those seeds that look like a star come there?" Then later, "And on the tree there came a bud. And the bud became a blossom, and the blossom became an apple, and I am eating that apple! If I eat its seeds will a tree grow?"

The question of how what got to the table is one of the best approaches to first science, first geography, first transportation, and first intelligent conversation. It starts with something the child is interested in, something that is happening to him, and then moves out into the wide world, taking him along, wide-eyed for the ride. For example, try these two books:

Milk
illus. by Christine Sharr
From milk at the table to mammals everywhere in no time at all.
Grosset & Dunlap, board, 4 colors, 6¼" x 7¾",
32 pp. (3).

Eggs
illus. by Esme Eve
The ones you eat and the ones (all kinds) that hatch.
Grosset & Dunlap, board, 4 colors, 6¼" x 7¾",
32 pp. (3).

See page 248 for some suggestions about kitchen chemistry and science lessons to be learned in the kitchen by the older pre-schooler. The possibilities are unending—yeast, baking soda, jello, pudding, soapsuds, food coloring. Check out the activity books in the next chapter for some good experiments.

THE BOY AND THE SPONGE

Despite almost universal agreement that spilled milk is not something to cry over, sooner or later spills do become an audible issue. After 93 patient mop-up operations as martyrs we tend to break forth and shout, "Watch out! Why don't you look what you're doing?" Or if we still manage to keep still about the spill, we hiss, "I said don't cry about it!" so venomously that the crying becomes louder. Nervous spills become more frequent, and we develop self-hate headaches from suppressed fury and rampant guilt.

For the child, crying over spilled milk is not nearly so harmful as the dread of the next spill, which amounts to fear of trying to learn. A few people hit upon the obvious answer spontaneously, but for the rest of us it took the whole Montessori movement to call our attention to the idea of the child-wielded sponge. Show him how to use one—how to dampen and squeeze one out, how to sponge up a spill with light circular motions, squeezing out the sponge and wiping again. What you think is a chore is a freedom to him, not only the freedom of a new skill, but freedom from a whole scene of tensions that impede learning and disrupt peace. This way he has the freedom to get out of his own predicament. We cannot shout or scold immaturity out of him. Mature coordination, judgment, and alertness come only with time and experience.

One parent reported the following results the first time she tried the sponge approach: "He had just spilled his paints for the fourth time in half an hour. I knew better than to get mad, but I felt angry and he was looking worried because he knew I was not happy. I was considering putting the paints away just to avoid another accident. Then I remembered about the sponge. I gave him one and said, 'How would you like to clean it up yourself this time?' He looked at me as if I had just given him a present. He was so relieved. 'Oh, Mommy, I love you!' he said. I didn't know whether to be sad or happy—it takes so little, but most of the time you just don't see it. Now whenever he is doing something in which spilling is a possibility I make sure that he has a sponge nearby."

Don't expect miracles right off the bat. It takes time to learn to use a sponge just as it takes years to outgrow spills (since when have we stopped spilling things ourselves?). Also, don't make sponging up a punishment. If you approach it that way, the child will for sure develop the idea that mopping up is for you and the birds, and never discover that it's a freedom.

Helping

Helping means being like Mommy and Daddy. And even before they know the words, they will aspire to that. Before the age of two they can, and will already appreciate the challenge of:

• *"Washing"* unbreakable dishes and vegetables and *drying* silverware
• *sponging* off cabinets (let her have her own sponge) and *dusting*
• *unwrapping* a stick of margarine (while you season the meat, put it in the oven, peel the potatoes, and wash his hands)
• *peeling* off the outer layers of an onion (while you peel and finely chop six)
• *breaking* the yolk of an egg before you beat it and *dumping* the pudding mix into the pan
• *telling* you when it starts to bubble
• *throwing* anything away
• *carrying* things from here to there (the littlest ones have a tireless love of missions and cooperative efforts)
• *putting* the bread on top and wrapping sandwiches

And so on. The more *we* cooperate, the more we will be inspired with the appropriate ideas at the appropriate times. And we will be blessed a hundred times over for our generosity in priceless companionship and incredible beauty—for there is nothing quite so grateful or so perfectly lovely as a child who is merely being allowed to learn.

Not helping

Worse than not allowing our children to help is expecting too much or insisting. This happens, too. You hear people hissing things like "Can't you do anything right? You're no help at all!" That is devastatingly not the point. Watch a child try to put a cloth table mat on the table for the first time. He will try to lift it from the bottom edge, not realizing yet that the material will flop down. All these things have to be learned. Then if he hasn't come to hate the failure connected with his efforts to be helpful he will indeed be a help.

See page 259 for suggestions about child-sized pots and pans and housekeeping equipment.

A monk told Joshu: "I have just entered the monastery. Please teach me."
Joshu asked: "Have you eaten your rice porridge?"
The monk replied: "I have eaten."
Joshu said: "Then you had better wash your bowl."
At that moment the monk was enlightened.

–*Zen Flesh, Zen Bones,* compiled by Paul Reps

Jesus said, "Therefore I say unto you, Take no thought for your life, what ye shall eat, or what ye shall drink; nor yet for the body, what ye shall put on. Is not the life more than meat, and the body than raiment? Behold the fowls of the air; for they sow not, neither do they reap, nor gather into barns; yet your heavenly Father feedeth them. Are ye not much better than they? Which of you by taking thought can add one cubit unto his stature? And why take ye thought for raiment? Consider the lilies of the field, how they grow; they toil not, neither do they spin: And yet I say unto you, that even Solomon in all his glory was not arrayed like one of these. Wherefore, if God so clothes the grass of the field, which today is, and tomorrow is cast into the oven, shall he not much more clothe you, O ye of little faith? Therefore take no thought, saying, What shall we eat? or, what shall we drink? or, wherewithal shall we be clothed? (For after all these things do the Gentiles seek:) for your heavenly Father knoweth that ye have need of all these things. But seek ye first the kingdom of God, and his righteousness; and all these things shall be added unto you.

–Matthew 6:25–33

Man shall not live by bread alone, but by every word that proceedeth out of the mouth of God.

–Matthew 4:4

When a hungry monk at work heard the dinner gong he immediately dropped his work and showed himself in the dining room. The master, seeing him, laughed heartily, for the monk had been acting Zen to its fullest extent. Nothing could be more natural; the one thing needful is to open one's eye to the significance of it all.

–D. T. Suzuki, *Introduction to Zen Buddhism*

Happiness and Understanding

In almost no time at all it becomes obvious that even our littlest children are seeking everywhere the same goals we are. Even the newborn baby already experiences himself to be one thing and life or other people or the outside another. When his blanket is unwrapped or he is lowered into his bed too quickly, he flails his arms and perhaps cries. Evidently he feels his *self* being unwrapped and exposed; he feels his *self* falling from some goodness. His startle reflex shows that this feeling of self as separated from something comes as a sort of unhappy shock. With this perception comes the experience of limitation (and lack) and the desire to overcome limitation—to sit, to walk, to crawl, to run, to fly; to find enough security, freedom, love.

Having discovered that he is a separate self he embarks on the struggle to get his *self* taken care of or to become an adequate separate self, one that can take care of itself. He does not know what he is searching for or even that he is searching, but we can see that everything he does is part of the search to understand what he is and what life is and how the apparent distance between is to be dealt with or overcome.

The great understanders or wise men of history, such as Jesus and Buddha, tell us that there is no distance between, no self and no other; hence, no separation or limitation. They say our only limitation is ignorance—that we and life are one and that our one nature is all good. They say that even if we could overcome all our *experiences* of physical, material, emotional, psychological, and intellectual limitation, to be happy we would still have to understand that reality (with which we are one) is infinite love, freedom, intelligence, harmony, beauty—in short, that there never was such a thing as limitation or a gap in the first place.

Well timed and at their best, toys are a means through which a baby or child can experience on a material plane certain of these spiritual realities. Through puzzles and blocks he experiences unity; through learning to walk or riding a trike he experiences freedom; through music and art, beauty; through books, meaning and truth; through pets and friends and family, love. When these experiences break in upon the child we see that he is happy. For a moment that sense of gap between self and other is overcome and the child rejoices. Without quite realizing it but *without doubting it either,* he learns that the unity, beauty, freedom, truth, and love he desires to find (because they are the truth about him, too) are *so.* That's why play is so much fun. Because the child's work with his toys brings him happiness, we call it play and buy more toys. But *having* toys is not the fun; it's the learning and experiencing of truth that is so happy. The toy is just a means. This is obvious from the fact that children lose interest in a toy as soon as they have learned all they can from it.

On an adult level we work more than we play. But we only call our work *work* because we have come to think that happy has something to do with having, rather than with finding out. That's probably why having a baby, for example, often comes as such a jolt. There are all kinds of reasons for *having* babies. Some people have them to be creative, some hope to fill a lonely space in their lives. But most of the motives are part of this human quest to establish one's separate self as a more adequate or self-sufficient separate self. This never works since the basic perception of separated selfhood (whether a having or a lacking one) is not happy. *Having* a baby cannot be happy: If we don't like our new parental role, we aren't happy because we don't like it; if we do like it, we still aren't happy because sooner or later it's going to be over and then what will we have left.

Another reason we call our work *work* is that we do not trust in the reality of the goodness we experience. If things go well, and our lives seem to flow smoothly for a minute, we call it luck or coincidence. When confronted with abundance, goodness, beauty, effortlessness, we say, "Oh, if only it would always be like this, if only it were really true." We do not go quite far enough to ask, *"Where did it come from if it isn't true?"* But we can take a cue from our children about this. On a higher level we are involved in the same searching to overcome gaps as our children. Now it is no longer a matter of simple experience, but of perception. After all, unity, freedom, beauty, meaning, and love are not things (toys) that we can have. They are ideas, which by definition can only be ours in understanding, through conscious realization, that they are so. So happiness depends on learning. We can see this from watching our children who are so clearly happy when they are learning.

A good toy is one through which a child experientially discovers principles; that is, he experiences their effects. This is the beginning of developing an appreciation of principles. Somewhere in the process of growing up, the joy in the experience of principle gets all mixed up with the thing or conditions through which this experience occurs. ("Why don't you take better care of your things? I laid out good money for that toy, and now you've broken it. Well, don't think I'm just going to run out and buy another one!") We get distracted. Instead of moving smoothly from experiencing to seeking to understand or realize principle, we get all involved with trying to acquire things or set up situations in which we can *have* the experiences. Detached from principle, these efforts fail, and we even begin to assume that the principles are not so. We are now as unhappy as we can be, for the true self, the soul in us, goes on yearning and will not give up seeking its truly happy idea(l) fulfillment, the overcoming of our sense of separation.

A child is not a toy but, as we have seen, a toy is not really a toy either. Properly understood, both are instruments through which principles are perceivable. The child so clearly demonstrates in his play that happiness occurs when truthful principles come together with the true self, and that therefore learning (the child on a material plane, the parent on a conscious plane) rather than having or doing is what leads to this happiness. Once we understand this we can proceed to find fulfillment in every moment and in any circumstance or activity in which we find ourselves.

Children are instrumental in our lives in many ways. Like good toys they express certain qualities of spiritual reality as being undeniably so. We know that they do not possess or understand these qualities; we know (if we are honest) that we have not put them there. Yet there they are. Marvel at it! This sourceless purity, beauty, intelligence, vitality, love reflected in our children with such startling clarity! If we can learn to look *through* our babies in this nonpersonal way, especially before they have learned very much about self and other, we cannot fail to observe this sourcelessness, the incredible is-so-ness of these qualities—peace in the sweet sleeping and still watching, love in the fearless expectancy of perfection, intelligence in the alert searching, vitality in the ever-aliveness, unity in the working together of all parts and all functions for good. Where did all this come from? Where is it located? What is it if it isn't so?

Just as a good toy invites a response from the child, children also have a way of personally involving us with these qualities and of eliciting them from us through their everlastingly happy expectancy which we do not wish to disappoint. So here we are confronted with the is-so-ness of goodness and the necessity and possibility of being good. In proportion as we give ourselves over to this goodness we begin to experience the overcoming of the self/other gap much as the child experiences unity when he participates in fitting a puzzle piece into a puzzle. If we proceed from here to perceive the truthfulness of this as principle, the very idea of gap disappears along with all experiences of separation, loneliness, lack, loss, limitation, and meaninglessness. So the work of the child and the work of the parent are the same. The objective is the realization of truth. On the child's level it is a matter of experiencing truth; on our level it is a matter of perceiving, validating, and ultimately realizing it as the one nature of self, other, and life itself.

To be helpful to our children and happy as parents we must perceive the true nature of play as work and discover that the pleasure of work is the learning principle. Once we discover that true fulfillment is spiritual understanding, we will be more beneficial parents and we will be as happy in our so-called work as the child is in his play.

Our attitude toward the newborn child should be one of reverence that a spiritual being has been confined within limits perceptible to us.

–Maria Montessori, *The Secret of Childhood*

Toys and Playtime

One of the most important things to know about buying toys is when not to. The key principle in good toy buying is love; a fundamental technique in carrying out this principle is toy avoidance. For the most part, toys are an unnecessary encumbrance for parent, home, and budget, and they can even become obstacles to the child's learning and happiness. Whenever a child is given the notion that he needs to be entertained, learning comes to almost a halt. If we keep in mind that the purpose of play is learning and that toys are tools in the process rather than possessions, we will be more successful in choosing appropriate toys. Children learn so quickly. If we treat them as objects of our affection by tossing them a lot of objects (toys) when we are at a loss for love, they will quickly catch on to the idea that they are themselves no more than objects and become quite miserable and difficult to live with. This is a painful object lesson all the way around.

The solution is mostly a matter of love. The child whose essential *spiritual* perfection is constantly beheld in the parents' consciousness will concentrate raptly, and develop speedily, securely, and happily. At the same time such a parent will be readily inspired with the right idea for the right activity or toy at the right time. Toys must be introduced as fruits of rather than as substitutes for understanding. Partly it is a matter of improvising, partly of literally offering our children tools instead of toys. And to a large extent it is a matter of providing a good work/play environment both spiritual and material. The principle of love is really the subject of this entire book. What follows are some practical suggestions for how to time, improvise, avoid, substitute, buy, and manage toys and playtime to best advantage.

Timing and reach

At first the baby is mainly reaching with his ears and eyes. He almost seems to be focusing his eyes with his ears, using his hearing to aim his face at you when you speak, then peering out for you through those incredibly sincere, intelligent, unfocused eyes.

When he begins to "speak" to us, we see this same reaching for focus—the generalized groping toward the specific. He sees you, smiles, and then his whole body reaches for the means of communication. The shoulders come forward, he exhales through rounded lips, and a soft lovely "Ho" comes forth—the purest, dearest sound ever. Answer it on its own terms with another soft "Ho" and you have had your first conversation. It's an astonishing miracle of love.

Slowly the hands come into play—first as unrecognized servants of the mouth, then more and more as a means of reaching out to explore the many things he now sees and hears.

This reaching is the crux. Everything follows from the reaching. It is meticulously and minutely ordered in favor of progress. For example, at a certain period a baby will open and close his hand several times when reaching for a desired object. He does not know to raise the hand and bring it down upon the toy. We watch compassionately as the opening fist actually pushes the toy farther from his grasp. He will soon become frustrated and rely upon our assistance for relief. But in the meantime we notice something wonderful. In striving to reach out for the toy, the baby now draws up one leg. This is the beginning of crawling! The very inadequacy of his grasp initiates his discovery of the possibility of mobility!

Likewise, at a certain point diaper-changing becomes difficult because the baby is suddenly overcome with the desire to see what is behind his head. He looks up, cranes his neck, arches his back, reaches with his arm, then with his leg—reaching, reaching. He doesn't know it, but this is the beginning of turning over. No one is as surprised as he is when one day—plop—he suddenly finds himself on his tummy.

The key to helping our babies is perceiving the reaching and responding to it in the most helpful—that is, the least interfering and most meaningful (to the baby)—manner possible. We can gauge our response by the happiness it evokes in the baby. For example, if we "ho" back to the "ho"ing baby we will see a smile and perhaps even a laugh of pleasure that seems to mean *mission accomplished. We have reached each other.* From "ho" we may move soon to repeated, one-syllable, explosive sounds—"Buh! Buh! Buh!"—which we find evoke almost startled laughter. But "hey diddle diddle" is still apparently too complex—just part of the background din that doesn't penetrate. We can see from the lack of reaction that such complicated sounds do not yet register at all.

Sometimes we bring an out-of-reach toy within reach to relieve the striving baby before he becomes discouraged. But sometimes instead, perceiving the link between reaching and crawling, we place our hands beneath the soles of his feet, helping him to discover the possibility of pushing off toward the desired toy.

Most of our assistance should not be given in the form of toys at all, but where toys are appropriate, the main guideline for what and when is reach. Month and age criteria are uselessly arbitrary and are part of a very detrimental tendency to question the unique perfection of our children and compare them (and ourselves) with each other. The time to introduce a toy is when the child is in fact or in principle reaching for it. It is most useful if we can see beyond the child's reach to the ultimate principle being sought. His desire to walk is the quest for freedom; his love of bright pictures and music is the quest for beauty; his urge to speak is the quest for truth and meaning; his wish to be held is the quest for love. If we appreciate that principle is the central issue, we need only to watch our children to perceive when a particular toy would be most helpful.

For these reasons most toys, books, and pieces of equipment have been organized according to the main principles they serve rather than according to chronological or circumstantial categories (although some effort has been made within each chapter to present things according to progressive difficulty). The hope is that this approach will make it easier for us to be more responsively helpful to our children, while at the same time fostering our own discovery that discovery is the secret of happiness.

The following chart gives a rough idea of when things might be introduced to babies and where they might be found in this book. Such charting becomes increasingly useless as the children grow and become more obviously different in their interests and pace. Once walking begins, in fact even before that, a chart is useless. You just have to watch what's going on.

	Freedom	Unity	Beauty	Truth	Love
Lying	crib gym being carried carrier carriage jumper	hand toys textures touching parents cribmobile	light plastic envelope mobiles bells music box lullabies records	picture books baby-talk (sounds)	hugging holding smiling laughing beholding knowing

Sitting-Standing	walker
	stroller
	back carrier
	safety gate
	safety locks
	wheeled things
	roughhousing
		kitchen stuff
		pounding bench
		stack and nest
		puzzle
		  (to take apart)
		telephone
		tinker tools
		sand, water
		bath boat
			low mirror
			pictures
			mobiles
			music box
			xylophone
			play dough
				books and
				  more books
				questions
				  and answers
				talk and
				  more talk
				wordbooks
					hugging
					holding
					smiling
					sitter
					dog
					zoo
					beholding
					knowing

Crawling-Walking-Running	back carrier
	bike carrier
	stroller
	walks
	push/pull toys
	swimming
	sliding
	swing
	ride-em
	  cars and trucks
	books about
	  transportation
	trike
		puzzles
		blocks
		construction sets
		spindlecraft
		free-form posts
		pegboard
		constructs
		tools
		books about
		  building
		sand, water
		play dough
			play dough
			paints
			crayons,
			pictures
			mobiles
			songbooks
			records
			kazoo
			xylophone
			dancing
			singing
				word and
				  concept books
				storybooks
				a little TV
				conversation
				library
					hugging
					holding and some-
					  times not hugging
					  or holding
					science
					plants
					animals
					friends
					pretense
					dolls
					costumes
					books about
					  everything

Not Buying Toys

Improvising

It doesn't make much sense to buy many toys for babies. Play is work, and the baby is supremely motivated to do this work, which involves a thorough sensory examination of all the properties of anything he can get his hands on. When this work is done, the object ceases to be interesting. This doesn't take very long because every baby works fast in his enthusiasm for growing. So, as much as possible, use things you find around the house—plastic measuring spoons, potholders, coasters, etc. Babyfood jars, plastic bottles, and boxes can be filled with colored water or split peas or beads or buttons *until* the baby learns to open or break them or *unless* he has an older toddler sibling who doesn't know any better than to do it for him.

From sitting to crawling is perhaps the easiest time of all. At this stage children like anything you put in front of them and they work with these things diligently—from patting to pounding to picking up to putting in and taking out and putting in and taking out. From standing to walking to running, things happen very quickly and busily. When he tries to walk set up a walking tour. Arrange a few chairs and low tables so that the child can progress from one to the other while still holding on. Put a cookie on one chair, a box with some buttons inside on another, some costume jewelry on another, a favorite toy on another.

Avoiding

Many toys that seem to be worthwhile at first are ultimately a disappointment. It is well to avoid or at least be cautious about the following:

Baby home learning programs—As soon as you have a new baby you are likely to find yourself on a surprising number of mailing lists, many of which want you to subscribe to their home learning program for your baby. They may offer to send new toys each month (pretested to suit the development of the child) plus wall charts or booklets for recording the baby's growth, and a sort of teacher's manual for the parent. There may be an exception or two, but most of these cost more than they're worth, and they often result in your receiving toys that are not well made, useful or attractive. Because all babies and parents are different, the time progressions of these programs are more arbitrary than helpful. In general, it is better to select what you need (very little) as you go along. Base your decisions on interests manifested by the child. You may want to look over the brochures you receive. To discover what is available and perhaps pick up some ideas for things to do with your child. But then go on your own way. And, if possible don't buy anything without seeing it first unless you know the dealer or manufacturer to be consistently reliable. □

One-act plays—Some beautiful, well-made, educationally sound toys that are valuable in a preschool are nevertheless not worth two cents as purchases for the home because the child will learn everything they offer in a few minutes. At least in the beginning, children are not interested in the having of toys (possessiveness is an acquired trait), but in what they can learn. As soon the child has learned all he can from a toy, he will lose interest in it. If he can learn everything in one sitting, he will be through with it in one sitting. Glenn Doman estimates that the average toy designed for the average 18-month-old lasts 90 seconds. (See Doman's book, *How to Teach Your Baby to Read,* New York: Random House, 1964.)

Babysitter toys—Sometimes a parent wants to find a toy that will "really keep her occupied so I can get some work done." This hardly ever works because the motive is tantamount to an open invitation to the child to cling. But if you are looking for something in this category that *will* work, here are some things to consider.

A lot of very expensive, very elaborate, "busy" toys bedazzle but are really not worth much. While an occasional busy toy will give exceptional mileage, big garage or farm or school sets take up tremendous amounts of space on a permanent basis, teach little, and are generally rather ugly. Partly it's that we buy them too soon—they are really more suited to 4-, 5-, and 6-year-olds who are more into pretending. Some younger children do play with them a lot, but usually the intense interest of the first day of ownership burns out quickly. Nevertheless, if you want one, try to test it out at a friend's house more than once. Buy one you think you can bear to look at for a long time. Share it or trade it with friends for other "busy" toys. Set it apart from the rest and give it a spot suited to best use. A model garage or farm will be much easier to use and more interesting to the child if set at eye level on a table. □

More effective and less expensive busy toys are such use-up activities as sewing cards, stick-em booklets, coloring books, and follow-the-dots. A small set of watercolors or a box of colored pencils and a pad of paper contribute more of lasting value while occupying the child better than almost any expensive thing you could buy.

Substituting nontoys

Every time you buy a toy, you make a commitment to having it around. You have to find a place for it, pick it up frequently, and, despite the fact that your child will probably lose interest within a few days, you will probably think you have to keep it for quite a while. The assumptions are that he may regain his interest or be followed by a younger sibling who will be just as interested in the toy as he was for 24 hours.

There's no question but that most toy purchases are a matter of parental weakness. If we paid more attention and were not quite so lazy, we would see many ways to amuse and educate our children with things that are already in the house. Two or three supervised sessions with your pincushion and a dish will satisfy your toddler's curiosity and give some useful information and increased dexterity. Between sessions, the pincushion can go on residing in the sewing box for which you have already allotted space. Instead of a bead-stringing set there is the button box. Bath toys can be made from empty plastic bottles, pull toys from juice cans, blocks from boxes. In the long run these things which you can toss out at will are certainly less expensive and undoubtedly less trouble than store-bought toys which you have to shop for and then have under foot so endlessly. Furthermore our children like to use our "real" things because they are trying to grow up into real people and accomplish real ends. Stringing buttons from your sewing box is much more obviously related to sewing per se than is plopping a lot of large wooden beads from a can onto a shoe lace.

Certain concept materials such as parquetry are worth purchasing because of their beauty and precision which are difficult to duplicate in the home and because over the years they can be used on many levels.

Otherwise, about the only legitimate excuses for buying toys are safety and expense. Children would probably occupy themselves tirelessly and to maximum educational advantage with grown-ups' tools and "real" equipment if we didn't have to interfere all the time because (a) they are in danger of getting hurt or (b) part of the learning process consists of breaking things and we can't afford that. So be watchful. When you are thinking of buying a toy, consider whether or not it is something you could match with materials you already have at home. Try some of the following nontoys:

Under one-year-old

• *Telephone*—the real one with the button taped down (only when the child is not in a banging phase).
• *Transistor radio*—they love turning the knobs and watching the dial move and hearing the stations and volume change.
• *Jewelry box*—with only good-sized safe and durable things inside. He will lift the lid and close the lid, take things out and put them in, and examine and examine and examine.
• *Kitchen drawer*—full of safe things to explore.

Over one-year-old

• *Old manual typewriter.*
• *Tool box*—minus sharp things.
• *Sewing box*—also minus the sharp things.

Any desperate rainy day

• *A ball of string.*
• *A roll of toilet paper.*
• *A little masking tape.*

Montessori teachers are past masters at setting up truly worthwhile nontoy activities. In a good Montessori classroom you will find dozens of children working at the most mundane tasks with the most sublime expressions on their faces. On one tray are a small bowl full of walnuts, an empty bowl, and a pair of tongs. Another tray, also with two bowls, includes some tinier objects and a pair of tweezers. Each of these activities is entirely

self-explanatory and offers the child a practical skill. Their arrangement on trays helps to bring about a sense of security, definition, and peaceful order that could never be expressed verbally. Once the child has transferred all the nuts to the empty bowl (and probably back again) he will almost certainly replace the entire tray on the shelf from which he got it. The whole procedure is carried out by the child independently, entirely free of adult intervention. Whatever they may lack of the garish appeal of commercial toys, such activities more than make up in their appeal to the child's intelligence and his innate love of order, freedom, and peace.

One of the loveliest Christmas gifts we ever heard of was a scrap of cloth with four buttons sewed onto it. A 2½-year-old child had done the sewing. In great secrecy, her 11½-year-old sister had taught her. Of course the greatest gift was the idea and patience shown by the older child. There are so many little things our preschool children would learn with joy if we did not think of them as dull work, too hard for the child, or too time-consuming for us. Children are often happiest by our sides, doing some modified version of whatever we are doing. How few toys we would buy if we really appreciated this!

Books about toy-making, and play

One last thing to consider before heading off to purchase a commercial toy is a good practical book on home-made toys and play activities. The true craftsman's books on toy-making are best reserved for enthusiastic grandparents and friends unless you already have the necessary skills or a mother's helper to take care of your preschooler while you learn to carve or sew or carpent. But the more improvisational books on toy-making and play activities are extremely helpful in inspiring us with well-tried ideas that can be done on the spur of the moment. One such book coupled with a little enthusiasm is worth a dozen toys and will probably cost half as much as one toy. The more general and improvisational books listed below are the most useful, but along the way we ran into some specialized books that are either too oddball or too excellent to be omitted. This is not a thorough listing; it just represents some of the interesting things we ran across.

American Folk Toys and How to Make Them
by Dick Schnacke
85 American folk toys, with clear instructions for the skillful whittler.
G. P. Putnam's Sons, hardcover, 1 color, 8⅜" x 11", 224 pp.

The Big Book of Soft Toys
by Mabs Tyler, photos by Gina Harris, line illus. by John Kingsford
Clear and precise instructions for making more than 200 toys involving sewing (dolls, puppets, mobiles, balls, blocks). Bright, full-color photos are what make this book both inspiring and expensive. Meticulously thought out.
McGraw-Hill, hardcover, 4-color photos, 1-color drawing, 7" x 10", 264 pp.

Big Rock Candy Mountain
ed. by Samuel Yanes and Cia Holdorf.
"Educational Resources for our education." Not specifically concerned with preschoolers or, for that matter, even with children, this follow-up to *The Whole Earth Catalog* includes extensive reviews and excerpts from writings germane to the new consciousness in education—from Krishnamurti, Gestalt and the Sufis to cardboard carpentry. An interesting little practical book within this book is the "Playground Book" by Jay Beckwith—10 pages of imaginative ideas for building playground equipment out of anything.
Dell, paperback, 1 color, 10½" x 14½", 192 pp.

Child Care Tips for Busy Mothers
by Nancy Carlyle
Practical tips to make life with children pleasanter and easier. From coping with slippery-soled new shoes, to finger paint recipes, to long car trips. Sometimes silly, but mostly very helpful.
Simon & Schuster, paperback, 4" x 7", 128 pp.

Finger Plays for Nursery and Kindergarten
by Emilie Poulsson
A reprint of an old-timer (first published in 1893), full of elaborate fingerplays. Wonderful old illustrations.
Dover Publications, paperback, 1 color, 6¼" x 9¼", 80 pp.

Hand Shadows to Be Thrown upon the Wall: A Series of Novel and Amusing Figures Formed by the Hand
by Henry Bursill
For the zealot. 18 hand shadows, including a bird that flies, a duck that quacks, and a dog that wags. Not easy. No instructions apart from very precise drawings showing hand position and shadow cast.
Dover Publications, paperback, 1 color, 6½" x 9¼", 40 pp.

How to Make Children's Furniture and Play Equipment
by Mario Dal Fabbro
Cribs, chairs, gyms, tables, sandbox, easel, playhouse, workbench—60 clear plans for the parent handy with some power tools.
McGraw-Hill, hardcover, 1 color, 7″ x 9¾″, 108 pp.

How to Make Whirligigs and Whimmy Diddles and Other American Folkcraft Objects
by Florence H. Pettit, illus. by Laura Louise Foster
A very beautifully done book of American crafts for the dedicated craft lover. Its approximately 2 dozen projects include wooden toys to carve and paint, a small quilt for a baby, pine cone birds, a wooden Eskimo mask, and corn shuck dolls.
T. Y. Crowell, hardcover, 1 color, 8″ x 9″, 368 pp.

How to Make Sock Toys
More than 50 dolls and toys to be made from socks (especially red-heel socks from the Nelson Knitting Co. of Rockford, Ill.). Includes a monkey, hobby horse, and happy/sad double dolls. Very clear, simple instructions.
Order from Clapper Publishing, Park Ridge, Illinois 60068. 1 color, 8¼″ x 10¾″, 48 pp.

I Saw a Purple Cow and 100 Other Recipes for Learning
by Ann Cole, Carolyn Haas, Faith Bushnell, and Betty Weinberger, illus. by True Kelley.
An endless variety of things to do and make with young children. Includes play dough recipe, finger plays, toys to make. Compiled by four mothers who seem to know what they're talking about.
Little, Brown, paperback, 2 colors, 9¼″ x 8¾″, 96 pp.

Just a Box?
by Goldie Taub Chernoff, illus. by Margaret Hartelius
Many things to make from the endless cardboard boxes everything comes in. A toothpaste-box alligator, oatmeal box cradle, etc.
Scholastic Book Services, paperback, 4 colors, 9″ x 7½″, 24 pp.

The Ladybird Book of Toys and Games to Make
by James Webster, illus. by Robert Ayton
23 toys to make from any old thing. Designed for older children to do by themselves, a bargain for mothers of preschoolers.
A Ladybird Book. Penguin Books, board, 4 colors, 4½″ x 6¾″, 56 pp.

* Learning with Mother
by Ethel and Harry Wingfield
Books 1 (up to 2 years), 2 (2–3 years), 3 (3–4 years), and 4 (4–5 years). Imported from England, these unassuming little books are unusually helpful regarding what to do and how to get along with the preschooler from babyhood until five. Arranged according to chronological development, the sequence is good, though many children will be ready for things sooner than the books suggest. As small activity books they don't contain many things to do, but each idea offered suggests a dozen other ways of helping your child to learn.
A Ladybird Book. Penguin Books, 4 colors, 4½″ x 6¾″, 56 pp., 79¢ each or $3.16 for all 4.

Making Things
by Ann Wiseman
A good craft and toy-making book that is mostly for older children but good to know about. Includes a wide variety of activities from printing, to xylophone-making, to carving wooden whistles.
Little, Brown, paperback, 2 colors, 8″ x 10¼″, 176 pp.

Nomadic Furniture
by James Hennessy and Victor Papanek
This is a wonderful, practical book of intelligent ideas for flexible living. It includes some children's things such as a hanging criblet, a toddler swing, tables and storage units which you might buy ready-made or try to copy on your own, plus many good do-it-yourself ideas."
Random House, paperback, 1 color, 8½″ x 11″, 160 pp.

A Parent's Guide to Children's Play and Recreation
by Alvin Schwartz
First published in 1963, this book is not quite up to date in the materials and prices it mentions. Nevertheless, it is an exceptionally useful introduction to the activities most children enjoy,

with rough guidelines for when and suggestions for how to provide appropriate equipment inexpensively.
Collier, paperback, 4¼" x 7", 192 pp.

The Playgroup Book
by Marie Winn and Mary Ann Porcher
A superb book about all the things preschoolers like to learn from doing. A totally useful resource for parents of preschoolers, whether or not you're starting a play group.
Penguin Books, paperback, 1 color, 5" x 7¾", 224 pp.

Play and Playthings for the Preschool Child
by E. M. Matterson
Just what the title implies: a useful book brimming with suggestions for providing young children with a good play/learning environment. Special emphasis for the handy parent-with-a-hammer on building shelves, benches, gym equipment (doesn't give specific plans, just ideas to improvise on). Very useful presentations of the particular worth of various kinds of play.
Penguin Books, paperback, 1 color, 5" x 7¾", 208 pp.

Puppet Party
by Goldie Taub Chernoff, illus. by Margaret Hartelius
All kinds of simple hand puppets made from paperbags, socks, paper plates, and cups.
Scholastic Book Services, paperback, 4 colors, 9" x 7½", 24 pp.

Ship Models and How to Build Them
by Harvey Weiss
Unusually clear instructions for building model boats, some quite simple and some harder. Besides its good instructions, what is distinctive about this book is its useful presentation of some of the principles involved.
T. Y. Crowell, hardcover, 1-color photos, 2-color drawings, 7½" x 9", 88 pp.

This Little Puffin
by Elizabeth Matterson
A good collection of musical games, action songs, and finger plays. The finger plays are especially useful with very young children and do not require musical skills on the part of the parent.
Penguin Books, paperback, 1 color, 5" x 7¾", 208 pp.

Round and round the garden
(Run your index finger round the baby's palm.)
Went the Teddy Bear,
One step,
Two steps,
(Jump your finger up his arm.)
Tickly under there.
(Tickle him under his arm.)

Round and round the haystack
Went the little mouse,
One step,
Two steps,
In his little house.
(Repeat the same actions for the second verse.)
From *This Little Puffin*

* Three, Four, Open the Door
by Susan M. Stein and Sarah T. Lottick
At once just about the most conscious and practical book of activities for young children: what they accomplish, how to do them, and when. Very well thought out in response to society's growing awareness of the very young child's eagerness, ability, and right to learn. Wonderful for parents or teachers.
Follett, paperback, a few 1-color illustrations, 6" x 9", 264 pp.

Toy Book
by Steven Caney
Clear instructions on how to make and get the most out of more than 50 toys and experiments. Many of the toys are for children older than preschool age, for whom much of the fun will be in the making. But the preschooler is growing up fast and in the meantime such things as soap crayons, tube telephones, sand combs, and a creature cage are wonderful.
Workman Publishing Co., paperback, 1 color, 9" x 8¼", 176 pp.

* What to Do When "There's Nothing to Do"
by members of the staff of the Boston Children's Medical Center and Elizabeth M. Gregg, illus. by Marc Simont
601 truly practical play ideas that really work with younger children. Expresses very well the possibilities of learning and playing without buying a lot.
Dell Publishing, paperback, 1 color, 5½" x 8", 168 pp.

Toy Buying

The first and last thing to know about buying toys is that buying toys isn't important. Love, that is, intelligent love, *is* enough. If you cannot afford to buy any toys, your children can still have every educational advantage. On the other hand, we can buy all the best toys in the world and they won't help a bit unless we are there, maintaining without reservation the loving atmosphere vital to all children.

Choosing what toys to buy is a small matter compared with the overall task of determining from moment to moment how to respond to our children in an intelligently loving way. When buying a toy seems called for, here are some things to consider:

• *Physical quality*. Is it sturdy and safe? Is it strong enough to last as long as the child's interest or as long as you think it should for the price you are paying? It is a mistake to stress the safety issue to the point of fear. Generally speaking, parental watchfulness is a better answer to risk than fearful prevention. But given what your child is likely to do with her new toy (throw it, mouth it, fall on it, take it apart), is it relatively safe?

• *Physical appearance*. Is it beautiful? There's no disputing tastes when it comes to beauty, but in general is it nicely designed and har-monious in appearance? Remember it will probably be around and in sight for a long time.

• *Span of usefulness*. How long at a time will the child enjoy it and how many times?

• *Educational value*. What does it teach and is what it teaches worth learning? Is a toy really needed to teach this or is the lesson one that will easily be picked up as a matter of course?

• *Your child's stake in the toy*. Does it meet a need or interest that your child is manifesting now? This is the hardest question of all, but the most important. Even the right toy at the wrong moment is the wrong toy. You can answer all the other questions by looking at the toy, but this one can only be answered by watching and knowing your child.

• *Cost*. Balancing the price against all the above and against the limitations of your budget and living quarters, is this toy worth buying?

We don't claim that the toys recommended in the catalogs are the best. We haven't tested everything and new things are coming out all the time. But we hope that at the very least, some of the comments will make it easier for some people to discern what's best for themselves and their children.

Direct-mail sources of toys and equipment

There seems to be a resurgence of enthusiasm for shopping by mail, and, indeed, if you know what you're doing, this can be a most efficient and pleasant way to buy precisely what you need. Sometimes, what with shipping and handling costs, it is still cheaper to get up and go, but often the trekking back and forth is both more troublesome and, in the long run, more costly.

All the following sources offer some of the things recommended in this book. Many are primarily suppliers of schools and other institutions, though most of these indicate a willingness to deal with individuals as well as institutions. Quite understandably, many require of private individuals a fee for the catalog, a minimum purchase (or handling charge for small orders), and advance payment.

This list is far from comprehensive. Specifically not included are any of the dozens of general mail-order houses which offer gurgling fish pitchers, super nose-hair clips, and a few children's toys and accessories. You can almost always find some things worth considering in such catalogs, but it didn't seem necessary to list them here since one tends to get on their mailing lists whether one wants to or not.

Additional mail-order sources are listed throughout this book according to the particular products they offer. To find still more sources, consult telephone directories. In regular phone books look under *child, children, childhood, early childhood, preschool, education, toys, play,* etc. In the classified pages see "Toys," "Education," "School Furniture and Equipment." Then, of course, there are the big three of mail order—Sears Roebuck, Montgomery Ward, and J. C. Penney—which offer between them many of the most popular (though not necessarily most worthwhile) toys in America. If you desire to obtain any of these catalogs consult the telephone directory for the nearest regional or catalog offices of these nationwide stores.

Dick Blick
P.O. Box 1267
Galesburg, Ill. 61401
A very large resource of art and educational materials. Blick has a number of catalogs starting with a 318-page listing of art supplies. Most relevent to the parents of preschoolers are Blick's "Early Learning Catalog," "Enrichment Aids," and "Invicta Educational Aids."

Childcraft Education Corporation
52 Hook Rd.
Bayonne, N.J. 07002
A large collection of toys and equipment for children, including many fine imported things not generally available in the United States. Childcraft offers most of the best there is, plus some less good or silly toys. There is an excellent range of fine puzzles, art supplies, and construction toys. Childcraft blocks are superior. The regular 48-page catalog is free. But the bigger institutional catalog is much more worthwhile and is now finally being made available to individuals for $1.50.

Child Life Play Specialties, Inc.
1640 Washington St.
Holliston, Mass. 01746
An excellent source of good indoor and outdoor gymnastic equipment for children. Especially good for preschoolers are the Child Life swings, doorway gym, and kinder climber. The Child Life wooden gym sets are among the best (discreetly natural and dark green finishes) and can be purchased assembled or less expensively in kit form. Also nice for the do-it-yourselfer are some carefully selected pieces of hardware and replacement parts —hitching rings for wooden doorframes and rafters, special hitching rings for tree limbs. The 24-page, black-and-white catalog is free upon request.

Community Playthings
Rifton, New York 12471
The wooden climbing equipment, furniture, and toys manufactured by this Christian community (Society of Brothers) are all beautifully made, superior products strong enough for nursery school use. Especially recommended for the preschooler's home are Community Playthings' blocks, wall easel, plastic-topped table, workhorse, Variplay House-Gym, and A-Frame climber. High quality has won the community so much business that a

delay of a month or so is not unusual. When ordering, be patient. The 64-page, black-and-white catalog is free.

Constructive Playthings
1040 East 85th St.
Kansas City, Missouri
A large early-childhood and special-education resource similar to Novo but handier for Western and Midwestern families. No orders under $10 accepted. 168-page black and white catalog, free.

Developmental Learning Materials
7440 Natchez Ave.
Niles, Ill. 60648
A highly selective catalog of excellent educational materials for young children. Of special interest and value to preschoolers are DLM's parquetry, wooden cubes, xylophone, rhythm instruments, and puzzles. DLM also offers a unique collection of learning materials specifically designed for Spanish-speaking grade school students. The 76-page, full-color catalog is available free.

Edmund Scientific Co.
800 Edscorp Bldg.
Barrington, N.J. 08007
"Astronomy, optics, science, hobbies, para-psychology, alternate energy . . . more than 4500 unusual bargains for hobbyists, schools, and industry." A wonderful catalog for experimenters of all ages, this does include a number of things to delight and inform the preschooler. 3-ft. toy parachutes, cardboard periscope, large assortments of prisms and magnets, gigantic balloons. Their magnetic tape could prove to be the world's easiest way to make any place a bulletin board. Satisfaction guaranteed or your money back. This 164-page catalog is free.

Educational Teaching Aids
159 W. Kinzie St.
Chicago, Ill. 60610
Items for early childhood and special education. Includes a wide variety of manipulative materials selected for "their educational merit in terms of providing concrete learning experience." Besides being the only direct-mail source we found for Creative Playthings, ETA distributes some fine European manipulative materials otherwise available in the United States only through overseas mail. The 196-page 1-color catalog is available to

individuals not connected with a preschool for a fee of $1.50 (deductible from first order totaling $25 or more).

Federal Smallwares Corp.
85 Fifth Ave.
New York, N.Y. 10003
A 65-page catalog that is just full of dollhouse furniture and wonderful tiny dolls and dollhouse accessories.

Folkways Records
701 Seventh Avenue
New York, N.Y. 10026
Excellent recordings for children.

J. L. Hammett Co.
Braintree, Mass. 02184
Toys, art supplies, furniture and storage equipment, gym equipment, music, math and reading readiness, science—some good things in every category. Another institutional supplier with many worthwhile materials for the preschooler at home. Ask for the "Hammett Early Childhood and Special Education Catalog" (136 pages, 1 color).

Learning Games, Inc.
34 South Broadway
White Plains, New York 10601
Math-related games and materials including Cuisenaire rods, Geoboard, and a small line of puzzles and board games. Prices seem fairly high, but descriptive brochure and the price list are free.

Mead School Products
2 Allwood Ave.
Central Islip, N.Y. 11722
Still another fine institutional supplier of play equipment, furniture, constructions, and education play materials for early childhood and special education. Worthwhile and not found in many other catalogs are the Gerico Quad Units ("Mouse House"), lefty scissors. "All prices are those prevailing at time of shipment, and all prices F.O.B. point of shipment." The 160-page, 1-color "Mead School Products Catalog for Early Childhood" is $1.

Montgomery Schoolhouse
Montgomery, Vt. 05470
All-wood children's toys at reasonable prices. Some of these are available only through small retail shops, but the "Beach and Sandbox Series" can be ordered by mail. The brochure for this series is free.

Novo Education Corp.
124 W. 24th St.
New York, N.Y. 10011
A very large supplier of educational toys, furniture and equipment, Novo has many of the same things as Childcraft, but it is worth comparing prices before purchasing. Their 96-page, 1-color catalog is free to schools, $1 to private individuals.

Scholastic Audio-Visual Materials
906 Sylvan Avenue
Englewood Cliffs, N.J. 07632
A 44-page catalog of Scholastic's records, cassettes, films, filmstrips, and posters. Free.

Posters from Scholastic
Scholastic's marvelous free catalog of audio/visual materials includes a 2-page list of posters, charts, and prints, nearly all of which are only $1 apiece. Write to above address.

Scholastic Book Services, Starline Editions
50 West 44th Street
New York, N.Y. 10036
A catalog of more than 800 paperback children's books. See pp. 217–18 for additional information. Free.

F. A. O. Schwarz
745 Fifth Ave.
New York, N.Y. 10022
A rather expensive, but fairly inclusive collection of fine toys including the snazzy Schwarz dollhouse, and giant Steiff plush animals, but also most of the more down-to-earth good toys more people can afford. Schwarz puts out two free catalogs per year —a small one for spring/summer, and a larger one for fall/winter.

Vermont Wooden Toy Co.
Old High School Building
Waitsfield, Vt. 05673
Beautiful but costly all-wood toys, including some infant toys and many vehicles. 34-page catalog, 25¢.

Be sure to consult the following catalogs, all of which include many sources additional to those listed in this book:

The Catalogue of Catalogues
by Maria De La Iglesia
An annotated and photographically illustrated list of more than 470 shops around the world from which it is possible to buy by mail. Dick Bruna wash mitts? Flexible dollhouse dolls?
Random House, paperback, 1 color, 8½" x 11", 192 pp., $4.95.

The Catalogue of American Catalogues
by Maria De La Iglesia
Just what it says, this time covering "more than 750 shops and sources from which to buy thousands of unusual and useful goods made in the United States." A place to buy balloons by the gross? Christmas-stocking stuffers?
Random House, paperback, 1 color, 8½" x 11", 272 pp., $4.95.

The Last Updated Whole Earth Catalog
A super guide to tools, books, and techniques for do-it-yourself and slightly off-beat living. "An item is listed in the *Catalog* if it is deemed: (1) Useful as a tool, (2) Relevant to independent education, (3) High quality or low cost, (4) Easily available by mail."
Portola Institute/Random House, 1 color, 10½" x 14½", 204 pp., $5.

The Physical Environment

Organizing and Storing Toys

The physical environment in which the child works with his toys is also a matter of considerable importance. Despite the fact that toys aren't really necessary, if we can afford it and probably even if we think we can't, by the time our children are only a year old we have accumulated quite a supply. Unless we discover an orderly way of storing them, we will slowly go crazy from looking at or trying to deal with the mess. Worst of all are the Toys of Many Pieces, irresponsibly packaged in flimsy cardboard boxes that self-destruct on opening. It isn't only the picking up that's so difficult, it's the endless sorting—pegs from parquetry from blocks from beads from tiny cars. More decision-making than it takes to make a stone wall, but with no lasting result. The toys become a useless jumble which we ultimately put away on a semi-permanent basis or throw away altogether.

To avoid this some parents make an arbitrary decision never to purchase anything with small pieces. This seems too bad since, if you're going to buy toys at all, it is often these small-pieces sets that tend to offer the most absorbing and edifying activity to our children. Other parents live with the mess—perhaps confining it to the child's room and simply chucking everything into one box at the end of the day to be dumped out all at once again in the morning. This is certainly too bad. As we learn to tolerate the mess, so does the child and strewing becomes the only thing he can do with such a jumble of toys.

One mother developed a system of paper bags—Monday, Tuesday, Wednesday, etc. This worked for a short while, but didn't prove to be a lasting solution. If toy manufacturers ever want to foster more constructive use of their products and better public relations, they will offer their small-parts toys in appropriately sized boxes that are sufficiently nice-looking to serve as permanent storage units.

In the meantime and anyway, it is important that we find some way of organizing and storing the things of childhood in a reasonably effortless and orderly way. A jumble of toys only expresses the idea of amassed possessions and the purpose of play as learning gets lost. Toys are tools of learning and they will not be useful if they are in an unmanageable jumble. And of course order is important as an expression of unity, a quality of life basic to man's fulfillment.

But order cannot be imposed, not on toys and certainly not on children. Efforts to impose order either fail because they are too arduous or because they only tyrannize and incite rebellion. Order must be rightly valued, sought, discovered, and allowed to reveal itself. Order already exists and we only have to find it. But there are practical ways for dealing with clutter while we share with our children the search for genuine order.

Children really appreciate order and, provided the order is appreciably apparent, they will usually help to maintain it. They like to find things in the same place; they like to know where things go. It's easier and pleasanter that way. Order is supposed to be like that, to make life easier. With toys the hard part is finding some sort of a rationale to go on—not merely a place for everything, but a sensible place for everything. Generally speaking, you can organize toys effectively into categories: small-parts toys and sets, small-to-medium single toys, medium-to-large toys, medium-to-large unorganizable toys.

Small-parts toys and sets—These can be nicely stored in *clear plastic kitchen containers*. They come in all sizes, look pleasant, and you can see what's inside at a glance. If you are giving a small-parts toy as a gift, it will be greatly appreciated if you take the trouble to purchase one of these in the right size as well. Such containers can be found in the housewares section of almost any hardware or department store.

Small-to-medium toys—Yo-yos, balls, and flashlights are almost as troublesome as small-parts sets. They defy organization and are too small and roll-y to have loose on shelves. The best thing to do is organize everything else and then put these into a couple of shallow drawers or boxes. Rectangular *plastic bins and basins* and *cat litter trays* make good toy drawers which can be set on shelves or actually mounted as drawers on glides under shelves. See the April, 1972, issue of *The Family Handyman* magazine for instructions on how to build glides.

Medium-to-large single toys—Such things as a cash register, pounding bench, or xylophone can each be given a specific place on a shelf.

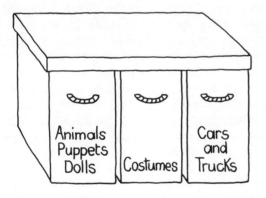

Medium-to-large unorganizable things— Dolls and stuffed animals can be sorted into categories and stored in *large sturdy cardboard cartons*. Cover the cartons with contact paper and place them on the floor under a shelf. They can be easily pulled out by the child and they thus act as well as look like drawers. Depending on what you have (and how much of it) you might want three boxes —one for dolls, stuffed animals, and puppets; one for cars and trucks; and one for costumes. For early reading label the boxes in large clear letters.

A big toy chest is not very useful and only leads to the very jumbling we are trying to avoid. Things get lost at the bottom and nobody has the strength or time to wrestle them forth.

Shelves—Built up rather than around the walls, they take up less play space. Besides it's wise to have some things out of reach so that not everything can be spread out in three aimless moments or at inappropriate times.

Closet—The closet in a preschooler's room may be much more useful as a *toy closet* than as a place for clothes. While it's good for children to have free access to their toys, having them out in the open at all times is a distraction that may result in the child's moving from one thing to another in a superficial way. Preschooler's clothes are so small and so few of them need to be hung on hangers that it's often more useful to turn the closet over to or at least share it with the toys. Line the closet with shelves bracketed to the walls. The child can still get things out at will, but they are less likely to be on his mind all the time.

Hooks—Placed here and there, they are handy for tanglers or danglers that don't fit in harmoniously anywhere else. And take the clothes you took out of the closet to make room for the toys and give them each a hook that the child can reach. From a Japanese import store you can buy bright-colored clothes hooks of plasic or china. Get a ¾ by 2½ by 18-inch board. Sand it, wax it, and screw in four or five hooks. If you are artistic and silly, you can paint ears on the board and eyes on the hooks to give the appearance of elephants. Wrap it up and give it to the child as a present. Then mount it at child level on the wall behind her bedroom door for her to hang her pajamas, jacket, raincoat, and bathrobe on all by herself. You'll be surprised at the daily difference it makes in both your lives.

Pick-up time—If you're overwhelmed by the task of picking up, just imagine how the child views it. For a quick pick-up and a chance for the child to experience the clean-up as happy and rewarding, give him a shopping bag into which he can put "everything you find on the floor" or "everything you find around the house that really belongs in your room." Then have a sorting session. It is as pleasant an activity for the child as a treasure hunt, and the difference is reward-ingly sudden and obvious for both child and parent.

A place to work

In fostering the best use of toys and playtime, a place to work is just as important as a place to put things away. The former is mostly taken care of by the latter since a little space is about all a child requires to do his work. Otherwise, the only pieces of equipment that might be considered crucial are a table and chair sized down to the child, and a step stool for sizing up the child.

A child-size table and chair are almost as valuable as a bed. While it's perfectly possible for children to work or study a book in high-chairs or junior chairs at adult-size tables, they are much more comfortable at tables and chairs that fit them. Activities that are under-taken tend to last longer at a child-size table than at a big one or on the floor. They can pick up what they drop, work standing up for a while, move around and work from the other side, or go off and pick out a new book or some other work. And somehow a clean visi-ble, reachable work surface inspires construc-tive activity in a way that a table they only see the underside of does not. In this way much greater concentration, independence, and freedom are possible, for the parents as well as the children.

Besides its function as a work place, a small table is just the thing when a friend comes for dinner. Let the parents have a good visit while dining in peace at the big table while the chil-dren have the privilege of eating *un*super-vised by themselves. It doesn't always work, but when it does it's a pleasant treat for everyone.

Heavy-duty plastic-topped tables such as those from Community Playthings have the best, most enduring surfaces, but almost any smooth surface will do. Adequate small formica tables with vinyl-covered chairs can often be found for less than $15 at big toy and discount stores. You can even turn your coffee table over to a child for a finger-painting session if you put a piece of vinyl over it for protection. A large piece of plywood (18 to 24 inches wide by 4 to 6 feet long) covered with matte-finished white formica is a counter/table/desk that can grow with the child to adulthood. All you have to do is change the base from low legs or cinder blocks to longer legs, more cinder blocks, small chests of drawers, or low filing cabinets. If you make a wooden table or cut down an old one, epoxy paint will give it a good, smooth, washable surface. A good minimum size is 20 by 30 inches. Most important is the relative height of the table and chairs. During the preschool years, 24 inches is a good height for a table, and 10 inches should be allowed for leg room between the table top and the chair. If possible have several chairs for visitors.

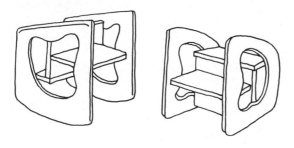

The merits of a step stool are infinite. A good step stool which brings the child up to sink, counter, toilet, workbench, and top bookshelf height can often more than replace a water table, play kitchen, small-size "potty," and the long, preoccupied arm of Mommy and Daddy. Almost any untippy stool will do, but the one pictured is uniquely versatile. □

KINDS OF PLAY

Facilitating the happiest and most fruitful uses of toys and playtime is a much greater issue than deciding what toys to provide. Discovery of the proper mental environment is a major concern of this entire book, but here are a few suggestions about pacing and paying attention.

When the days get long, often what's needed is not a new toy or a change in the weather, but a shift in the type of play that is going on, a change of perspective. There is a time for . . .

Playing alone—while we should never abandon our children or push them aside, we must nevertheless stand back as much as possible, remaining available, but not interfering, helping and encouraging, but becoming ever more irrelevant. It is also of the utmost importance that we treat our children and their work with courtesy and respect, never abruptly interrupting a child at play anymore that we would interrupt a fellow adult in his work.

Playing beside each other—This is the most common mode of play throughout the preschool years. He does his work; you do yours. Do not interfere with his work, but share the joy of working, understanding, learning, accomplishing. You are nearby in love.

Playing together—Doing the same thing together. This can be anything from rough-housing, to an educational activity, to cooking or making something together. Often it is something requiring two that exposes the child to the benefits of cooperating and augments his sense of possibility. Whatever the activity is, it should be characterized by joy and a sense of appreciation.

Planned play—You have an activity planned in advance, usually something you would think would be both fun and edifying for the child. With toddlers it is almost crucial to have some specific activities planned each day. They are now too mobile, and too thirsty for learning, for us to respond adequately to them on an entirely moment-to-moment basis. You will feel sick and tired of each other at the end of any day in which you do not have some planned time. Easiest are activities planned around things you have to do—a tray of black and white buttons to sort while you sew, for example, or a session with play dough while you cook.

One time of day that is often unfortunately trying for small children is the early morning. They wake so expectantly, so totally glad to see us, so eager to get on with the business of growing; and then they have to wait so long while we pry ourselves out of bed and reluctantly carry out our endless "work." The child on his way to the park at 10:00 is often fairly discouraged, a different individual from the one that woke so brightly four hours earlier. So set something up after he goes to bed—a project or a toy the child hasn't seen for a while, or his cars all lined up to play with in a new place. Just this little bit of thoughtful-ness expresses love and can help to give everyone a happier start in the day.

Going out—This is another thing you will almost have to do at least once every day. It helps you to keep from believing that life is just a matter of you and the child revolving around each other. When you go out, try to arrange for the child to do some walking or climbing on his own. While a ride in a grocery cart or a quick tour of a pet store is as good as a trip to a musuem, long shopping trips are a trial for everyone and must be counted as a unique form of child (and parent) torture. For your sake and your child's, try to avoid such expeditions as much as possible. Besides outdoor walks and romps, try museums, the library, the firehouse, an airport, a factory, a pajama walk just before bed. And don't think rain means you have to stay in. Hardly anything is more fun than a pair of boots, a puddle, and permission to splash.

Active play—A time to allow for climbing. You are available now, so the safety gate can come off the stairs and he can practice. Dancing. Marching. Walking like a duck or an inchworm. He does exercises and you copy him. And, indoors or out, just some running around and jumping and climbing.

Quiet play—Private times for each of you separately. Quiet times together. A time to be still, to listen to the wind or a watch or what she wants to say. To look out the window, up at the stars, down at the street, into the woods. To walk once around the house before bed and hear the insect music. If you should want your child to learn to pray, don't teach her what to say, teach her how to be still and listen when there doesn't seem to be anybody talking at all.

Receptivity

*You road I enter upon and look around! I believe
  you are not all that is here;
I believe that much unseen is also here.*

*Here the profound lesson of reception, neither
  preference or denial . . .*

–Walt Whitman, *Song of the Open Road*

We spend so very much time trying to get our work done—the laundry, dishes, freelance work, what-have-you—with the idea that once all that is out of the way we'll be able to "devote our full attention" to our children. But then, in those rare moments when our sense of self-importance is diminished or satiated enough so that we feel we can take some time off, we suddenly find that we are uninspired. We sit down to "be with our children" and find the moments almost awkward. This indicates that our idea of "being with" is invalid in some way.

Many of us believe that the purpose of being with our children is twofold; we take care of them, and we entertain them. This narrow subject/object outlook leads to all kinds of unhappinesses such as the idea of being taken advantage of by our children, neglecting them, never having enough time for anything, etc. But the only valid and rewarding motive for ever being with anyone is learning, the furthering of understanding of both parties. Understanding of what? Oh, love, life. Why? To be fulfilled, happy.

Children who, of course, do not consciously know this, also never doubt it. They are learning machines, ceaselessly seeking new understanding of anything and everything. That is one reason they will not play with their toys and leave us alone for very long. Learning is their work and they love it. Furthermore, their learning is existential; they especially want to be learning what relates to their living. And for the toddler this usually means whatever we are doing.

We, however, have long since divided our work and our learning time into categories. Work is supposed to be the most time-consuming of all, and learning (which means reading an educational book or taking a course) is another. "I have so much work to do I don't have any time to improve my mind anymore!" Medical science even suggests that learning is children's thing. Their brains are young and growing; ours are already deteriorating. But it seems more likely that we are not learning more because we no longer think that learning pertains to us. And if we *are* interested in learning we certainly do not expect to learn anything from changing diapers or folding the laundry.

But what the child has to learn is more obvious to us only because so much of it is so physical. If we allow our 1½-year-old to "help" us fold the laundry he will learn something about buttons, zippers, snaps, where things go, the physical properties of cloth, what happens when you drop it, how easy or hard it is to carry compared with everything else he has ever carried, what clean clothes smell like, how a big towel can turn into a small bundle, how the small bundle you just folded can turn into a big towel again, plus any songs you care to sing or stories or related or unrelated facts you care to pass on. If we are cheerful and responsive, he may also go on assuming that orderliness is an agreeable aspect of reality and that it's a joy to be together. And he may *not* yet begin to think that he is only a nuisance.

So it's easy to see that it is good for our children to be included in our work whenever possible. And, practically speaking, no matter how unhelpful the help of a toddler is, we will almost certainly get the task done faster with him than by trying to keep him busy in some other room.

In the meantime, what can we possibly learn from folding the laundry? It *is* possible to learn happiness while folding the laundry. But first probably we must relearn how to learn. For this it is good to pay attention to our children.

The learning child unconsciously assumes two things that are crucial to learning. The first assumption is that *there is nothing standing between him and happiness but what he hasn't learned yet.* At least for a while, he does not think that having or doing something else would be nicer. As long as he's learning he's happy. He lives to find out. The second assumption is that *whatever comes along next is the next thing he needs to learn.* He does not doubt the fulfilling nature of life. These two assumptions are crucial to receptivity. And receptivity is crucial to learning.

Accepting these assumptions for the moment, what might there be for us to learn when we are trying to fold the laundry (which we may think is a bore) and the task is being made more difficult by the fact that our toddler is aggressively in the way?

The basic issue in folding the laundry is orderliness. If folding the laundry is the task

with which we are presented, it is likely that a right appreciation of orderliness is what we need to learn. And perhaps the interruption by our children signifies the truth that the perception and expression of love are even higher aspects of our lives. Or perhaps we need to see that love and order are not in conflict with each other. The possibilities are infinite, and we can learn some new dimension of reality each time we are confronted with this situation. Perhaps while the child is exploring the physical properties of cloth or material, we will come to see that what we do is *im*material, or that life is *un*foldment and that expressing life (in this case love, order, humility) is fulfilling. When we understand whatever there is for us to understand while folding the laundry, we will either be happy folding laundry or else we will be lifted into some other task altogether.

Like us, our children will become fulfilled, happy adults only in proportion as they come to understand and express life aright. We cannot teach them what is life is or, for example, what orderliness is even if we come to understand it ourselves; one day they will have to find out for themselves, just as we are doing. But as manifestations of life, they enter this world with a natural expectation or unconscious appreciation of order. As parents we can foster this appreciation and help it to become conscious. Then when our children become Young Men and Women Searching, order will be one of the realities they seek to discover and understand.

But the simple lesson of orderliness is only a small part of what we teach our children. The unspoken lesson for us all in our right appreciation of even the smallest tasks is that life—every minute detail of it—is significant and meaningful and worthwhile, that understanding (and, more fundamentally, receptivity) is the secret of happiness and that ultimately happiness is.

Lay Disciple Ho said:
"My daily activities are not different,
Only I am naturally in harmony with them.
Taking nothing, renouncing nothing,
In every circumstance no hindrance, no conflict . . .
Drawing water, carrying firewood,
This is supernatural power, this marvelous activity."

–Huston Smith, *The Religions of Man*

Paul said: "Set your affections on things above, not on things on the earth."

–Colossians 3:2

Jesus said, "Suffer the little children to come unto me, and forbid them not: for of such is the kingdom of God. Verily I say unto you, whosoever shall not receive the kingdom of God as a little child shall in no wise enter therein."

–Mark 10:14–15

Suzuki said: " 'Childlikeness' has to be restored with long years of training in the art of self-forget-fullness."

–Eugen Herrigel, *Zen*

Freedom

Jesus defined freedom as understanding when he said, "Seek ye the truth and the truth shall make you free." Here again we can see that the issue at hand is a spiritual or ideal one rather than a material one. The newborn infant, unable even to hold up her head, is almost completely restricted by the limitations of her physical body. As an immature physical human being she is further in bondage to the physical presence of her parents. As she learns to feed herself, to walk, and to climb, she experiences emancipation both from her own physical limitations and from her physical dependency on parents. Each of these attainments increases her freedom and, more importantly her awareness of freedom.

As with everything else the child experiences freedom on a material plane whereas the adult must come to perceive freedom—idea(1) spiritual freedom—in consciousness. But although the child's experience of freedom occurs at a material level, it is not material freedom which is being experienced or sought. What the running, jumping child celebrates so run-jumpingly is not the power of her body but the unfolding awareness of the possibility of transcending the limitations of that body.

This can be confusing if it is not properly understood. There is a tremendous difference between the dawn-to-dusk physical exercise of a child and that of a man in a gym. The child and man may work equally hard, but because she is happy in it we call the child's work play and the man's strenuous work exercise. Whereas the man is seeking physical fitness (adequacy or superiority as a separate material self), the child is seeking physical freedom, that is, freedom from her sense of physical limitation. The man seeks to confirm himself as a body. The child seeks to transcend her body. The man experiences effort, the child joy.

This is not to say that the child is more understanding than the man. In fact, the child understands virtually nothing. Nevertheless, she provides a good example for us since she has not yet acquired much in the way of conscious error either. We have already discussed the fact that while the child's initial play with her toys is enjoyed purely for the understanding it brings, sooner or later, it is fairly inevitable that the having of toys and pleasurable material experiences will become a central concern. Likewise the sprightly youngster will almost inevitably pass into a stage in which the idea of freedom is a material one. She will begin to seek freedom *as opposed* to something—to have a car and go places as opposed to staying home, to do as she pleases as opposed to what parents or spouse desire; to have her rights.

But to become truly happy—truly free—eventually each of us must discover that the nature of freedom is spiritual rather than material and that in reality nobody and nothing other than ignorance (which is no body, no thing) was ever there to hold us back.

The first part of the practical section of this chapter is concerned with mobility and the possibilities of going places together with our babies and young children. Included are evaluations of such equipment as carriages, carriers, and strollers, as well as some tips on traveling with young children. The second part discusses agility and the child's unfolding freedom to get somewhere on his own. This section treats first a few small hand toys for the baby who has not even learned to reach, and proceeds to jumpers, walkers, gyms, swings, and tricycles. Also included are some suggestions regarding freedom and safety.

Interspersed along the way are some practical suggestions for purchasing, improvising, and utilizing these items, as well as some more philosophical commentary intended to facilitate growth and understanding as various issues arise. Especially interesting when considering parent and child as co-seekers of freedom is the way that parents and babies are often released from each other in the very act of going somewhere together. The child's need for release from himself (physical limitations) is fairly obvious. His need for both mental and physical release from his parent is also fairly obvious.

Less obvious but even more important is the need for the parent to find release. Most of us are completely taken in by the child's early physical dependency on us. We may experience a sense of physical and mental bondage to the child based on our beliefs of personal responsibility. This is not something that having children brings upon us. What happens is rather that the experience of parenthood renders our longstanding existential yearning for true freedom suddenly more acute. Only as the parent discovers the nature of freedom is it possible for the child's inborn quest for freedom to unfold harmoniously. Without a rightful perception of freedom on the part of the parent the child's growing need for freedom (even so small a thing as the freedom to sleep) will be frustrated, and the result will be a painful bondage for both parent and child. If we pay attention to the significance of what happens to us now and to the significance of our children's strivings, we stand a good chance of discovering true freedom which will benefit us and our children beyond all imagining.

Wheels and Wings

GOING PLACES TOGETHER

The obvious purpose of a carriage, a stroller, and a carrier is for you and your baby to move out into the world. As with any form of mobility, freedom is what is implied. Any mother can attest to the seeming miracles that can occur from simply shoving off and going for a stroll.

After hours of struggling, a restless, wakeful baby may fall instantly asleep when he is put in the carriage and wheeled out the door. The motion? The background hum of outdoor sounds and the carriage rolling? The lulling effect of passing sights? No such explanation seems adequate. Perhaps it has to do with the turning of our attention outward, away from the problems, to the rolling along. More specifically perhaps, the secret lies in switching our orientation from steering the baby to simply steering the carriage. Maybe he falls asleep when we let him.

"So I finally gave up and decided to take him out for a walk, and do you know what happened? I put on my coat, got the carriage out, and when I went to pick him up—there he was, fast asleep!" Did he finally "wear himself out" or was he simply at long last allowed to sleep? Mothers who understand the principle involved here probably take fewer and shorter walks, get more done, and still spend more time just enjoying their babies.

But it's still good to take walks often. The baby may sleep the whole time and she probably doesn't *need* the fresh air. But the parent—that's the point—it is so good for our perspective. The first time one mother took her new baby out for a walk, she thought he was going to be annihilated—by the sound of a jackhammer; the fumes from passing cars; the visible, greasy dirt that fell out of the air onto the baby's beautiful, clean, pure cheek. She remembers suddenly being struck glad by the realization that all those other mothers, all those storekeepers, drivers, passers-by, all those thousands upon thousands of fellow city dwellers had actually survived babyhood. Different parents have different fears, but walks are good for most of them.

Carriages

To try to sort out the issues regarding the purchase of carriages and strollers we went to the Albee Baby Carriage Company at 93d Street and Amsterdam Avenue in New York City. Albee's has the widest selection we know of and among the lowest prices. Best of all, several salesmen there have been in the business for 25 to 40 years and are as generous with their time, when they have it, as they are experienced.

The man we talked with pointed out that most first mothers have some sort of dream, see, of what this carriage should look like, so it's very hard to give practical advice. But he went on to explain that there are three basic types of carriages: inexpensive, moderately priced, and expensive.

Inexpensive—These start at around $20. They tend to be a bit heavy and do not last as long as the more expensive ones. But if you are concerned about budget and know that you will not be using your carriage extensively or lifting it a lot, then you should be able to find something perfectly adequate for under $50. The main thing to look for in this type of carriage is sturdiness. The wheels and wheel base are the most important parts. Accessories are not.

Moderately priced—These carriages run from $60 to $90. They include well-built, lightweight carriages, and heavier models which can be converted from carriages to strollers. The carriage-to-stroller type appears to be more of an encumbrance than a bargain. The well-made, lightweight kind, have sturdy but collapsible metal frames, and

the beds can be used as car beds or bassinets. These are nice-looking, highly useful carriages, and seem to be the best buy for most people. □

Expensive and fancy—For anywhere from $90 to several hundred dollars (if you like suede or fur!). These are elaborate yacht-like affairs. They are durable and include some accessories (e.g., built-in storage pouches), but they offer little other practical advantage over the mid range carriages and they are not as adaptable.

Mattresses—are generally not included in the price of the carriage. Purchased separately they range from $5 to $10, varying in thickness and propability.

Accessories—If you come across them you may want a *storage basket* to fit the wheel base, a *carrying bag* to hang from carriage bed or handle, a *carriage seat* for a toddler sibling, *clips* for hanging purse or shopping bag from the carriage (or stroller) handle, a *harness* for sitting/standing babies or toddlers, or a *rain cover* for the carriage bed (comes with some carriages). □

Strollers

More than anything, the man from Albee's wanted to stress the fact that a stroller is a much more important purchase than a carriage. This is undoubtedly truer for city dwellers than non-city dwellers. Many country families never use a stroller especially if a back carrier is used. What with cars and the fact that supermarket carts have child seats built in, a stroller is just plain unnecessary for some people. But in the city a stroller is used constantly and for a much longer period of time, and by a much heavier and more active child. While the carriage may be used for 6 months to a year, the stroller is expected to last about 2 years. Strollers range in price from about $15 to $100.

Least expensive—These strollers are light, collapsible, and generally flimsy. Some people buy them as auxiliary strollers. Others use them almost as disposables. The theory is that you can use one until it wears out, buy another, and maybe even another, and still come out cheaper in the long run. This seems doubtful, but we haven't tested it.

Moderately priced—Included are the lightweight, totally collapsible, umbrella-type strollers of which the best known in this country are made by Cross River and Gerry, and the sturdier folding ones such as those made by Headstrom and Strollee.

The advantage of the umbrella type is its extreme lightness and collapsibility. It can be collapsed in seconds, hooked over the arm, and carried by anyone up and downstairs or on and off buses and escalators. They are ideal auxiliary strollers and may be used as the only stroller if necessary (e.g., you live in a walk-up apartment) or if only average use is required. But they are not quite as sturdy as the standard strollers and cannot be loaded up with many groceries or sand pails. And they are too tippy to be left unattended with a child aboard. □

Generally speaking, moderately priced, sturdy, folding strollers are a good buy for most city people. They are heavier than the umbrella strollers and can be collapsed flat enough to store in a closet or load into a car trunk, but they are not easily carried on and off buses with a child in tow. Things to look for are sturdy construction (especially of the wheel base), a place for sand pails and groceries, a sunshade (not crucial), reclining position for seat (not crucial unless long stroller outings are planned), and a small tray for toys or feeding. Tubular frames are strongest. Most of all be sure to try pushing any stroller you are considering purchasing. Some are unbearably difficult to push and steer. □

Baby carriers

A baby carrier is a wonderful way for a parent and baby to be together without revolving around each other. Sometimes a baby and a parent seem to be holding each other captive. The child cries the minute he is put down and yet the parents have a sneaking suspicion that their very efforts to put him down are precisely what are keeping him up. A carrier of some sort often breaks this vicious circle, releasing the parents to carry on with their work while allowing the baby to be close but unfussed with. Usually what happens is that the baby falls asleep as soon as he is put in the carrier.

Back or front infant carrier—In Japan and Taiwan, this type of carrier is used everywhere all the time. It is worn on the back with the straps crossed in front and, sometimes, twisted into a rope which goes between the mother's breasts. The straps are then divided again and tied behind the back. Used constantly until the child is 2 or 3 years old, it thus replaces the carriage Gerry-type back carrier, stroller, and often even the babysitter. It folds into a purse-sized nothing and is considered to be almost as indispensable as diapers.

In the United States it is usually sold and used as a front carrier. Some women here feel uncomfortable about having the baby out of sight or about crossing the straps between their breasts to carry the baby on the back. But as a front carrier it is less comfortable for both mother and child than as a back carrier except for very young babies who sleep blissfully there as between the mountains of paradise. However you wear it, it can still be a handy problem solver if you happen to live in a walk-up apartment or if you're trying to houseclean when the baby is fretful. And it is

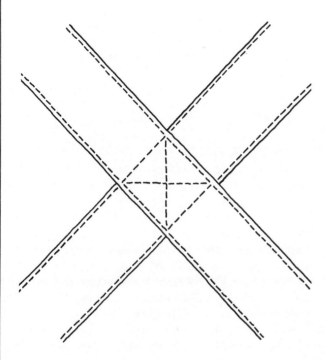

wan and is now wearing her second baby on her back, sends the following instructions for making a carrier like her mother-in-law's. What could be easier?

A-ma's model is much simpler and just as adequate as the purchasable models—two long strips of cotton cloth about 12 inches wide and 5 or 6 feet long, sewed together like this (just a cross). The double part goes on the baby's bottom—two straps under the baby's arms and over the mother's shoulders, two straps between the baby's legs and around the mother's waist, then crossed in front of the mother and tied. Many people use just one long strip of material to bind around the baby and mother.

In cold weather a blanket is tied on, too—on top of the carrying straps. Some blankets are made with hoods for the baby's head, and many times a baby looks completely smothered and out of sight!

I'm all for this back carrier—for convenience, closeness, etc. My only criticism is that here in Taiwan it is sometimes overused with older babies who need more freedom and time to crawl. But it is certainly soothing for the baby and freeing, in a way, for both the baby and the mother.

Back carrier with frame—For carrying on
without a lot of carrying on
in the woods
at the zoo
on a bicycle
on an escalator
in a store
at the beach
to the laundromat
in a museum
on the stairs of a
   walk-up apartment,
and in the home
or backyard,
there is nothing like a back carrier with a

very useful for hiking and cycling families before the baby is old enough to sit in a frame-type carrier.

Three versions are available in this country, any of which is wonderful if you are comfortable wearing it. They are great for the babies, much nicer in many ways than the rolling beds we otherwise push them around in. You just have to consider before you buy it, whether or not you really will use such a thing. □

For next to no money, you can make your own. An American mother who lives in Tailight metal frame. The big advantage, and the best proof of its worth, is that babies and toddlers are so happy up there. You can tell two ways. In the first place, they smile and laugh all the time they are awake, and second, they fall asleep there without a peep—suddenly, anywhere, anytime, whenever they are sleepy.

For some families the use of the back carrier indoors simply brings order back into their lives. When the baby is too tired to be happy on the floor but not ready to sleep, you *can* quickly get the dinner dishes (or the ironing, or vacuuming, or leaf raking or lawn mowing) out of the way with him on your back. When you are finished he will probably already be asleep, and you can snuggle him into bed without an hour of ritualistic nursing or bottle feeding. It's such a nice way for both of you to go about your individual business together, without interfering with each other. When the guests are hungry and dinner is ready (at your house or at someone else's), you can wear him to the table. He will enjoy it and be enjoyed, and again probably conk out in no time flat.

Like any back-packing, this *does* take getting used to. But if you have to use a carrier, you do get used to it. And once you discover the possibilities, the freedoms, you will find it difficult to imagine toddlering without one. A five-month-old is about ready for backpacking, you can start about a month earlier if you sandwich the baby in with a pillow for a little extra support. The carrier may be used as long as you can stand it—most people find 1½ years or about 25 pounds the limit.

One mother's favorite, early parenthood memory is two under one umbrella, three hands on the shaft. She can't say which version is better—being one of the two under the one umbrella, or looking from under a separate umbrella at father and son—saturated, rainy day colors, sunny day laughter. The three of them so private and safe somehow, traveling dry and warm and cozy along the wet city sidewalks, the rain pat-patting so friendly. You can hear snow falling on an umbrella, too. □

Bike carriers for children—Some people say that cycling is dangerous and that cycling with a child in tow is too dangerous. On the other hand, those who do go bike riding with their children aboard find this one of the happiest and most harmonious ways imaginable of being together. At first, parent-borne carriers such as the Happy Baby Carrier can be used. As the child becomes heavier, a bike-mounted carrier is preferable.

Bike-mounted carriers are of two major types—front and back. Front carriers attach to the handlebars and thus make steering a bit more arduous, though probably to no greater extent than a loaded bicycle basket. Front carriers are generally not considered adequate for children much heavier than 30 pounds. The advantage of this type of carrier is the better view for the child and the companionship.

Aside from its convenience we just love the way our daughter sits in this seat. She is way up high by the front handlebars. She can see everything and participates in the ride so fully. It is so easy to hear what she has to say and this enriches the ride for all of us greatly.

In addition, it seems to us that the rider is very secure in this seat. Our daughter is up high but she is right between our arms and we are aware of all her movements. We can give directions if need be.

It is also a beautiful sight to see my husband and daughter riding toward me on a bike—the one resting so serene and secure inside the other, and both looking so interested. It is an image of parenthood.

Some have said this seat is tippy—that it is hard to handle the bike with it. This is true, but to us the advantages far outweigh this disadvantage. We are just careful to balance well and turn carefully.

A good rear carrier should, of course, have a secure means of holding the child in the seat, and foot rests. It is also desirable that there be some protection against the child's putting her foot into the spokes of the rear wheel.

Car-seats and safety restraints

Despite fuel shortages and high costs, new and improved car seats are coming out all the time. As far as we know none is ideal, and the hope is that something better will be available by the time this book is published. Ideally you should look for something that is safe, comfortable to sleep in, and not too much of a hassle to install or to load your child in and out of. Aspects to consider when selecting a car seat include:

• *Safety*. All car seats on the market must meet certain Federal standards, but many people say these standards are not adequate. Safety factors include: strength of seat, secure attachment of seat to car, and secure and safe attachment of the child to the car seat. Seats are attached to the car either with the car seat belt plus bars wedged under the back cushion of the passenger seat or by bolts to the frame of the car (usually plus car seat belt). Children are attached with seat belts, harnesses, or more shieldlike affairs. The main concern is to hold the child securely but in such a way that he is unlikely to be injured by the restraint itself or by whiplash in an accident. Simple waist seat belts are considered hazardous.

• *Rigamarole*. Bolting requires the drilling of a hole in the frame of the car, usually from inside the trunk. This is reasonably simple unless your car's engine happens to be located in the rear, in which case you may have to hire someone at a garage to do it for you. Depending on how it's done, attachment through the use of seat belts which are attached to the car frame may be just as adequate. Bolting may be worth the trouble but it's useful to be aware of what is involved with whatever model you purchase. Also under the heading of rigamarole is the fact that some of the safest car seats on the market today are such mazes to get in and out of that some parents become negligent about using them for short trips. Look for the easiest possible safe restraint.

• *Comfort*. From the standpoint of sanity, this is a most important factor. If you are doing any significant amount of traveling, it seems desirable, if not necessary, that the child have a seat which is not only safe but comfortable and a good place to sleep. If possible, there should be a reclining position as well as a more erect one for looking around. Some children think trips are a time to throw up; others think that traveling is sleeping time. The latter is definitely preferable. Alas, at the present writing it seems that the safest car seats are the least comfortable, while the least safe are as cozy as can be. Hopefully this will have changed by the time this book is published. If not, load up with pillows to make your safe seat as comfortable as possible. □

Trip tips

Leave shortly before a nap time or, if possible, even when the nap is slightly overdue.

If it's going to be a long trip, see if there is some place to stop off that will be of interest to the children. With a toddler it is better to take a picnic to the local playground of any strange town than to have a greasy lunch and a wrestling match in a restaurant. Twenty minutes in a sandbox or on the swings and slide with a little snack will refresh and settle much better than his first milk shake and french fries in a restaurant where he doesn't know how to behave.

Plan to take some things along that will entertain the child and expedite maintenance on the trip. For example:
• *A roll of paper towels* (should be standard equipment in a car).
• *A sopping wet washcloth* in a plastic bag and a clean hand towel, or the prepackaged wash-ups called Wet Ones. (Most other prepackaged wash-ups taste awful and leave the skin soapy and sticky.)
• *Some magnetic letters or shapes* and a *small metal tray*. Spray the metal tray with chalkboard paint and take along some chalk.
• A few *colorforms* to work with on the window.
• Any *toy* that is currently particularly absorbing to your child.
• *A magic drawing board*—those gray boards with acetate sheets on top. You draw with a wooden stick, and then erase the drawing by lifting the acetate.
• A *story anthology* which you can read or tell stories from.
• *Diapers* (yeah, well, sometimes they get forgotten).
• *Plastic spoons, paper cups, and plates*. If you keep some of these in the car, you can shop for your lunch in any supermarket or grocery store instead of taking a picnic or going through the treasure hunt for a suitable restaurant.
• *Snack food*—individual boxes of raisins, fresh raw vegetables or seedless grapes.
• *A bib*—even for the fairly grown-up toddler, a bib is handy for snacking in a carseat.
• *A basket* attached to the arm of the car seat for all these things you are taking with you.
• *A mechanical sparkler* or *small flashlight* for the child to play with if you will be traveling after dark.
• *Tripkit*—Buy a small rectangular metal lunch box. Paint or decorate it to your liking and spray the lid with chalkboard surface. Pack it with colorforms, magnetic shapes or letters, colored pencils, chalk, a box of raisins, a small pad of paper, a box of tiny children's books—just anything you can think of that your child might enjoy.
• *Surprise package*—Gift-wrap some of the above things to be opened at various points along the way. If you are familiar with the route you are taking and if the child is old enough, assign the sighting of certain landmarks as package times. "Open the next one when you see the white church with the bell in its tower." Otherwise introduce the packages whenever you see fit.
• *Knapsack*—Make a knapsack small and light

enough for even a two-year-old to carry. Let her take on trips anything she can personally carry in her little knapsack. She will appreciate and learn from the experience and you will be happily relieved of some of that endless paraphernalia. We don't have a pattern to follow, but if you're handy enough to attempt this, you can probably improvise a plan—a drawstring bag or a snap-closed cloth envelope with webbed shoulder straps? Instead of snaps or buckles for closures try the new Velcro self-gripping fasteners (pieces of bristly plastic that stick together when pressed). Webbed strapping can be purchased by the yard.

GETTING SOMEWHERE ON THEIR OWN

They shall mount up with wings as eagles; they shall run, and not be weary; and they shall walk and not faint.

–Isaiah 40:31

"Whither, oh whither, oh whither so high?"
"To sweep the cobwebs from the sky . . ."

–Traditional nursery rhyme

One of the prime and most obvious frontiers of our children is physical. They want to overcome all limitations, and the first and most perceptible ones they encounter are physical. They want to get up, then they want to go, then they want to go higher and faster and farther and upsidedowner and arounder. But they can climb no higher than we aspire, so it is important that we cultivate the highest possible appreciation of what their climbing means.

At first their motives are purer than ours are likely to be. They do not climb to prepare for competition or to be physically fit or to put gray hairs on our heads or to break their necks or to knock over our favorite lamps. They climb for understanding and for freedom, for the pure joy of becoming less limited. Ultimately at issue are certain life principles and laws which our children, as living beings, would like to make peace with, then understand, and if possible transcend altogether.

A baby first becomes aware of the law of gravity through conflict with it. Through trial and error and some minor bumps and tumbles, he makes a sort of intuitive truce with it and becomes able to walk. Too often this is as far as our appreciation of the existential value of his efforts goes. Either we lose interest in his efforts altogether or else we begin to channel them according to our own less valid motives. Climbing, we say, is or is not good because it fortifies or endangers bodily well-being. Or, the point of learning to climb well is to be better than other people. Neither of these is any way to invent an airplane, and yet that, too, is one step in man's efforts to overcome the limitation imposed upon him by the law of gravity.

With freedom the question of when to give what toy or piece of equipment must be settled the usual way—mostly by watching the child. At first a few things to learn to see and reach for will satisfy any gymnastic needs not met by the baby's incessant kicking, waving, and playing with her parents. After that there's the desire to get up and going, perhaps in a jumper and a walker, but very soon on her own. Then there's swinging and climbing and the sky is the limit. One whole category of equipment that is often overlooked for the preschooler is indoor gym equipment. Probably it is deemed too expensive and space-taking, but these ideas may be myths. Indoors, where the young child must wait so long so often to be taken out, a good piece of gym equipment may replace years-ful of toys that are constantly being spread over whole floors. Outdoors the dirt, trees, fences, and grass are really all you need, but here, too, a swing, a ladder, thoughtfully placed are better than almost any toy you can buy.

Of course the most important contributions we can make to our children are mental ones. By constantly calling to mind the child's ideal self, his essential perfection we keep him free to pursue true freedom. True freedom is, of course, not freedom from anything, but there is much bondage to be avoided. At the same time that there is a need for protection and comfort, there must be freedom from fear. At the same time that there is a need for guidance and teaching, there must be freedom from domination. At the same time that there is a need for reproof and correction, there must be freedom from guilt and blame. At the same time that there is discernment, there must be freedom from classification and comparison.

So it is not good to neglect, to hinder, or to overly direct our climbing, running, jumping children. Our fears are largely groundless and our directions either pointless or misleading since we ourselves do not yet know what true freedom is or what more than the invention of an airplane it could mean if realized. We can only recognize and appreciate the fact that freedom from limitation *is* the issue, in this case really the only valid issue. Then as we help and refrain from helping our children we can study what freedom really is, where it comes from, who finds it, how.

Pennant
Come up here, bard, bard;
Come up here, soul, soul;
Come up here, dear little child
To fly in the clouds and winds with me, and play
*   with the measureless light.*

Child
Father, what is that in the sky beckoning to me
*   with long finger?*
And what does it say to me all the while?

Father
Nothing, my babe, you see the sky;
And nothing at all to you it says. But look you, my
*   babe,*
Look at these dazzling things in the houses, and see
*   you the money-shops opening;*
And see you the vehicles preparing to crawl along
*   the streets with goods;*
These! ah, these! how valued and toil'd for, these!
How envied by all the earth . . .

Child
O father, it is alive—it is full of people—it has
*   children!*
O now it seems to me it is talking to its children!
I hear it—it talks to me—O it is wonderful!
O it stretches—it spreads and runs so fast! O my
*   father,*
It is so broad, it covers the whole sky!

Father
Cease, cease, my foolish babe,
What you are saying is sorrowful to me—much it
*   displeases me;*
Behold with the rest, again I say—behold not
*   banners and pennants aloft;*
But the well-prepared pavements behold—and mark
*   the solid wall'd houses . . .*

Child
O my father, I like not the houses;
They will never to me be anything—nor do I like
*   money;*

But to mount up there I would like, O father dear—
*   that banner I like;*
That pennant I would be, and must be . . .

–Walt Whitman, *Song of the Banner at Day-Break*

Indoors

Crib gyms—These tend to be more trouble and expense than they are worth. Those that attach with straps across the crib get in the way and are hard to put on and take off. Musical ones tend to break. Many are cluttered and merely exciting rather than helpful. And even the plainest ones (which don't get played with very much) usually cost around $6 or more. One thing that nevertheless seems worthwhile is pictured. □

Otherwise or anyway you can make one. Get a stick ½ inch wider than the crib. Notch it in two places and attach with heavy rubber bands as shown. Either notch the stick in several more places or screw in eye hooks from which to hang an endless and changing variety of things—soft, hard, circular, trans-

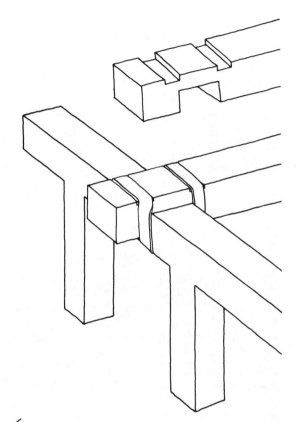

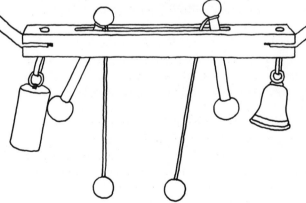

lucent, ringing, knocking things. If you hang some of these from something elastic they will spring about nicely.

Jumper—Before our first son was born we were against this on the general principles that it was a contraption and that he could learn to walk without it. We were also afraid that any such thing might become a crutch that would actually deter him from making progress. Nevertheless, at about 4 months— when his desire to be upright became a yearn-

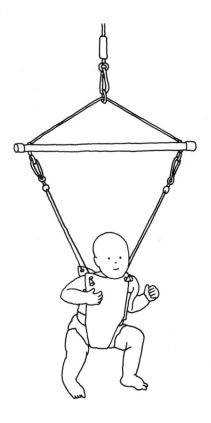

gins to discover the possibilities of turning and jumping. Once he really gets going, the jumper is good for about two or three months, two or three times a day. It will last longer each time if he has something to do with his hands—a toy tied to the jumper perhaps.

But a jumper is not a place to put a child away. Be with him as much while he's jumping as if you were holding his hands to help him stand. Hang it in the kitchen doorway while you're fixing supper. Play music, sing. And he will find it hilariously wonderful if once in a while you will jump with him.

By the way, this is one toy that outlasts its usefulness, so pass it on. Ours has been through four bouncing babies and is still going strong. □

Walker—There is no full-time substitute for walking around holding onto our hands, but, like the jumper, this contraption brings a great deal of pleasure and added freedom to the pre-walking, sitting child. It offers him the experience of mobility and thus an early appreciation of the possibility and value of walking by himself. Don't substitute a walker for all finger-holding practice, and never keep the child in a walker against his will, or you will teach him to associate walking with confinement and isolation from you instead of with freedom and independence. Dependency on either the walker or the parent will not occur if we have a full appreciation of mobility as a freedom for the child rather than as a hazard for him or an inconvenience for us. □

Indoor swing—The child with no backyard stands to gain the most from indoor gym equipment. This is especially true of the preschooler who can't go to the park by himself. A doorway swing is ideal—both for budget

ing—we tried it, and we have to be grateful for all the squeal-happy hours of practice it gave him. He could see better and turn around on his own. And he jumped and jumped for joy for about three months, until he was stricken with the desire to go forward as well as up and down.

As with anything, the best success can be had with a jumper if it is properly introduced and used. The first few exposures will last only a minute or so (less than the time spent in saddling up). The child will just hang there fascinated, drooling on his toes until he be-

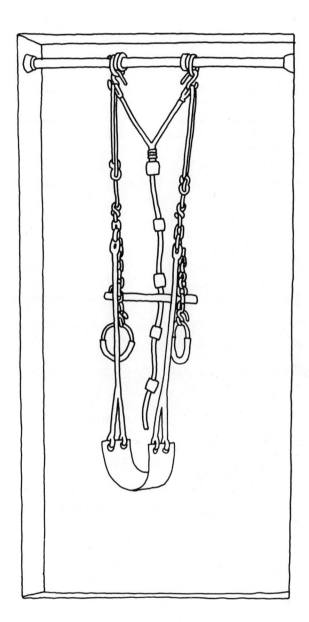

and for space. Unlike park swings, which must be used by children of all ages and heights, the indoor swing can be hung low enough so that even a 1½-year-old can experiment with it alone. He will do lots of things on a low swing that he can't attempt on a standard swing. The most popular position for preschoolers who don't yet know how to pump is the flying position—hanging by your tummy, watching how the floor goes by. And dangling like that is so much better than hanging around for hours, waiting to be taken to the park and pushed.

A homemade swing is the obvious answer. The more space you have around the swing the better, but if you don't have a handy rafter or beam, a doorway is fine. If the door frame is wooden, the swing can be suspended from good-sized eye hooks. If the door frame is metal, you will need a doorway gym bar which could also be used in a hallway with sturdy walls. See also *Nomadic Furniture* for a duck-and-dowel safety swing you could make for a baby. □

Almost more desirable than a seat swing is a trapeze bar (made from 17 inches of broomstick), especially if you have a landing mattress below. Invent something new and better or send to Child Life for the wonderful Doorway Gym including a rubber belt swing, trapeze rings, bar, and blocked climbing rope. □

Mattresses—Old ones that are free are cheaper than real tumbling mats and, if they have innersprings, more fun. If you can get a double-bed mattress with box springs, you have something safer than a trampoline but nearly as much fun. Cover it with a shag rug, bedspread, or bright-colored mattress cover. The floor of a whole room could be done this

way, with the child's bed being a raised foam mattress for jumping from as well as sleeping.

Indoor climbing gyms—The small indoor toddler gym/slide combinations available from a number of sources are outgrown too quickly to be worth the space and money for most families. More useful and for longer is a real climbing gym of some sort. Such a thing is especially valuable for city children. There are many wonderful gym/playhouse/slide combinations available. A horizontal or folding-ladder climber takes up less space and can also be used with a slide or as a playhouse scaffolding. Even smaller, less gymnastic pieces are available, such as rocking boats and small multipurpose units that can be used as tables, chairs, or for climbing. Space, budget and personal preference are the determining factors. □

If you're handy, there are things you might build yourself. (See especially *How to Make Children's Furniture and Play Equipment*, p. 72.) Wouldn't a whole wall environment be nice—a floor-to-ceiling climbing thing? The children are so small. You could easily divide their rooms into two levels. Let there be a balcony at the top with a foam cushion or covered mattress for a combination floor and bunk bed, and all the books up there on shelves, and a good reading light. Let there be ladders for going up and a slide and a pole through a hole for coming down. A swing thing underneath and interchangeable platforms, a tunnel, a door, a cave, a secret place. If possible, there should be movable parts so the children can revise and restructure.

Maybe simple is even better. We have seen children's rooms designed almost as dance sets. Platforms and ramps built roughly out of wood, yielding caves and open spaces and a high place to sleep or leap from, the whole affair covered in shag rug with deep padding underneath. There are so many ways—as many ways as days, as many different possibilities as snowflakes. But there is only one time to do it in: now.

Outdoors

You can drive through miles and miles of suburbia and see hundreds and hundreds of bright metal gym set combinations in well-kept backyards and *nary a child* on one of them. If you look into the bushes or behind garages or in culverts or empty lots or up in trees with a very sharp eye, you will begin to spot the children. With the exception of the wonderful ones from Child Life, has there ever been an outdoor gym set that seemed genuinely inviting or anything but an eyesore in the backyard? It's somehow different on a playground designed for children coming together. At first it is hard to put a finger on what is wrong with these things that parents feel they *have* to buy; but the hiding/climbing children remind us that freedom, which is the issue in climbing, is the factor lacking. The child seeks freedom from the ground to fly like the birds into and over the trees. Flying is beautiful. And he seeks freedom from his dependency on us.

A bare pipe structure in full view of the kitchen window does not inspire the child with any sense of freedom. If one had a piece of wooded property, it would be lovely to hide the play facilities or at least to spread them around in nooks and clearings. The swing should hang from or beneath the trees, with a far view if possible. It should be unobtrusive since, after all, the flying is the thing, not the swing. And perhaps there would be a tree house somewhere—a high-up private place, as safe as necessary. The sandbox could be in another clearing and offer the choice of shade or sun. In between there would be paths. But you wouldn't have to put them there; they would mysteriously appear with surprising speed.

Of course the littlest ones are not ready to go off alone like this, but it's good to give some thought to their growing needs and to plan for them materials that inspire.

Climbing gym—Outdoors such a thing is probably a luxury rather than a necessity, but if you're going to get one a real climbing apparatus is much better than a metal swing/slide/seesaw combination. Get nothing or get a real jungle gym of some sort. Child Life wins the prize for having the most inviting, diverse, and unobtrusive assortment at relatively reasonable prices. Some of these include ladders, rope net, movable platforms, and pulley-assisted hoists. Other simpler climbers for indoor or outdoor use are available for less money from Child Life and others. □

Outdoor swings—In accordance with the belief that a swing should be mounted separately from other play equipment, we looked for seats and mounts and hitches rather than full swing sets. Obviously, if you have the right tree and a piece of board, and some tire rubber to protect the tree limb, you don't need to buy anything but rope (nylon is best). Otherwise you will probably be grateful for some of the mounts and parts available from, yes, again, Child Life. □

Don't think you even need a backyard. Make a good length of clothesline a regular part of your picnic equipment. If it's long enough you can even make two swings—one with each end of the line. Sling it over a tree branch and tie it close enough to the ground so that the child can step into the loop. Any two-year-old can learn to stand in this loop on one foot. Tell him to reach as high as he can before stepping up. If the knot is located above the child's reach you can pull the end of the line to give a nice ride. Remind your child not to step off unless the swing is still. And take it easy—let him tell you when he wants to go higher.

How do you like to go up in a swing
  Up in the air so high?
Oh, I do think it the pleasantest thing
  Ever a child can do!
Up in the air and over the wall
  Till I can see so wide,
Rivers and trees and cattle and all
  Over the countryside—
Till I look down on the garden green,
  Down on the roof so brown—
Up in the air I go flying again,
  Up in the air and down!
–Robert Louis Stevenson, The Swing

Ride-ems—Most pre-trikes or kiddie cars are built too low to the ground. By the time the child is ready to propel himself along on them, his legs are too long. Undaunted, our children do manage with kiddiecars, but they are unnecessarily awkward. The best pre-trike vehicles seem to be the lightweight, plastic-wheeled motorcycles, horses, Snoopy dogs, etc., which the children ride from almost a standing position. In city parks tiny children ride them with astonishing speed and delight.

Just why they have to be so ugly is beyond comprehension. The motorcycles generally come in Merthiolate pink and have horrendous, roaring noisemakers which augment the false idea that power rather than freedom is the virtue of vehicles. We can imagine and would like to find some more free-form, plastic riding things designed simply to express the freedom, beauty, and grace of movement. They could be in bright, attractive (not neon) colors—Child Steeds! □

Tricyles—To get some expert advice on purchasing tricycles, we went to Morris Toyland at 1896 Third Avenue in New York City. Morris Toyland looks like a tiny storefront on the outside, but once inside you find that it goes on and on and on. It is located in East Harlem where Morris says people "shouldn't spend" too much on toys, "but they do." Educationally, Morris Toyland isn't Childcraft or Creative Playthings, but Morris is concerned with value. He has the interest of the children and the budget of the parents at heart. He knows they are going to want to buy what they see on television. "Some mothers buy these enormous dolls," he says. "They take the doll home and give it to the kid and the kid thinks the doll is the mother." Morris tries to find reasonably priced versions of the best that his customers desire.

He also sells and repairs bicycles in unbelievable numbers. Morris has even recovered a number of stolen ones. "A kid comes in for parts," he says. "I recognize the bike, and I know he isn't the one I sold it to. So I hold the bike overnight for repairs and try to get it back to its original owner."

The bike department of the Morris toy store is a whole floor. It isn't everyone who is allowed up there. About tricycles, Morris said, "Well, I suppose I could tell you what to look for in the wheels and construction, but the best advice I have is, you go where you trust the salesman and you take the kid. Surprises are no good with tricycles. Also you never buy a bike or a trike in a box with the idea that you're going to put it together at home. Go buy a whole one. Buy where they service bikes and trikes as well as sell them, either in a bike shop or a big toy store where they specialize in selling *and fixing* bikes." The point seems to be that it's okay if the store buys its bikes in boxes just so long as they sell it to you fully assembled.

Morris went on to say that the best size trike is a 10- or 12-incher. He said the big 16-inchers are silly, because by the time the child is ready to ride one that big, he could better move to a real bicycle (with or without training wheels). Further about size, Morris said to be sure "you buy for the kid, not the parent. Buy a trike that fits, one that he can ride and enjoy now." No blocks until he grows into it. He will never grow into it if he doesn't enjoy it. Morris also said not to worry much about the passenger provisions on a tricycle because the child who belongs on a trike is not big enough or well-coordinated enough to carry a passenger. It's only big kids on little kids' trikes who can manage the extra weight.

Finally about price Morris said that a good midrange tricycle, just right for the average use-time of a tricycle, should run somewhere between $15 and $20. "Don't spend more than $20. Put it toward a good bike when the time comes." We asked Morris if he could suggest any midrange tricycles. He recommended any 10- or 12-incher by Headstrom or Murray.

That's what Morris said, and he certainly seemed to know what he was talking about, and to care.

Trike handle—Most children do not use a tricycle for real travel. It is not until the bike stage that the real traveling mentality usually hits. So most trikers sort of pedal and stop and tool around and get off and on. This is not always handy. When you're crossing a big city intersection and the light turns yellow and you have an armload of groceries, it is not the most convenient thing in the world to bend down and pull your stalled tricycle, complete with foot-dragging passenger, the rest of the way. It happens a lot. You don't want to keep your child confined to a stroller for all the walking you do in the city, but it is not pleasant to walk around with your underpants showing, pushing a tricycle up and down curbs and spilling groceries all over the place. For such situations, the trike handle which hooks over the handlebars and acts like a wagon handle, is a boon. You can fashion one from a couple of heavy coathangers or buy one in a good city bike store.

Model transportation toys—Indoors or out transportation toys do not add anything immediate to the child's freedom and their inclusion here is somewhat arbitrary. Most children show only momentary interest in cars and trucks, though some are intensely interested—perhaps because of a fascination with mechanics or perhaps because they are taken with the possibilities of freedom which are expressed in these toy vehicles. Hopefully, they are not already overinterested in power and possession.

So many well-made models are available that it isn't necessary to discuss who makes the best. On the youngest level, generally the ones that get played with most are those that do something—cranes that lift, bulldozers that push, trenchers that trench, and dump trucks that dump. Tonka's metal cars, trucks, and machines are tops, and good wooden ones can be purchased by mail from Montgomery Schoolhouse and Vermont Wooden toys (see pp. 76, 77).

Good ridable toy vehicles are available from Community Playthings, Novo, Childcraft, and Hammett.

Do resist the temptation to buy an electric or mechanical train for a toddler. It is a ridiculous idea that can only bore or frustrate the child. If you buy any toy train at all, try to find one with open cars that can be loaded with real pebbles or dirt or such.

And don't forget the girls. Just as many girls are as interested in cars and trucks as little boys. And just as many little boys are *not* interested as little girls. If you will, buy a few cars and trucks for boys and girls at well-spaced intervals. But don't get carried away unless you perceive that their interest is unusually keen and constructive.

Walks

In theory, at least, walks are also an exercise in freedom—and, for that matter, in peace, beauty, and love. For children and parents, it is desirable for walks and picnics to be almost a way of life. But, especially if you like walking, it may take some new understanding before you can appreciate the ways in which walking with your lagging ("carry me!") toddler has anything to do with freedom. For many parents and very young children walks are pure hassle because the children keep stopping, hunkering down to look up at the tall trees or buildings—and the parents keep wanting to keep moving. Some people drag their children; others manipulate, baiting the children with promises of what they might see around the next corner or what they will have to eat when they get home.

What most of us don't realize is that by about the age of 2½, the child, too, all of a sudden gets the idea that a walk is a matter of going somewhere. Quite spontaneously, he will begin taking your hand and walking down the street with you, viewing things as he passes them instead of stopping to study each cellar door, each fuel intake, and every different balustrade. But first he simply must examine these things. So in the meantime, before you set forth, decide which kind of a walk it's going to be. If it's a walk-walk for *him*, prepare to stand still a lot yourself. The walk can be very short in distance and very long in time. It can take an hour and a half to go around the block at his pace. So if you want it to be short in time, don't plan to go far. On the other hand, if you are really trying to go somewhere, plan to take a stroller or a carrier or to be quite firm. Take both kinds of walks, and learn to appreciate both kinds.

Books

[*Note:* Numbers in parentheses indicate comprehension levels (not age) as outlined on pp. 7–9, 195, 197, 201, 207. Starred titles are those deemed superior for a preschoolers' home library. See pp. 6–7, 193–94 for additional information regarding book notations and selection.]

* Airplanes and Trucks and Trains, Fire Engines, Boats and Ships and Building and Wrecking Machines
by George Zaffo
Composed of six single Zaffo titles (the best ones), this book is unmatched in its suitability for vehicle-minded preschoolers to grow up with. Impressively large-scale and dramatic pictures make these fascinating for the youngest children. Parts of the texts are difficult and not for straightforward reading aloud to most every young child. But as increasingly technical questions arise in the child's mind, any parent will be grateful to find the answers in the detailed text (if you aren't interested simply for your own sake).
Grosset & Dunlap, hardcover, 1 and 4 colors, 8¼" x 11", 292 pp., (2 up).

The Book of Airplanes, The Big Book of Real Boats and Ships, The Big Book of Real Building and Wrecking Machines, The Big Book of Real Fire Engines, The Big Book of Real Helicopters (not incl. in above), The Big Book of Real Trains, The Big Book of Real Trucks
by George Zaffo
Good individual titles (all included in the volume above). There are others, but these are among the best. And Zaffo's Grosset titles are definitely better than his comparable ones for Doubleday.
Grosset & Dunlap, board, 1 and 4 colors, 8¼" x 11", 32 pp., (2 up).

* Be A Frog, A Bird, Or A Tree
by Rachel Carr, photos by Edward Kimball, Jr., illus. by Don Hedin
A unique exercise book that appeals to children's fondness for mimicry. Poetic instructions, drawings of animals, and photos of children express clearly how to assume each pose.
Doubleday & Co., hardcover, 1 color, 7" x 10¼", 104 pp., (3 up).

Boats
by Ruth Lachman, illus. by Lenora and Herbert Combes
A good little introduction to boats and boating and shipping.
A Little Golden Book. Golden Press, board, 4 colors, 6½" x 8", 24 pp. (2).

Busy Wheels
by Peter Lippman
Through the day, everywhere, all the things that go on wheels. A good concept book with slightly too sophisticated artwork.
Random House, paperback, 4 colors, 8″ x 8″, 32 pp., (2).

Red Light Green Light
by Golden MacDonald, illus. by Leonard Weisgard
The dawn-to-dusk story of stopping and going. Very simple text. Nice mood.
Doubleday & Co., paperback, 2 and 4 colors, 8¼″ x 7″, 40 pp., (2).

Additional books for interested parents

How to Make and Fly Paper Airplanes
by Ralph S. Barnaby
Just what it says, for the parent who happens to be really interested in flying paper airplanes. A pioneering aviator himself, Barnaby knew the Wright brothers and designed and built his first real glider in 1909. More recently he was first prize winner at the International Paper Airplane Competition sponsored by *Scientific American*.
Bantam Books, paperback, 1 color, 4¼″ x 7″.

The Paper Airplane Book
by Seymour Simon
Designed to teach the principles of flight and airplane design to older children through experiments with paper gliders, this little book offers some good techniques for glider flying with clear explanations (for the preschooler's parent) of why what works which way.
Viking Press, paperback, 1 color, 7½″ x 9″, 48 pp.,

25 Kites That Fly
by Leslie L. Hunt, former kite-maker for the U.S. Weather Bureau
Clear instructions on how to build and fly kites. 70 illustrations.
Dover Publications, paperback, 1 color, 5⅜″ x 8⅜″, 126 pp.

FREEDOM AND SAFETY

Child-Proofing the Home

To some extent the matter of safety can be dealt with in a preventive way. It is certainly intelligent to take some safety precautions, but it is equally important not to carry this to any fearful extent lest self-fulfilling prophecies become a factor. Freedom is a good principle to be guided by when considering what safety measures to take. Freedom and safety belong together. When considering how best to protect your home and your children from each other, keep freedom in mind. Otherwise your efforts will result only in retarding and frustrating your child's eager development and in long years of inconvenience for you.

Baby-proofing is a breeze; you just don't put the baby down where she might fall off or where anyone might step or anything fall on her. But toddler-proofing is another matter. You have to protect both the toddler and the house while maintaining the freedom of both —the "right" of the home to be lovely and pleasant for everyone and the right of the child to learn and grow.

Don't resort to a playpen. One mother used a playpen as a place to do her free-lance artwork while her two infants were on the loose in the apartment. This is the best use we ever heard of for a playpen. The mother doesn't need to move around and touch things; she already knows how to walk and, physically at least, "where she's at." She is busy with ideas. But the child is, after all, learning to walk, and his acquaintance with the physical world —with distance, shape, weight, texture, what breaks and doesn't break, and (oh how amazing!) what bounces and rolls—is vital. She not only needs to find out, she needs to develop her faculties of finding out. So don't cage her —make way for her. Put things that might get broken or hurt her out of reach. Close off places where she might fall. And plug or cover up places where she might get a shock or a burn. Good child-proofing frees the child to learn, the parent from worrying and nagging futilely, and the home from destruction and disarray.

Outdoors if there is traffic nearby, a *fence* around the yard is handy if you can manage. But a companionable watchful eye is still necessary for the wee ones. They are, above all, interested in finding out about us (that is, about what will become of them) and do not like to be left alone for very long. □

Indoors you will find *safety latches* for cupboards and drawers an indispensable way to keep small children from getting into cupboards and drawers containing dangerous or breakable things. But try to have one or two low cupboards and drawers that are all right for the child to explore. The pulling-out-and-dumping-all-over-the-place stage doesn't last

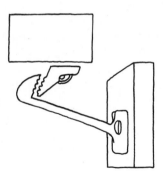

long, and evidently something is learned from it. *Socket caps* are a must for closing off open electric sockets which small children cannot otherwise resist poking things into or trying

to open with metal keys. Put gates across doors and stairs where it is not safe for the child to go. Consult *Consumer Reports* for the most up-to-date coverage of the quality and type of gates available. Don't use gates or doors to keep the child away from you. Another extremely important freedom is that of the child to move away from you when she is ready. Shutting her away deprives her of this freedom, and possibly even worse of the desire for it. □

But don't go overboard and revise your whole home to suit the unsteady and not-very-wise toddler. It is sensible to make some adjustments and take a few precautions, but there's no substitute for vigilance, and at this stage you have to be pretty close by most of the time anyway. Furthermore, though it may seem endless at first, it takes only a minute or two for the child to grow up. At 9 months she may bruise her head on the coffee table trying to stand up, but at 1½ she can already open the door and dash out! It is simpler to make some adjustments along the way, but it is not necessary to become fearful or to change your whole life for what is only a momentary stage.

Accident-Proofing the Child

Mother, may I go out to swim?
Yes, my darling daughter.
Hang your clothes on a hickory limb,
But don't go near the water.
–Traditional nursery rhyme

Be careful about "Be careful!" Almost against our will the cry "Be careful!" leaps into our parental vocabulary. The child is backing off the bed, standing up in his high chair, teetering heedlessly at the top of the ladder to the slide. Some parents are so fearful of these occasions that they virtually keep their children chained up. On New York City playgrounds dozens of children more than 2 years old can be seen harnessed into their strollers *next* to the sandbox, *watching* other children play. Other, more permissive parents are so terrified by precarious moments that they even become angry with their children, shouting such things as "What's the matter with you? Do you want to kill yourself? See? It's your own fault that you got hurt. I told you to be careful!"

All these children are in danger of becoming overly reckless, timid or, worst of all, apathetic. For most of us the problem does not become so extreme, but we are nevertheless unhappy with our responses. We want to keep our children safe from harm, yet the last thing in the world we hope for them is that they will become full of care. It's a dreadful phase really. So what are we to know? How can we teach safety without teaching fear?

As with everything else, the answer lies in greater awareness on our part. Even as the child crawls toward the open fireplace, he is not trying to destroy himself—quite the opposite in fact. He is purely and rightfully interested in learning, which is life-fulfilling and even life-saving rather than life-risking. Once he knows what the word *hot* means and that the fire is hot he will not try to crawl into the fireplace. In the meantime safety is our business. We do not have to teach safety at all. We must simply as uninterferingly as possible, protect him from his ignorance, at the same time fostering the awareness he needs to exercise better judgment. In this task there is a place for prohibition and prevention, for explanation, for assistance, and more and more for letting go. But there is no place for fear, and we must seek all the understanding we can to refrain from teaching fear or self-doubt.

In any endeavor we must first try to see what positive things might be learned and then exercise judgment as to how best to assist in this learning process. Simply avoid situations which the child is not ready for or in which you find yourself too fearful to be helpful. Avoid having to issue too many instructions, and state your suggestions in concrete positive terms—"Step here, honey" instead of "Watch out behind you!" Don't be lazy—many crises and shouted warnings can be avoided if we are willing to be there, stepping in silently with a helping hand when it is needed.

But the best protection of all comes from what we know more than what we do or say. We can marvel at the unfolding abilities of our children and their enthusiastic life-seeking and we must seek awareness of reality as life-affirming, a gentle teacher. There is a well-known phenomenon of correlation between accidents and fearfulness (worst fears coming true). Likewise there is a correlation between an atmosphere of confidence, assurance, and appreciation and the safe and full unfoldment of confident, assured, and grateful children.

Another thing not to make too much of are the small (and even most of the big) bumps and bruises that may occur along the way. Comfort when they happen but then let them be forgotten. Don't worry the child with poking and checking and asking if it hurts. A kiss or a hug for comfort is usually the only medicine that's needed. Couple it with a quick change of subject and you have almost a healing. The younger the child, often the quicker the cure—long suffering is a learned attitude. One family refers to small injuries as *minor mishaps.* Their crying 2-year-old receives a quick look and a generous hug, and then the parent says, "Did you have a minor mishap?" The child finds this a fascinating idea—much more interesting than the hurt. "Yes!" he says, "I had a minor mishap with the stairs." Another child is satisfied with a little comfort and a brief identification of the problem followed by the simple suggestion that it is all better. "Oh dear, did your toe get bumped?" "Yes." "Is it all better now?" "Yes, it's all better!" (Beaming smile and running off to play again.)

It is not good to belittle or to be negligent, but it is good to help our children let go of pain. Mostly these hurts arise in the process of learning. What hurts and startles most about them is the interruption of the learning that the child is trying to do. The child wants to be released from the experience so that he can go on learning. It is important, therefore, that fear not be introduced in these moments. Fear is an absolute obstacle to learning. Help the child to carry on.

Because he cleaves to me in love,
  I will deliver him;
I will protect him, because he knows my name.
When he calls to me, I will answer him;
I will be with him in trouble,
I will rescue him . . .
—Psalms 91:14, 15

Humility

When a child begins to learn to walk, he succeeds in fits and starts, sometimes falling flat out, sometimes momentarily teeteringly staying upright. To anyone without a knowledge of the law of gravity this would appear unfair, and it might seem reasonable to blame the hidden force of gravity for being unreliable and hurtful. But, of course, this is foolishness. Contrary to appearance the principle of gravity remains a consistently beneficial law. Partly through suffering from his ignorant conflict with the law, the child slowly awakens to its nature and reliability. He comes into harmony with it and, instead of its seemingly working against him, he now finds it working for him. Now he walks.

If freedom is a spiritual issue, the only obstacles to our discovering freedom must be cognitive. Freedom is not something that can be obtained, but rather a state of being and knowing to be discovered. Jesus said, "Except ye become as a little child ye shall never enter the kingdom." He wasn't talking about *cute* or *little* or *helpless* or *ignorant*: he was talking about the child's most outstanding ability, the ability to learn. Partly, as we have already seen, this is a matter of receptivity. The child expects to learn, doesn't think there is anything better to do than learn, and assumes that life is indeed learnable.

One aspect of this tremendous teachability of the child is his lack of pridefulness. Though he may be tearful when he falls, he is not embarrassed. His disappointment is that *this* experiment in walking didn't work, not that he is personally a failure. His disappointment is more a reflection of enthusiasm than discouragement. Nor does he assume from his momentary failure that the possibility of walking is unreal or doesn't apply to him. He is neither insulted nor despairing. He is not egotistical enough to take either success or failure personally. In short, he is humble. The urge to walk and the conviction that walking is a possibility remain stronger than self-concern. In the child they govern the self. Hence, after only a moment of tearfulness he tries again.

Genuinely humble and supremely motivated to walk, children thus fall a lot but learn quickly. This is a fact really worth taking note of. The child does not begin to fall until he becomes seriously interested in walking, until he actually begins learning. Falling is thus more an indication of learning than a sign of failure. Also worth noticing is this—that once the child has learned to walk in the house, he can walk more or less anywhere. The physical principles of gravity

and balance remain consistent and the child's new-found harmony with these principles will work for him almost everywhere. What a wonderful freedom! The falls along the way are nothing compared to this freedom. Thus the child's receptivity, especially that aspect called humility, is life-transforming, the secret to freedom. There are many important freedoms, but the most fundamental one of all is the freedom to learn.

For us it is a little more difficult, partly because we are having to learn higher principles than the law of gravity and partly because over the years we have become so prideful. Mostly we are not even aware that learning is the issue. Whereas our preconceptions about parenthood may have been filled with images of ourselves and our children being loving toward each other, we may find ourselves more subject than ever to momentary irritation and outbursts of anger. Depending on whether we interpret this as a flaw in life or in ourselves, we feel either angry or guilty. It scarcely crosses our minds that we do not yet have sufficient understanding of what love is. Love? Of course we know—the question is why doesn't it (or don't I as a loving parent) work?

How much easier for us it would be if we could view increased disharmony in our lives as the double sign of what we need to learn and what, in fact, we are learning—just as the child's tumbles indicate his readiness to learn to walk. As parents, many of us are suddenly more highly motivated and urgent about love than we have ever been before, ready to sacrifice anything—perhaps even our illusions for the sake of our children. We want to be effectively loving. No wonder we run into difficulty—we have never tried so hard before. If we can keep from getting side-tracked by self-conscious concerns—success or failure, guilt or anger—we may struggle and suffer a bit just like the child learning to walk, but then finally discover what is really worth knowing—i.e., that love is, that we are in it and of it. Just as the child who learns to walk in his living room can thereafter walk anywhere, once we learn to truly love our children (behold them in love) it will be easier to be loving toward everyone, to find love everywhere.

In the meantime, it is important to remain humble about the apparent abundance of disharmony in our lives and our ability to achieve greater understanding and harmony. Without humility we may become bitter. Sometimes we become discouraged because we are not the patient parents we thought we would be or because things do not go as smoothly as we anticipated. We may feel discouraged or fearful, angry or guilty. But discouragement, fear, anger, and guilt are all stepping stones to bitterness and stumbling blocks to learning.

Sometimes a child becomes afraid of falling or angry with his momentary failure to learn to walk. Then briefly he ceases to try and to learn, until his natural need to walk becomes more urgent than the fear of falling. And it *will* become urgent; he must learn to walk. Likewise since it is our nature to need to understand, and since bitterness is effectively the refusal to seek further understanding, it is clear that bitterness is at least a painful and unnecessary indulgence in self-concern. Furthermore, if all the discord we suffer is only ignorance and if bitterness is

the refusal to learn, it becomes excruciatingly clear that this is a cognitive mistake we cannot afford. Humility is both the easier and the wiser way.

The experience of parenthood and of human existence altogether is very likely for the sake of our awakening. So we should not become discouraged if our experiences indicate that we have not yet understood. Of course we haven't. Nor do these experiences signify that there is no truth to the idea that reality is ultimately harmonious and fulfilling. We do not understand for the sake of solving life's problems; rather we live that we may learn to understand. The fact that problems fall away as we understand is certainly a benefit, but it is not the ultimate point. The child does not learn to walk so that he may stop falling, but rather that he may be increasingly free.

Problems themselves do not reflect the nature of reality. They only reveal our specific ignorances of reality. As we do now and then reach new understandings, we will not find that our problems have been solved but rather that they have been *dis*solved. In the light of truth they were never the substantial problems we thought they were any more than the toddler ever really had a problem with the floor leaping up and hitting him in the face.

In seeming contrast to Jesus' recommendation to "Seek ye the truth and the truth shall make you free," it is written in Zen literature, "Search not for the truth; only cease to cherish opinions." In reality these statements do not contradict each other at all. Both suggest that the most basic freedom of all is the freedom to learn, to understand. Jesus' statement calls us specifically to that aspect of receptivity which may be called gratitude (appreciation of truth as valuable) or prayer. The Zen calls us to humility or fasting. If we value the truth (set our hearts on it) as Jesus says, and if we are willing to give up our personal minds as the Zen says, then the truth which is the one mind becomes ours, is what we are. Then, already, we are free.

I believe that man must get rid of illusions that enslave and paralyze him; that he must become aware of the reality inside and outside of him in order to create a world which needs no illusions.

Freedom and independence can be achieved only when the chains of illusion are broken.

–Erich Fromm, *Beyond the Chains of Illusion*

Be a lamp to your self,
be like an island.
Struggle hard, be wise.
Cleansed of weakness, you will find freedom
from birth and old age.

–Buddha in *The Dhammapada*, trans. by P. Lal

In clearness comes freedom from all pains;
in those whose minds are free of all
pains, understanding is utterly steadfast.

–The Bhagavad-Gita

Unity

For many people the least obvious aspects of reality are its underlying unity and reliability. We experience life as chaotic, unreliable, fragmentary, precarious, even meaningless. What order we do perceive seems worrisome, for we are sure that it will bring us a mixture of bad and good. Yet as living beings, it is unity we yearn for and, in an endless variety of mistaken ways, it is unity we seek. We wish to find unity in life and become one with it. Not finding it, we try to take life in all its perceivable pieces and make it one with us. Believing ourselves to be separated —that is, un- or dis-united from goodness—we take the seeming pieces of reality—self, other, and circumstance—and try personally to arrange them so that we can bring about unity in such a way as to have only good experiences. We try to cause unity, but always on the assumption that it isn't there in the first place. Our efforts are analogous to and about as successful as a very young child's first attempts to assemble a puzzle.

If you present a child of less than a year with a knobbed wooden puzzle such as those pictured on page 122, he will first lift out the pieces, his attention being attracted by the protruding knobs. The simple fact that the whole can become parts is revelation enough for him. He may not be at all concerned with trying to put the puzzle together again, perhaps trying instead to stack or stand the pieces while totally ignoring the puzzle tray. When he does awaken to the possibility of putting the pieces back into the puzzle, he will try simply to push them in anywhere. He is totally oblivious to the fact that each piece has its own hole or that there is any relationship between the outer edge of a particular piece and the inner edge of its particular hole. Only gradually does he learn the secret that all he needs to do is to align the pieces with the holes—at which point the fitting, the unifying, occurs by itself.

It can be stated rather humorously as follows: if you align the parts with the holes, the parts become whole and the whole becomes evident. What the child is discovering on a material plane with his puzzle we must sooner or later discover on an ideal or spiritual plane, in consciousness. In the end we will have to learn that unity is a principle, an already existing aspect of truth which can come into our experience through the alignment of our thoughts and ourselves with what truly is—through understanding that disunity is experienced only as we in ignorance violate inviolable principles.

All the toys and materials discussed in this chapter are helpful in the child's long quest, now barely begun, toward making this discovery. On an adult level, puzzles are usually done as a sort of intellectual activity, a fantasy confirmation of the sense of personal mental power. The adult seeks to confirm the adequacy or superiority of his separate personal intelligence—in this case specifically as a unifier. But on the preschool level the unconscious motivation is totally different and considerably better. The preschooler who has not yet learned to believe in disunity has also not yet ceased from his unconscious assumption that unity is. He is receptively delighted with all demonstrations of unity, and his experience of unity is existential. He not only delights in the demonstration of the unity of many different puzzle pieces as a whole, but he also experiences his part in fitting the pieces together as the unity between himself and life. He doesn't know it yet, but he is right.

A Playskool advertisement nicely points up one aspect of this key issue in puzzles. "Puzzles," the ad says, "reinforce a conviction necessary to learning: that things make sense." The preschooler's joy in his puzzle goes even one step further: the preschooler enjoys being part of (united with) the sense of things.

The toys and materials covered in this chapter offer children such demonstrations and experiences of unity on a material plane. They are presented roughly in progression from the most specific to the most general, the most concrete to the most open-ended and potentially abstract. Among small unity toys a rattle is a whole comprised of parts. Any infant hand toy with parts that do not come off demonstrates the parts/whole idea (*It is apart from me but I can pick it up*). Anything with moving parts also demonstrates the parts/whole idea (*It has parts but it is one thing*). Stack and nesting toys, puzzles, pegboards are all wholes that can become parts, all parts that can become wholes. Blocks and construction sets are parts that can express the infinitude of the possibilities of unity (*With the same set of parts I can make many different things*). Tools implement the parts/whole idea. Mud, sand, and water are the most amorphous materials of all and are thus of the longest-lasting usefulness and the best teachers of both the fact and the infinitude of unity and reliability.

In working with any of these materials, the child also has the experience of making the transition from apparent disunity to unity, from unreliability to reliability. He learns the impossibility of trying to force seemingly conflicting puzzle pieces together and instead to let go, gently easing, effortlessly allowing them to fit into place through proper alignment. He learns that the water in which he sinks while struggling fearfully will support him once he can give up his struggling and rely instead on the true buoyancy of the water.

Of course, the child is not yet conscious of the significance of these experiences, so they do not yet become generalized in his life as understanding. But they are happy times which foster positive expectancy and the development of adaptability. As he grows toward consciousness such experiences will become evidence for him that unity and reliability are facts of life, that contrary experiences are only belief, that it is possible and worthwhile for him to make the transition from one to the other. It should thus be possible for him to make this transition with optimum ease.

In the meantime, the responsive parent who concentrates on the significance of his child's play and his own role as a parent in the light of unity will not only be a beneficial parent, but he may also make transforming discoveries about himself and life in consciousness. The more we perceive unity rather than, say, personal power, personal intelligence, or personal responsibility as the issue, the more likely we are to discover unity. In this way it is possible for our lives to become less fragmentary and more harmonious. Ultimately it is the self that we must see as part of the whole or a reflection of it. The sense of separation and all the fragmentation that accompanies it can be finally overcome only by the realization that instead of personal mind there is One Mind.

Parts and Wholes

Small Unity Toys

For babies

It almost seems silly to speak about what makes a good rattle or other hand toy for a little baby, and yet even on this level there are toys that work and toys that don't. Partly it's a matter of when they are given to what child, but there are a few things worth considering when trying to choose a toy for a little baby.

As with anything else, you have to pay attention to the baby—what she can do and

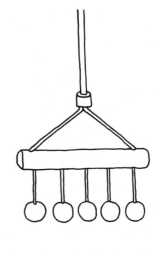

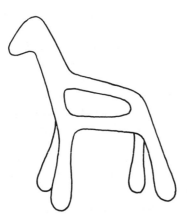

what she's trying to do. To help the baby learn to grasp things, choose something that's easy for a tiny hand to hold. The little dumbbell-type rattles are best for tiny babies—they can hold them before they know about holding. In fact, it is often the sound of a rattle in her hand that seems to call the baby's attention to the fact that either the hand or the rattle is there in the first place.

Obviously a baby's toy must be safe—not small enough to swallow, not sharp or breakable or soluble in the mouth.

Less obviously if you're buying a few toys you don't want them to be redundant. Look for variety. Buy or make something that will help the baby learn to grasp and pick up, something bright-colored that will help her learn to use her eyes, something with a pleasant sound (not too loud and not an ugly one such as those squeakery things that come in some rubber toys) that will help her learn to use her ears. Find something with moving parts, something that rocks, something that slides, something that rolls, things of different shapes. Find something hard and something soft in hand or mouth. Most toys do several of these things, but see if they do them differently.

You *really* don't have to buy anything because your house is full of inspiring things already, but pictured at left is a variety of small toys we know most babies enjoy. And of course you can make things! □

• A *soft block with a bell inside* (see page 128). Springy, ringy, chewy, and—hurray—absorbent.

• A *cribmobile.* This crib or carriage toy was made of nylon cord and wooden things found

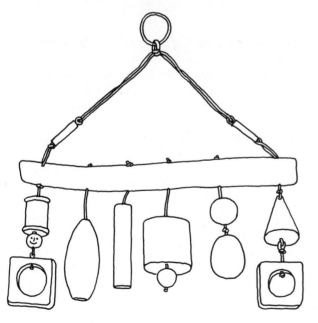

around the house. From left to right: napkin ring and spool, darning egg, package handle, candlestick and bead, cork fishing float and whittled-down knob of wood, napkin ring and wooden cone from broken toy. The crossbar is a 12-inch stick from the woods. All parts were finely sanded. Knots can be secured by melting the nylon string over a flame. Cost: about 30¢ for the string.

• An *empty film can* with some split peas inside.

• Some *big buttons or wooden spools* on a ring of nylon string.

• A *homemade cloth book* with, say, four pages of bright shapes sewn on by machine. Use various textured materials (fake fur, wool, satin, corduroy, oilcloth), and don't bother to hem, just use pinking shears.

• A *shape sheet.* Sew a few wonderful things like enormous round shiny buttons, a plastic costume jewelry bracelet onto a small piece of sturdy cloth for the baby to hold. Or do the same thing around the edge of a larger quilt or blanket for her to lie on.

Once you start, where can you stop? The possibilities are endless.

Pre-puzzles

Gradually the child becomes ready for parts/whole toys that really come apart and can be put together. On the way to doing puzzles and even after that the following may be useful for a time.

Pole and rings—Most children find the stacking of discs or doughnut-shaped rings around a center pole an interesting activity at some point (1 year old, more or less), though not for very long. Just don't buy one

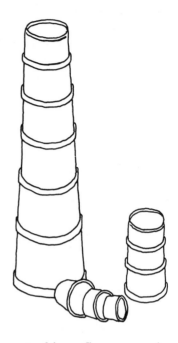

with a great many rings (you may come to hate it) or a tapering center shaft. The purpose of the tapered shaft is to force the child to discover seriation—the big one goes on first, the smallest one last. But the activity of removing and replacing the rings appeals to children long before they are ready to select for size. The tapered pole only baffles and frustrates the 1–2-year-old. □

Stackable/nestable cups or boxes—Seriation comes a little earlier and more effortlessly with these than with the stacking rings described above. If you are choosing between a pole and ring setup or these, the cups or boxes will give you more mileage. Besides stacking and nesting, they are also good for putting (things) in, out, on, and under, all of which are activities of interest considerably

earlier than stacking. Games can be played with them, such as hiding an object beneath an overturned box or cup and then guessing which one it is under. Don't fall for an expensive set of beautiful nesting boxes made of cardboard or wood covered with marrable, chewable, soak-offable paper. Two breeze-easy ideas for homemade versions are as follows. □

Silver tuna tower—The world's easiest-to-make set of nesting cups for the very youngest ones. Buy a 3½-, a 7-, and a 13-ounce can of tuna. Throw away the tops, eat the tuna, and wash and save the cans. If you have a good can opener, the edges will be smooth; but check the inside of the can and pound down any sharp edges. Don't even paint or decorate unless you want to. These look very pretty in natural silver, and if you buy Bumblebee tuna, the edges and inside will even be gold. Put them inside each other in a cardboard box. Gift-wrap the box loosely, and give it to your baby when she wakes up from her nap.

Super tower—The stackable cans that Puss 'n'Boots catfood comes in make wonderful sets of stacking units. Put strips of red, orange, yellow, blue, green, and purple contact paper (1⅜ inches wide) around them—such a spectrum of colors results in a beautiful striped tower. Carefully fitting them together, it is possible to build a tower taller than an adult. For a sturdier base and an even taller tower, try nailing the bottom can to a board. Or you could make a puzzle column by depicting a clown or other figure on a stack of four or five cans to be scrambled and reassembled. For the older preschooler, these cans also make perfect units for basic math exercises: build a one, build a two, build a three, build a stairway up to ten.

Shape sorter—A box or container with geometrically shaped holes that admit only objects of the same shape. A worthwhile and absorbing activity. Good wooden ones are available. We saw one designed to look like a mailbox which turned out to be frustrating because, unless the door was closed, the objects fell to the floor, making the door impossible to close. Plastic would be fine, but the only ones we've seen have too many holes and surfaces for a child of the appropriate age to work with. Try it yourself before buying one, if you want to be certain of how hard or easy it is likely to be for your child at the time. □

Homemade shape sorter—You need a lidded cardboard box and some solid geometric shapes: a ball, a spool, a small block or two. If you can't find enough geometric objects around the house, you can make them from wood or styrofoam. (See Additional Information for p. 132.) Design the box so that, once the objects are inside, they can be removed by the child either by lifting off the top or through a door or hole cut in the side. You can even cut the bottom out altogether and just let the objects fall to the floor. Choose according to what you think the child would like best. Cover the box with paper, or paint it. Trace the geometric objects on top of the box, and then cut holes in those shapes.

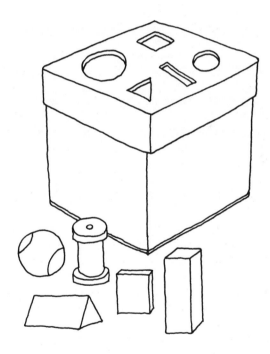

Pegboards—With tiny, tweezerlike fingers and surprising strength, the baby begins tweaking tiny patches of skin on your neck. Smile while you wince; he's developing dexterity. This is also part of his progress in checking things out. Do they come apart? Do you? Pegboards and pegs are marketed for older preschoolers, but if you're willing to sit by and supervise (no swallowing and no scattering) you might want to buy one now. For a brief period well before a year he will find the task of simply picking out the pegs an absorbing challenge. When he is 1½ or so he will again become briefly interested, this time in trying to maneuver the peg into position in his hands and then fit it into a hole. It's fascinating to watch. It looks the way it feels to unbutton a coat with freezing hands.

A pincushion does as well as a pegboard at 1½ and offers the advantage of not being an extra thing around the house. But if you want to buy a pegboard, a plain one with regularly spaced holes and colored pegs (used later for math, color, and design work) is most useful. When your child is older he will enjoy having a design to follow. Copy the board on paper, drawing one circle for each hole. Have this sheet photocopied and then make various designs by coloring in the circles to match the different-colored pegs. □

Puzzles, parquetry, and then some

Knobbed wooden puzzles—These are ideal first puzzles for children. Made of plywood, they include a number of different cutouts of geometric shapes or realistically painted animals or objects. These puzzles can be introduced soon after the baby can sit up alone.

They will continue to be of interest for a long time, both as puzzles and as sort of first books from which to learn to talk. □

Imported from Holland, simplex knobbed wooden puzzles are about the best and most abundant. See especially the farm animals and first things puzzles. Also ideal is the geometric-form puzzle offered in the United States by direct mail from ETA (see p. 76).

The farm animal puzzle pictured here is an unusually fine one to start with. For several months the newly sitting child will be concerned with simply trying to lift out the pieces. At the same time he will enjoy learning to recognize and eventually say the names of the animals and the sounds they make. Then for a while the puzzle may cease to be a challenge—perhaps while the freedom to walk is being first discovered—but in a month or so the idea of fitting the pieces back into the puzzle will dawn on him. Work with the

child. Give him the puzzle at the end of a meal in his highchair and help him with it. (Turn it! Turn it! There it goes!) You can also eventually use the animals as play figures, making up stories about them or using them for simple hide-and-seek games. You can even make up and act out little stories. The simplex farm animal puzzle lends itself to a story such as this:

Once upon a time the duck and the hen went for a walk on a sunny day. [Child takes these pieces away from the puzzle and walks them.] Dum—teedum—teedum—teedum [a good strolling noise]. After a while they sat down to rest in the shade of a tree. [Child puts pieces down somewhere.] Next the cow and the crow decided to take a walk. Dum—teedum—teedum—teedum. Pretty soon they came to the tree where the duck and the hen were sitting. What a surprise! They were very glad to see each other. So they all sat together in the shade. [This goes on until the child has seated all the animals under the "tree".] "Well," they said, "what a nice surprise! If

only we had known we could have brought a picnic." For indeed by now the animals were all very hungry. Just then the hen looked up. "What do you know!" she said. "We do not need a picnic, for the tree we are sitting under is an apple tree and it is full of apples!" So the duck and the hen and the cow and the crow and the dog and the pig and the lamb and the sheep and the rooster and the cat and the goat and the goose and the rabbit all had an apple picnic party under the apple tree in the sunny day. Then very happy and very full they all went home.

Some of these knobbed wooden puzzles are also designed for teaching reading. The printed name of each object is revealed when the piece is lifted out. But all of these puzzles were selected on the basis of their appropriateness for children just learning to talk (simplicity, diversity, and subject interest) since the reading-ready child is usually ready to manipulate more difficult puzzles.

Simple wooden picture puzzles—Puzzles in which each piece is a whole shape in the picture are the next step after the knobbed whole-object puzzles just described. In this category are lots of perfectly adequate American-made puzzles, but unfortunately they are mostly rather ugly. It is desirable that anything which is going to be worked over and looked at as much as these first picture puzzles should be lovely in appearance. You do not need many of these, for they will be quite satisfying for some time if introduced soon enough. □

First jigsaw puzzles—By the time the child is ready for these puzzles in which the shape of the pieces does not correspond to the subject matter of the picture, he understands enough about the process of puzzling and has acquired enough manipulative skills so that quantity is almost more important than material quality. While two, three, or four of the puzzles listed so far should be ample, when the jigsaw stage is reached you almost cannot have too many if you select ones that are appropriately challenging (but not too hard) to the child.

Difficulty depends on size, number, and distinctive shape of the pieces. Start with puzzles that have only a few large pieces, all easily distinguishable from each other in shape. Work up gradually to smaller, more similar pieces, depending on the development of the child's ability and his continuing interest.

Good, wooden puzzles are always nice, but for many people cardboard jigsaws are a more practical idea at this point. The child will no longer work the same puzzle so many times over because he no longer learns anything from doing so. So the durability of wooden puzzles is no longer so important, and a whole boxful of cardboard puzzles is probably worth more than one or two wooden ones. Cardboard puzzles will be more easily managed if they include a frame and backing, and, of course, it is still desirable to select puzzles that are pretty. This last criterion is hard to fill, since most of the cardboard puzzles available for young children are rather unlovely. Keep your eye out, though; new ones are being manufactured all the time. In the meantime, Child Guidance puts out quite a number of simple cardboard jigsaw puzzles that are just right for the age level and pocket book.

Beautiful homemade jigsaw puzzles—With your child, select a pretty and interesting picture from a magazine. Or use one of the lovely Mother Goose prints available from Hubbard Press (see page 159). A puzzle will be more successful with a preschooler if it has a tray, or at least a frame, around it. Take two pieces of cardboard that are sufficiently larger than the picture to allow for a ¾ to 1 inch margin. With rubber cement glue the picture to one of the pieces of cardboard, leaving straight margins all the way around. With a single-edge razor blade or mat knife cut around the picture, leaving the whole cardboard frame intact. Glue the frame to the other piece of cardboard. Cut the mounted picture into pieces that are appropriate in number, size, and shape for your child. For durability, you may also give the surface a coat of spray varnish.

Parquetry—The official verb that describes this type of activity is "to tessellate," that is, "to form of small squares or blocks, as floors, pavements, etc.; form or arrange in a checkered or mosaic pattern." For this, many sets of lovely, wooden, colored tiles are available, from giant size for working on the floor, to almost pocket size for working anywhere, to basic medium size. Parquetry tiles are enjoyably used in making anything from the simplest random arrangements to sophisticated exercises in the study of symmetry and optical illusion. □

For children under 2 years old a big part of the challenge is simply manipulating individual pieces together without pushing others already-placed out of position. The bright-colored wooden shapes are attractive to children, the results are beautiful, and in working with the tiles the child gains an intuitive understanding of relationships that serves for both math and reading readiness.

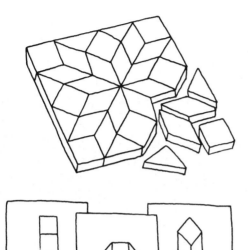

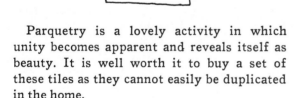

your child is or will be attending a nursery school which provides guided exposure to the above materials, it is probably best to stick to the spontaneous at home. The colored inch cubes, pegs and pegboard, parquetry, geometric inset board, and geometric design board described elsewhere, are all math-related materials which double as something else that is fun to do.

If you want a more formal head start in math, the Cuisenaire type of kit may be what

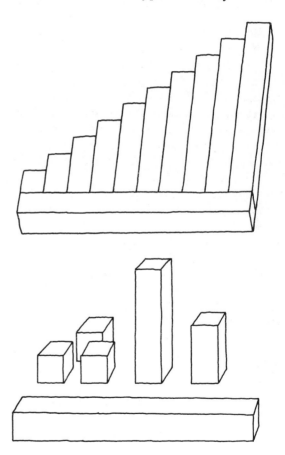

Parquetry is a lovely activity in which unity becomes apparent and reveals itself as beauty. It is well worth it to buy a set of these tiles as they cannot easily be duplicated in the home.

Math materials—Much can be done with math on the preschool level. Through guided work with materials such as the Cuisenaire rods, the Montessori materials, and those by Stearn and Unifix, many children learn to solve quite complicated mathematical problems. It is certainly possible for preschoolers to reach a sound understanding of some basic mathematical concepts and relationships and how our number system works. □

Most teachers agree that you can give the preschooler just about as good a home start in math with improvised materials, and if you want. But do not buy such a thing unless you are reasonably certain that you will be a faithful partner to your child in working with him and studying the teaching materials.

A bigger variable than the aptitude of the children and worth of the materials is the skill of the parent as both an understander of math fundamentals and a fosterer of spontaneous learning. Whatever you do, formal or informal, it is most important that the learning remain joyful. The main thing is to be as aware as possible of the learning potential of any situation. Try to recognize that unity, *beautiful* unity—rather than brains, success, or competition—is the issue in math. All work should be play; all play should be work, and all of it, if we pay close attention, should reveal to us that unity is, and that it is beautiful.

Geometric design board—By stretching brightly colored rubber bands from nail to nail on this simple toy, it is possible for the preschooler to make lovely designs and have

a good time while incidentally making some basic geometric discoveries. To make one, sand and finish (wax or varnish) a board approximately 5 x ¾ x 15 inches. On a piece of paper the same size, draw as accurately as possible two 5 or 6 inch squares. Using a compass, draw a circle inside one of the squares (the diameter of the circle should equal one side of the square). Divide the circle and the square into equal segments. Tape the paper to the board and drive a 1- or 1½-inch finishing nail (that's the kind with hardly any head) through each dot and through the corners of the squares. Remove the paper. Screw an eye hook into one end of the board for hanging when the board is not in use. This is the safest way to store this toy and, besides, it looks pretty. Give it and a box of colored rubber bands as a gift to an older preschooler or to an elementary school child.

Or you can buy a plastic Geoboard from Learning Games, Inc. (See p. 76).

Construction

Blocks

Our youngest block-builders are, of course, entirely unconscious of motive, and almost completely without skill. It takes a highly understanding eye to view their crude buildings as models of truth and beauty. Nevertheless, as builders they are themselves models for us. True inspiration is not a matter of mere amplification of purpose or technique, but rather of purity of motive. To become truly inspired and creative in any endeavor we have to somehow make a move from self-

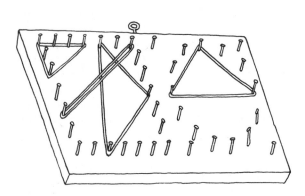

confirmatory motives to an existential or spiritual one. Children express this motive spontaneously without having to make any such move. They build without preconception —not to prove anything, not to please anyone —they build to find out. With such a motive revelation is automatic—understanding (on however primitive and material a plane) rushes in. We see before us models of creativity and demonstrations of inspiration that should, if we truly appreciate what we see, transform our lives.

The child is not yet conscious enough to benefit from his own demonstrations of creativity. It is almost inevitable that he must first become as intellectual and self-conscious as the rest of us before one day, hopefully, he will consciously seek the purity of motive he manifested spontaneously as a child. We can foster or discourage this growth as we sit beside him on the floor or in the sandbox. In every way we must ourselves cultivate appreciation of the revelation of principle rather than human achievement.

In building, the ultimate issue is probably dwelling place; man seeks his true or ideal dwelling place. If the body is not an adequate habitation, what is? If we teach our children to build towers for praise or a sense of power, we have all but done violence to them. We have led them astray. On the other hand, if we join with them on their frontiers, rejoicing in the small revelations of balance, stability, order, line, we will first of all learn much ourselves and we will at least leave open the possibility of our child's most harmonious unfoldment.

Practically speaking, this can mean anything. Mostly it means don't. Don't channel, don't instruct, and at first don't even build anything very spectacular to "show the possibilities." If you build spectacularly, he may respond appropriately by becoming a spectator. See what he tries to do with his blocks. Many children first "draw" with them, making long lines of blocks placed end to end. Help if you will, but don't change course. Appreciate whatever understanding you see coming along.

You will suddenly find that you are having a good time, too, and even that more creative ideas for building are occurring to you. Once the ball is rolling, of course, it is okay for you to build something individual, too. Go ahead. But watch your motive. What happens when your baby uses your castle to discover that a jumble of blocks can happen again more quickly than the castle did? A little twinge of disappointment? Or a genuine appreciation of the revelation of your child's growth?

Once the interest in building is established, here is a nice game to help the preschooler discover new building techniques. The whole family can sit down and enjoy doing this together. Decide in advance how many blocks each individual may place at one time—two or three are about right. Then take turns working on the same building, with each member of the family adding the prescribed number of blocks to the construction any way he likes. It's a surprisingly pleasant activity of equal enjoyment for a variety of ages at once. This educational game, which also provides a good first experience in taking turns, can be played very nicely with the Cuisenaire rods as well as with blocks.

Here are some blocks and building toys that seem worthwhile on the preschool level.

Soft blocks—Cover some foam shapes with bright pieces of cloth sewn together by hand or machine. If you have a small unbreakable container, you can put a bell inside and slip this into a hole in one of the blocks. These are just right for babies, but with great big pieces of polyurethane foam you could make fabulous blocks for older children—whole play environments!

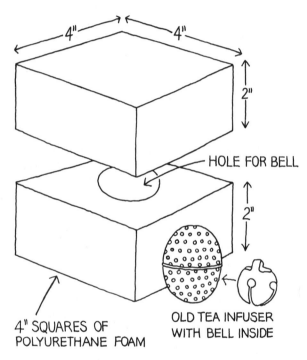

4" SQUARES OF
POLYURETHANE FOAM

HOLE FOR BELL

OLD TEA INFUSER
WITH BELL INSIDE

1-inch wooden cubes—Bright-colored 1-inch wooden cubes designed for teaching math are available from a number of sources. But they are perfectly delightful for the preschooler to use in tabletop or highchair building and designing experiments. Little babies love them, too, so they can be bought early and used a long time for teaching colors and math or building small sets for housing and fencing miniature animals or cars.

One 4-year-old we know uses these cubes to invent and play wonderful games with his 2-year-old sibling. Same/different: "You build what I build" (or the other way around), so patiently, block by block. "Is this the same? Is this? No, that's different. Which one looks like this?" Colors: "Can you find another *red* one?" Numbers: "Now let's count them. Hey, let's build a stair!" Relationships: "Let's make a pattern: "Here's a blue one, here's a red one, blue one, red one—can you find the one that goes next?" □

Cardboard blocks—Wonderfully big and lightweight are the corrugated cardboard blocks that you have to assemble yourself (easy, and once and for all). They are large enough so that a stack of three is already rewarding. They are light enough to be managed easily, strong enough to be climbed on, and when they fall down nobody gets hurt. Cardboard blocks are available from a variety of places. Almost any educational mail order house has them.

Wooden block sets—The small cubes and large cardboard blocks are adequate for the preschool building days, but, as the child grows, almost nothing compares with a good set of wooden blocks from which more complicated structures can be built. There are a great many sets to choose from. The main thing to avoid is buying three or four different sets as the child grows. A little anticipation of what will ultimately prove most useful is helpful.

Basically the choice is between tabletop sets (small pieces which are good for the floor as well as tabletops) and floor sets (big pieces). The bigger pieces of the floor sets are significantly more satisfying to build with and are really not much more space-taking. Some places it is possible to buy a starter set and then add individual pieces or additional partial sets as needed. Try to see the blocks before you buy—some are better finished (smooth-sanded, rounded or planed edges) than others. And do be sure to buy modular ones, with each block relating to the others in direct ratio. Among the toys you might buy, a set of good blocks is worth the extra money you have to pay. □

Homemade wooden blocks—Pieces of 2 x 4-inch lumber (hard or soft wood) can be scaled and cut in direct proportion to each other and then sanded well to make a fine set of blocks. But watch out! These days a 2 x 4 is really only a $1\frac{5}{8}$ x $3\frac{5}{8}$. (It's only 2 x 4 before they plane it.) So to have a square unit that is equal to twice the thickness of the wood (this is the objective) you either have to be good at adding fractions or else measure carefully one block at a time, using a piece of wood as your measure. This is easiest anyway since, fractions or no fractions, you can't mark off a whole board at once and expect to come out with a stack of equally proportioned blocks. You have to allow for the sawdust. If you cut a 12-foot board into four equal pieces they will not be 3 feet long. In summary, *do scale all the blocks in direct proportion to each other (they should all be evenly divisible by the narrowest dimension of the wood), and do measure and cut one block at a time, cutting each time to the outside of your mark.* Check

commercially made sets to see what variety of pieces is most useful. Most commercial sets seem to have about twice as many rectangular (double-square) units as squares.

Non-block construction sets

It is useful to understand that the more open-ended a thing is the more you can do with it. Thus although a gaudy plastic busy toy may occupy your child intensely for a few hours, it is to plain blocks, or even better, sand, clay, paints, hammer, and nails that he will return again and again. In the long run, one of the best things you can do for your preschooler in the area of construction is to let/help him learn to saw and hammer as he becomes able.

Wood scraps are more open-ended than blocks; blocks are more open-ended than construction sets. But in the whole hierarchy of toys construction sets tend to be more interest-sustaining than most, and can contribute much to a child's pleasure, sense of spatial relationships, manipulative development, and repertoire of ideas of how things can fit together.

In buying a construction set, select the most open-ended one you can find while still taking your child's present skills into account. Additional Information at the back of this book lists a variety of sets suitable for preschoolers. Some we have tried ourselves, others have been recommended by nursery school teachers and parents. A few were found in catalogs—things that appear to be unique in some worthwhile way bearing further investigation. These sets are presented roughly in order of increasing difficulty and sophistication. □

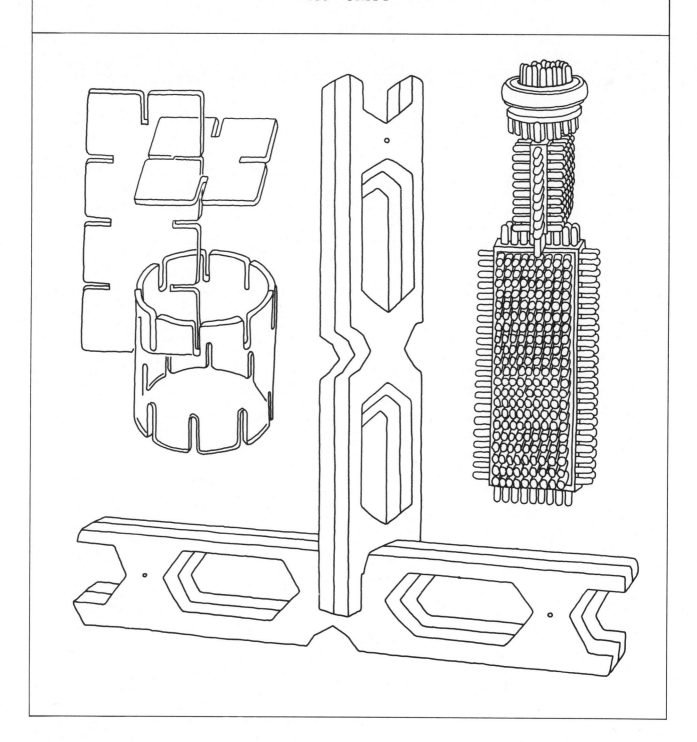

Real tools and carpentry

As always there's nothing like the real thing and real skills. A *pounding bench* is one of the best toddler toys around, good for children around the age of 1, and *play tools* can be fun. But by the time they are 3, most girls and boys are capable of using a hammer and saw and drill on soft wood, if *we* are only game. They do love it so! There are perfectly gorgeous *tool benches* available which are lovely to have if you *know* you will fork up with a steady supply of wood, plenty of per-

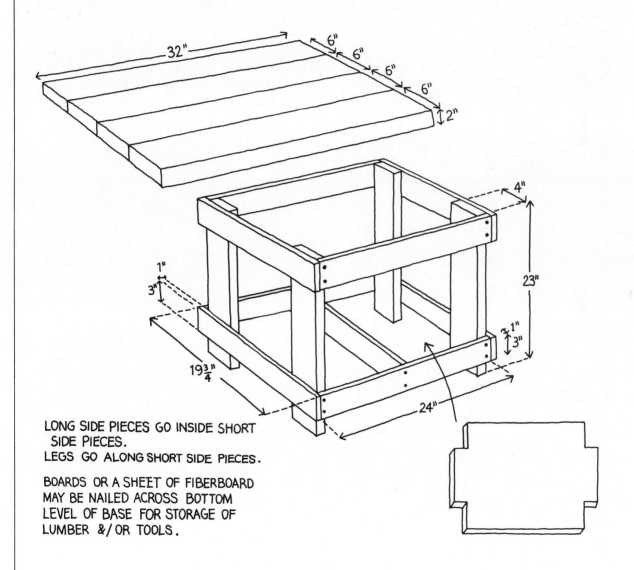

LONG SIDE PIECES GO INSIDE SHORT
  SIDE PIECES.
LEGS GO ALONG SHORT SIDE PIECES.

BOARDS OR A SHEET OF FIBERBOARD
MAY BE NAILED ACROSS BOTTOM
LEVEL OF BASE FOR STORAGE OF
LUMBER &/OR TOOLS.

mission, and a fair amount of help and guidance. (It is very bad to purchase these things and not follow through because this teaches irresponsibility and materialism.) □

Teaching the proper care of tools is important whether or not a tool kit is purchased. Be sure to set up a good place for her tools or for the ones you share with her.

Mostly the child will be happy just to pound in nails (hang up a "Bent Nail" original) and make cuts. Give him some wire or rubber bands to entwine and stretch into designs on a board of nails. And keep some glue available. When hammering and sawing become discouraging, gluing is glorious. □

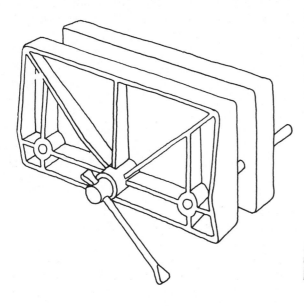

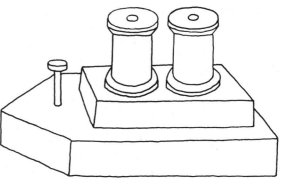

All you really need, besides a small 12–18-inch *crosscut saw* and a medium-sized *hammer* and maybe a *drill,* is a *vise* to hold the wood. A vise makes a tremendous difference in the preschooler's sawing success. While an older, stronger child can manage fine without one, the preschooler needs two hands to saw and thus depends on something or you to hold the wood steady. Woodworking vises (the kind with plates) are rather costly and C-clamps will do. The main advantage of the vise over the C-clamp is that the child can mount the wood in the vise by himself, which is not possible with the clamps. □

Besides all this it is a good idea to guide the child through a few finished carpentry products. A bath boat that really floats is wonderful. Also a hook thing for neckties or kitchen utensils.
• The child cuts the board. (You may have to start the cut.)
• Together you sand it—perfectly (but make the sanding the issue, not the child's willingness to stay with it).
• Supervised waxing and polishing.
• What a beautiful, smooth piece of wood this has become! How wonderful!

• Screw in the hooks (L-shaped) after careful measuring. You start and finish; he gives a few turns in the middle.
• Give it (gift-wrapped) to someone, if possible someone who will really hang and use it.

Of course, it's like anything else—there's a time to help and a time to refrain from helping, a time to demonstrate and a time to refrain from demonstrating, a time for experimentation and (more rarely) a time for finished products. You have to be guided by the child to see what he is ready to learn. You also have to be ready for his idea of what a finished product is. As long as the atmosphere is appreciative, you know you're on the right track.

Padlock and Key and Other Mechanical Wonders

From small hardware items to tools and machines, mechanical things also fascinate children and inspire them with increased awareness of the fact and possibilities of unity. Anything you can find that a child can safely work—an eggbeater, a crank, a typewriter—is a happy and edifying activity for him. Hardware stores are full of toys for children. A great big nut and a bolt is a beautiful thing to a toddler.

Almost all children have a fascination for keys. They jingle nicely for babies and provide a growing challenge for the growing toddler who likes to fit things into things, and the older preschooler for whom opening and closing a padlock is an absolute wonder and a joy. Buy a good-sized padlock and hide the extra key. Even better also buy a latch and

mount it on a board. Even better, cut a door out of the board and attach it with real hinges. You can also buy a lock box from Creative Playthings with all kinds of latches on it. But it seems better to introduce these things one at a time as inspiration suggests. Just a padlock and a key will do. As a gift it's better than two dozen junky toys.

Along the same lines, never miss an opportunity to dissect an old machine with your youngster. An old toaster or clock that is ready for the junkyard is a whole afternoon of investigation, the perfect opportunity to see, first of all, *that* things work, a little bit of how, and to demonstrate and practice the use of screwdrivers, pliers, and other real tools.

LOCK AND KEY: A MEDITATION

In *Alice in Wonderland* there comes a point at which Alice wants to go through a door into a beautiful garden. She has the key and there is a door, but she is too big to go through. She drinks something that makes her very tiny, small enough to pass through the door (small enough to be born?). But now she finds that she cannot reach the key, which she has left upon the table. So she eats something that makes her grow very very big, bigger than before. Now she can reach the key, but she is much too big to get through the door. "She could just manage, by putting her head down close to the ground, to *look* through with one eye!" After crying forth a pool of tears at last she obtains from a rabbit a fan which, when she uses it, makes her small once more.

It is such a strange story and goes on so mysteriously, but this part, at least, seems suggestive of our life course. The young child of ours to whom we bend in these days of parenthood, is small enough, humble and innocent enough to get through the door to the kingdom, yet he does not seem able to grasp the key that would open the door. We nourish him and he grows as we have grown until, like us, he has the key but is too big, too self-separate and self-confirmed to go through the door. As adults, it is only when we bend down very low to the ground again and look *with a single eye* that we can even begin to glimpse the beautiful kingdom to which we have the key. Is not the child our keyhole? Just what is this fan and where is it to be found that blows away the enormous sense of personal selfhood?

Seek and ye shall find.
Knock and it shall be opened.
–Matthew 7:7

Water, Sand, and Mud

Man on earth never really outgrows sand, mud, and water, nor can he begin his exploration of these materials too young. The more amorphous the material, the more can be done with it, the longer it will sustain interest, and the more can be learned from it. There are no toys for sale to equal these simple materials in entertainment and educational value, or in long-lasting appeal. Like everything else in the material world water, sand, and mud are significant of ideas far beyond themselves. So even when we become old men and women, if we have grown at all wise we will still be contemplating and learning from these materials as symbols.

Children don't need to be bathed every day for cleanliness, though regular bathing may contribute to their appreciation of order and provide certain mental purification. But the bath is one of the best places for the very young child to enjoy some quiet and uniquely private play. One mother tells of living in an apartment in which the only bathroom was off the kitchen. It was totally inconvenient in every way except one. Strategically it was the best possible location for her toddler's bath. She could fix dinner while keeping an unobtrusive eye on her child, and she found that all the best bath toys came from the kitchen. "I want da collander, please!" her 2-year-old would call. Given a simple trickle of running water to work with, the child played happily for nearly an hour each day before supper. Mother and child were equally refreshed by this period of quiet independence.

So take advantage of the bathtub, sink, a sand or water table, sandbox, the hose in that patch where the grass refuses to grow anyway, a rainy day, and the beach above all, amen.

Sticks and stones and leaves and popsicle sticks are more than enough equipment to keep a child busy with sand and water, but here are a few toys you might make or buy and some activities you might set up.

Sponge boats—You make them with sponges and scissors.

Plastic tube—For blowing noisy bubbles in the bath. Less than a $1 for 2 feet of fish tank tubing from any pet store.

Tiny tea set—A little plastic blister-wrapped one for less than $1 in almost any supermarket, dime, or toy store.

Cups, collanders, ladles, funnels, and measuring cups—All such utensils from the kitchen are marvelous for sand or water.

Bubble bath—Many children are somewhat fearful of this at first, but after a time or two they all discover the fun of shoveling, modeling, land- and seascaping, and wearing the bubbles.

Boats—Most cheap plastic bathtub boats are not a bargain because they capsize or sink. If they fill up with water, they also mildew inside. So, as with any real boat, it matters that a toy boat be leakproof and buoyant. Buy a wooden one. Some not too expensive and very nice ones are available from wooden toy manufacturers listed on pp. 76–77. Instructions for how to make rubber-band-powered paddle boats can be found in *American Folk Toys* by Dick Schnacke (described on page 71). □

Montgomery Schoolhouse has a whole line of toys specifically designed for beach and sandbox use. Includes all kinds of wooden traffic (toys though, oddly enough not many real earth movers such as bulldozers and graders), entirely free of plastic or rustable metal parts. Especially useful for really enthusiastic junior road engineers is their assortment of loading ramps, platforms, tunnels, and bridge units.

Sand painting—See page 168.

Sandbox—Buy or build a wooden one (1″ x 8″ boards are about right), or make one from a half-sunk tractor tire. And don't forget, just a washtub full of sand (or rice or corn meal) and a few small kitchen cups and spoons on the porch can be tremendously satisfying. Think about a sandbox in the basement for the winter.

Also of interest is a "sandbox pond liner," a 5-foot square of heavy polyethelene with "instructions for use as a shallow pond in sand or earth" ($1, from Montgomery Schoolhouse). The idea sounds so good that even if you don't buy it, you might want to try out the idea with a piece of old shower curtain.

Sand pile—You don't have to have a sandbox at all, you know. You don't even have to have sand. A mound/mountain of sand or soil in a corner of the yard may be even more fun to climb and work on. Just shovel it back together again from time to time to make it last a little longer.

Sand pail and shovel—If you are a parkgoer, buy an inexpensive plastic pail and shovel. No matter how hard you try, these things seem to get lost somehow. Flexible plastic pails and shovels are a little safer than hard metal or wooden ones in a sandbox with several not-very-experienced preschoolers.

Sand combs—for drawing designs in the sand can be purchased, but they can be cut for nothing from empty plastic bottles, which also make good scoops.

Earth movers—Among model vehicles the earth movers are the most useful, especially in a sandbox or pile of dirt. A vast variety of well-made metal ones is available. A bulldozer is nice because it's easy to operate and to understand its purpose. Tonka road machines make even the youngest kids' eyes light up (with first greed?). A trencher is nice because there is something to do with it at each end. This makes it a very good toy in a sandbox where the idea of sharing with other kids often comes up for the first time.

A baby simply likes to move the moving parts. Toddlers often don't even know what a bulldozer is for yet, but they know it can do something and they think it is amazing. Sometimes the first thing a group of toddlers will do together with such a toy is bury it. They know it has something to do with sand, but they aren't quite sure what. Please remember that little girls love and learn from this type of activity just as much as little boys. Playing with trucks has nothing to do with wanting to be a truck driver. At this stage a truck is simply a tool for finding out about living and moving on the earth.

Bubbles—To get a *giant soap bubble* rub a wet piece of soap along the side of your wet index finger and thumb. Close thumb tightly around index finger. Open slowly into a ring. Blow softly and steadily. If the ratio of water and soap is just right, you will now be able to softly blow a giant bubble, equaled in size only by your own and your child's wide eyes. Bubble blowing is beautiful. The bubbles are beautiful, and it is even more beautiful to watch the beautiful children beautifully watching the bubbles or running with a wake of tiny bubbles behind. You will find that the bubbling power of different brands of bubble stuff varies. Blow some for a tiny baby and see how he smiles and reaches.

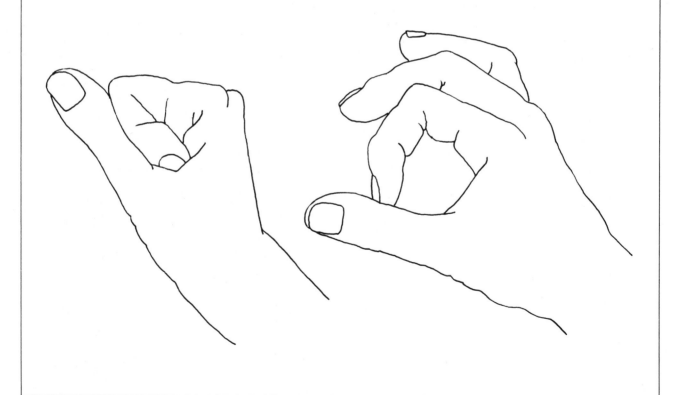

Super bubble mixtures can be achieved by adding a drop of glycerine (which is safe and available in drugstores) to your mixture of soap and water.

Bubble pipes seem like a nice idea, but don't buy one until you know your child knows the difference between sucking and blowing. Yuck! Phooey! Betrayal.

Water machines—There are a number of toys available that demonstrate the power of water. Among "busy" toys the Kohner Busy Bath is successful, and in summer watch for such wonderful, inexpensive plastic toys as a pail with a real pump and water-wheel machinery. □

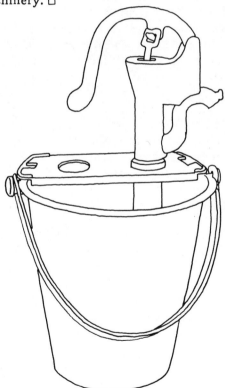

Books

The following short bibliography includes some books that have nothing to say about unity directly, but they do relate to the tools and toys through which a child first experiences the principle of unity on a material plane.

[*Note:* Numbers in parentheses indicate comprehension levels (not age) as outlined on pp. 7–9, 195, 197, 201, 207. Starred titles are those deemed superior for a preschoolers' home library. See pp. 6–7, 193–4 for additional information regarding book notations and selection.]

Bam, Zam, Boom!
by Eve Merriam, photo design by William Lightfoot
The demolition of an old building and the construction of a new, high-rise apartment building.
Scholastic Book Services, paperback, 1 and limited 4 colors, 7½" x 9", 40 pp., (2–3).

Castles and Mirrors and Cities of Sand
by Lillian Bason, illus. by Allan Eitzen
A useful enrichment on the subject of sand everywhere. Touches on beaches, deserts, sand castles, cement, glass, timers, icy roads, sand paintings. A good library book, if not to buy.
Lothrop, Lee & Shepard, hardcover, 2 and 4 colors, 8" x 9¾", 40 pp., (3).

Machines
by William Dugan
A little bit about 17 vehicular machines (crane, bulldozer, plow).
A Little Golden Book. Golden Press, board, 4 colors, 6½" x 8", 24 pp., (2).

* Machines
by Anne and Harlow Rockwell
A beautifully simple and useful book about machines and what they are specifically for. Includes sprocket, gear, lever, pulley, wheel, jackscrew.

Enlightening to mechanically ignorant parents as well.
Macmillan, hardcover, 4 colors, 9¼″ x 8¼″, 32 pp., (2–4).

Tommy Takes a Bath
by Gunilla Wolde
See page 197 for a complete listing of this good book.

Tommy Builds a House
by Gunilla Wolde
Also see p. 197 for a full description of this book.

* The Toolbox
by Anne and Harlow Rockwell
Approximately 15 tools and what they do. A simple picture and single sentence about each. Like *Machines* by the Rockwells (see above), this book has a special and appropriate quality of reverent appreciation for the tools and the fact that things work and for the child learning.
Collier, paperback, 4 colors, 9¼″ x 8¼″, 24 pp. (1 up).

What Makes It Go? Work? Fly? Float?
by Joe Kaufman
Too hard for most preschoolers, this book about how everything (motorcycles, vacuum cleaners, telephones, clarinets) works is, nevertheless, a boon for parents who are going to get asked these questions sooner or later.
Golden Press, board, 4 colors, 10¼″ x 11¾″, (4 up).

Discipline

Most children are not greatly distressed by the tumbling of sand castles and block towers, or the failure of water to remain in a leaky or overturned vessel. Over and over the castles are built, gradually better and better, until the properties of sand and the laws governing its behavior are at least partially understood. For the most part progress is made harmoniously and the sandbox remains a pleasant place to play.

The secret of this harmonious unfoldment is our lack of personal sense regarding material laws. We understand that sand behaves according to reliable physical principles, so we do not teach our children to take this behavior personally, neither do we too often take personally our children's ignorance of these laws. From the start we say "that's how it is" and "that's what happens when," and the child does not develop the notion that through exertion of his personal will he can somehow successfully take exception to physical law if he so desires.

We are not so enlightened regarding the less tangible but higher laws of being. We do take life in general, our children in particular and ourselves above all, very personally. It is for this reason that most of us have difficulty with our children in the area we call discipline. We have a whole battery of techniques, which we fire at our children "for their own good," ranging from old-fashioned, punitive insistence, through all the more subtle forms of manipulation, coercion, and bribery, to hands-off permissiveness. (The golden mean between these extremes is undoubtedly the cruelest and most detrimental of all.) The results vary accordingly from fearful compliance and passivity through anxious uncertainty to broad anarchy and rebellion, often moving from one extreme to the other, especially in adolescence.

Since none of our approaches is successful, most of us wind up trying a little of everything. The reason none of them works is that each is wrong. Less obvious is that they are also all the same. Each of those disciplinary techniques is based on an idea that personal mind is the basic issue and reality. We believe we are personally and causally responsible for the existence of our children and for the way they behave. We also believe that life and living are matters of personal opinion.

In the sandbox we express a certain degree of faith in the sand as teacher and the child as learner, but we assume full personal responsibility for just about everything else. In fact, the less we know about something the more personal responsibility we assume. In ignorance we constantly violate higher laws of being and thus invite experiences of disharmony that reinforce our belief in lawlessness. Misinterpreting our own ignorance of higher law as the fact that there is no higher law, that reality is lawless, we undertake the awesome responsibility of personally authoring and enforcing law. When it comes to our children (whom we also believe we have authored), we even believe we *must* take this personal responsibility. In adhering to this misconception, the biggest lesson we are teaching our children is that personal will (be it compliant or defiant) is the basic issue. This places us and our children in immediate conflict with life and therefore with each other.

In reality, however, we too are but children in the sandbox. Our children and the situations in which we find ourselves are like the sand, relentlessly—but not maliciously—manifesting certain principles of existence as law. We are to each other both sand and fellow diggers in the sandbox. As diggers we are responsible only for reflecting or expressing those laws in our lives. But in neither case are we *personally* responsible. We do not create the laws, nor can we vary them, nor force anyone to live by them. We are responsible only in the sense that we are able to respond to the laws both in understanding and in our mode of being in the world. These laws are the truth about us; we do not make them true.

What does this mean regarding our role as parents? How can we avoid the years of struggling, frustration, anger, disappointment, and even tragedy that plague so many wholeheartedly well-meaning families in this area called discipline?

It is important to remember that it is what we know (in principle, in truth) that makes the difference, not what we do or say. Sand castles will tumble one day and tower the next in a bewildering fashion unless the builder is aware of the difference between wet and dry sand. Though from a material standpoint sand is characteristically shifting, in ideal terms it is constant; it is reliably shifty. It always expresses the laws of its being. So it is most important to make a continuous effort in consciousness to discern the truth that is being revealed in any situation—not the facts or details or cause but the underlying principle.

For this we must maintain an unceasing vigil over our thoughts, distinguishing with relentless honesty between our ignorant personal moods and whims and what is a matter of genuine law or truth. This is especially true with regard to our little children who are so easy to push around. Insofar as we understand the truth of any situation it will be possible for us to remain as constant as sand in our loyalty to those principles without making it seem a matter of personal will. For example, knowing the properties of sand to the extent that we do, we are not tempted to interfere overmuch in our children's experimental struggles in the sandbox. Nor do we feel impelled to make them accept our word for it that this is what will happen.

Best of all it seems that what we truly know is somehow transmitted to the children through consciousness and does not have to be spoken of or enforced at all. Insofar as we can see that law, one law, is operating for us and for our children we can more easily let each other live and learn without being swayed (through false fears and personal responsibility) by the ups and downs of our inadvertent compliance with and violation of these laws. Our assured non-interference is conveyed to the child as a sense of confidence in both himself and reality that, despite all appearances and experiences to the contrary, reality is reliable, and he can know this too.

So the first answer to the problems of personal sense is silent seeking and knowing. This involves letting go of our misconceptions and exaggerated personal sense, and receptively turning our attention toward the revelation of principle.

The second answer to the problem of personal mind is the demonstration in our lives of those principles we understand, our appreciation of their value and validity, and above all our confidence in the fact of their existence.

On the one hand this means simply practicing what we preach—an easy matter if we really know what we're talking about, otherwise more difficult. We have dominion over our children much as we have dominion over the sand, not through domination but through understanding the dominion of principles. For the most part our children will behave in accordance with our values, reflecting positively or negatively the ideas we cherish most. Any truths we fully understand, and thus demonstrate in daily living, will be picked up by our children. This means that although the child is not yet conscious enough to understand the principles *per se* (we are only beginning to discover them for ourselves), he will nevertheless be drawn to them, and live in accordance with them, and thus experience their fruits. This is a happy way to grow up and a joyful way to be a parent.

Sometimes, however, we do not know the law ourselves much less the principle behind the law. In such instances, both for our own sake and for the sake of our children, affirmation in the face of uncertainty is called for in order that learning may occur; we affirm that truth *is,* that the sand does behave according to law even though it is not immediately clear to us why this particular sand castle has just caved in or why at this particular moment our child seems to be having a tantrum. In fact it is not possible for us to have any personal difficulty with our children any more than we truly have difficulty with the sand. The only difficulty we can ever have is with error, the ignorance of truth.

For example, if we do not understand the laws behind the behavior of sand we may try to force it to behave in accordance with our erroneous preconceptions, quite against its own nature, or to fling it about in frustration. As long as we continue to cling to our error and believe that the problem is with the sand, the sand will only be able to manifest our error. It will be shifty, unreliable, hurtful to the eyes. Likewise, when we run into difficulty with our children, we are often inclined to try to change them rather than our thoughts. As with the sand, we are thus keeping them in bondage to our errors, contrary to the truth of their own as yet unconscious being. At best it is a bewildering experience for both parent and child. Worst of all, since the child, unlike the sand, is growing in consciousness he not only manifests the error, but sooner or later he will begin to adopt it in the form of a conscious, but false, belief.

So it can be seen that the acknowledgment of discord as error or ignorance of truth is a vital first step toward relinquishing error and its accompanying problems. For the child just this one small step already means tremendous release from the false lessons of personal badness and conflict. There is little worse that we could hope to spare our children. Affirmation that truth exists, whether we yet know it or not, is called faith. In our children it will be expressed as confidence, enthusiasm, and happy expectancy, the freedom to live and learn. In our own lives the practice of known or acknowledged principles will be accompanied by our firsthand discovery of their validity.

So with regard to discipline, the removal of personal sense from parenthood means first of all the silent seeking and knowing of principle in consciousness and, second, the practice and exemplification of principle in experience as law. But is this enough? Do knowing and exemplifying substitute altogether for teaching? Of course not.

Much, if not most, of the intruding and interfering and bullying that passes for what has been called discipline is done away with in silent knowing and demonstrating. But there remains for the parent a very important role as guardian and teacher, a very constructive one once the error of personal sense is removed. With children, by and large this is the setting forth of certain precepts or laws.

Whatever is not communicated through silent knowing and example must be reduced to laws. Laws are a temporary measure necessitated by the imperfection of our understanding of principle and by the fact that our children, who are by definition largely unconscious, cannot receive principles, which by definition can only be understood in consciousness.

As consistently as possible we must try to see that the laws we set forth are based on principles that we consciously understand. This will help us to avoid the problems of personal sense and the accumulation of an excessive number of mutually conflicting laws. At the same time we need to keep in mind that such laws are at best an imperfect reflection of principle and often even a temporary substitute for the awareness of principle. We will thus be ready to revise or relinquish any law in the light of greater understanding or the growing readiness of our children to move from regulation toward principle. Once we begin to appreciate that the apparent destructiveness of the toddler in taking apart a flower or knocking down sand castles is in fact a constructive effort to understand unity, we are able to revise our view of the situation, moving from reprimand and prohibition to the intelligent channeling of his efforts and the fostering of discovery. Perhaps instead of "don't touch," we may now be inspired to give him one flower from the centerpiece to examine. Or we may offer to rebuild (demonstration) the same sand castle several times in a row, allowing the child the freedom to knock it down and find out.

Likewise, we are ready to revise or relinquish any of our laws as the child himself grows in understanding. At first we protect our children and our property from each other by not allowing any hazardous opportunities to arise. Dangerous and breakable things are kept out of reach and our babies are kept physically out of danger. But as the child grows, a progression occurs from protection and prevention to admonition and advice. More and more the child is allowed to discover and prove things for himself through trial and error (depending, of course, on the possible danger of any given situation).

This does not mean that leaping forth into the formulation of laws as principles is ever called for. As we have seen, it is not in the definition of the child to become fully conscious of principles as principles. That is the task of maturity. It is true that we can and should verbally express from time to time in front of our child the few principles we genuinely understand as principles, but only as sowers, letting the ideas fall as seeds in consciousness to sprout and bloom later when he is ready. But we cannot expect the child to infer anything about his behavior on the basis of principle. Therefore, it is important for all laws to be formulated in the most concrete terms possible.

Initially this means not even using words, as in the physical protection of the physical baby from physical harm. Later it means expressing laws as do's and don'ts. For example, when children first begin to play with each other they have great difficulty sharing. They do not, they even cannot, understand what sharing is or its possible value. Yet somehow we have to help them overcome the problem of fighting over cherished toys if they are to have a happy social experience and ultimately discover the joy of sharing. A helpful and effective law that can be set forth at such times is, "No one may take anything out of anybody's hands." With older children such a law only reduces sharing to competitive snatching and conflict, but for the youngest children it is wonderful. It is concrete, comprehensible, and it works. At the right time such a principle-based concrete law is a tool with which the child can validate for himself the underlying principle on an experiential level.

It is also wise in formulating laws to express them as positively as possible. For example, it is almost universally known that, on a nonverbal level, it is easier to stop a child from repeatedly heading for an electric socket or banging the glass coffee table with his xylophone if something more interesting is presented to take his attention away. The same thing is true on a verbal level. While there is certainly a place for taking a firm, stern stand against error as error, in most instances it is wise to express laws in positive terms. One incident that comes to mind has to do with kicking. Like most children, one little boy used to kick his legs while his diaper was being changed. As he grew bigger and stronger, the kicking became painful and also playfully purposeful. Saying "Don't kick" and "Stop it!" only fixed the idea in the forefront of his thoughts and made it impossible for him to turn to anything else. Then another idea occurred to the parents. "Kick leaves," they said, "not people." The idea itself was a distraction and also suggested an additional possibility. The kicking stopped.

But there is more than technique working in this illustration. The principle behind the effectiveness of this technique is that true behavior is always to our good. Sacrificing error does not mean loss, but rather fulfillment. The living child cannot be concerned with how not to live, but only with living.

Finally, in formulating laws for our children the most important thing to keep in mind is the removal of personal sense. It is truth that is at issue, not personal will or mind. There isn't anything more important that we could do for ourselves than to realize this, and there is nothing more that we could do for our children than to spare them a too-persuasive indoctrination into the personal point of view. Bad and good behavior does not imply badness or goodness on the part of the child, nor is it bad or good because we say so or because we do or do not like it. In fact, there is not good or bad behavior at all. There is only that which works existentially and that which doesn't, that which is valid and that which isn't, that which is harmony-accompanied and that which is discord-accompanied. The opposite of true isn't bad, it isn't even really false; it is only ignorant. Both in order that we may truly realize this and in order that our children may not come to think otherwise with too strong a conviction, it is helpful to delete the misleading personal words of "I" and "you" as much as

possible when setting forth laws or instructions for our children.

This means first of all casting all discordant behavior into the category of mistake—error—irrelevant. It has nothing to do with the true child and nothing to do with the truth of life. It is no way to be. It is nothing. Another name for this realization is forgiveness. Instead of "Why did you do that?" or "You shouldn't do that" or "You are a bad girl!" or "I told you not to do that" or "Don't you ever let me see you do that again!" we say, "That was a mistake" or, more concretely, "Hitting is a mistake—it doesn't work." This way the issue is understood to be ignorance, and the assumption is that the child would not do such a thing if she genuinely knew better. This leaves open the possibility of learning. It is even possible in many instances to spell out positively the lesson that, say, "Hitting breaks things. Now the glass is broken."

Likewise, it is a good idea to delete "I" and "you" from all commands and positive rules and regulations. At first this seems awkward, for we rightfully realize that we do not know the principle behind the laws we are setting forth. It may be clear to us what must be done even though we don't clearly see the underlying principle that makes this so. We know that the sand must be wet if there is to be a tunnel, but we do not have a precise understanding of the principle that makes this so. So, to our personal way of thinking, it seems presumptuous to set forth anything as a law. Trying hard to be realistic and democratic, we struggle to choose between "You have to do this because I said so, don't ask me why," and long, drawn-out, incoherent explanations that are mostly incorrect and which don't mean anything to the child anyway. It is hard to say which of these two approaches is more tyrannical and irrelevant. But since truth *is,* an immediate here-and-now reality revealing itself here and now, we can most truthfully say, "This is not a good time or place for" thus and such, or "Now is the time for putting on coats," or "Right now it seems best to go home for supper." Even if it remains necessary to pick up the child and bodily cart him off, the issue will not become a matter of personal dominance. Such phrasing is not better because it is less offensive; it is less offensive because it is more truthful.

Perhaps at first it seems stilted and cumbersome to speak in this manner, but the fruits are well worth the effort. By making such a conscious effort to speak in precisely truthful terms, we are keeping the quest for truth as the central issue. It *is* the central issue. This most valid of all existential orientations will transform our lives and the lives of our children.

Behind the laws there stands the Law, which is greater and more perfect than the laws and which the laws must serve. Behind the Law there stands principle or truth, which is purer and more perfect than the Law and which the Law must serve. Only truth is ultimately redemptive. Even though redemption in our lives depends upon our conscious, individual realization of truth, truth is not personal. Neither is it impersonal. It is transpersonal. The best way to reach the realization of truth for ourselves, and as parents to foster our children's growth toward this realization, is through silent knowing, exemplification, and teaching.

The highest of these is silent knowing, which is the pure concern in consciousness with pure principle. Its fruits in our lives are revelation and redemption. Its fruit in the lives of our children is the maintenance of a wholesome and happy environment for growth. Another name for silent knowing is prayer.

The second way to reach realization is through exemplification, the affirmation, practice, and demonstration of principle in daily life. In our lives its fruit is the discovery and validation of principle in experience as Law. In our children's lives this is the providence of healthy models of being in the world and the maintenance of the desire and freedom to be healthy. Another name for exemplification is witness.

Finally there is teaching. On the highest level this means voicing realized truth in the presence of anyone sincerely interested, but as parents it is mostly the concern with what to do or say *in the meantime*—until we know, until our children are ready to seek to know. This is the most confusing of all because it is the farthest from the truth, the most human and temporary. It is made much easier by the removal of personal sense, and it is largely replaced by silent knowing and exemplification. In our lives the fruit of teaching is learning. In our children's lives, it is easier growth.

So the true disciplinarian of us all is truth. The true discipline is the following after or seeking of truth. The best way for us to discipline our children is not to discipline them at all, but rather to be ourselves disciples of truth. The true answer to the problems of discipline is thus discipleship.

The One is none other than the All, the All none other than the One.
Take your stand on this, and the rest will follow of its accord;
To trust in the Heart is the "Not Two," the "Not Two" is to trust in the Heart.
I have spoken, but in vain; for what can words tell
Of things that have no yesterday, tomorrow, or today?

–Seng Ts'an in *The Religions of Man,* by Huston Smith

Hear, O Israel: The Lord our God is one Lord.

–Deuteronomy 6:4

Mountains and rivers, the whole earth—
All manifest forth the essence of being.

–*The Gospel According to Zen,* ed. by Sohl and Carr

So we, being many, are one body in Christ,
and every one members one of another.

–Romans 12:5

Kabir said: Behold but One in all things; it is the second that leads you astray.

–*The Way of Life, Lao Tzu,* trans. by R. B. Blakney

Beauty

Since "beauty is in the eye of the beholder," it is the eye that must be trained, first to see, then to see beauty. Ultimately there is another eye altogether with which to see. The real objective in the quest for beauty is the discovery of this eye. To see anything clearly beyond the tip of one's tiny nose, to see beyond the surface of a picture, beyond difficult circumstances and seemingly ugly personalities of this life are all steps toward this objective.

". . . *the eye* of the beholder,"—the use of the singular form, *the eye,* rather than the plural, *eyes,* is a most profoundly significant aspect of this very wonderful statement. The eye that beholds the beauty is the single eye, the inner spiritual one rather than the material two. The same is true of hearing. What the two ears receive is merely sound and noise. It is only the inner ear, the spiritual one, that hears the beauty that is truthful, the truth that is so beautiful. And what the nonmaterial eye and ear see and hear is ideal or spiritual truth, which, even in art and music, is entirely free of both sound and image. Spiritual truth is always a matter of qualities—infinite qualities—harmony, order, flow, goodness.

What is important about this is not only what we see and hear when we see and hear with the inner eye and ear, but even more of what we become in the moment of inner seeing and hearing. In such an instant we become what we truly are—one with the One Mind, one with the infinite qualities of the One Mind. Instead of a separate material self thing (id entity) controlled by material impressions we become individual (literally *undivided*) expressions of infinite reality, undivided from our source of being. When we perceive order, we become orderly; when we perceive harmony, we become harmonious. Perceiving spiritual reality, our lives become spiritual, leaving no room for material discomfort or lack. Perceiving oneness we become one, leaving no room for dualistic conflict of any sort. Perceiving truth, we become truthful; perceiving beauty, we become beautiful.

What of our children—our littlest babies who cannot even focus their new eyes on the material world yet and to whom all sounds are probably a sort of undifferentiated background din? What is all this to them? Not more but neither less than an unconscious yearning—a profound, existential, but unconscious, yearning. No one born escapes it; everyone is blessed and burdened with it. Music and art can be part of the path toward fulfilling this yearning. We can perceive the yearning in our children's enthusiastic responses to music and art.

Even before they learn to speak words, they talk in music, and dancing for them is not a recreation; it's the only way to travel.

We may want our children to like music because of its cultural and social merit. But, while it is true that music offers certain worthwhile benefits in physical, social, and intellectual development, such motives could never evoke the rapt and happy enthusiasm most children have for music and art. The child's interest is spontaneous and more profound, and it lasts either until it has served her purpose (probably forever) or until we suffocate it with our purposes. Unconsciously she is seeking the same harmony, flow, order, beauty in life we yearn for. These qualities are part of her secret nature as a living being, and part of the secret nature of life. They are also characteristic qualities of good music and art. When the child encounters them in music and art, a reunion takes place and she reacts with pure joy, dancing and clapping and smiling and laughing.

So it is good for us to foster our children's appreciation of music and art. And it is even better if we can learn the secret of joy from them.

Oddly enough, in human experience the two eyes and two ears must be well trained before the true eye, the true ear (the One Mind) can be appreciated or consciously sought and discovered. The baby has to learn to see and hear through her eyes and ears before she can begin to appreciate songs and pictures, and that long before she can begin to look beyond music and artwork to the qualities expressed so beautifully there.

The practical sections of this chapter are largely concerned with this process. Broken arbitrarily into separate sections on music and art, the main issues are invitation and inspiration and letting be. There are not a lot of things to buy. Art supplies should be in infinite supply, and records should be as abundant as possible since they constitute both an invitation and an inspiration, charming the child into participation and fostering his awareness of the possibilities of beauty. A variety of pictures and prints is desirable but otherwise you don't need much—a few songbooks, perhaps a musical instrument or two, and maybe an easel.

Letting be is harder, but if we keep in mind the ultimate objectives of the child's quest in art and music, we will be well-guided in how to help and not help, and most of all how not to interfere or deter.

If it is arbitrary to separate music and art from each other, it is positively erroneous to subdivide these fields into separate categories of hearing or seeing and actively doing as we have for convenience' sake in the following pages. Whether performing or creating, listening or looking, the objective should be the same. While the spectator's task is more contemplative and the performer's more expressive, the true concern of both should remain the perception of ideal reality. This fact sheds light on the parental issue of praise and encouragement.

In the beginning, at least, discovery is both the child's objective and his reward. Later in life we have to learn that this is really so. The child does not seek personal praise at first and it should not be given. If we watch closely, we can easily see that all the play activity of the child is directed toward learning. This is entirely valid. Understanding is the reward that brings the child delight, and it is understanding alone that will most facilitate his existence.

Personal praise is thus a distraction. If we teach our children that praise is any reward at all, we are in fact impeding their learning progress. Through praise we may be able to get them to *do* more, but only at the costly expense of perverting their motive. Each time they turn to us for praise, they are turning away from what they are learning. And worst of all, in fostering a desire for self-acclaim, we have introduced the possibility of self-doubt. In this way an appetite develops that will be less and less easy to satisfy as the child grows. Sooner or later it is almost inescapable that some of both will creep into the child's motivation (our whole society is founded upon nothing else), but it is not necessary to introduce these elements prematurely, and with awareness it is possible to minimize them when they do come.

What then must we offer our children as they endeavor to learn (be it music, art, dressing themselves, or whatever)? The answer is love and gratitude. Love cheerfully assumes and reflects confidence in both the child's perfect potential to learn and life's built-in tendency to reveal itself as goodness and beauty. In the spirit of love we can and should join our children in expressive encouragement for whatever is being attempted and substitute for praise a joyful appreciation of whatever is being revealed and perceived. (See pp. 167, 245 for concrete examples.)

Sounds and Sights

*i thank You God for this most amazing
day: for the leaping greenly spirits of trees
and a blue true dream of sky; and for everything
which is natural which is infinite which is yes*

*(i who have died am alive again today,
and this is the sun's birthday; this is the birth
day of life and of love and wings: and of the gay
great happening illimitably earth)*

*how should tasting touching hearing seeing
breathing any—lifted from the no
of all nothing—human merely being
doubt unimaginable You?*

*(now the ears of my ears awake and
now the eyes of my eyes are opened.*
–e.e. cummings, *Poems 1923–1954*

MUSIC: GOING FORTH WITH JOY

*For ye shall go out with joy, and be led forth in
peace; the mountains and the hills before you shall
break forth into singing and all the trees of the
fields shall clap their hands.*
–Isaiah 55:12

Just Listening In

Crib bell—One family had a bronze wind chime from Japan hanging over their son's crib almost from the first day they brought him home. He obviously loved its musical sound. The only thing they had found to hang it from was so low that the chime's paper sail was in reach of his foot. Within a week or two he began accidentally ringing the bell, usually when he cried or was excited. This surprised and pleased him so much that he often stopped in mid-cry to listen. He came to notice that there was a connection between his excitement and the lovely sound. They could see him working on the problem. Gradually he discovered that general movement, and then specifically kicking, was what did the trick. Before long, as his vision sharpened, he began moving around and grabbing the sail with his hand. Then they had to change to a sturdier bell and cord. From then on he announced nearly all his wakings by ringing instead of by crying. It was a cheerful and educational accident that might be worth trying to repeat on purpose.

Music box—This is one of those things you will probably receive five of as gifts or not any. It is nice to have one to wind up and play for stilling moments. Don't get those that are operated by pulling a string—they usually break. The main thing, of course, is a lovely tune, preferably one long enough so that it is not repeated excessively before the movement runs down. ☐

Records—These are invaluable and unsurpassed in the many contributions they make to children through music. A lively tune well performed inspires the child to dance, and it is through movement after all that the child can first really participate in and feel the facts of music. Records are valuable, not only in the development of musical skills and appreciation, but even more basically in language and concept development. And through listening to records, parents and children easily learn songs together. You don't have to be musical, you don't even have to try; eventually you discover you know the songs.

Records also seem to be more effective than television in eliciting participation and, of course, with records you have the advantage of being able to select what your child hears.

In fact, there are so many children's records that walking into a record store to select one is bewildering. Although there are large listings of children's records such as the Schwann juvenile catalog, it is wiser as a start to consult a more selective listing such as the good one in some educational toy catalogs. Scholastic offers a number of fine records and record/book combinations including many wonderful Folkway recordings of Pete Seeger. Burl Ives, Pete Seeger, and Woodie Guthrie are basic to a good library of children's records. ☐

There are many musical toys and instruments to buy for very small children (drums, pianos, horns, etc.). They are all fine to introduce at some point. But for a start for a baby, a xylophone, a bell, a music box seem sufficient. Wait until the real singing and dancing begins before adding other things.

Children especially appreciate times of singing and dancing together when the harmony of music becomes the harmony of people together. It is a special kind of wealth to a small child to see his parents join with other adults and children to sing some of the songs he knows and even dance together. Sometimes you can see a child's face become positively radiant with happy amazement on witnessing such a wonder for the first time. Such things can't and mustn't be forced, but if they occur without too much self-consciousness they're nice—just one family or two, the children jumping for joy, the parents for love. Then you might want some rhythm instruments. Pots and pans, spoons and forks, sticks and stones, etc., ad infinitum will be perfectly adequate, but, if you really get going, a selection of well-made rhythm instruments adds a lot. ▢

Chiming In

Xylophone—Probably the most satisfying first musical instrument for the home, and it is one of the few toys for a baby that may last well into childhood. As soon as he can sit, the baby will understand the hammering motion that produces the lovely sound. He can (and will) hammer happily to his heart's content without driving anyone nuts, since even a badly played, decently made xylophone sounds cheerful and musical. Furthermore, it is a simple instrument on which most parents can pick out a tune even if they can't read music. ▢

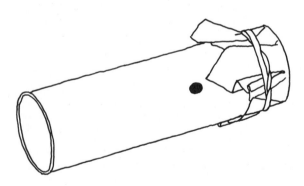

Kazoo—Because it is easiest to play (and easiest to make) the kazoo is the best instrument around for getting a good music session going. Many people like to sing, but most are ashamed of the quality of their un-

trained voices. Because it serves as a disguise, the kazoo is an irresistible invitation to sing. If there are enough kazoos to go around or enough already cut strips of waxed paper to fold over enough combs almost any adult who knows a tune will be happy to hum it—especially if someone else starts first. For

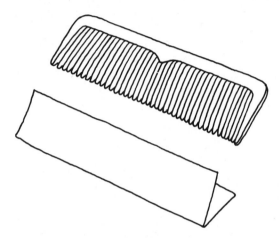

some reason, very young children are also more likely to buzz aloud with a kazoo than to sing aloud the songs they know. Both homemade and manufactured kazoos vary in design and quality. The objective is ease. A good kazoo should kazoo with just a soft hum to kazoo on.

Private concerts—Ask (hire? invite?) neighboring grade-school children who are learning to play musical instruments to come and show their instruments to your preschooler and play a little tune or a scale. Ask the older child if he will let your child touch his instrument and perhaps even try to play it. "Maybe you could blow, while she pushes down one of the keys?"

Song Books and Singing

Song books

If you think you are not musically inclined and have not learned to read music, don't buy song books that contain many unfamiliar songs. On the other hand, don't think you have to be able to play the piano or the guitar to use a song book with your child. Just sit down on the sofa with a nicely illustrated song book and sing. Even if you do play the piano, this sofa system is often much more harmonious with the littlest ones who otherwise insist on helping you to play the piano. One mother found that using a back carrier made it possible to have some wonderful singing and playing times at the piano with her very young child. He was happy up there, where he could see and sit comfortably and rock to the music with his mother. Quite often that was how he fell asleep at night.

In buying a song book remember that size is not necessarily an advantage and may even be a drawback if you have to spend five or ten minutes between songs hunting for another that you know. Look for singable songs, with (if you also play) arrangements that are at once musical and not more difficult than you can play and not too hopelessly out of your singing range. With traditional songs, be sure that most of the tunes in the book are the traditional ones.

A vast number of song books are available for young children. Some of the best are really better suited to group work than to the home; they contain songs that are just right for nursery schools but that you wouldn't be so inclined to sing around the house. Most of the books listed below have been selected partly on the basis of their usefulness in the home, where singing is more spontaneous.

The Fireside Book of Children's Songs
compiled by Marie Winn, musical arrangements by Allan Miller, illus. by John Alcorn.
An excellent selection of songs that appeal to children—67 of them—divided into chapters: Good Morning and Goodnight, Birds and Beasts, Nursery, Silly, and Singing Games and Rounds. The rather stylized art is less appealing to youngsters than the songs themselves. Guitar chords and easy piano arrangements.
Simon & Schuster, hardcover, 3 colors, 8⅜" x 10⅞", 100 pp.

The Fireside Book of Folk Songs
compiled by Margaret Bradford Boni, piano arrangements by Norman Lloyd, illus. by Alice and Martin Provensen
Not specifically for children, this is listed here just as a good book of folksongs for the family. Includes traditional ballads, work songs, Christmas carols, marching songs, hymns and spirituals. Easily playable piano accompaniments. Guitar chords.
Simon & Schuster, hardcover, 8" x 11", 324 pp.

* The Golden Song Book
selected and arranged by Katharine Tyler Wessells, illus. by Gertrude Elliott
If you want one all-purpose song book of the old familiars for children, this one (in its twenty-fourth printing) is hard to beat. Unlike those in most simple song books, the piano arrangements in this one are fairly simple yet musical. 56 songs including some hymns. The illustrations and the use of color bars behind the musical score in some places give this book a slightly more inviting appearance than many song books.
Golden Press, board, 2 and 4 colors, 8¼" x 11", 72 pp.

* Jim Along, Josie
compiled by Nancy and John Langstaff, illus. by Jan Pienkowski
A perfectly superb selection of 81 singable danceable, versatile folksongs and singing games for

young children at home or in groups. Simple, *musical* piano arrangements by Seymour Barab. Guitar chords by Happy Traum. Very successful and unusual black-and-white silhouette illustrations.
Harcourt Brace Jovanovich, hardcover, 1 color, 8½″ x 11″, 136 pp.

Play It In Spanish
compiled by Marianna Prieto, piano accompaniment by Elizabeth Nielsen, illus. by Regina and Haig Shekerjian
17 readily singable and playable Spanish games, dances, and folksongs for children. Includes English translations.
John Day, hardcover, 2 colors, 8½″ x 11″, 48 pp.

Playtime with Music
lyrics and text by Marion Abeson, music and arrangements by Charity Bailey, illus. by Sally Michel
If you want a little collection specifically for working with a preschooler (or a preschool group), this small one is an interesting choice. Only 16 songs, easy to play, good for dancing and acting out.
Liveright, board, 4 colors, 8¼″ x 11′, 48 pp.

The Sesame Street Song Book
by Joe Raposo and Jeffrey Moss
If your child watches "Sesame Street" and *if you are a musical parent,* this is nice enrichment material. The up-to-date music is quite difficult for young singers and mediocre piano players, but the 36 songs are happy and educational. Guitar chords included.
Simon & Schuster, hardcover, 1 color, 9″ x 11″, 136 pp.

Sesame Street Songbook, Vols. 1 and 2
Respectively 17 and 19 "Sesame Street" songs in two unillustrated paperback volumes. Otherwise the comments on *The Sesame Street Song Book* apply to these as well. Between them, they include many of the same songs as the above.
Quadrangle, paperback, 9″ x 12″, 72 pp. ea.

Sing Through the Day
compiled and edited by the Society of Brothers
90 songs for younger children, including some traditional ones and some that are original or that have new tunes. A bit on the sweet side and perhaps

more useful to nursery schools than the home, but reflective of the dedicated spirit of the Christian community in Rifton, N.Y. This community supports itself through its work as the Plough Publishing Company and Community Playthings which manufactures superior children's equipment and toys.
Plough Publishing Co., hardcover, 1 and 2 colors, 10″ x 10¾″″, 152 pp.

Songs to Grow on
compiled by Beatrice Landeck, illus. by David Stone Martin
Approximately 60 American folksongs arranged with suggestions for dances and rhythmic activities suitable for young children.
Edwin B. Marks and William B. Sloane, hardcover, 2 colors, 8½″ x 11″, 136 pp.

* What Shall We Do and Allee Galloo!
collected and edited by Marie Winn, musical arrangements by Alan Miller, illus. by Karla Kuskin
A superb collection of 47 activity songs, all perfectly suited to preschoolers. The book is divided into categories: follow-the-leader songs, word-play songs, finger-play and motion songs, and simple games. Easy piano arrangements and guitar chords.
Harper & Row, board, 2 colors, 8¼″ x 9½″, 104 pp.

See also Lullabies and Night Songs, *by Alec Wilder and Maurice Sendak (p. 48).*

Picture song books

There are a number of picture books which are simply illustrated editions of single children's songs. As a picture book editor I never particularly appreciated these, but as a mother I have discovered that they can be a source of great delight to young children who have learned the songs but often do not understand the lyrics and who, in any case, like to see more about something already familiar. Reading these books, singing them, and talking about the pictures is pleasant and helpful.

Always Room for One More
by Sorche Nic Leodhas, illus. by Nonny Hogrogian
Based on a Scottish folksong, this one also has merit as a story in its own right. A happy tale of hospitality. Tune included.
Holt, Rinehart & Winston, paperback, 3 colors, 9″ x 7½″, 32 pp.

The Erie Canal
illus. by Peter Spier
Meticulously researched and beautifully rendered depiction of 19th-century American life along the canal from Albany to Buffalo. As much for art- and history-appreciating adults as it is for singing children. Tune included.
Doubleday & Co., paperback, 4 colors, 9¼″ x 7″, 40 pp.

The Foolish Frog
by Pete Seeger and Charles Seeger, illus. by Miloslav Jagr
If you have the delightful Seeger record of Birds, Beasts, Bugs, and Bigger Fishes this picture book of one of its most rollicking songs is a must.
Macmillan, board, 4 colors, 8″ x 9¼″, 48 pp.

The Fox Went Out on a Chilly Night
by Peter Spier
Another beautifully detailed work by Mr. Spier, and a song children adore. Tune included.
Doubleday, paperback, 4 colors, 9¼″ x 7″, 40 pp.

Frog Went A-Courtin'
intro. by John Langstaff, illus. by Feodor Rojankovsky
Tune included.
Harcourt Brace Jovanovich, paperback, 2 and 4 colors, 7½″ x 9″, 32 pp.

Hush Little Baby
illus. by Aliki
A folk lullaby about what papa would buy to keep his baby happy. In a way the lyrics are awfully materialistic, but the emphasis should be placed on the love of fathers for their children. Lovely illustrations reproduced from paintings on wooden boards. Tune included.
Prentice-Hall, paperback, 4 colors, 7″ x 9″, 32 pp.

The Little Drummer Boy
illus. by Ezra Jack Keats
Especially useful for parents who want to introduce their children to the Christmas story. This book lovingly portrays the giving spirit of Christmas. Tune included.
Collier, paperback, 4 colors, 9″ x 7½″, 32 pp.

London Bridge Is Falling Down
illus. by Peter Spier
Again the whole picture/story behind the song, accurately researched and minutely detailed. Historical note at the back tells how the 1789 restoration of London Bridge was finally transported in 1971 to Arizona for $7.5 million.
(One day hopefully there will be an anthology of Peter Spier's work for children to grow up with.
Tune included.
Doubleday & Co., paperback, 4 colors, 9¼″ x 7″, 48 pp.

Old Macdonald Had a Farm
illus. by Moritz Kennel
Nice colorful picture of a farmer caring for his livestock. Tune not included.
A Little Golden Book. Golden Press, board, 6½″ x 8″, 24 pp.

One Wide River to Cross
adapted by Barbara Emberley
Woodcut illustrations of an old slave spiritual. Tune included.
Scholastic Book Services, paperback, 2 and 4 colors, 9″ x 7½″, 32 pp.

People in My Family
by Jeffrey Moss
A popular, singable song from "Sesame Street." This book is especially nice because of the helpful story told separately in the pictures. Two families (muppet and monster) independently set out for a picnic on a city park hill. On meeting unexpectedly at the top, the muppets are at first afraid. Then it is discovered that the monsters are really just another nice family on an outing. The two families share picnics and have a better time. Tune not included.
A Golden Shape Book. Golden Press, 4 colors, approx. 8″ x 8″, 24 pp.

Made-up songs

The very best songs are the ones that you and your child make up together. Singing a song about anything, *especially* the most routine activities, reinforces the child's experience of life as harmonious, flowing, joyful, orderly. The lyrics don't have to rhyme; the tune can be different every time (or use an old tune). Narration or nonsense, one-line repeater or long-drawn-outer, a song will relieve some situations and enhance others. But its real, invaluable contribution lies in the sharing of a sense of joy between you and your child.

One family's best song—from a winter walk:

Soft, soft snow is falling on my hair (face) (hand).
Soft, white snow is falling everywhere (everyplace)
  (on the land).
I hear the crow calling.
I hear the snow falling—soft, white snow.

ART: WALKING IN LOVELINESS

When Nancy, a beloved high-school baby-sitter, returned from a trip to the Far East, she brought one of her small charges a gift: an unusually beautiful, hand-made bamboo box with a lovely painting of a tiny bird on it. Every detail of the box was exquisite. It was even lined with a highly polished veneer of bamboo. What an unusual gift for such a young child. The parents were somewhat puzzled.

On Nancy's next visit she took the child on a long walk in a city park. Some time after she had gone home, the parents happened to look in the box. Inside were two beautiful heart-shaped leaves from a beech tree. Now the parents understood. The box had been given with the idea of helping the little boy to come to an early, conscious appreciation of beauty. And, without saying a word, Nancy had added a wonderful dimension to the parents' understanding as well. There are several new, small examples of beauty in the beauty box now. Perhaps this child, who (like all young children) delights so in beautiful things, is beginning already to have an idea of what beauty is.

Sometimes the whole emphasis on spiritual significance seems silly, contrived, or, at least with the little children, irrelevant. But, after all, there isn't anything else that is of ultimate relevance. And, as the following story illustrates, on the practical level, even with the youngest children, what the parent understands can have a transforming effect on the child's life—much more so than saying or doing even the psychologically right thing. This story reveals that when the parent's focus is spiritual it is possible for the child to receive direct, fresh inspiration about a concern that the parent may not even be aware the child has.

A spiritually alert mother was going to town to do some errands, taking her 3½-year-old son with her. She suggested to the child that they look for beauty during the walk. "Perhaps you might even try to collect some beautiful things to make a collage with when we get home," she said. It was autumn. There were many beautiful things to find—leaves, acorns, and a red-and-white striped cigarette pack that caught the child's attention. As they trudged home up the hill the boy became increasingly awed by the vast number of beauty-full things he saw to pick up. "Look, Mommy!" he said as he scrambled about on the ground, "this is beautiful and this is beautiful and this is beautiful. I could pick up everything for my collage!" Suddenly his attention was lifted from the many beautiful things on the ground to an entire outstandingly beautiful tree, aflame with autumn colors. He stood still and stared. "Oh, Mommy!" he said softly. "The whole world is beautiful. There's nothing to be afraid of!"

Looking On

Mobile—Be sure to hang something pretty and moving over the crib and changing table —a lightweight mobile, out of reach, suspended from a cloth-backed stick'em hook. Mobiles can be purchased in many places, or you can make them yourself. The more they move the better. And it's nice to change them from time to time. Be sure to give some thought to the baby's perspective on any mobile you are considering. Most are nearly invisible when viewed from below. Either choose ones that are best viewed from below or else hang them to the side or over the foot of the crib rather than directly above the baby's face.

Here is a very simple mobile to make from concentric paper rings and circles (two colors), and a thin stick (bamboo skewer) or piece of wire. Line up the circles as in the picture. Put a drop of glue in the center of each solid circle and at the top and bottom of the rings. Lay pieces of strong black thread through the drops of glue. (Add more glue if necessary to cover the thread.) Tie the strings of rings to the stick as shown and

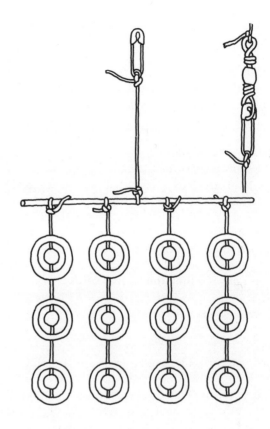

put a drop of glue over each knot to prevent sliding. To add mobility to any mobile tie it to a small swivel clip (used in fishing tackle). In fact, if you have one of these hanging from the ceiling at a good height, it will be very easy to switch mobiles from time to time without the use of a ladder. *See also* Crib-mobile (page 119), and Five Finger Exerciser (page 118).

Clear plastic envelopes—Transparent plastic envelopes with safe, rounded corners can be bought in most dime and office supply stores. These make excellent pre-books. Put bright pictures, postcards, wrapping paper, or photos inside and change them from time to time. With the youngest babies, high-contrast, black-and-white designs seem to be most easily perceivable and interesting. Wonderful for the baby on his tummy. It won't roll out of reach, and it isn't uncomfortable if he gets tired of holding up his head and puts his face down on it.

Sunnyside up or down?—There are lots of medical theories (orthopedic and gastrointestinal) over whether it's better for babies to sleep on their tummies or on their backs. But tummy-lying is definitely good for much of a baby's waking time. The view is better. Dropped toys remain within reach so you don't have to pick them up as often.

Pictures on the wall

Some of the best windows to the world and beyond for wide, young eyes are the pictures we hang on the nursery wall. It is here, during those most private moments on both ends of a nap, that little children may take their first solo flights, examining and memorizing every detail of each picture, stepping through the frame and traveling into the world and beyond.

Many publishers are now making reproductions of favorite book illustrations available. These are wonderful enrichments, and in some cases they offer almost more than the books themselves. Hubbard Press offers fourteen perfectly beautiful prints of single animals, each with the name of the animal printed below in large roman type. These are taken directly from the Hubbard book, *My Zoo*. Rotate the pictures, or hang a group of them (say, three rows of three), nicely framed, on one wall of the child's room. The words may even become memorized along with the pictures.

Not all the pictures in a child's room should be childish. We can be so grateful for the availability of reproductions of great masterpieces. It is feasible to hang some of the best works of history in a child's room. (The framing will probably cost more than the picture.) Choose nothing that might be scary, for the painting last viewed before the child's eyes fall closed must surely sometimes accompany him into his dreams. Peace, beauty, joy, harmony—again, these are what to look for in selecting a painting or reproduction for a child's room. The beauty he lives with will become the beauty he appreciates when he grows up. Landscapes seem particularly appropriate.

Except for the few really lovely pictures of lasting value which may remain a more or less permanent part of a child's room, most pictures should be changed fairly often. Less good ones or those of uniquely young appeal will be used up as the child learns all he can from them or moves to new interests. Keep the child's eye level in mind when hanging pictures. Hang some close to the floor in a hallway for the crawling child.

Good framing is expensive, and there's almost no getting around it. Yet framing does make an important difference. Masking tape all over the place is not desirable; it looks messy and devalues the picture. Large posters can be mounted on stiff pieces of cardboard and wrapped in sheets of acetate from an art-supply store.

Clear contact paper is also useful for protecting low-hanging pictures from finger-prints, drool, and food marks. The contact paper is applied directly to the surface of the picture (mounted on cardboard). It does dull the picture, but it can be washed with soap and water as necessary.

Very reasonable, ready-made frames in all sizes are available at Woolworth's, as are ready-cut mats.

Lucite box frames are a lovely way to display pictures (they are especially nice for pictures children do themselves). Although less expensive than custom-made frames these are nevertheless quite costly. But it is very easy to change the pictures in them. For example, one family received a box of beautiful notepaper with illustrations of woodland animals. They bought one lucite frame to hang next to their diaper-changing table and then slipped in a different notepaper every few weeks. Try hanging a 9 x 12-inch Lucite box frame in your dining room to display your child's latest drawings and paintings.

Brackets are another handy way to mount small posters or prints. For these you may purchase a sheet of glass the size of your picture (most art stores have them precut to standard sizes). Sandwich the picture between the glass, a piece of cardboard cut the same size, and clip a pair of brackets to top and bottom. You might also look into the sectional, aluminum frames, which you can buy in parts and assemble yourself. □

Some good pictures and posters

* Mother Goose Picture Set I
13 full-color, 8½" x 11" prints from the classic Volland edition of *Mother Goose,* by Frederick Richardson.

Hubbard Press, order No. 6550. An amazing bargain at $1.75.

* Mother Goose Picture Set II
Same as above, but including 13 different Mother Goose prints from Richardson's beautiful book.
Hubbard Press, order No. 6551, $1.75.

Mother Goose Posters
Full-color 28" x 24" posters (Old King Cole, Little Boy Blue) from the Richardson book.
Hubbard Press, order No. 6868 and 6566, respectively. $1.50 each.

* Zoo Animals
14 captioned, full-color, 8½" x 11" prints from the book *My Zoo,* by Hermann Fay. Perfect in every way.
Hubbard Press, order No. 6576, $1.75.

The ABC Frieze
by Michael Spink
A full-color foldout alphabet in 2 parts. Total dimensions—13' x 8½".
E. P. Dutton Co., $2.50.

The 1–2–3 Frieze
by Michael Spink
A full-color, illustrated, foldout frieze of the numerals 1–10. 13' x 8½" (in 2 parts).
E. P. Dutton Co., $2.75.

Peter Rabbit and His Friends
A portfolio of 8 full-color portraits of such lovable Beatrix Potter characters as Jemima Puddle-Duck, Jeremy Fisher, and Mrs. Tiggy-Winkle. 13" x 17" trimmable.
Frederick Warne & Co. $3.95.

Peter Rabbit Wall Frieze
A full-color mural (in 3 parts) of Beatrix Potterland.
Frederick Warne & Co., $1.95.

Busy Town
by Richard Scarry
A full-color blow-up of 2 pp. from Scarry's book *What Do People Do All Day?* 32" x 24".
Random House, $1.50.

* Words to Grow On
by Harry McNaught
A full-color composite blow-up of 12 pp. from this artist's excellent word book, *500 Words to Grow On.* 24" x 32".
Random House, $1.50.

Winnie the Pooh Posters
3 full-color posters of Christopher Robin, Winnie-the-Pooh, and friends. 20" x 32".
E. P. Dutton Co., $4.95.

The Very Long Train
by Eric Carle
A full-color, foldout book or wall frieze showing very many animals aboard a long train.
T. Y. Crowell, $1.95.

Ezra Jack Keats Posters
3 full-color posters of children together in school.
2' x 3'.
Macmillan, $4.95.

Arts and Crafts

Though they sometimes require more parental supervision than toys, hardly anything is quite so fruitful, fulfilling, absorbing, and inexpensive as crayons, felt-tip pens, play dough, watercolors, finger paints, etc. Crayons and play dough can be introduced any-time beginning around 1, and the rest according to your child's readiness and your willingness to cope. Be willing. Set things up so that you don't have to be defensive about walls and furniture. This means either sticking close by or putting the child in some place where disasters are improbable. For the very youngest the highchair is good and augments concentration. Try the bathtub for finger-painting. As he grows, having his own table will be handy and an easel wonderful.

This section is not a complete guide on arts and crafts. Many more ideas and instructions can be found in the books listed on pp. 71–74 (especially, *I Saw a Purple Cow and 100 Other Recipes for Learning, Making Things, What to Do When "There's Nothing to Do,"* and *Three, Four, Open the Door*), and *The Little Kid's Craft Book* (page 170). What follows is just an introduction to some possibilities, a few ideas to get the ball rolling.

Crayons—Store these safely out of reach if you aren't fond of interior graffiti, but make them available any time after about 1 year. Don't make a big deal out of broken crayons or peeled ones or even eaten ones. One book suggests peeling and breaking in two all crayons before starting to use them, claiming that half of a peeled crayon is the most useful crayon in the first place.

Don't start by suggesting that the object is to draw something. The understanding of making a picture that represents something is a much later stage and will come (and hopefully also feel free to go) of its own accord. Just demonstrate things like dots! wiggles! lines! scribbles! If you take up a crayon at all, let it be to share with your child the discovery of *what happens when you do this with that?* Sometimes the child will be most interested in what he is doing with his hands, sometimes he will pay attention to the colors. After a while he will begin to *read* his pictures. "Hey!" said a 2-year-old, "I drew many tiny fingers!" Try to see what he is trying to see and appreciate the discovery.

Good old Crayola crayons are fine. (A small set is as good, as if not better than, a big one.) But you might also like hexagonal ones that don't keep rolling off the table or Chubbi Stumps, which are wonderful short, fat crayons imported from England. □

Felt-tip pens—These are highly satisfying to preschoolers because the colors flow onto the paper so easily and so brilliantly. Get the fat kind, and make sure the inks are washable. By the way, washable doesn't mean that it comes off with a quick sponging or hand-washing, but it does come off "by tomorrow" (a couple of hand-washings and a bath) and comes off clothes in a washing machine. □

It's well to begin to teach the idea of putting the tops back on, but since felt tips will dry out if left open for extended periods, don't make a federal case out of it, and be prepared to help a lot. If he is interested in his work, he will forget to put the tops on—be glad for the interest.

Finger painting—Recipes for finger paint are included in several of the books listed above. Small finger-paint sets are generally not worth the money. You need a lot of paint to make one painting, and the small sets have a lot of box and very little paint. Maybe homemade paints are the answer, but large quart and pint jars of finger paint are available from most big art-supply stores for a good bit less than your time is probably worth.

Some very glossy paper is necessary, either special finger-painting paper or glossy freezer or shelf paper.

Many children are hesitant at first about putting their hands in the goo. Why, tell me, why? They are so willing to cover themselves with food! Anyway, don't insist. Just demonstrate the joys of finger painting yourself, put the paints away, and hang your painting up. You may even have to do this more than once before the child finally dares to dig in.

Here's the how-to:

• Wet the paper by dipping it in water or soaking both sides with a wet sponge.
• Place the paper on a large baking pan or edged cookie sheet to confine the mess.
• Spoon a tablespoon of paint, or lesser amounts of different colors, onto the paper.
• Spread the paint around with hands or forearms and then paint in it (you could say "unpaint") with fingers.
• That's the conventional way. Sometimes it's nicer and a little less messy to put a spoonful of each color on a plate or paint tray and dip and paint with single fingertips.

Tempera paints—These tend to be more successful than finger paints with preschoolers at home. This is another thing you can make yourself from dry pigments, but not very successfully unless you buy tempera medium and use a blender . . . once for each color—let's see now, that's—You figure it out. No matter how little you think your time is worth, it is still probably cheaper and surely easier to buy unbreakable plastic pints of premixed paint. Quarts and gallons are even less expensive, but unless you're going to work your way to the bottom very quickly the last quarter or third may dry up before you use it. Small sets of temperas with small brushes are a slightly better investment than the small sets of finger paints because less paint is used per painting, but you still wind up buying set after set and accumulating many half-jars of certain colors. It pays in the long run to buy good-sized jars from which to serve up just the needed amount. Also worthwhile are Flex-Flo Dispensers from Childcraft—unbreakable polyethelene storage bottles with nozzles for easy pouring.

Temperas can be used nicely at a table with

small brushes and perhaps a small paint pan. An easel with great big, school-type poster brushes is also nice.

A good way to introduce tempera painting to a 1½ or 2 year old is one color at a time. When more colors are used, it is well to have a separate brush for each. It is also advisable not to put big jars before the child until the principle of not mixing colors in the jars is fairly well understood. Use smaller jars (baby food, junior size, is perfect), lidded juice cans, muffin tins, or paint pans. □

Watercolors—For sheer pleasure, ease, and inexpensiveness hardly any paints can equal a small cheap set of watercolors. It is surprising how early a child can learn to dip her brush in the water before touching it to a new cake of color. To make it easier, put a few drops of water on each color before the very young child starts to paint. During most paint sessions the temptation to run her brush across the whole box of colors, playing it like a xylophone, is irresistible. But no matter, the paints can be cleaned off (more economically with a damp paper towel than under running water) and it will soon be time to buy a new set anyway. We can afford to be generous regarding anything that offers so much quiet, constructive activity at less than a $1 a set.

Paper—If possible, never be in a position in which you have to refuse a child a piece of paper. Keep a small pad or notebook and perhaps a set of colored mini-pencils in your purse, and have a big pad of newsprint and a stack of construction paper at home. A big roll of shelf paper is wonderful. Trace the whole child and let her decorate herself. Shelf paper makes good wrapping paper, adequate finger-painting paper, and a giant surface for all kinds of creative activity on the wall or floor. On a rainy afternoon invite another preschooler over. Spread out enough shelf paper so that they can sit on it and make drawings all over the place. Draw a landscape for play: railroad tracks for a toy train, fences to keep in toy animals, roads for cars, airstrips for airplanes. Build houses out of blocks beside the roads. Hang a big sheet in the hall and let every member of the family who wants to add something to the mural. From smaller sheets of paper make books for your child to fill in. Use newsprint, note cards, shirt cards, paper bags—and brown wrapping paper is beautiful to paint on. Just don't run out of paper.

Easels—A good easel is a worthwhile purchase, if only because it makes painting so much easier on the parent and therefore more available to the child. Ideal is a standing back-to-back easel for two with adjustable heights and removable paint trays. Some are also chalk boards. Painting on a back-to-back easel is a pleasant way for two not-yet-quite-socialized youngsters to be together happily and busily—also nice for siblings to share. More compact wall easels are also available. But you don't have to buy something expensive; you can improvise or buy a modified version, trying to meet as many of the qualifications listed as you conveniently can. ☐

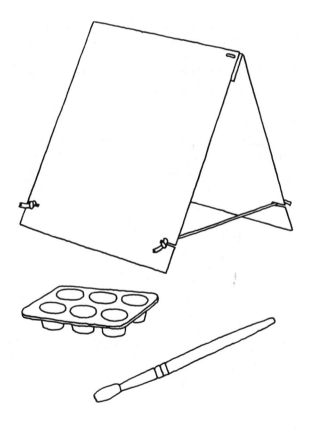

Chalk board—A chalk board is a must. The kitchen is a nice place for one—with a high stool beside it. It's easy enough to draw a picture or write a message for the child while you're waiting for something to come to a boil, and she will enjoy drawing and, in a minute, learning to form letters by your side. If you like, hang another one low down in a hall or on his bedroom wall.

Modeling materials—In the beginning (between 1 and 2 years) a soft play dough (Play-Doh or your own homemade) is best, as most of the nonhardening clays are too stiff for the child to work with. Don't teach him to make something (though it's perfectly all right for you to make things for him), just help him to find out what he can do with the clay—squeeze it, poke it, pinch it, stick Tinkertoys in it, cut it, scratch it. Make a slide for him that a bunch of little balls will roll down. Give him an egg slicer, dull knife, rolling pin, apple slicer (the type illustrated),

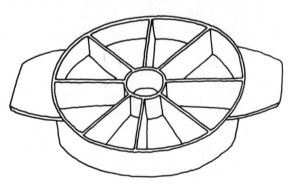

and some of the Play-Doh Shapemakers and the Play-Doh Fun Factory. Around 3 years old he may become interested in making "things." Now a slightly stiffer modeling ma-

Printing with a pad—Printing with a real ink stamp pad is fun, though fairly indelible. A large office-size stamp pad is more satisfactory than a small one. Try brushing tempera paint onto the stamp. For stamps try anything. Vegetables are great (dry them with a paper towel first). Or try pressing a leaf to the pad and then on paper. To avoid fingerprints, use two index cards for this: one to press the leaf to the stamp pad, one to press the inked leaf to the paper. These cards are also very nice for printing on. If you use a big sheet of paper you tend to wind up with just a hodgepodge of stamped impressions, some good, some bad, but all in all not worth hanging up.

terial is nice; dough models tend to slump and sag. ☐

Printing with a brayer—One way is to take a still-very-wet painting and cover it with a clean piece of paper the same size but placed at a different angle. Roll the brayer back and forth to make a print. One picture may not be much, but (especially if the print is in a different position on its piece of paper than the original) the two mounted and hung together may look terrific. ☐

An alternative method is to scratch a picture with a nail into a block of soap or very soft balsa wood. Roll the brayer in some water-base printing ink (from any art-supply store) on a smooth surface (a piece of glass or a metal tray). If you don't have printing ink, you can try thick paint. Roll the inked brayer over the etched surface of wood or soap. Make a print on the paper. Experiment.

Printing with a screen—Cut the lid of a small cardboard box so that only the sides and a little bit of the top remain intact. Inside the box top place a piece of window screen (larger than the top) and staple it securely to the side of the top. Place a piece of paper with a cutout or object on it in the bottom of the box and put the screened top on the box. Dip a toothbrush in paint and scrub it across the screen until the object has been silhouetted.

Rubbings—Go on a texture hunt with a piece of paper and a crayon or a pencil. Sidewalk, brick wall, wooden table, tree trunk, the bottom of a pair of rubber boots, leaf, the bathroom floor.

Usually it works best to put the paper onto the block, but you may find it better sometimes to work the other way around. Try rubbing the back of the paper with a spoon while it is in contact with the inked block. Thin ¼-inch sheets of balsa can often be purchased in art-supply stores; they are ideal for small printers. A child less than 3 will readily enjoy this activity.

THE WHOLE POINT ANYWAY

While creative freedom in artwork is crucial and should even be counted sacred for children, it is important that sloppiness not become a factor. There is one basic principle that can help to avoid this: the valuing of beauty as it is sought and expressed in their work—not as accomplishment, not as pretty good for a little kid, but as beautiful. It isn't silly to say that the work of these little ones is beautiful. It is only necessary to develop an appreciation of ideal beauty to find beauty in children's art. Spontaneous motion, brilliance of light and color, and striking form are often clearly present in the drawings and paintings of unhindered children, who are so receptively creative. Remark on this—"How bright that picture is! How happy that looks! . . . Oh, see how nicely those lines go around together. . . . That is wonderfully straight. This picture is especially graceful."

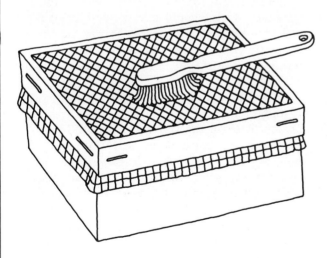

Do not confuse such comments with praising the child. The shared discovery and appreciation of what is beautiful is worth ten times more than praise and will further his creative growth where praise (by distracting) would actually stunt it. Of course, the fact that you value the work enough to hang it will fortify the child regarding his ability to express beauty. Having truly seen what is lovely in a particular picture, you will rejoice to hang it—not just to make your child feel good, but because it is lovely and you would like to see it on your wall.

Mount and frame it nicely, as you would any professional, purchased work, setting off the beauty as clearly as possible for the observer. Since children are prolific, you may wish to have a frame or two in which to put new pictures from time to time. One must, of course, exercise judgment. Much of the work is not beautiful and should not be preserved; but do be on the lookout for what is worthwhile. Where we really help our children is in fostering their awareness that beauty is both the issue and the reward that fulfills.

Children's paintings also make nice gift wrapping. Use a finished painting or wrap a gift in white shelf paper and invite the child to decorate it with felt-tip pens. It looks nice, and children like to participate this way in the giving.

Sometimes after painting happily for a while, a child becomes aimless and sloppy in his work and begins obviously messing around. Perhaps all that is needed is a little companionship or a little help. See if he can tell you what he is trying to do, or just work beside him for a minute, focusing appreciatively on whatever beauty may be happening in his work. While artwork is something children will often do for prolonged periods without supervision, it should not be used simply for getting them out of our hair. If the restlessness persists despite the arrival of a little helpful companionship, clean up immediately. He may be through, or it may be the wrong moment for this project. Whenever beauty isn't happening beautifully, it's time to stop. Always try to finish and thoroughly clean up while the spirit is happy.

Finally, when a craft project is being undertaken with specific results expected, make sure that the activity is something the child can do and that the end product will work. In a summer craft class for preschoolers the project for one day was to make hats out of paper plates. The children worked all morning gluing things to the plates and painting them and decorating them according to their individual inspirations. But when the strings attached to the hats were tied under the chins of the little milliners the hats fell off. Nothing short of glue could have made those hats stay aboard the silky heads. It was terribly disappointing. No one cried, but it was demeaning. In a way it profaned the idea of arts and crafts.

Lots of things can be done with scraps and trash, but the results should never be trashy. The children in the above story would probably have been quite happy with the fruits of their work if they had understood that they were making something to hang rather than something to wear. It is one thing to make a pile of scraps while practicing how to use scissors, but when the objective is to make *something* or create something beautiful the end product should work (if that's what it's supposed to do) or be beautiful (if that's what it's supposed to be). With crafts this involves careful planning and paying attention to the readiness of the child to do the work required and to the prospects of getting a worthwhile result.

Cut, fold, staple, and punch

An hour of cutting, folding, stapling, or punching holes in paper is as good as receiving a $15 play garage with a real elevator and a greaser, and it will prove to be of infinitely more lasting value. To the child who is just ready to learn (in fact, even slightly before he can manage) scissoring is an activity in itself—not for making anything, just scissoring for the sake of scissoring. Partly it is the joy of simply using a tool, and this could therefore be listed under unity just as well as beauty. But of course the skill is one that will soon serve in his efforts toward artistic expression.

We tried to find blunt-tipped, child-sized sewing *scissors* which we imagine would be much easier to operate than the usual two-finger scissors, but we couldn't find them. Maybe someone will invent them. But it's surprising how young a child can learn to use even the two-fingered ones—well under 3 years if given a good chance. □

Obviously, the better the scissors, the more easily a child can learn to cut, and adults' scissors are usually better made (sharper and easier to manipulate) than those available for children. It's really worth it to sit by for safety and let the very young child practice with adult scissors (the semi-blunt-tipped kind) until he is skillful. One child of only a year and a half learned to snip and tear with his mother's scissors. By the age of 2 he was able to manage on his own with the safer but somewhat duller and more awkward children's scissors. He enjoyed working for as much as an hour a day simply cutting up old newspapers and folding the pieces into small interesting shapes. It's amazing what such a small skill can contribute to the child's creativity and to the freedom of both parent and child from each other.

Scissorlike *paper punches* are mostly too hard for the preschooler to operate, but if you have a press-down desk model, your child will have a heyday with it and will enjoy making designs by folding the paper and punching through several thicknesses at once.

Likewise, while the hand-held *staplers* require more strength than most 3-year-olds have, a desk-top model is manageable and can be used to make envelopes, paper wallets and purses, hats, books, or even clothes for a small doll.

Glue

Glue is almost as much a medium as it is a tool in creative expression. Give a child a small bottle of Elmer's glue and he will simply draw with it. This isn't very worthwhile unless you add food coloring, as the glue becomes transparent when dry. But we are told that food-colored-glue paintings can be nice and sand-and-glue paintings are fabulous (see below). Even before using scissors, a child can tear and glue. With scissors, he can make a scrapbook (save colorful magazines and catalogs). There are hundreds of things children love to do with glue. Here are a few.

Collage above all—Try making collages with torn paper, cut shapes, indoor things, outdoor things. Ahead of time cut a variety of bright-colored triangles—just triangles—for the child to fit together and glue in a design. The child tears or cuts construction paper into shapes he can glue down. An outdoor collage: sand, grasses, leaves, seeds, flower petals, road dust, tree bark. An indoor collage: rice krispies, coffee grounds, lentils, split peas, all kinds of beans, popcorn, corn meal, sawdust, wood shavings (a great beard for Santa Claus, wonderful hair), pencil shavings, string, packing materials. See also *playboards* on page 260.

Trashcan sculpture—Make trains, houses, boats, and free-form sculptures by gluing saved-up cardboard tubes and boxes together. As another activity paint them.

Wooden sculpture—Buy a bag of wooden parts or some wooden scraps from a lumber yard, and let the child glue them together into a structure or sculpture. The results are usually quite pretty. They may be left plain or, as another activity, painted. With a little extra parental help and some parts from a hardware store, a nice lamp for a child's bedside could be made this way. □

Sand painting—Dye some sand with food coloring in paper cups. Spread the colored sand out on paper plates to dry in the sun (or plan to wait a little longer before actually sand painting). Draw or paint with glue on paper, and sprinkle the colored sand over the glue (one color at a time). Shake off the excess sand. Elmer's glue drawings result in Jackson Pollack-type pictures. Brushed-on glue or paste yields more surface-covered pictures (à la watercolor landscape). *This is a perfectly wonderful activity, much nicer in many ways than finger painting.* The results are beautiful. Children as young as a year and a half can begin to do it. It is such a satisfying activity for most children that it is worthwhile to dye enough sand in the summer to last through the winter.

Collage bin—Keep a bin of everything glueable—jar tops, beads, cartons, tree bark, etc. Collecting things for this bin can be as enjoyable as later working with them. Try to arrange it so that by age 3, if he is interested, your child knows how and is allowed to work with these materials at will and without supervision. Only simple procedural experience and equipment is necessary.

• A table to work at and, if necessary, a covering to protect the table.
• An apron to protect clothing.
• A sponge for spills and some training in wetting, wiping, rinsing, and squeezing out.
• A place to put finished works for drying.
• A place for trash.
• The obvious: glue, paste, scissors, paper.

Art-related toys and games

A few art toys are available for preschoolers that can enrich the child with greater color and design awareness and are thus worth considering as extra purchases. The parquetry tiles and colored inch cubes mentioned in an earlier chapter are perfect examples. Etch-A-Sketch and Colorforms are also favorites. And with all these things you can invent games that increase awareness. □

If you just want to help your child to discover what color is and augment her perceptual skills, get some colored paper and cut it into equal-sized rectangles. Then cut all the rectangles in half. Give the child one square to look at. Then place three or four different squares in front of her, including the mate to the one she has. Let her try to choose the one that matches. This can become very difficult if you have many similar shades of color. The game can also become more complicated by putting out more wrong choices along with the correct one. Beautiful papers can be bought in art-supply stores (glue to cardboard and cover with clear contact paper for permanence, if you like). Or you can buy a little packet of origami paper.

Art-related books

Of course, a good art book for children is not a book about art or a book that teaches colors or a book of art and craft projects. A good art book is a beautiful book with inspiring pictures. Beautifully illustrated books for children are slightly easier to find than beautifully written, meaningful ones, but not *that* easy—not if you mean beauty that is truly beautiful and at the same time meaningful to the child. Any books we found that meet these standards (nothing much leaps to mind) are to be found among those listed in the chapter called "Truth." On page 6 there is also a little more discussion of what makes a good illustration for children. But many very beautiful-looking books are not listed here because their stories were not substantial enough to be worth purchasing at hardcover prices. One such example is *Honschi* (by Aline Glasgow, illustrated by Tony Chen, Parents' Magazine Press). So the following is a rather slim list of a few art-related books, including two specifically concerned with suggesting arts and crafts projects. (See also the practical books on play activities listed in Chapter II, many of which include substantial sections on arts and crafts.)

[*Note:* Numbers in parentheses indicate comprehension levels (not age) as outlined on pp. 7–9, 195, 197, 201, 207. Starred titles are those deemed superior for a preschoolers' home library. See pp. 6–7, 193–94 for additional information regarding book notations and selection.]

All-Around-the-House Art and Craft Book
by Patricia Z. Wirtenberg
Straw construction, hanger sculpture, shoe-polish banner, sugar-cube art, sand-casting, and "take-away" bleach pictures are some of the surprising suggestions in this book of projects. Many are not for preschoolers, some are only for the daring, but the book as a whole opens the reader to lots of new possibilities and will prove useful over the years. Clear black-and-white photos and precise instructions throughout.
Houghton Mifflin, paperback, 1 color, 7½″ x 9″, 120 pp.

Black Is Beautiful
by Ann McGovern, photos by Hope Wurmfeld
This book was designed to help black children appreciate the idea that black is beautiful, but it makes a very good color awareness book. It's best to take it and read it at face value, teaching the perception of beauty rather than racial consciousness. "Black is beautiful. A black bird singing in the morning. On the pond, a black swan gliding. And beyond, in tall grass, crickets hiding. Black is beautiful."
Scholastic Book Services, paperback, 1 color, 9¼″ x 7¾″, 40 pp., (3).

Ed Emberley's Little Drawing Book of Farms
Though this is mainly for older children some preschoolers are interested enough to learn to draw the 12 simple figures (e.g., triangle, dot, circle) on the first page of this book. Any who can may enjoy

following with their parents the step by step demonstrations of how to make 50 different pictures using only these few figures. There are other equally ingenius and delightful Emberly books in both hardcover and paperback, but this little one is good for a start.
Little, Brown, paperback, 4 colors, 7½" x 5", 16 pp.

Is This You?
by Ruth Krauss and Crockett Johnson
A book for older preschoolers, who can draw representational pictures. "Is this your family? (snowmen, royalty, horses) Get some pages of paper all the same size and draw your family on one of them." And so on. A nice idea. Keeps asking questions about you and your life and encouraging you to draw pictures. The child who is ready for this should wind up with a clearer self-concept and a self-illustrated book. He'd need a little help from his mom and dad along the way, though.
Scholastic Book Services, paperback, 2 colors, 7½" x 9", 40 pp., (3–4).

The Little Kid's Craft Book
by Jackie Vermeer and Marian Lariviere
Its painfully high price notwithstanding, this book proceeds from start to finish with art, craft, and science projects that are consistently practical and enjoyable for preschoolers. Especially useful are two recipes for cookie dough which can be modeled, baked, and eaten. A very useful book.
Taplinger Publishing Co., hardcover, 1 and 4 colors, 7¼" x 9½", 132 pp.

Mr. Rabbit and the Lovely Present
by Charlotte Zolotow, illus. by Maurice Sendak
A sweet story about a little girl trying to find the right present for her mother who likes red, yellow, green, and blue. Her rabbit friend (Harvey-sized, but visible) tries to be helpful, but in the end it is the child herself who discovers just the right thing. Along the way, of course, colors are well rehearsed.
Harper & Row, board cover, 4 colors, 8" x 6¾", 40 pp., (3).

My Slippers Are Red
by Charlotte Steiner
A book in rhyme about the colors of things familiar to most young children.
Pantheon Books, paperback, 4 colors, 32 pp., (2).

Shopping Cart Art
by James E. Seidelman and Grace Mintonye
Art projects from everyday supermarket supplies. Very useful for older children and offers a few good ideas for preschoolers, too.
Collier, paperback, 2 colors, 7½" x 9", 48 pp.

Where Is Everybody?
by Remy Charlip
This is another book that demonstrates possibilities. It is a story told in one simple picture progressively altered and embellished with more and more details. "Here is an empty sky [a white page]. A bird flies up into the sky [bird added]. The sun shines in the sky [sun added]. These are the hills against the sky [hills added]." And so on with people and animals until ultimately a heavy rainstorm hides everything from view.
Scholastic Book Services, paperback, 1 and 2 colors, 9" x 7⅜", 48 pp.

Gratitude

A young child was looking at a picture book. At the edge of one page was an illustration showing only the tail and hind legs of a dog. The child frowned. "Oh dear," he said. "He is broken." The picture was then explained to him. "But where is the front of him?" asked the child. "Is it lost? Did it get cut off? How did it get cut off? Did he get deaded?" He could not see the picture as indicating that the dog was walking away.

One day a mother drew a picture of a child. She asked her 2½-year-old daughter, "Now, can you draw some clothes on this boy?" The child said, "I will draw a sweater for him." She took up her crayon and carefully drew a line around the whole drawing of the child. This was her way of expressing the idea of a sweater. It was the truest way she could think of. Her picture of the child and of the sweater was more whole than what she saw in the flat drawing. *A sweater is warm and cozy and goes all around me.* Spontaneously the child's concern was more with truth than appearance.

It is important to learn to see beyond the senses. The child in the first story was not yet able to do that. Most very young children cannot. This is something we have to learn. Therapists and special educators have discovered that partial pictures can be extremely upsetting to some seriously disturbed children. Unable to look beyond what their eyes see on the paper, they can only see brokenness. Evidently brokenness is much more real (truer) to them than wholeness. They are terrified of the appearance of brokenness.

Of course, most children quite effortlessly come to see beyond what is shown in a picture to its significance. We can help our children in this process. For example, whenever her child was restless in bed and found it difficult to fall asleep, one mother used to tell stories about a picture that hung on the bedroom wall. It was a picture of a boy with a flower in his hand, standing in a field of tall grass. "What kind of shoes do you suppose that boy is wearing?" the mother would ask. And then she would go on to make up a story about what was happening down in the grass around the boy's feet—perhaps a little ant was on his way home, perhaps a mouse passing by stopped to collect some seeds that fell from the boy's flower. ". . . And the boy didn't even know that the mouse was there or that he had helped to feed him!" The child always fell still, and he came to learn to look beyond the picture and to see with other eyes what might have been happening there.

On a material plane this faculty of looking beyond is usually called imagination. It is important for the child to learn of this possibility. But by itself imagination is not useful, for what the so-called imagination imagines may produce as much disturbance as peace. What the imagination sees is only a reflection of the underlying concept of reality of the imaginer. Thus, while the seriously disturbed child can only imagine more brokenness, only the child for whom wholeness is real can imagine wholeness. So we see that the ability to imagine is not necessarily healthy and may even be harmful when divorced from a healthy concept of reality.

In all the above illustrations the object of the imagining, whether on paper or in the imagination, is material. Learning to see beyond what materially appears to our material eyes on the material piece of paper is only part of our unfoldment. The child must not simply move from seeing half a dog to seeing a whole dog, but to seeing the dog going somewhere. And there is even more to be seen after that, for the idea of brokenness (which must be overcome if there is to be happiness) remains a possibility for even the "healthy" child as long as his concept of reality is at all material.

This is where our own growth comes into discussion, since the transition from a material to a spiritual concept of reality must be made in consciousness and hence only on an adult level. As long as we base our impressions on material appearances, receivable by our material senses, we are like the disturbed children who can see only brokenness. While material wholeness seems better than material brokenness, it nevertheless includes the idea of brokenness. Whatever is material is breakable; it cannot last. Therefore, material wholeness is not really wholeness at all.

Sometimes it happens that on hearing a great piece of music greatly performed we are suddenly overcome with its beauty. We are so overwhelmed that, without understanding what is happening to us, suddenly we find that we are crying. There is a mixture of joy (it is so beautiful, so grand) and profound melancholy, a terrific yearning. It does not even take a full orchestra to effect this in us. It can be the clarity of a bird's call, a child's pure singing for pure joy, a special place in the middle of a rock ballad. Everybody has such experiences. When they happen we say that we are "moved." We speak of being transported into another world, uplifted.

At their finest, music and art are symbolic representations in materially perceivable form of ideological (or spiritual) qualities. Through music and art, eternal qualities such as order, flow, harmony, rhythm, purity, light (that is emanation), and unity become experienceable or appreciable. These qualities, which are beyond brokenness, are represented in audible and visible terms, that is, in terms perceivable through human eyes and ears. Sight and hearing are somehow slightly less material senses than touch, smell, and taste. Perhaps it is just that we have fewer preconceived ideas about them. Whatever the reason, to some extent we allow the eternal to reach us through these senses; we see what is not specifically visible, we hear what is not specifically audible. The eternal qualities reach through what is eternal in us, the soul. There is reunion, communion, the momentary overcoming of our sense of brokenness. The truth of all being touches the truth of our individ-

ual being, and we are lifted beyond brokenness into eternity.

The beauty of these moments is not to be found in the sound or the sight (any more than music can be found in the radio or time in a clock) but rather in the significance of the sounds and sights, in the eternal, *unbreakable* truth being expressed. Our joy is joy in the truth, the momentary realization of the is-so-ness of what we have been yearning for all along. The sorrow or melancholy that so often accompanies this joy is only our imagination that this beauty is only our imagination. We wish it to be so, but we doubt it; or if we believe it is so, we imagine we are far from it and that it is unattainable. And yet we have felt its is-so-ness, a moment when there was no break between us and eternal goodness.

It is significant that the study of the beauty of art and music is called art and music appreciation rather than art and music imagination. In imagination there is the concern with seeing what isn't or might not be, whereas in appreciation there is a concern with perceiving what is, that is, with truth. In the study of art and music appreciation we seek to see what is beyond sight and hearing with vision and hearing that are beyond and definitely other than eyes and ears. *Appreciate* is an excellent word that means more than merely to like. It begins with valuing, proceeds with seeking, and is fulfilled in perceiving. Appreciation is a synonym for gratitude which also does not mean merely liking, or being happy with, or glad about something. Gratitude is thankfulness for what is so (the givens in life) rather than for what is imagined or wished for. It has to do with grace. It is only in the moment of gratitude that grace can become effective.

Now it is possible to see the importance of gratitude or appreciation as a redemptive force in our lives. It is often recommended that in times of stress or even as a general policy we should take time to count our blessings. Mostly this is understood as a psychological or sentimental device for consoling oneself or trying to feel better. One version says, "Well, at least we have thus and such so we shouldn't feel too badly." This is like telling the child, "Well, at least there is still half a dog, and that's better than no dog at all." Another version runs, "Well, maybe this or that other good thing will happen instead," which is like trying to make up for the missing half-dog by imagining the rest.

Both these versions of the idea of gratitude completely miss the mark, and anyone who has ever tried them can attest to the fact that they don't work very well and are not much comfort. The flaw in both is materialism. They are both concerned with the material dog. But whether you have one half or two halves of a material dog, even if both halves are together, the idea of brokenness remains and the true significance of the picture cannot be perceived.

In the long run, whether the dog is already "deaded" or whether it is a dog that can be "deaded" does not make much difference. In point of fact the very illustration that appears to depict a "deaded" dog really signifies the vitality of the dog. Half a dog expresses the dog's goingness, his vitality, perhaps even better than a picture of a whole dog would. But it is only as one turns from appearance to significance, from the material to the ideal or spiritual that the truth becomes perceivable. Perhaps it can even be said that once the on-goingness of the dog is perceived, the image of the dog is no longer necessary at all.

So true gratitude is the concern with significance, with spiritual rather than material reality. It means first, valuing; second, seeking, and finally, perceiving (that is, finding out for sure) the eternally true. It is one of the most important keys to overcoming the sense of brokenness in our lives. Gratitude is not only a sentiment, the being glad of the unworthy self with some sort of booby prize. Gratitude is an important aspect of true cognition. Its prerequisite and partner is humility, the letting-go or laying-aside of all material claims, concerns, worries. True gratitude is not possible without humility; true humility is not possible without gratitude. Another name for this combination is prayer (gratitude) and fasting (humility). They are not sentimental; they are logical.

It is clearly logical that eternal, spiritual reality cannot dawn upon us when we are entirely focused on material brokenness. In the moment of true gratitude (when all material concern is set aside) it is not only the perception that is made whole but the perceiver as well. When the attention is turned from material preoccupation to spiritual significance, the separate (fragmented, limited, broken off, lonely, scared) material mind is stilled and the One Mind takes over. Creatively this is called inspiration. Existentially it is revelation and redemption. It is the disappearance of the sense of brokenness and the realization of eternal oneness.

Instead of the broken dog expressing deadness or isn't-ness, the half-dog expresses vitality, ongoingness, is-ness. The truth is just the reverse of what appears to be. The dog does not express himself, but rather God. If you start with a G and go backwards you get Dog—a thing capable of dying. If you start with a G and go frontwards you get God—eternal being.

Then I said, "I covet truth;
Beauty is unripe childhood's cheat;
I leave it behind with the games of youth";—
As I spoke, beneath my feet
The ground-pine curled its pretty wreath,
I inhaled the violet's breath;
Around me stood the oaks and firs;
Pine-cones and acorns lay on the ground;
Over me soared the eternal sky,
Full of light and of deity;
Again I say, again I heard,
The rolling river, the morning bird;—
Beauty through my sense stole;
I yielded myself to the perfect whole.

–Ralph Waldo Emerson, *Each and All*

The five colors can blind,
The five tones deafen,
The five tastes cloy.
The race, the hunt, can drive men mad
And their booty leave them no peace.
Therefore a sensible man
Prefers the inner to the outer eye:
He has his yes—he has his no.

–Lao Tzu in *The Way of Zen*, by Watts

I hearing get who had but ears,
  And sight, who had but eyes before,
I moments live who lived but years,
  And truth discern who knew but learning's lore.

I hear beyond the range of sound,
  I see beyond the range of sight,
New earths and skies and seas around,
  And in my day the sun doth pale his light.

–Henry David Thoreau, *Inspiration*

"I AM THAT I AM"*: A MEDITATION

We shall not all sleep, but we shall all be changed—in a moment, in the twinkling of an eye . . .
–I Corinthians 15:51–52

"The eye is the lamp of the body. If therefore thine eye be single, thy whole body shall be full of light. But if thine eye be evil, thy whole body shall be full of darkness. If therefore the light that is in thee be darkness, how great is that darkness! No man can serve two masters; for either he will hate the one, and love the other; or else he will hold to the one, and despise the other. Ye cannot serve both God and mammon."
–Matthew 6:23–24

I and my Father are one.
–John 10:30

We shall not all sleep, but we shall all be changed—in a moment, in the twinkling of an I . . .

The I is the lamp of the body. If therefore thine I be single, thy whole body shall be full of light. But if thine I be evil, thy whole body shall be full of darkness. If therefore the light that is in thee be darkness, how great is that darkness! No man can serve two masters; for either he will hate the one, and love the other; or else he will hold to the one, and despise the other. Ye cannot serve both God and mammon.

Eye and my Father are one.

* Exodus 3:14

Truth

The value of truth is the transformation of our lives—from darkness into light, sickness to health, slavery to freedom, ugliness to beauty, emptiness to fulfillment, sorrow into joy, hatred and loneliness into love, failure into creativity, conflict into harmony, lack into abundance. It is merely a matter of seeing life aright—of recognizing and relinquishing misperception in favor of a truthful or realistic awareness of reality. Ultimately this whole process or event must occur on an ideal, mental, or spiritual plane. To a large extent language is the means. But language is useful only insofar as it is employed for its proper purpose. Purity of motive, sincerity are crucial.

There was once a little girl whose parents were very eager for her to learn to talk. They were diligent parents and spent much time trying to teach her the names of things. "Kitty!" they would exclaim. "Cup!" "Chair!" The child was delighted with the kitty, cup, and chair, and especially with her parents' enthusiasm, but she did not learn to talk. Finally, one day the cat walked in and she said it: "Kitty." Great joy was registered on the faces of the proud parents. Hugs, kisses, delight! She said it again. More hugs and delight.

A number of days went by and the little girl kept saying *kitty,* but did not acquire many new words. The parents' enthusiasm began to wane and suddenly the little girl began to call everything *kitty*—cup and chair included. Now the parents registered discouragement. "No," they said. "Not kitty. Doggie!" Sooner or later the little girl said "Doggie" and the hugs and kisses were renewed. But the parents were very disappointed to find that, with

the coming of *doggie, kitty* disappeared. Now the little girl called everything *doggie.* Even the cat. The parents were mystified and worried.

Most people have a secret desire for their children to talk early so that they can show how smart they are or (more accurately) how smart the parents are. Likewise many of us like to speak because we like to be listened to. But, until all too soon they learn otherwise from us, children become interested in speaking largely because they are interested in finding out. The idea of talking to show what you know is absolutely useless to children, who are mainly and rightly interested in learning what they don't know. A child will learn to talk early if somehow he discovers what speech can do for him—how it facilitates his existence.

The little girl in the story obviously thought that the purpose of speech was to get hugs and kisses from her parents. But such an idea did nothing to help her crack the code —to discover what speech is and does. Furthermore, she was being exposed to the dangerous idea that personal praise, rather than understanding, is the object of learning.

In this light it can easily be seen that we must cultivate a right appreciation of speech as a means of communication rather than for showing off if we wish to be helpful to our children. To communicate is generally defined as to make known, divulge, or impart—in short, to tell. But a higher definition has to do with communion or communing, since communication requires something on the part of the listener as well as the speaker. The answer is useless without the question. The speaking is meaningless without the hearing.

In some branches of Christianity communion is taken to mean participation in what is called the eucharist or breaking of bread. But if the bread of life can be understood to be truth, then it can be said that communion or communication is the sharing of truth. The true purpose of speech then would have to be truth-seeking, and truth-revealing. The most practical of these two aspects of communication is truth-seeking. So the question (which is the key to learning) can then be seen to be the material key to discovering speech. Sincerity is the spiritual key.

If we can teach our children, who are infinitely receptive, that speech is the means of formulating their endless questions, and if we can learn from our children sincerely to ask questions and be receptive, our lives will be greatly enriched. Our children will talk sooner and learn more, and we will talk less and learn sooner.

Oddly enough, this chapter is less directly concerned with the content of truth than almost any other in the book. Instead, its more elementary concern is the development of the child's ability to perceive truth. Since truth is idea(l) and has to be known, it follows that language by which we express and understand ideas is the faculty of truth. Expressing ideas is not so important as finding them out. Ideas (both questions and answers) are formulated in language. If reality is spiritual (that is, ideal) then happiness or fulfillment depends upon consciousness or understanding. Language is the means through which we understand.

A major objective that we should have for our children is the development of the ability to look beyond what seems to be for significance and meaning, and ultimately (when they are older) for truth. Language skills are prerequisite to this. Topically, therefore, this chapter is concerned with books and conversation, the means through which a child can develop his ability to express questions and conceive of ideas. He must learn to talk, build a strong vocabulary of words and concepts, and learn to read and write before he can begin to formulate his questions about life and look beyond for the answers.

What can be said that could possibly express the value of booktime with babies and young children. Books are a car, a plane, a spaceship to any tired little striver who cannot yet even crawl. You know he's tired; you pick him up and try to hold him close, yet he struggles out of your arms and wriggles away after his yearning to learn. But just snuggle him into your lap, open a big book so that it's almost a room around him and see what happens. After hours of looking at nothing but the floor without craning his neck, here suddenly is the world in vistavision. And a whole new view of it on every page—all different and amazing.

The first time you show him a book he will probably try to pick up the things pictured on the pages. But after a time or two he will switch to simply patting the pictures. What a thing to learn at 6 months—those round things are flat! Those flat things look round! He will also try to grab the book, and if you aren't careful he may tear the pages. This doesn't mean he's too young for books; it just means you need to be there. Protect the book. He will soon understand that a book is for looking, and once he knows how to turn the pages, the tearing will cease.

Of course children will not all become interested in books at the same time, but if we are responsively ready at the earliest flickerings of interest, the interest will develop faster and more fruitfully. So start experimenting with books early—at 5 or 6 months of age. *Never insist*—interest can be stifled all too easily. Don't give up too quickly either. Try at different times of day with different types of books—cloth, board, large, small, with busy pictures, with simple ones, familiar subject matter and unfamiliar. No interest? OK, forget it for now, but try again next week.

The point is not to push our children or to fill them up with as much information as possible at the earliest possible moment. Language is the thing. Perhaps, once we really know, language is not so necessary anymore, but along the way, for finding out, understanding without language is inconceivable. In the meantime (perhaps because they serve so well the quest for truth) books can provide us and our children with wonderful hours together. Once you and your child are at home together with them, books will be a channel for some of your very finest and most inspired times together. It isn't only what's in the books (in fact, there really aren't so many very good ones), it's also what happens between you—your mutual growing awareness, your knowing of your child, the facilitation of your conversations with each other, and the broadening of perspectives.

The first half of this chapter deals with techniques and books that may be used to help our children develop basic language skills. It begins with some very first books for the child who doesn't know what a book is.

Then there are some books for learning to talk, some for expanding vocabulary and concept awareness, and a few specifically designed for teaching reading and math. Mother Goose and some other poetry books are included in this section because of the so far unequaled contribution they make to happy language development.

The second half of the chapter centers around storybooks, through which the child can further develop his language skills and begin putting them to use in the task of seeking significance and a healthy and truthful concept of reality. The books in this section are divided roughly into four stages of conceptual difficulty. Part of what distinguishes these books from those in the first half is their more substantial content. They should be used along with (not after) the books of the first half.

Throughout this book an effort has been made to show the relevance of every childish phase and activity, not only to the long-range fulfillment of the child, but also to the immediate fulfillment of the parent who must oversee it. In every case it can be seen that what the child is trying to learn on a material plane corresponds directly to something we need to learn on a spiritual plane. Thus paying attention to the child at play becomes worthwhile and beneficial to the parent. With books and language, the time spent in helping the child ceases to seem boring or self-sacrificing in any way and becomes instead an opportunity for the parents' fulfillment as well when viewed in the light of the universal quest for truth.

As with every principle of life, the child's experience of truth even in language is largely material. Yet we can see that his underlying concern is with reality. He wants to see who he really is, what the world is really like, and how he should be in it. He specifically, naturally, hopes to find that goodness is the truth.

Truth includes all of the objectives presented so far in this book—happiness, freedom, unity, and beauty. Happiness is the experience of all these goals as truth. Although language is a slightly less materialistic channel of perception than the toys and activities discussed in earlier chapters, the child's experience of truth through books and language is still largely material; that is, it can only reach him when expressed in material terms (terminology). Yet if we consider the fact of language and the content of books and the fact of our children's interest in these things in the light of truth, we will find our own spiritual needs being met. Everything is to be gained from a truthful awareness of the purpose of language. Observe that the preschool child's interest in everything is an interest in reality. He listens unconditionally to every story with a view to discovering *what is so.* If we follow his example on a conscious plane, viewing everything in the light of ideal truth, we will both help our children with their so valid strivings and will ourselves draw nearer to the realization of ideal reality.

Learning to Talk – Beginning to Read

Helping Them Learn to Talk

If our appreciation of the purpose of speech is correct and our motives for wanting our children to learn are pure, we will be readily inspired with good ideas for helping them. But here are a few suggestions.

Do not simply teach the names of things. To be able to say *fish* at the sight of a fish will not do anything for the child's existence. To have to say it again and again for every relative or friend of the parent will do even less. But to find out that that bright wiggly flippery thing is named *fish* will please and serve him very well. This need of his to find out is as strong as his need to eat and, in the long run, as vital. There is no difference between his asking for and his asking about something.

By the time our babies are 3 or 4 months old it is a good idea for us to talk to them in phrases, mostly questions and answers about the things we perceive they are momentarily interested in. "Do you see the fish? Is that a fish? Yes, that's a fish!" The repetition of the word fish will not escape him, but what we are really after is his discovery of what the rest of the words are about. For this the use of analogy is helpful. We hide and say, "*Where's* Daddy?" We pop up and say, "*There* he is!" Later, as we look at a picture book with many pictures on one page, we say, "*Where's* the bear? *There's* the bear!" or

"Do you see the bear? Is that the bear? Yes, *that's* the bear!" Tap the picture of the bear with a finger.

Suddenly we can see that our question and answer tone is making sense to him. He knows vaguely what "where is?" or "what's that?" means; it means seeking. And he knows what "there it is" or "yes, that's a" means; it means finding or discovering. The question expresses this desire he has to understand. The answer expresses the joy of finding out. He may still learn to say a few single words first, but the question will come quickly "Whassa!" (what's that?). He has cracked the code, and from now on the words will tumble forth with astonishing speed.

Reading to Them Before They Can Talk

If the first use of books is helping children to learn to talk, the second use is further developing their abilities to cope in this world. On the lowest level this is simply a matter of informing the child about his environment— what this is, what that is, what it is called, what it does, how it works. This is the business of building a vocabulary of words and material concepts, equipment the child needs to live in this world and to grow to higher levels of understanding. He can learn all these things when he's older and he will just by roaming around outside. But he is interested in learning them long before he is able to move about very much on his own, and he can learn through books.

The younger the child the more important it seems to be to feed him when he is hungry. Sometimes if we do not have lunch ready at the moment of peak hunger, the child's appetite decreases, becomes diffused, or is rechanneled. Then he eats restlessly, consuming little, slowly. The meaning of this phenomenon is not clear, but it seems to apply to learning as well. Apparently children learn certain things most effortlessly at certain times. All over the world it is being discovered that much of the toilsome learning of school days can be accomplished joyfully on the preschool level—not by teaching, but by simply responding to the child's own manifest interest. Books are an especially fine medium for both detecting and responding to these early interests. And, of course, the deeper significance of this early learning is that it awakens the child to possibilities for himself—his own potential and the potential of life.

Techniques

• *Read the child more than the book.* At the very beginning of our children's book experience the printed text will be virtually useless. In these months our reading consists almost entirely of off-the-cuff conversations about the pictures. When reading a word book, for example, it is not helpful to simply pronounce the one-word captions—*ball, bear, book.* If the child isn't talking yet, she won't know what we mean; if she has begun to talk, she may become quickly bored. When reading a simple storybook we cannot merely read or even summarize the text either.

In fact, it is perhaps better if we do not think of ourselves as reading books at all. It is more helpful if *we* read our children who are reading the pictures. Then we shall be readily guided in what to say. Watch the child to see what her interest is and then speak about that in whatever terms she can understand and to the extent that she remains interested. It is easy to tell when we are going astray because the child will become restless and crawl away.

• *Fingers.* A very obvious, but often neglected technique in reading to nonverbal or barely verbal little children is the use of the pointing finger. It may not be polite in society, but in reading to little children always point. Even tap. Even if she's listening, at least half of what you're saying probably means nothing to her. So if there are twenty-five animals on the page and you are talking about the mouse, point to the mouse. Besides making things clearer, this becomes a fun activity in itself. In one family there even evolved a game or two from this—a sort of pictorial hide-and-seek. "I see a mouse on this page, do you?" The child looks all over and then points delightedly to the found mouse, perhaps even calling out "There's the mouse!" Later there came a sillier version which involved "walking" suspensefully on two fingers all over the page to find whatever it was.

On a more advanced level, when you are trying to help your child discover the continuity of a story, these finger dramatics can be the key to understanding. Trace occurrences as you read, pointing to the characters and showing who threw the ball and where it went. This is especially helpful in explaining the appearance of the same character in several pictures. It is not immediately obvious to the small child that these are the same character. Unless we show with our fingers that this bear walked out the door with his hat on here and then went for a walk here, most children will think for some time that this is a book full of many bears that look alike.

• *Question and answer.* The merits of the question-and-answer form in helping the child to discover what speech is have already been discussed, but this is only the beginning. Simple questions encourage the child to verbalize and help him to discover the usefulness of books as a means of finding out. Through this device something happens that is even more important to his learning: you find out where he is. This obviously makes it easier for you to be a helpful teacher.

From the simple "where is the—?" type of question you can move to unspoken questions in which you occasionally pause in your reading and silently invite the child to fill in the blank. This should always be left as an invitation, however, never insisted on or pressed for in any way. Many children also find it hilarious when you intentionally misread words, leaving it to them to make the corrections.

These basic little techniques may or may not be accompanied by obvious gains in understanding and verbal development, but we will never be able to measure the infinite value for both parent and child of this sharing of book reading and the practice of dialogue. Of course, we must never stop with mere technique. The motive of truth-seeking and truth-finding must always be kept in mind. This maintaining of a pure motive will spare us and our children the excessive rehearsing (for display purposes) and intrusive questioning which may otherwise arise to disrupt or retard the learning process.

• *Pantomime.* Don't stop with the pointing finger. Simple acting out of words and events can make all the difference in whether the child knows what's going on or not. She may know the meaning of *throw,* but have no recognition of its use in the past tense. A simple throwing gesture when you read "He threw the ball" may make it perfectly clear—also livelier and more fun.

• *Translation.* Whenever possible make use of the child's existing vocabulary and understanding to introduce new words and concepts. See page 193 for a fuller explanation of what this means and how to do it.

• *Expression.* After children are born to us almost all of us begin to speak with greater animation than before. As a result of trying to communicate with our little ones, we often find ourselves less shy with small children in general—more generous, more easily silly, less reserved. Realizing that our children do not know specifically what we are saying, we try to convey its significance (say, our enthusiasm) through a more animated, joyful tone of voice. This small, new freedom is a little fruit of love for which we are grateful. It is helpful if we carry this freedom over to the way in which we read aloud. First of all it makes the reading more interesting, and second, it provides clues as to the significance of the baffling barrage of words we are reading.

• *Abbreviation.* Some people say you should never speak to children in anything but full sentences. This seems silly. Of course it is good to use full sentences some of the time, but when helping a child to learn what talking is, it is helpful to abbreviate. When reading, concentrate on the significant subject. You can fill in more words as she becomes ready to understand them.

• *But yes, don't correct. Yes* is a very useful word in helping a child develop the faculty of speech. If she points to a telephone and says "Dophone," don't say, "No, that's a *tell*-a-fone." Say "Yes [i.e., I understand what you mean and it's true!] that *is* a *tell*-a-fone!" *No* is not only discouraging, it is downright misleading. The child may think, *oh, that's not a telephone?* Children who are first attempting words of more than one syllable often get the sounds completely backwards. For example, one child would crouch down behind a bed and then jump up shouting, "B'kee!" His parents recognized that he was trying to say *peek-a-boo.* "Yes, peek-a-boo!" they would respond. "There's Tommy." *B'kee* became *buh-ka-pee,* and finally *peek-a-boo.* The parents realized that they did not need to correct their son but only to demonstrate perfect pronunciation. They realized that the main issue was communication, and they were thus able to respond helpfully and enthusiastically to their son's first understandable efforts to talk.

Very First Books: Something to Eat?

One way to tell if you are starting books soon enough with your child is whether or not she gives them the taste test. If she doesn't already know that a book is not something to eat you are starting on time. At this point (6 months or younger) you can use almost anything with bright pictures. It doesn't matter if it is too difficult. Just see what catches the child's interest. At first it is the book itself as a thing, a toy almost more than anything else. An *old telephone book is* a totally disposable practice book which will outlast its usefulness no matter how much it is torn, crumpled, drooled on, eaten, scribbled or painted. It is a large magic block that turns out to be really made of a thousand smooth, flat, thin things that can be flipped over and that sometimes flop back by themselves in a delightful way. Children do not learn that books are for tearing from this experimenting. Once they have explored all the physical properties of a book and have more or less learned to turn pages they lose interest in the telephone book.

Cloth or plastic books—These may be used, as extra purchases for the child who cannot yet be trusted alone with a book. They should not be used ahead of or instead of regular books (which are generally better in content) but as supplements. While they may be used later, the main time for these is when the child is gnawing, that is, somewhere between sitting and walking.

Most of those available are either inanely condescending or too difficult to be useful, or they have drool-soluble illustrations. Especially silly are the cloth books on the subject of Baby Himself—what baby can do, what he has—which either show him doing things babies *can't* do (tying shoes, running, dressing) or are so revoltingly cutsie in art and text as to be unbearable. We never did find a really satisfactory book about babyhood—too bad, too, it would be useful. But a few are included below that don't run and are more or less all right for the age level.

Board books—Also included in this list are a few board books, that is, books with heavy cardboard pages and covers. It is almost as difficult to find nice board books as it is to find good cloth ones, but as with cloth not many are necessary. In the beginning books are mainly for you to share with your child,

but a few indestructibles are handy for when your back is turned.

[*Note:* Numbers in parentheses indicate comprehension levels (not age) as outlined on pp. 7–9, 195, 197, 201, 207. Starred titles are those deemed superior for a preschoolers' home library. See pp. 6–7, 193–94 for additional information regarding book notations and selection.]

Animals
by C. R. Schaare
Horse, goat, cow, pig, hen, dog, squirrel, rabbit with young. What does the so-and-so say (moo, meow, etc.) is one of the best pretalking activities for babies.
Hubbard Press, fully washable cloth, 4 colors, 10 pp., 8¼″ x 6½″, (0–1).

Baby's Things
by Thomas Matthiesen
Nicely presented, full-color photographs of familiar objects such as key, ball, and flower. This is abridged from Matthiesen's *ABC: An Alphabet Book,* which is quite good. There is also a cloth abridgement of this book. Obviously you would not want all three, but one is very useful. *ABC: An Alphabet Book* (see page 184) is much more comprehensive, but you may prefer one of the sturdier abridgments.
Platt & Munk, board cover, board pp., plastic comb binding, 4 colors, 6½″ x 8″, (0–1).

Farm Friends
by Percy Reeves
Cow, mule, horse, cat, pig, dog, bull, sheep, cat. Nice pictures.
Hubbard Press, fully washable cloth, 7½″ x 9″, 10 pp., (0–1).

In the Forest
by Hilde Heyduck-Huth
An unusually beautiful-looking board book that is almost indestructible. Not quite as young in appeal as some, but interesting for longer. One-line captions describe paintings of deer, squirrels, berries, and other woodland sights.
Harcourt Brace Jovanovich, hardcover, board pp., 4 colors, 6¾″ x 8″, 20 pp., (1–2).

Pat the Bunny
by Dorothy Kunhardt
Although in no way indestructible, this old-timer (first published in 1940) is a tried and true favorite with the littlest, a uniquely happy introduction to books. On each spread there is something to do. Judy and Paul can do it and now so can you (peek-a-boo, look in the mirror, etc.). A gimmick book that works.
Golden Press, light cardboard pp. and cover, 4 colors, 4¾" x 5⅜", 18 pp., (0–1).

When the Sun Shines
by Hilde Heyduck-Huth
Another unusually pretty and sturdy board book by this artist. And there's more content than is first apparent if you depart from the text and take time to "read" the pictures, naming all the things on the cover, the numbers on the clock, etc.
Harcourt Brace Jovanovich, hardcover, board, pp., 4 colors, 6¾" x 8", 20 pp., (1–2).

From Words to Concepts

Books for from learning to talk at all to getting ready to read:

* ABC: An Alphabet Book
by Thomas Matthiesen
A single word for each letter illustrated with a bright, clear, straightforward photograph. Useful with children less than a year old. The objects pictured include a great many of those first recognized by children. *Insect,* for example, is especially useful to the very young child because insects are so interesting and observable. A good very first book.
Platt & Munk, hardcover, 4 colors, 6½" x 8", 64 pp., (0–1).

ABC Book
by C. B. Falls
A simple alphabet with one animal illustration for each letter. Its biggest contribution is artistic. The old, 4-color woodcuts are lovely, expressing beauty, simplicity, and careful design. Extra use can be had from this by pausing to make up a short song or story about each animal. It is so wonderful that books like this are being made available in paperback form. The Falls ABC cannot be said to be indispensable and yet it offers so much as an additional enrichment.
Doubleday & Co., paperback, 4 colors, 7" x 9¼", 30 pp., (1–3).

A B See
by Lucille Ogle and Tina Thoburn
A carefully thought-out small book for children who are ready to take first steps toward reading. A phonetic alphabet picture book that illustrates both the variety of ways each letter can look and the variety of sounds it can have. Included at the back is a helpful list of supplementary learning games.
McGraw-Hill, hardcover, 4 colors, 4" x 8", 128 pp., (3,4).

* Best Word Book Ever
by Richard Scarry
If you had to buy only one book for the first 2 years, this should probably be it. It is really a first encyclopedia as much as a word book. There are ways in which it could be better—less male chauvinistic, less frantic, less confusing in places. But few books on the market will last through as many readings. It can begin as one of the child's very first books (at less than 1 year old) and will last throughout the preschool years. This is one of the first books children will "read" by themselves, poring over the pictures and coming out only to ask questions.
Golden Press, board, 4 colors, 10¼" x 12", 96 pp., (0–4).

Hop, Skip, and Jump Book
by Jack Kent
In this delightful "First Book of Action Words" there is one picture for every word, and the one-word caption is always a verb! Very useful and charming.
Random House, paperback, 4 colors, 8" x 8", 32 pp., (2–4).

* Fast-Slow High-Low
by Peter Spier
Described as a book of opposites, it is that and much more—an exceptionally original and superbly useful word and concept book. All kinds of opposites are portrayed in the pictures, a page full of each. For example, one page shows about a dozen paired illustrations of heavy/light, another

of dark/light. Lots of humor along the way. To make use of this book discuss its pictures with the middle and older preschooler—"What's different in this picture? What's long and what's short in this one?" But it can certainly also be put to good use with younger children as a word book.
Doubleday & Co., hardcover, 4 colors, 10¼" x 8", 48 pp., (1–4).

* 500 Words to Grow On
illus. by Harry McNaught
A gem for the price or for more. 500 very basic words grouped and illustrated according to context (kitchen words, people words, country words, house words, etc.), with very realistic, beautifully rendered paintings. Perfect for the child who is just breaking forth into speech. Not confusing or cluttered or simple-minded.
Random House, paperback, 4 colors, 8" x 8", 32 pp., (0–3).

I Spy
by Lucille Ogle and Tina Thoburn, illus. by Joe Kaufman
"A Picture Book of Objects in a Child's Home Environment." And a good one, too. 356 everyday objects grouped according to use but illustrated singly. Easy-to-handle, small, oblong format.
American Heritage, hardcover, 4 colors, 4" x 8", 192 pp., (0–2).

Little Golden Picture Dictionary
by Nancy Fielding Hulick, illus. by Tibor Gergely
A good little word book for its low price.
A Little Golden Book. Golden Press, board, 4 colors, 6½" x 8", 24 pp., (0–2).

Mi Diccionario
A Spanish/English edition of *My Pictionary* (*see below*).

My Pictionary
by W. Cabell Greet, Marion Monroe, and Andrew Schiller
A straightforward, well-thought-out word book. Literal, full-color illustrations with single-word captions and some nice progressions such as "goose, geese," and "man, woman, men, women, people."
Scott Foresman, paperback, 4 colors, 96 pp., (0–3).

Primary Dictionary #1
by Amy Brown, John Downing, John Sceats, illus. by Mance Post
First in a series of 4 dictionaries for children. Designed to help reading children develop dictionary skills, but very useful as a word book for children learning to talk. 160 single words with single illustrations. Low price.
Pyramid Communications, paperback, 4 colors, 4¼" x 7", 96 pp., (1–2).

See and Say, Guarda e Parla, Regarde et Parle, Mira y Habla
by Antonio Frasconi
61 words and some phrases illustrated with woodcuts and translated into 4 languages. A useful introduction to the fact of many languages.
Harcourt Brace Jovanovich, paperback, 4 colors, 7" x 9", 32 pp., (2–4).

Things in My House
by Joe Kaufman
A very simple first-word book at a bargain price.
A Little Golden Book. Golden Press, board, 4 colors, 6½" x 8", 24 pp., (0–1).

Dictionaries

In the beginning a child uses a word book to learn what words are—the names of things he knows. Later, when he understands what language is, he can use a word book to learn about things he has never even seen before. Much later he will come to use words as a means of transmitting *ideas*. Many of the books listed above were prepared for use as dictionaries by children who have already begun to read, but they have been included here (and graded accordingly) for their usefulness in helping children learn to talk and expand their speaking vocabularies. The following books might also be used this way, but they are more useful once reading has begun. These are also very helpful for the child who is learning to write and who may enjoy copying the words printed in boldface.

The Cat in the Hat Beginner Book Dictionary
by Dr. Seuss, illus. by P. D. Eastman
A silly, fun dictionary for beginning readers. Each word illustrated with a picture and often an almost-story phrase or sentence. 1,350 words alphabetically arranged, with more than that many pictures. Certain characters can be followed throughout the book.
Random House, board, 4 colors, 8″ x 11″, 144 pp., (3–4).

A First Ladybird Key Words Picture Dictionary
by J. McNally, illus. by R. Ayton
A dictionary companion to the Ladybird Key Words Reading Scheme (see page 1 7).
Penguin Books, board, 4 colors, 4½″ x 6¾″, 56 pp.

The New Golden Dictionary
by Bertha Morris Parker, illus. by Aurelius Battaglia
1,262 words defined, used in context, and illustrated with more than 2,000 pictures.
Golden Press, board, 10¼″ x 11¾″, 120 pp.,(3–4).

Richard Scarry's Storybook Dictionary
Just what it says. Each fully illustrated word entry includes an explicit or implied storylet that illustrates the word's meaning. Much information and lots of fun.
Golden Press, board, 4 colors, 10¼″ x 11¾″, 128 pp., (3–4).

Learning to Read and Write

Since most of us learned to read in grade school with a Run Spot Run! and an ABC!, the idea of teaching reading means to us teaching letters and words. If that's what we understand, we should definitely not teach our preschoolers to read at home; we will simply stifle their interest. On the other hand, the notion that parents should not under any circumstances try to teach their children to read or they will develop complexes is a lot of hogwash. Given a good and pleasant exposure to books, most children will develop a desire to read, and if you have started very early with books this may well happen before the child goes to school. The main thing to keep in mind if you want to help your child learn to read as soon as possible is that your teaching must always be in response to the child's own expressed interest.

Teaching reading really begins with teaching the value of reading, and this we must do, giving the littlest ones lots of books and, even more important, lots of hours of reading aloud and talking about books, plus maybe a little "Sesame Street" to chalk off the basics. Let them discover and help them to see what reading can mean to their lives. Help them to learn that words are another way to picture ideas and things. Offer good materials and point out signs, and give free demonstrations. Don't miss an opportunity to demonstrate— "H-E-L-E-N.   Huh-Eh-Ul-Eh-Nnn.   Helen! See? That's your name." Do everything you can to bring the child to the point where she is trying to learn to read. Then you won't have to teach her, you will just have to answer her questions.

Here are some specific things you might do when the time comes.
• Point out all the places where words and letters are helpful. "Push this button—the B button—we are going to the basement." "This says PUSH. We have to push this door to open it." "This letter has your name and our address on it. That's how the mailman knew to bring it here for you."

• Write things down for your child. Captions for his pictures. Short messages (e.g., Today we will _____). Stories he dictates.

• Try to teach the sounds of letters as well as the letters themselves. English is not a consistently phonetic language, but many words can be sounded out. Once the child catches on to the idea that he can sound out words his ability to read will develop quickly.

• Try to make your child aware of both big (capital) and small (lower case) letters.

• When your child shows an interest in writing help him along by providing examples of words he needs at the moment to copy. Holiday cards provide high motivation. He will like to copy the name or the first letter of the name of the person the card is for. This is slow, difficult work for him. He will not like to do it for long at a time. But once he is able to copy what he sees with some ease he will begin to do it eagerly.

• Provide dotted examples of words for him to connect. His name is John. Write JOHN. "Now can you write it once by yourself."

• If he becomes really interested in writing, buy him a small lined notebook; his word treasure book. Let him copy words into it from books with big captioned pictures. If he asks you for a word, write it in his book for him to copy. Make cards of some of the words and put them in a word box (a decorated cardboard box with a hole in it). Play the game of reaching into the box for a card and trying to read the word that is on it.

Writing and reading come hand in hand. Some children get motivated to read on the basis of their interest in learning to write. Others work from reading to writing. Provide clear demonstrations of both, suggest possibilities for the child, but never push. Not ever. If you say, "Shall I write down your name so you can copy it on your picture?" and he says, "No, I don't want to"—*don't.* When he understands what it's all about and when he thinks he *can,* he will. It's that simple.

In researching this book, several series were discovered which have been quite popular and which are rather interesting to preschoolers as read-aloud materials, but which have been designed specifically for teaching reading. One is a series of graded readers called the "Ladybird Key Words Reading Scheme." On the order of Run Spot Run, these little books employ 12 most frequently used English words repeated in a planned fashion, and very literal, full-color illustrations, and for subject matter the daily affairs of two young children. While they might be boring to first- and second-graders, smaller children identify with the characters and listen with real interest to find out more about their own possible future as growing children.

Another series of inexpensive, reader-type books available are the Ant and Bee books by Angela Banner and imported from England by Franklin Watts. It takes an especially generous parent to read these loose-jointed, strung-together, but highly eventful adventures of two cartoon characters. But young children do like to hear them and just might pick up some reading awareness along the way. In this series key words are individually introduced and illustrated, and then repeated many times in the story in red type.

From each of these series here is a list of the titles that seem most suitable for children under 4 years old.

Play with Us (la), We Have Fun (2a), Things We Like (3a)
by W. Murray
All about Peter and Jane. In each successive book the children are slightly older and farther from home. The length of text and number of new words also increases while previously introduced words are carried over and repeated. There are titles going all the way to 9a in difficulty (mostly too old for preschoolers) and another whole list beginning again at 1. Each book carries a listing of other titles available in the series.
Penguin Books, board, 4 colors, 4½″ x 6¾″, 56 pp., (2–4).

Ant and Bee and the ABC, Ant and Bee, More Ant and Bee, Ant and Bee and the Kind Dog
by Angela Banner
Alphabetical stories about Ant and Bee—how they met, what happened to them, and what happened after that.
Franklin Watts, hardcover, 4 colors, 4½″ x 3½″, 112 pp., (2–4).

Once real reading begins quite a wonderful wealth of material is available at reasonable prices, most of it considerably more readable and relevant than what we grew up on. Harper's "I Can Read" books are informative, literary, well illustrated and entertaining. Random House's "Beginner Books" are zanier and children love them. From Grosset & Dunlap come "Easy Readers," wonderfully tailored to the interests of K-3 readers by reading experts and offered for the generously low price of 69¢ a book. Follett has an extensive line of easy-to-read titles including a big list of pre-primers. The pre-primers seem good but it was not possible to recommend specific titles since we had an opportunity to see only a representative sampling of three. Single titles from some of these series are recommended elsewhere in this bibliography strictly on the basis of their story merit and suitability as read-aloud materials for very young children.

Math

On both the very lowest and the very highest levels, math is a matter of truth and communication. That's why the few basic math books recommended are included here, instead of under Unity where certain mathematically useful things are presented.

Just through repeating counting-out rhymes and listening to "Sesame Street," a child learns to say the numbers 1 through 10 without much effort. This is fine; it's nice to acquire these tools so effortlessly. Discovering what the numbers stand for, what quantity and counting *are,* is another matter. Just keep illustrating them and suddenly one day you see that the child begins to know what's being talked about.

The best way to introduce kids to math is to do it with them, in situations, with things, not on paper or through reading about it. Don't forget that geometry is math—learning about shapes and sizes and how things fit together is math. Seeing how things balance each other on scales, how the liquid from one measure doesn't fit into a smaller measure, and how a pulley works—all this is math.

What with "Sesame Street" and the big word and concept books which all touch on counting, straight counting books don't seem worth the money unless they offer something more than counting for content. Except for a few titles, the books listed below are special interest books for preschool children and parents who really get turned on to math early.

Animal Counting Book
illus. by Moritz Kennel
"Over in the meadow in a nest in the sun lived an old mother beaver and her little beaver *one*. Beave, said the mother. We beave, said the one. So they beaved all day by the light of the sun." A delightful adaptation of a joyful old rhyme that takes us from 1 to 10 while presenting 10 different animals in their natural surroundings.
A Little Golden Book. Golden Press, board, 6½" x 8", 24 pp., (1–2).

Bigger and Smaller
by Robert Froman, illus. by Gioia Fiammenghi
Shows how size is a relative matter. Requires quite a sophisticated vocabulary, and many examples will be clearer to children familiar with a school classroom situation. For exceptionally interested preschoolers only.
T. Y. Crowell, paperback, 1 and 3 colors, 8½" x 8", 40 pp., (4).

* Count and See
by Tana Hoban
A totally useful book for helping children and their parents to understand what numbers mean and how our counting system works. Each number is represented in numerals, words, dots, and a photograph that shows the number in mundane sets: e.g., for 100 there is a picture of 10 peapods with 10 peas each. With this book children do get inspired to count and they do see.
Macmillan, paperback, 1 color, 9" x 7½", 32 pp., (3 up).

Do You Know What Time It Is?
by Roz Abisch, illus. by Boche Kaplan
If your child is really interested in learning to tell time, this book could be helpful.
Prentice-Hall, paperback, 3 colors, 8¾" x 8", 32 pp., (4).

Fractions Are Parts of Things
by J. Richard Dennis, illus. by Ronald Crews
A good introduction to the idea of fractions for the child who is ready.
T. Y. Crowell, paperback, 1 and 3 colors, 8½" x 8" (4).

One Bright Monday Morning
by Arline and Joseph Baum
"One bright Wednesday morning on my way to school I saw 3 blades of green grass growing, 2 pretty flowers blooming, 1 maple tree just budding near a little pool." A cumulative counting book from 1 to 7 and from Monday to Sunday that all adds up to spring.
Knopf/Pantheon, paperback, 9" x 7", 32 pp., (2–3).

1 Is One
by Tasha Tudor
"1 is one duckling swimming in a dish, 2 is two sisters making a wish . . ." Bedecked with sweet birds and old-fashioned children by a noted illustrator.
Rand McNally, paperback, 1 and 4 colors, 9" x 6¾", (1–2).

Telling the Time
by M. E. Gagg, illus. by J. H. Wingfield
A first book for learning to tell time—easier than *Do You Know What Time It Is,* but less comprehensive. Concentrates on the hours.
A Ladybird Book. Penguin Books, board, 4 colors, 4½" x 6¾", 56 pp., (3).

Understanding Numbers, Words We Need for Numbers, More Words for Numbers, and Everyday Words for Numbers
by J. McNally and W. Murray
Books 1–4 of the "Ladybird Words for Numbers Series." An intelligent verbal and pictorial introduction to basic mathematical ideas of quantity: least/most, full/empty, weeks/months/year/calendar, etc. Work around the Britishisms.
Penguin Books, board, 4½" x 6¾", 56 pp., (2–4).

Weighing and Balancing
by Jane Jonas Srivastava, illus. by Aliki
Especially useful if you take the time to make the simple balancing scale for which the instructions are given in the book.
T. Y. Crowell, paperback, 1 and 3 colors, 8½" x 8", 40 pp., (3–4).

What Is Symmetry?
by Mindel and Harry Sitomer, illus. by Ed Emberley
Since the idea of balance is basic to an under-

standing of this book, it seems sensible to work through *Weighing and Balancing* (above) first. Then try using this book in conjunction with parquetry (see page 124).
T. Y. Crowell, paperback, 1 and 3 colors, 8½″ x 8″, 40 pp., (4).

Mother Goose and Nursery Rhymes

Although the stories they tell are often silly or incomprehensible and the values they express either undetectable or poor, the Mother Goose rhymes offer the young child much that's useful. A good collection of these traditional rhymes is an unmatched resource for fostering the language and concept development of the young child, at the same time providing parent and child a pleasant and constructive way of being together. Through rhyme, rhythm, and repetition, mastery of the basic speech sounds is fostered. A basic vocabulary of words and concepts is built through contextual use and graphic illustration. And the silly little story/poems provide the child with first experiences in story continuity and general exposure to the diversity of the wide world.

The search for a good anthology presents us with a poor-little-rich-girl situation, for almost every publisher has at least one Mother Goose collection. The key difference seems to be the quality and quantity of artwork.

The illustrations should be beautiful since we hope along the way to instill in our children high standards of artistic appreciation and since we will be looking at these pictures so thoroughly and often. But of course the beauty must be of a sort appreciable by the child. Many perfectly lovely editions of Mother Goose are too sophisticated and static

for anyone but adult collectors or as supplementary materials for use with the children. In general, appropriate art for children includes qualities of liveliness, brilliance, and youthfulness.

The most useful—that is, the most communicative—Mother Goose anthology will also have a large quantity of illustrations which the child can "read" to herself and which will help to explain and embellish the text as you read it aloud. So look for an anthology in which each rhyme is illustrated with at least one picture.

Not much needs to be said about how to use Mother Goose, since simply sitting down and paying attention to the child is usually more than enough to get the ball rolling. Long before any rhyme is understood, the heavily illustrated Mother Goose book can be used as a word book. Find and talk about familiar objects in the pictures and name the unfamiliar ones. When the child is interested, recite the rhymes and repeat them at other times without the book. Most enjoyable will be those you rehearse again and again, and the child may like best those with tunes and actions, such as "One Misty Moisty Morning" ("with a how do you do and how do you do and how do you do again?"). Be choosey. "One Misty Moisty Morning" is a nice one to memorize since it expresses a spirit of friendliness, and effortlessly teaches children how to shake hands.

Superior big collections

* The Golden Mother Goose
illus. by Alice and Martin Provensen
367 rhymes and about 400 illustrations. Though you may like other illustration styles better this

is one of the most useful editions of Mother Goose rhymes available because of its good ratio of full-color pictures to rhymes.
Golden Press, board, 4 colors, 9½" x 12¾", 100 pp.

* Mother Goose
illus. by Gyo Fujikawa
306 rhymes illustrated in full-page composites or individual vignettes. This ranks with the Provensen book for its usefulness with little children. Many illustrations that are very appealing to children. Fujikawa's pictures are always done in nice colors and have a gentle happy look. It's just too bad that the publisher didn't find a way to do the whole book in color.
Grosset & Dunlap, 1 and 4 colors, 9" x 12", 128 pp.

* Mother Goose
illus. by Frederick Richardson
"The Classic Volland Edition." Perfectly beautiful, vividly printed, full-page illustrations. 293 rhymes, 108 illustrations. Ideally it would be nice to own both this (or *Favorite Rhymes*—paperbound selections from this book) and either the Fujikawa or Provensen edition, which more helpfully offer an individual illustration for nearly every rhyme. Page-size prints of many of these old-fashioned illustrations are also available (see page 159).
Hubbard Press, hardcover, 4 colors, 9" x 12", 168 pp.

Mother Goose and Nursery Rhymes
illus. by Philip Reed
Too expensive and too sophisticated to be recommended as a wise priority for many young children, this edition is nevertheless such a beautifully wrought book in every way that it should be mentioned. Beautiful layout, handset typography, and lovely, 6-color wood engravings throughout.
Atheneum, hardcover, 6 colors, 7¾" x 10¾", 64 pp.

The Real Mother Goose
illus. by Blanche Fisher Wright
306 rhymes and 170 illustrations. First published in 1916, this tried-and-true edition of Mother Goose rhymes has illustrations that are lovelier than those

in many other collections, though perhaps a little static for the preschooler.
Rand McNally, hardcover, 4 colors, 8¾" x 11½", 136 pp.

Smaller collections

A First Ladybird Book of Nursery Rhymes, A Second Ladybird Book of Nursery Rhymes, and A Third Ladybird Book of Nursery Rhymes
illus. by Frank Hampson
About 24 Mother Goose favorites in each volume, each rhyme illustrated in primer style with real-looking children and grownups.
Penguin Books, board, 4 colors, 4½" x 6¾", 56 pp., (0–4).

* Favorite Rhymes of Mother Goose
illus. by Frederick Richardson
A good selection of 35 rhymes (23 illus.) from the beautiful big Richardson Mother Goose.
Hubbard Press, paperback, 4 colors, 32 pp., (0–4).

The Little Golden Mother Goose
illus. by Feodor Rojankovsky
75 rhymes and about 100 illustrations. Rojankovsky at his best is superb. If a big collection is not feasible, this is a good substitute.
A Little Golden Book. Golden Press, board, 4 colors, 6½" x 8", 24 pp., (0–4).

To Market to Market
illus. by Peter Spier
An amazing little book in which approximately 20 of the old familiar nursery rhymes are arranged to tell the dawn-to-dusk story of a market day in 19th-century America. Meticulously detailed, beautiful, humorous illustrations for the older preschooler. A treasure for adults, too. See other Spier books on pages 155, 184.
Doubleday & Co., paperback, 4 colors, 9¼" x 7", (0–4).

The Tall Book of Mother Goose
illus. by Feodor Rojankovsky
An excellent, easy-to-manage, and beautifully illustrated basic collection of about 100 rhymes with about 200 illustrations.
Harper & Row, hardcover, 5" x 12", 128 pp.

Picture Story Mother Goose

In these books each rhyme is carried over several pages and illustrated as a story. Usually only 1–4 rhymes per book. Classic in this category are the old Greenaway, Brooke, and Caldecott gems. Published in hardcover by Frederick Warne, many of these (to Warne's dismay) are in public domain and available in paperback. Given all the books you might like to purchase for the preschooler, these seem best to borrow from the library or to purchase in paperback.

The House That Jack Built
by Randolph Caldecott

The Queen of Hearts
by Randolph Caldecott

Buckle My Shoe Book
by Walter Crane
All paperback reprints of old classics.
Mulberry, paperback, 4 colors, 7¾" x 5¼", 64 pp., (2–4).

More poetry for preschoolers

Except for the Mother Goose rhymes most of the poetry written for children is for older than preschool age. And much that is written expressly for preschoolers is really only *about* them and requires the child to have a higher degree of self-conscious awareness than preschoolers have. But some preschoolers who have had a lot of book time do develop an appreciation for the sound and harmony of poetic language. For the child and parent who are interested, a heavily illustrated anthology of poems is a good way to begin. Here are one big one and a few small bargains worth considering for a start.

A Child's Book of Poems
illus. by Gyo Fujikawa
This is the most useful big book we found for use with preschoolers. It is a good collection of some best poets' poems for children, heavily illustrated in a style most appealing to the youngest children. As in the Big Mother Goose anthologies, the many pictures in this book serve to make it a useful word book with the youngest children and to translate the poems for older, verbal preschoolers.
Grosset & Dunlap, board, 1 and 4 colors, 9" x 12", 128 pp.

Don't Tell the Scarecrow
illus. by Talivaldis Stubis
34 lovely, old Japanese Haiku poems especially selected for young children by the understanding editors of Scholastic's Lucky Book Club.
Scholastic Book Services, paperback, 2 and 3 colors, 9" x 7¼", (3–4).

Father Fox's Pennyrhymes
by Clyde Watson, illus. by Wendy Watson
Though not really for the very youngest, this book of fox family, Mother Goose-like rhymes is nevertheless so original and so sure to endure that is has to be mentioned. Some rhymes may become quickly memorized household chants. New England-o-philes will especially love its cozy portrayal of woodsy, loving, family country life.
T. Y. Crowell, hardcover, 4 colors, 8" x 9", 64 pp.

Nibble Nibble
by Margaret Wise Brown, illus. by Leonard Weisgard
If you go to the library for poetry anthology you will find many good ones to choose from, but you might not happen to meet this little collection of Margaret Wise Brown, a lady who knew almost better than anyone how to talk (in a whisper) to little children. Even *her* poems may fail to captivate the busiest young ones, but if you've ever been grateful for *The Sailor Dog* or *The Golden Egg Book* you might like to give this collection a try.
Young Scott, hardcover, 2 colors, 8¼" x 10½", 72 pp., (4).

The Rooster Crows
by Maud and Miska Petersham
A cheerful collection of "American Rhymes and Jingles," including a number of the old ones brought over from England.
Collier, paperback, 2, 3, and 4 colors, 7½" x 9", 48 pp., (3–4).

One by one the leaves fall down
From the sky come falling one by one
And leaf by leaf the summer is done
One by one by one by one.

–Margaret Wise Brown, *"The Leaves Fall Down," Nibble Nibble*

Let the fall leaves fall
And the cold snow snow
And the rain rain rain 'till April:
Our coats are warm
And the pantry's full
And there's cake upon the table.

–Clyde Watson, *Father Fox's Pennyrhymes*

From Events to Significance: Real Story Books

How to Read Them

Many of the storybooks on the following lists were classified by their publishers as suitable for children from kindergarten through third grade. Yet we found they were appreciated by many children under 3 years of age. What all the children had in common was an early, thoughtful introduction to books. What the books have in common that makes them workable with such young children is concreteness. Most of the stories can be distilled to a sequence of events and details largely within the ken of preschoolers.

When introducing these stories to very young children, it is often wise the first time around to strip away the more difficult details. Boil down and translate the story into a sequence of words and events you know he can understand. Then once the tracks have been laid, you can begin to run the whole train over them, adding car after car at whatever pace seems appropriate. As soon as the child has a general idea of what is happening, he will happily listen to even the most sophisticated words and details. So throw them in, too, explaining what you can but knowing that even the words you don't explain will eventually come clear. He will guess many from their context and the rest will unfold sooner or later, perhaps from hearing them used in other situations.

We explored these books for older children partly because we ran out of good things for preschoolers, but in the process a better reason was discovered. It's nice if a child's book experience can keep pace or even anticipate his living experience. A good children's book, like an onion, has layers and layers of meaning to peel off and understand. The child's interest will last through endless readings of the same book, not because children like repetition but because he still finds something new there to understand. A superior children's book will inspire the parent at the same time that it edifies and entertains the child.

Once he has understood everything he can find to question, his interest will taper off suddenly. He will ask for a favorite story and, before you have read three pages, will begin to wriggle away. You will sense he now knows all he can appreciate of what is coming up. It's time to retire that book and find another. Sometimes the retirement can be temporary and in a few months the child will have matured enough to discover a new layer of meaning. It may even happen that years later, a book loved as a little child will suddenly come to mind, bringing with it the very understanding most needed in that moment.

Fantasies Should Be Realistic

Why do children like stories? A fair guess seems to be that stories pull the pieces of their impressions together into meaningful order. Meaning is ultimately what is being sought and so it is important that we not deceive our children by giving them meaningless or trivial stories. Where we know the difference we should exercise discrimination. The difficulty lies in our knowing the difference in the first place.

"Be realistic" is usually understood to mean "don't be so idealistic—take all the bad in the world into account." In this book, however, reality is understood as that ideal state of peace and harmony all mankind basically seeks to *realize*. War, poverty, sickness, disharmony are byproducts of error which disappear in proportion as truth or reality is realized. Reality, then, is not the so-called hard facts of life, but rather the ideas or values that can, if rightly understood, harmonize our life experience.

In this light it can be seen that all books for children should be realistic. Children are very interested in what will become of them. This means that they are first of all interested in what life is like and, as they become more self-conscious, how they are supposed to behave in this life. So it is very important that the books we give our children depict the highest concepts of mankind and existence. Very first books should foster a happy expectancy of what life is like, and the storybook characters should be healthy models with whom the child can identify. The highest purpose of books is to foster the child's ability to discern the difference between values that work and those that don't, between what is existentially valid and invalid. Fantasies, oddly enough, can be the most realistic or the least.

Bad Books for Good Children

Reading aloud, we are constantly confronted with the purity of the young listener. We are suddenly aware of the negative values expressed in what we are reading, and we are painfully reluctant to write them upon the clean slate beside us. In *Babar* the mother elephant is shot and killed by a hunter; in slapstick humor people throw pies at each other and laugh, or they laugh at fat people, or are simply unwilling to help each other. In *The Three Little Pigs* the smart little pig boils alive the wolf who would otherwise have eaten him up. Especially in these old nursery tales the values are old-fashioned—the reality of evil is never questioned, and the techniques for dealing with it are trickiness and cruelty.

This is all news to that little lap-sitter you love. He has probably never thought of the possibility of a mother disappearing; he did not know about hunting and killing, about hurting, about too fat, about dead, about anyone wanting to eat anyone up. The revelation of this purity is startling, the quandary is immediate. One mother recalls her hesitation the first time she introduced her child to Humpty Dumpty who couldn't be put together again.

Here are some assurances and suggestions that we have found helpful.

• Most of the broad violence simply washes off the back of the preschooler.

• Reverse the storybook evil if you can—use it for teaching better values. For example, the hunting, the shooting down of Babar's mother is a mistake. The hunter did not understand about kindness. This way of treating evil is very useful. It points up the idea that evil doesn't work in life, that it isn't happy. This puts it in the "oh" category of irrelevant behavior where it belongs. Here the child can dump all the erroneous values that you and he have inspected and rejected in favor of better values such as kindness and letting be.

• Seek for yourself the positive value and then capitalize on it in your own consciousness. For example, though it need not be mentioned to the child unless he questions it, Babar clearly gets along fine without his mother. He even becomes king. Does this suggest that life itself is the mother?

• Timing. Of course we must exercise judgment about good timing. We do not want to frighten or sorrow our children by introducing disturbing ideas too early or at times when they are particularly sensitive or worried about certain matters. But timing is most of all a matter of our own readiness. For example, once we overcome the notion that we are indispensable to our children as mothers we are not so traumatized by the idea of Babar losing his! Our ease is effortlessly transmitted to our children as a sense of assurance.

• Immunization. While we do not want to disillusion our children unnecessarily, we must also not send them into the world unprotected or ignorant. Evil is neither to be feared nor ignored. It is not even to be fought against. Instead it must be transcended. At the same time that we do not want to drug our children with truly misleading books or television programs in which evil is made attractive and convincing, if we are alert we can use some of these things to help our children rise above evil. In the early years when our children are close by, we can be very grateful for the help both books and television give us in helping to teach them that evil is ignorance and how—with understanding—it can be overcome.

Stage-One Stories

For the child who has a vocabulary of single words (25 badly pronounced ones are good enough for a start). As first real stories or anticipating them, these can be used as word books, then as connected ideas, and finally most of them as real stories. They should be used along with the word- and nursery rhyme books listed in the first half of this chapter. Not many suitable stories are available for this stage, but the few that do work are good for an almost endless number of readings.

Elsewhere in this book Stage One comprehension level is indicated by (1) at the end of each book description.

The Animals of Farmer Jones
by Leah Gale, illus. by Richard Scarry
All the animals on the farm are hungry and say so one by one. Farmer Jones feeds them and they are thankful and say so one by one.
A Little Golden Book. Golden Press, board, 4 colors, 6½″ x 8″, 24 pp.

Anybody at Home?
by H. A. Rey
What lives where. Folded half pages, which the child can unfold to see what is inside, and the useful question-and-answer approach make this inviting to young children. The text is too long at first; just boil it down.
Houghton Mifflin, paperback, 4 colors, 5½″ x 6½″, 22 pp. (with 11 foldouts).

*Are You My Mother
by P. D. Eastman
Although designed as a story for beginning readers, this tale of a bird who hatched while his mother was out and went looking for her is invariably successful as a first story if carefully abridged. Long before they understand what any story is all about, small children enjoy the simple question-and-answer encounters of the baby bird with other animals and things. Throw out the text at first. Instead try: He meets a kitten. Is the kitten his Mommy? Nah! He meets a dog. Is the dog his Mommy? Nooo! Before long the child may learn to join in. You say, "What's this?" "Cow." "Yes, a cow! Is the cow the Mommy Bird?" "No." "No, of course not!" Random House, board, 3 and 4 colors, 6½″ x 9″, 72 pp.

The Boy with a Drum
by David Harrison, illus. by Eloise Wilkin
One by one the animals follow a little boy playing on a drum. One of the few books from which you can read the text verbatim to the youngest children. Just be sure to point. The only drawbacks are a few pages in which there is a discrepancy between the animals mentioned and those in the pictures.
Golden Press, board, 4 colors, 9¼″ x 12½″, 32 pp.

The Early Bird
by Richard Scarry
A little bird sets out to find a worm for a friend. Some elements in the story are contrived and confusing, but the pictures are Scarry-terrific and youngsters identify with the little bird at large.
Random House, board, 4 colors, 6½″ x 9″, 44 pp.

The Golden Egg Book
by Margaret Wise Brown, illus. by Leonard Weisgard
A bunny finds an egg but can't get it open. Finally the egg hatches, but the bunny has gone to sleep and the duck can't get him to wake up.
Golden Press, board, 4 colors, 9¼″ x 12½″, 32 pp.

Hi, All You Rabbits
by Carl Memling, illus. by Myra McGee
Question-and-answer rather than real story. Lots of enjoyable repetition and rhyme. "Hi, all you ducks. What do you do? 'We quack and we paddle. Quack and paddle. Quack and paddle. That's what all ducks do.'" Nice pen and wash illustrations.
Parents' Magazine Press, hardcover, 4 colors, 48 pp.

The Little Farm
by Lois Lenski
All about Mr. Small and his work on the farm. See other Lenski books listed on p 263. The publisher lists these for ages 4–7, but if boiled down a bit many of them are greatly loved by much younger children. Their subject matter is interesting, and Mr. Small, a man who looks like a child, is easy for children to identify with.
Henry Z. Walck, paperback, 1 and 2 colors, 7″ x 7″, 48 pp.

Springtime for Jeanne-Marie
by Françoise
A little girl and her sheep Patapon have a hard time finding their lost friend Madelon, a little white duck. The text of many words should be reduced to a few for the littlest ones.
Charles Scribner's Sons, paperback, 2 and 4 colors, 7½″ x 9″, 32 pp.

The Three Birds
by Hilde Heyduck-Huth
"By the river there was a town. In the town there was a garden. In the garden stood a tree. Among the branches was a nest. In the nest there were three blue eggs. From the eggs came three little birds. The three little birds flew over the house. A boy watched the birds from his window. He saw three birds fly home to a nest." That is the whole story. If you want a very sturdy book with a very first story you don't have to boil down, this one might be just right.
Harcourt Brace Jovanovich, board cover and board pages, 4 colors, 6¾" x 8", 18 pp.

Tommy Builds a House
by Gunilla Wolde
The complete story of how Tommy got his tools and materials and built a house. The text is hard for this level, but the subject matter sustains interest. Tell only the bare essentials. Don't read, "Father is busy too, reading all the news in the newspaper. But he promises to help Tommy if he needs it." Instead say, "Tommy says good-bye to his Daddy."
Houghton Mifflin, board, 4 colors, 6" x 6", 28 pp.

Tommy Takes a Bath
by Gunilla Wolde
All about Tommy and mud and water and baths. As with *Tommy Builds a House,* the subject matter appeals and can be understood sooner than the full text can be comprehended. It is thus useful for a long time if introduced early.
Houghton Mifflin, board, 4 colors, 6" x 6", 28 pp.

Where Have You Been?
by Margaret Wise Brown, illus. by Barbara Cooney
Not quite a story—just simple question-and-answer rhymes about where each of 14 animals have been. Helpful, pleasant repetition and rudimentary story elements, with difficult words to be enjoyed now for their sound and understood later. " 'Little Old Cat, Little Old Cat, where have you been?' 'To see this and that, that's where I've been,' said the Little Old Cat."
Hastings House, board, 1 color, 5¼" x 4¾", 32 pp.

Where's My Baby?
by H. A. Rey
The same foldout format as *Anybody at Home.* An adult animal is shown and when the page is unfolded the young of that animal are revealed. Rey's art is not the prettiest somehow, but children love these books.
Houghton Mifflin, paperback, 4 colors, 5½" x 6½", 22 pp. (with 11 foldouts).

* Who Knows the Little Man?
by Walburga Attenberger
The ideal first storybook. Simple pictures tell the simple yet adventurous story of a little man (who looks like a child) who goes out for a walk and comes home having gone swimming and caught a fish. Use it as a word book, letting the child name the many basic, familiar things in the pictures; then slowly introduce him to the idea that this is a connected story. The full text can be understood quite early.
Random House, board, 4 colors, 6" x 6", 32 pp.

Stage-Two Stories

Some of these have a lot of words, but they are all basically composed of concrete events which can be told in a few words and understood quite young. Don't worry if your child doesn't get the main point, he will nevertheless enjoy the story sequence—seeing *that* things are connected if not how. As with any books for preschoolers, first read the story as a sequence of events, then, later, begin to fill in the details.

Elsewhere in this book Stage Two comprehension level is indicated by (2) at the end of each book description.

Angus and the Cat
by Marjorie Flack
Angus, the dog, is curious about cats until one moves in; then he would soon do anything to get rid of her. But when she mysteriously disappears, Angus misses her. Reflects the ambivalent

experience some people have with the entry of new friends or brothers or sisters into their lives, and underscores the likelihood of positive resolution.
Doubleday & Co., paperback, 1 and 4 colors, 9¼" x 7", 32 pp.

Angus and the Ducks
by Marjorie Flack
Another story in which it is shown that even when things in the big world seem scary and unfriendly nothing really terrible happens. We are equipped to find out and survive.
Doubleday & Co., paperback, 1 and 4 colors, 9¼" x 7", 32 pp.

Angus Lost
by Marjorie Flack
Away from home the little dog encounters one scary thing after another and gets lost. He is glad to be home in the end. At first glance this seems a discouraging story for the child getting ready to go forth, but there is a great underlying *nevertheless* that encourages. Nevertheless nothing terrible really happens, and after a fascinating adventure on his own he succeeds in finding his way home again.
Doubleday & Co., paperback, 1 and 4 colors, 9¼" x 7", 32 pp.

Ask Mr. Bear
by Marjorie Flack
A boy seeks a gift for his mother's birthday. Each animal he meets offers him something she already has. Finally, far from home, a bear suggests the perfect thing—a bear hug. Maybe a little trite, but it suggests the important idea that the true gift everyone can give is love. Nice pictures.
Collier, paperback, 4 colors, 7½" x 9", 40 pp.

* A Boy, a Dog, and a Frog
by Mercer Mayer
After foiling all the attempts of a boy and a dog to catch him, a lonely frog follows their tracks to a joyful bathtub reunion. A unique textless picture story for hours of conversational exploration.
Dial Press, paperback, 1 color, 4½" x 5½", 32 pp.,

* Go, Dog. Go!
by P. D. Eastman
A strange non-story with not particularly appealing pictures that seems to captivate most children at some point and while entertaining them puts across

useful paired concepts of in/out, over/under, up/down, night/day, and stop/go.
Random House, board, 4 colors, 6½" x 8¾", 72 pp.

The Country Noisy Book
by Margaret Wise Brown, illus. by Leonard Weisgard
Muffin, the dog, goes to the country with his family and hears many new sounds. Children identify with Muffin, who doesn't know where he's going or what will happen next, and they like to guess the sounds that Muffin hears.
Harper & Row, hardcover, 3 colors, 7" x 8½", 48 pp.

Feed the Animals
by H. A. Rey
Another Rey guessing book with fold-out surprise pages. Guess whom the zookeeper is going to feed in this cage?
Houghton Mifflin, paperback, 4 colors, 6¼" x 5½", 22 pp. (with 11 foldouts).

Flap Your Wings
by P. D. Eastman
A helpful boy places an egg from the path in a bird's nest. The surprised birds undertake the overwhelming parental responsibilities of hatching, feeding, and teaching a baby alligator to fly. Very funny; also presents helpfulness as a matter of course, and all turns out well for everyone.
Random House, board, 4 colors, 6½" x 9", 44 pp., $1.95.

The Indoor Noisy Book
by Margaret Wise Brown, illus. by Leonard Weisgard
Because of being sick, Muffin, the dog had to stay in his room all day. He could not see what was going on downstairs, but from the sounds he could guess. Children love to guess the sounds.
Harper & Row, hardcover, 3 colors, 7" x 8½", 44 pp.

Let's Find Charlie
by Lois Morton, illus. by Elissa Scott
Amy's pet mouse is lost somewhere in her house, which is full of doors (cupboard, closet, oven, garage) that really open as she (and we) search.
Random House, board, 4 colors, 6½" x 9", 26 pp., $2.50.

The Little Fireman
by Margaret Wise Brown, illus. by Esphyr Slobodkina
A big and a little fireman respectively put out a big and little fire in their big and little ways. But falling asleep, at last the big fireman dreams a little dream while the little fireman dreams a great big dream. Besides entertaining and teaching the difference between big and small, this expresses the ideas that worth and usefulness do not depend on size and that, in fact, the least may have the greatest vision. The old-fashioned art is kind of homely, but it doesn't matter.
Scholastic Book Services, paperback, 2 colors, 7½″ x 9″, 40 pp.

* Little Fur Family
by Margaret Wise Brown, illus. by Garth Williams
To Margaret Wise Brown furry must have been a way of saying lovable. This is a warm, simple story of the little fur child (a bearlike fellow from a bearlike family) and his wonderful, ordinary/extraordinary day in the wild wood. "The fish didn't have any fur and they didn't have any feet and they swam around under the river. The little fur child watched them for a long time."
Harper & Row, board, 4 colors, 6¼″ x 8¼″, 40 pp.,

The Little Train
by Lois Lenski
Mr. Small is an engineer in this one. In simple language a lot about trains and how they work.
Henry Z. Walck Inc., paperback, 8¼″ x 7″, 1 and 2 colors, 48 pp.

Little Turtle's Big Adventure
by David Harrison, illus. by John Parr Miller
The pond home of a turtle is bulldozed in to make way for a highway. The turtle searches endlessly for a new home until at last a boy carries him to a perfect new pond home. Much incidental information, a happy-ending journey into the unknown, and the boy provides a healthy example of letting be. Very useful.
Random House, board, 4 colors, 6½″ x 9″, 36 pp.,

Meet Babar and His Family
by Laurent de Brunhoff
A pleasant, eventful introduction to the beloved de Brunhoff society of elephants. Not strong in plot, but children do love these elephant friends.
Random House, paperback, 4 colors, 8″ x 8″, 32 pp.,

One Monday Morning
by Uri Shulevitz
A king, a queen, a prince, and their retinue make seven trips to a boy's city tenement home before finally catching him in. Could mean a lot to a city child.
Charles Scribner's Sons, paperback, 4 colors, 7½″ x 9″, 40 pp.

* Play with Me
by Marie Hall Ets
Though she only wants to play with them, the woodland animals all flee from a little girl as long as she tries to catch them. When at last she gives up and sits quietly the animals voluntarily come to her—even a baby deer. A rare, lovely story that both appeals to children and expresses the art of receptively letting be.
Viking Press, paperback, 4 colors, 7½″ x 9″.

* The Runaway Bunny
by Margaret Wise Brown, illus. by Clement Hurd
"If you become a bird and fly away from me," said his mother, "I will be the tree that you come home to." Each time the little bunny thinks of something he will run away and become, the mother bunny thinks of something she will become in order to be with him. This rather amazing story is either haunting, oppressive, and misleading or beautifully true and reassuring, depending on our concept of love and motherhood. If we understand that the mother of us and the mother in us is love, then we can rightfully and gratefully assure our children that the mother, that is, the love they need, will be with them always in whatever place or form necessary. It is not necessary and not wise to explain this in detail to the child, only to be quite clear about it ourselves.
Harper & Row, board, 1 and 4 colors, 8″ x 6¾″, 48 pp.

Whither shall I go from thy spirit?
Or whither shall I flee from thy presence?
If I ascend up into heaven, thou art there;
If I make my bed in hell, behold, thou art there.
If I take the wings of the morning,

and dwell in the uttermost parts of the sea,
Even there shall thy hand lead me,
and thy right hand shall hold me . . .

–Psalms 139:7–10

The Snowy Day
by Ezra Jack Keats
The adventures of Peter, a city child, in his first snowfall. Striking artwork.
Viking Press, paperback, 4 colors, 9" x 7½", 40 pp.

The Very Little Boy
by Phyllis Krasilovsky, illus. by Ninon
How the little boy who was smaller than everything grew big enough to do anything a child could care to do. There is a slightly too-girly companion volume to this, but it seems better to use this one for both boys and girls, viewing the boy simply as a child.
Doubleday & Co., paperback, 3 colors, 5¼" x 7¾", 32 pp.

Stage two—might also enjoy

The Happy Man and His Dump Truck
by Miryam, illus. by Tibor Gergley
A happy man gives a lot of animals a happy ride and a slide in his dump truck.
Little Golden Book. Golden Press, board, 4 colors, 6½" x 8", 24 pp.

Home for a Bunny
by Margaret Wise Brown, illus. by Garth Williams
A rabbit finally finds a cozy home for a rabbit, with another rabbit to be cozy with.
Golden Press, board, 4 colors, 9" x 12", 32 pp.

Just Me
by Marie Hall Ets
A boy pretends to walk like the animals until his father calls him for a boat ride—then he runs like himself.
Viking Press, paperback, 1 color, 9" x 7½", 32 pp.,

The Mouse Book
by Helen Piers
A photographically illustrated story of two mice

who find each other and a home in a dolls' house custom renovated by a boy.
Scholastic Book Services, paperback, 4 colors, 6" x 8", 64 pp.

The Night Before Christmas
by Clement C. Moore, illus. by Sergio Leone
Santa Claus, of course. There are many editions to choose from. This one is very inexpensive and does the job satisfactorily. But we wish that Norman Rockwell would do this poem so no one would ever have to do it again.
Grosset & Dunlap, board, 4 colors, 6¼" x 7¾", 24 pp.

The idea of Santa Claus can be used beautifully with children. Introduce him as someone who expresses the spirit (and the joy) of generosity. Though Santa is a personification of this idea, use him as an opportunity for your child to experience gifts coming literally from "out of the blue" instead of personally from you. The idea of goodness coming from anywhere but his parents may be a new one to your child, but it is an important idea for us all to learn. Use Santa as a disguise while studying to realize that "Every good endowment and every perfect gift is from above, and cometh down from the Father of lights, with whom there is no variableness neither shadow of turning." (James 1:17)

See the Circus
by H. A. Rey
Yet another of the Rey surprise, fold-out books. This one surprises the child with circus stunts.
Houghton Mifflin, 4 colors, 6¼" x 5½", 22 pp. (with 11 foldouts).

Umbrella
by Taro Yashima
A Japanese-American girl waits and waits for a rainy day in which to use her new boots and umbrella.
Viking Press, paperback, 4 colors, 9" x 7½".

Whistle for Willie
by Ezra Jack Keats
Another well-illustrated story of Peter and how he finally learns to whistle.
Viking Press, paperback, 4 colors, 9" x 7½",
32 pp.

Stage-Three Stories

Longer than the stories in Stage Two, these range farther from home, but for the most part they are still quite concrete. By now the child is ready for a greater number of stories with somewhat fewer repetitions of each one.

Elsewhere in this book Stage Three comprehension level is indicated by (3) at the end of each book description.

Birthday Presents
by Eugene Fern
Many children receive elaborate presents, but Joseph receives a simple song. The elaborate presents fall apart, but Joseph's song goes on and on. He can give it away and still have it. And he does—to his children, his children's children, etc.
Farrar, Straus & Giroux, hardcover, 4 colors, 6½" x 7", 64 pp.

Blueberries for Sal
by Robert McCloskey
A girl and her mother and a bear cub and his mother get all switched around while blueberrying on Blueberry Hill. A funny mixup that resolves itself with reassuring smoothness.
Viking Press, paperback, 1 color, 9" x 7½", 64 pp.,

Caps for Sale
by Esphyr Slobodkina
A cap pedlar angrily tries to regain his caps from some monkeys in a tree. Not until he discards his only remaining cap in disgust do the mimicking monkeys throw down the stolen caps as well. A seemingly unassuming old-timer that children love. And it's wiser than its hero. Though the man feels that the monkeys are out to get him, they clearly mean no harm and know nothing at all of his needs and wishes or even his anger. Furthermore this

story illlustrates the idea that a cherished concern must often be completely surrendered before a problem can be solved.
Young Scott, hardcover, 4 colors, 6¾" x 8¼", 48 pp.

Charlie
by Diane Fox Downs, illus. by Lilian Obligado
An underfed cat finds paradise in a city courtyard.
Golden Press, board, 4 colors, 6½" x 8", 24 pp.

The Cow Who Fell in the Canal
by Phyllis Krasilovsky, illus. by Peter Spier
Hendrika wanted to see the marketplace and by accident she finally did, floating down the canal to town on a raft. Beautiful illustrations of Holland.
Doubleday & Co., paperback, 1 and 4 colors, 40 pp., 9¾" x 7".

Horton Hatches the Egg
by Dr. Seuss
For substantial story lines, the early Seuss seems to be the best Seuss. A faithful elephant agrees to egg-sit for a lazy bird, and he does so through thick and thin. At the last minute the bird attempts to claim her offspring, but the baby is an elephant bird, clearly belonging to Horton.
Random House, board, 3 colors, 8" x 11".

Indian Two Feet and His Horse
by Margaret Friskey, illus. by Ezra Jack Keats
Though he cannot find a horse of his own, when an Indian boy learns all he needs to know to care for a horse, a horse finds him. Not as pretty as *Indian Indian* but more significant. It would not be redundant to have both.
Scholastic Book Services, paperback, 2 colors, 6" x 8", 48 pp.

Jacko
by John S. Goodall
A delightful, textless picture story set in 18th-century England. An organ grinder's monkey runs away with a sea captain's parrot to face high-sea peril before a joyful homecoming to a bemonkeyed, beparroted, people-free island. Alternating half pages lend a movielike dimension to this beautifully detailed book.
Harcourt Brace Jovanovich, hardcover, 4 colors, 6¾" x 4¾", 32 full and 13 half-pp.

* Katy and the Big Snow
by Virginia Lee Burton
The simple but, to many youngsters, enthralling story of a red crawler tractor that plowed out a whole town after a snowstorm.
Houghton Mifflin, paperback, 4 colors, 9″ x 8″, 40 pp.

A Kiss for Little Bear
by Else Homeland Minarik, illus. by Maurice Sendak
A friendly/silly story of how a chain of animals cooperated in passing along a kiss from Grandmother to Little Bear. And there are more Little Bear stories as beautifully illustrated for sooner or later.
Harper & Row, board, 3 colors, 5¾″ x 8½″, 64 pp.

Little Bear's Visit
by Else Homeland Minarik, illus. by Maurice Sendak
Little Bear spends a happy day alone with Grandmother and Grandfather and he hears two stories. This and *A Kiss for Little Bear* seem to be the strongest, best-suited Little Bear stories for preschoolers.
Harper & Row, board, 3 colors, 5¾″ x 8½″, 64 pp.

The Little Brute Family
by Russell Hoban, illus. by Lilian Hoban
The grumbly, growly Brute family discovers the joys that come with sincere politeness and gratitude.
Collier, paperback, 3 colors, 5¼″ x 7¾″, 32 pp.

The Little Engine That Could
by Watty Piper, illus. by George and Doris Hauman
Parents don't love this slightly saccharine story, but the total affection of children for it can't be ignored. Evidently they identify with, and are encouraged by, the little engine who agreed to try to pull the broken-down train full of toys over the mountain, saying, "I think I can, I think I can." They must surely also identify with the passengers who have to wait so long for someone willing to help out.
Platt & Munk, board, 4 colors, 8″ x 7″, 48 pp.

The Little House
by Virginia Lee Burton
Children have insisted on this one enough times for it to go through 20 printings. It is the story of a house in the country and how it became a rundown house in an enormous city before being rescued. Because of its negative view of city life, you might not want to read it to your child if you plan to remain city dwellers, but if you live in the country or are about to move there, this will certainly be of interest to your child at some point.
Houghton Mifflin, hardcover, 4 colors, 9¾″ x 9″, 52 pp.

The Little Red Lighthouse and the Great Gray Bridge
by Hildegarde Swift and Lynd Ward
Thinking it has been replaced by the beacon of the towering new bridge (the George Washington Bridge), the little red lighthouse is grateful to learn that it is still very needed. "Quick let your light shine again. Each to his own place, little brother." A tremendous favorite with youngsters.
Harcourt Brace Jovanovich, paperback, 3 colors, 6¾″ x 8¼″, 64 pp.

There are a lot of modern stories about young children who are experiencing uncertainties or fears of one sort or another. Yet few of these books seem to reach the children the way such old-timers as *The Little Red Lighthouse* and *Mike Mulligan and His Steam Shovel* do. Or if they do reach the children, they often seem to suggest and confirm rather than solve the problem at issue. As an editor I used to think these oldies were successful with us because they were the only things available when we were growing up. But try them out on some modern children and you will find that although they may have infinitely more books to choose from they still love many of these old ones best. Perhaps it's because contemporary books often present psychological problems *as* psychological problems, offering very little by way of concrete event. The point of view is not concrete enough and requires a higher degree of self-awareness and conceptualization than young children have. The "problem" will probably disappear anyway from the child's behavior if the mistaken parental idea it expresses is corrected.

Anthropomorphism has been out of style for a few years, but perhaps that is a mistake. Preschool children are not nearly so interested in other children as they are in machines and animals. Maybe it's easier to identify with a lighthouse or a steam shovel or a duck to whom something really happens than with another child who doesn't *look* like *me* and who thinks about how he feels and what *might* happen to *him*.

Lorenzo
by Bernard Waber
An intelligently curious fish gets separated from his fellows and sees many wonderful things before rejoining them.
Scholastic Book Services, paperback, 2 colors, 6" x 8", 48 pp.

* Make Way for Ducklings
by Robert McCloskey
Along with *The Sailor Dog,* this is one of the all-around best books ever for this level. A pair of ducks settle in Boston, hatch out a family of eight on the Charles River, and then with the aid of a friendly policeman migrate on foot (the ducklings can't fly yet) through the heart of Boston traffic to the public garden. Everything is just right: the story describes an adventure far from home and yet is concrete. The children identify with the ducks (the little among the big, the new in the unfamiliar). And the policeman is a model of helpfulness.
Viking Press, paperback, 1 color, 7½" x 9", 64 pp.

Mike Mulligan and His Steam Shovel
by Virginia Lee Burton
Another child-winning favorite. Mike Mulligan and his steam shovel, Mary Ann, are being put out of business by the gas, electric, and diesel-powered diggers. Finally they get a job digging the foundation of a town hall, for money if they do it in a day, for nothing otherwise. They succeed but in their haste dig themselves into the hole. All problems are solved by converting the steam shovel to a furnace and Mike Mulligan to the superintendent of the town hall.
Houghton Mifflin, hardcover, 4 colors, 9¼" x 8½", 60 pp.

Moon Mouse
by Adelaide Holl, illus. by Cyndy Szekeres
A small mouse goes to see what the moon is made of and, at least to his satisfaction, finds out that it is delicious. Lovely illustrations.
Random House, paperback, 2 colors, 9" x 7", 32 pp.

Mousekin's Christmas Eve
by Edna Miller
After Mousekin's people move away he must find a new home. He succeeds on Christmas eve, following a rainbow of beautiful colored lights into a happy house with a Christmas crèche of small animals and people for him to spend the night with.
Prentice-Hall, paperback, 4 colors, 7" x 9¼", 32 pp.

Mousekin's Golden House
by Edna Miller
This time Mousekin's wonderful house is a discarded jack-o'-lantern. Lovely woodland illustrations.
Prentice-Hall, paperback, 4 colors, 7" x 9", 32 pp.,

Not This Bear
by Bernice Myers
A fur-clad boy in winter is mistaken for a bear by some bears. Good for laughs.
Scholastic Book Services, paperback, 2 colors, 6" x 8", 48 pp.

The Old Bullfrog
by Berniece Freschet, illus. by Roger Duvoisin
How the heron crept closer and closer and closer to the old bullfrog and didn't catch him is the gist of this beautifully illustrated and suspenseful story.
Charles Scribner's Sons, paperback, 4 colors, 7½" x 9", 32 pp.

* Pippa Mouse
by Betty Boegehold, illus. by Cyndy Szekeres
Six just-right stories about a little girl mousechild who wants to try things—like making a door to keep out the rain or sleeping out overnight—and who does. The results are a healthy fifty/fifty mixture of success and failure that any small child, boy or girl, would be happy to call adventures. Perfect for reading aloud to the little ones or for easy reading by beginning readers.
Pantheon Books, board, 1 color, 5½" x 8¼" 72 pp., (3–4).

* The Sailor Dog
by Margaret Wise Brown, illus. by Garth Williams
One of the finest stories for preschoolers ever. Scuppers, the dog, wanted to go to sea and did. He got wrecked on an island and needed a house, so he built one. He needed tools, and he found some. He needed supplies, so he fixed his ship and got some. "And here he is where he wants to be/ a sailor sailing the deep green sea." Wonderful pictures, an exciting adventure, and a valuable, luxurious sense of order and possibility.
Golden Press, board, 4 colors, 9" x 12", 36 pp.

Stop Stop
by Edith Thacher Hurd, illus. by Clement Hurd
How an old babysitter named Miss Mugs wanted to scrub everything in sight until an angry elephant convinced her that there's such a thing as being too clean.
Scholastic Book Services, paperback, 3 colors, 6" x 8¼", 64 pp.

The Story About Ping
by Marjorie Flack and Kurt Wiese
Rather than receive a spank for being the last on board his Chinese junk home, a yellow duckling chooses to stay behind. After some adventures and a narrow escape he finds his boat again and opts to return, spank or no spank. Children seem to appreciate this story of the freedom to make choices and survive consequences.
Viking Press, 4 colors, 9¾" x 7".

The Story of Babar
by Jean de Brunhoff
How Babar the elephant grew up and went to the city and came home in clothes to be crowned king and marry Celeste. The classic beginning of an elephant storybook civilization that has lasted

through two authors (father and son), more than a dozen volumes, and thousands upon thousands of children.
Random House, board, 4 colors, 8" x 11", 56 pp.,

Swimmy
by Leo Lionni
A little black fish among many red ones. They are too bite-sized to go out and see the world safely until Swimmy shows them how to swim in formation as one big fish. He serves as the eye.
Knopf/Pantheon, paperback, 4 colors, 7" x 9", 32 pp.

Will I Have a Friend?
by Miriam Cohen, illus. by Lillian Hoban
The straightforward story of a boy's first day at nursery school and how his first friend happened to happen along. Reassuring and informative.
Collier, paperback, 4 colors, 9" x 7½", 32 pp.

Stage three—might also enjoy

All in the Morning Early
by Sorche Nic Leodhas, illus. by Evaline Ness
On his way to the mill a boy is joined by dozens of creatures and folk. A well illustrated, cumulative counting tale from Scotland, retold in prose and rhyme.
Holt, Rinehart & Winston, paperback, 2 and 3 colors, 9" x 7½", 40 pp.

Blaze Finds the Trail
by C. W. Anderson
When a lost boy on horseback runs out of hope, his horse finds the way home.
Collier, paperback, 1 color, 7½" x 9", 48 pp.

The Bird in the Hat
by Norman Bridwell
Trouble begins when a bird moves into a cat's hat and ends when both cat and bird discover how to share the hat and help each other.
Scholastic Book Services, paperback, 2 colors, 8" x 6", 32 pp.

Choo Choo, the Runaway Engine
by Virginia Lee Burton
A train learns that to be useful is to be happy.
Scholastic Book Services, paperback, 1 color, 7¾" x 10¾", 48 pp.

The Circus Baby
by Maud and Miska Petersham
An elephant mother learns that it's better for her
baby to behave like an elephant than like people.
Collier, paperback, 4 colors, 7½" x 9", 32 pp.

Clifford the Big Red Dog
by Norman Bridwell
The enormous advantages and a few funny disadvantages of having a dog so big that he can't even
hide behind a house and must be bathed in a
swimming pool.
Scholastic Book Services, paperback, 2 colors,
8" x 6", 48 pp.

Clifford the Small Red Puppy
by Norman Bridwell
A tiny, weak puppy suddenly grows bigger than a
house when his little girl owner says she loves him.
Another gigantic shaggy-dog story by this author.
Scholastic Book Services, paperback, 2 colors,
8" x 6", 48 pp.

Clifford Takes a Trip
by Norman Bridwell
Clifford's family will never leave him behind again
after all the hilarious chaos he causes on the way to
join and *rescue* them on vacation. There are several
other Clifford stories for children to read by themselves in due course. This and the two above were
selected as being the best for reading aloud to
children under four.
Scholastic Book Services, paperback, 2 colors,
8" x 6", 48 pp.

The Country Cat
by Norman Bridwell
A happy country cat is a miserable nuisance in the
city until he meets a friendly boy who happens to
be moving to the country.
Scholastic Book Services, paperback, 2 colors,
8" x 6", 32 pp.

Crictor
by Tomi Ungerer
A silly story of an old lady in France who received
a boa constrictor as a present and grew quite fond
of it. Very amusing pictures.
Scholastic Book Services, paperback, 2 colors,
7½" x 9", 32 pp.

The Fat Cat
adapted from the Danish by Jack Kent
A folk tale about a cat who ate everything in sight
until a kind woodcutter literally helped everyone
out.
Scholastic Book Services, paperback, 4 colors,
9" x 7", 32 pp.

Fish Is Fish
by Leo Lionni
When a tadpole turned frog recounts his land
adventures to an old fish friend the fish gets only a
fishy mental picture. After leaping ashore to see for
himself the gasping fish is grateful to be helped
back into his watery world which he suddenly
realizes is beautiful.
Knopf/Pantheon, paperback, 4 colors, 7" x 9",
32 pp.

Goggles
by Ezra Jack Keats
Two city children escape with their treasure (some
glassless goggles) from some bigger boys who are
trying to steal it from them.
Collier, paperback, 4 colors, 9" x 7½", 40 pp.

The Happy Egg
by Ruth Krauss, illus. by Crockett Johnson
An egg that couldn't do anything got sat on and
sat on and sat on until one day it was ready to walk
and sing and fly! Could be read to even younger
children, but it is better appreciated at this stage.
Scholastic Book Services, paperback, 2 colors,
6" x 8", 32 pp.

Hi, Cat!
by Ezra Jack Keats
Slapstick mishaps occur when a stray cat adopts a
city boy at an inconvenient time.
Collier, paperback, 4 colors, 9" x 7½", 40 pp.

How, Hippo!
by Marcia Brown
A close call with a crocodile for a little
hippopotamus growing up. Lovely woodcuts.
Charles Scribner's Sons, paperback, 2 and 4 colors,
7½" x 9", 32 pp.

Johnny Crow's Garden
by Leslie L. Brooke
A rhyming nonsense tale of an animal gathering in

Johnny Crow's garden, by a classic children's illustrator.
Grolier, paperback, 1 and 4 colors, 5¼" x 7¾", 64 pp.

Little Boy with a Big Horn
by Jack Bechdolt, illus. by Aurelius Battaglia
Because his tuba music annoys everyone, a boy finally rows out to sea to practice. There his music saves a ship from being wrecked in a fog. This makes him a hero and wins him the reward of a scholarship to music school.
A Little Golden Book. Golden Press, board, 4 colors, 6½" x 8", 24 pp.

My Mother Is Lost
by Bernice Myers
Everybody is relieved when two lost and rambunctious boys in a department store are reunited with their mothers.
Scholastic Book Services, paperback, 2 colors, 8" x 6", 48 pp.

Nobody Listens to Andrew
by Elizabeth Guilefoile, illus. by Mary Stevens
Andrew has a bear in his bed, but can't find anyone who will listen to him.
Scholastic Book Services, paperback, 2 colors, 8" x 6", 32 pp.

Noisy Nancy Norris
by Lou Ann Gaeddert, illus. by Gioia Fiammenghi
An apartment-dwelling girl struggles with the problems of how (and when and where) to be at once a happy child and a considerately quiet one.
Doubleday & Co., paperback, 2 and 4 colors, 5½" x 7", 64 pp., 75¢.

Nu Dang and His Kite
by Jacqueline Ayer
After giving up his search for his lost kite, a Thai boy finds that the kind wind has already blown it home to him.
Harcourt Brace Jovanovich, 9" x 7½", 2 and 3 colors, 32 pp.

Pet Show
by Ezra Jack Keats
A friendly story about a city neighborhood pet show, starring Archie, Peter, and Willie of other Keats books. As usual, Keats' bold colors are a luxury.
Collier, paperback, 4 colors, 9" x 7½", 32 pp.

Rich Cat, Poor Cat
by Bernard Waber
Some cats live in comfort, but Scat barely gets by until suddenly he is happily adopted into the very lap of luxury.
Scholastic Book Services, paperback, 2 and 4 colors, 7½" x 9", 48 pp.

Rosie's Walk
by Pat Hutchins
Minding her own business, a little hen never even knows of her narrow escapes from a hungry, but deservedly accident-prone, fox. Positive values and good introductions to such concepts as under, over, around, and through.
Collier, paperback, 3 colors, 9" x 7½", 32 pp.

The Sky Dog
by Brinton Turkel
A boy's wish for a dog like the one he sees in the clouds comes true.
Viking Press, paperback, 3 colors, 7½" x 9", 32 pp.

Thy Friend Obadiah
by Brinton Turkel
A small Quaker boy of old Nantucket comes at last to love the gull that has befriended him.
Viking Press, paperback, 4 colors, 9" x 7½", 40 pp.

Timothy Turtle
by Alice Vaught Davis, illus. by Guy Brown
A turtle gets stuck on his back and no one can turn him over until at last the frog suggests a surprising and effortless solution. Illustrates the need for looking at a problem from an entirely fresh point of view.
Harcourt Brace Jovanovich, paperback, 3 colors, 7½" x 9", 32 pp.

What Good Luck! What Bad Luck!
by Remy Charlip
"WHAT GOOD LUCK! There was a haystack on the ground. WHAT BAD LUCK! There was a pitchfork in the haystack. WHAT GOOD LUCK! He missed the pitchfork. WHAT BAD LUCK! He missed the haystack." A dramatic, slapstick adventure told entirely through this formula of sudden reversal.
Scholastic Book Services, paperback, 1 and 2 colors, 7½" x 9", 40 pp.

Whose Mouse Are You?
by Robert Kraus, illus. by Jose Aruego
A fantasy in which "nobody's mouse" rescues his entire family one by one from disastrous predicaments and winds up both beloved and be-baby-brothered.
Collier, paperback, 3 colors, 7½" x 9", 32 pp.

Who Took the Farmer's Hat?
by Joan L. Nodset, illus. by Fritz Siebel
How the kind farmer's favorite hat became an old, brown nest with his tacit consent.
Scholastic Book Services, paperback, 4 colors, 9" x 7½", 32 pp.

The Winter Picnic
by Robert Welber, illus. by Deborah Ray
While his mother is too busy for him, a little boy prepares a picnic to share with her in the snow.
Knopf/Pantheon, paperback, 4 colors, 9" x 7", 32 pp.

Stage-Four Stories

Some of these are simply longer than those in Stage Three. Others are not necessarily longer, but conceptually harder. Included are some seemingly oddball books with lofty underlying values which the children will probably miss now but may come to understand through the memory of these stories when they are older. Another reason for their inclusion is their potential to inspire us as parents. If we watch closely now, we can see that our so young children are already beginning to peer through the facts into the realm of ideas and values.

Elsewhere in this book Stage Four comprehension level is indicated by (4) at the end of each book description.

The Blind Men and the Elephant
retold by Lillian Quigley, illus. by Janice Holland
Six blind men meet the same elephant, and each encounters a different aspect. They disagree totally about what the creature is like. "A wall! A snake! A spear! A tree! A fan! A rope!" They learn that, although they all are right, each of them is wrong. Such a wise, old Indian tale.
Charles Scribner's Sons, paperback, 4 colors, 7½" x 9", 32 pp.

Bread and Jam for Frances
by Russell Hoban
A little badger finally gets her fill, and then some, of the only food she thought she really liked. Several other excellent Frances books are available from Harper & Row.
Scholastic Book Services, paperback, 2 colors, 7½" x 9", 32 pp.

* The Camel Who Took a Walk
by Jack Tworkov, illus. by Roger Duvoisin
The beautiful camel went for a walk in the beautiful day. A tiger prepares to pounce on her, and a chain of smaller animals prepares to pounce on the tiger and each other. But the sun keeps getting higher, and just before the camel reaches the spot where "the shadow of the tree falls across the road," she decides to turn back. Nobody pounces and everyone bursts out laughing except the tiger, who slinks away, and the camel, whose beautiful walk remains unmarred by even the thought of violence. A gem. Totally suspenseful and entertaining, but beneath it all profoundly and mystically true. Ranks with *The Sailor Dog* and *Make Way for Ducklings* as an all-around, topnotch book for preschoolers.
E. P. Dutton & Co., paperback, 1 and 3 colors, 7" x 9¼", 32 pp.

* Charlie the Tramp
by Russell Hoban, illus. by Lillian Hoban
Allowed to choose to be a tramp, Charlie Beaver builds a most beautiful pond for his own good reasons. "Sometimes I like to tramp around, and sometimes I like to make ponds." A lovely lesson for parents, and a happy story for children.
Scholastic Book Services, paperback, 1 color, 7½" x 9", 48 pp.

* The Fire Cat
by Esther Averill
A beautiful account of the life path of most of us disguised as the simple story of a little bully alley cat who becomes a good and skillful firehouse cat and then must still learn to be kind. He reflects,

"Once I chased a little cat up a tree. Oh me! Oh my! Why did I do that?" Especially loving and accepting; dismisses badness as ignorance.
Harper & Row, board, 3 colors, 5¾" x 8½", 64 pp.

Frederick
by Leo Lionni
When the other mice are storing up food for winter, Frederick appears to be doing nothing. But he is really meditating on what is beautiful, storing up thoughts of light and color for which the mice are grateful in the dark, gray winter.
Knopf/Pantheon, 4 colors, 7" x 9", 32 pp.

* The Goblin under the Stairs
by Mary Calhoun, illus. by Janet McCaffery
To the child who spies him through a knothole in the wall the boggart is a "wee frisky man," a playmate. To the mother he appears "a good servant elf," and to the father "a house-plaguing goblin." The most violent predictions prevail until the father gives up trying to get rid of the boggart and the mother serves up some of the hospitality a tidy servant elf deserves. A wonderful yarn, charmingly told, and valid.
William Morrow & Co., hardcover, 4 colors, 9" x 7¾", 40 pp.

The Happy Lion
by Louise Fatio, illus. by Roger Duvoisin
The beloved lion of a French zoological garden is bewildered by the startled and unfriendly response he receives when he takes a stroll among his friends outside the garden. Only the zookeeper's son greets him kindly and saves the day.
McGraw-Hill, hardcover, 2 and 3 colors, 8" x 10", 40 pp.

The Happy Lion and the Bear
by Louise Fatio, illus. by Roger Duvoisin
Mutual fear threatens to spoil the possibility of friendship between the Happy Lion and the new bear.
McGraw-Hill, hardcover, 2 and 3 colors, 8" x 10", 40 pp.

The Happy Lion Roars
by Louise Fatio, illus. by Roger Duvoisin
"Why am I alone in my house?" The Happy Lion is so *un*happy until a lady circus lion mysteriously disappears from the circus to elope with him. There are five more enjoyable Happy Lion books to read along the way. This and the two above seemed the most worthwhile and appropriate for preschoolers.
McGraw-Hill, hardcover, 2 and 3 colors, 8" x 10", 40 pp.

* The Little Island
by Golden MacDonald, illus. by Leonard Weisgard
On the surface this is a pleasant story of an island day by day, season by season, plant by plant, and creature by creature. But tucked away to be understood later is the amazing thought which a kitten must take on faith that the island which seems separately afloat is really a part of the land and, like the kitten himself, at once "a part of the world and a world of its own."
Doubleday & Co., paperback, 1 and 4 colors, 9¼" x 7", 48 pp.

* Little Pear
by Eleanor Frances Lattimore
Sooner than you think, the child who has been thoughtfully exposed to books is verbal enough to enjoy a story without seeing many pictures. There are no two better for preschoolers than this collection and Margery Clark's *Poppyseed Cakes*. Little Pear is a Chinese child just beginning to go off alone after his own curiosity. He makes dreadful mistakes and gets into scrapes while learning, but he is always so obviously loved and forgiven. This book contains nine of his adventures, and you will be sad to see them come to an end. Fortunately there are more, another whole book for a little bit later.
Harcourt Brace Jovanovich, paperback, 1 color, 6¼" x 8¾", 152 pp.

Little Raccoon and the Thing in the Pool
by Lilian Moore, illus. by Gioia Fiammenghi
On his first solo trip to the pool, Little Raccoon is warned by many animals about the "thing" he will find when he gets there. He is a bit frightened by the time he arrives and sure enough, there is a fearful "thing" staring back at him from the pool. After all his attempts to scare the "thing" result only in his getting scared himself, he runs home to his

mother and learns that the way to tame the "thing" is to smile at it. Sure enough, it works.
McGraw-Hill, hardcover, 2 colors, 6¼" x 8¼", 48 pp.

* A Little Schubert
by M. B. Goffstein
A short happy book that makes the astonishing point that "Franz Schubert heard music when his friends heard nothing, and Franz Schubert heard music that no one had ever heard before." Record included.
Harper & Row, hardcover, 1 color, 7" x 7", 40 pp.

Lyle, Lyle, Crocodile
by Bernard Waber
The story of a brownstone-dwelling crocodile and how he lived among and annoyed and won over and was beloved by a variety of people.
Houghton Mifflin, paperback, 2 and 4 colors, 7½" x 9", 48 pp.

Lyle and the Birthday Party
by Bernard Waber
Lyle remains sick with envy over Joshua's birthday celebration until, through comic events, he winds up in the hospital and finds himself helping others.
Houghton Mifflin, paperback, 2 and 3 colors, 7" x 9", 48 pp.

The Magician
by Uri Shulevitz (adapted from the Yiddish of I. L. Peretz)
At Passover a magician appears to provide a feast for a needy couple, who realize soon that they have been visited by the prophet Elijah. A nice statement of the way that spiritual understanding appears as magic to the world. This story is beyond most of us, but still a good yarn and a valuable brick to lay for future understanding.
Collier, hardcover, 1 color 7" x 9", 32 pp.

Millions of Cats
by Wanda Gag
A tall tale of millions of cats who eat each other up in an argument over who is prettiest. Only one humble cat survives to be loved and grow truly beautiful. Somehow, this truthful story, already a classic, is fascinating to children.
Coward-McCann, hardcover, 1 color, 9½" x 6¼", 32 pp.

Obadiah the Bold
by Brinton Turkel
A Quaker child of old Nantucket learns a better reason for going to sea than to be a pirate.
Viking Press, paperback, 4 colors, 9" x 7½", 40 pp.

A Pocketful of Cricket
by Rebecca Caudill, illus. by Evaline Ness
It's hard to nutshell this story of a child who (like most children with the opportunity) studied the whole beauty of each new thing he found. "The stripes on every bean were different from the stripes on every other bean." This is the story of one boy's peaceful and private observations, his beloved cricket, and the first-day-at-school experience of learning to share them gladly without giving them up. Beautiful, expressive illustrations.
Holt, Rinehart & Winston, paperback, 2 and 3 colors, 7½" x 9", 48 pp.

* The Poppyseed Cakes
by Margery Clark, illus. by Maud and Miska Petersham
Seven little stories about Andrewshek or Erminka getting into some trouble or other having to do with scrumptious poppyseed cakes. Warm reminiscences of predictable/accidental naughtinesses in two loving Slavic-American households. Charming, bright illustrations and decorations. An excellent collection to be used with even younger children than Little Pear.
Doubleday & Co., hardcover, 1, 2, and 4 colors, 5¾" x 7¼", 160 pp.

* The Tiger in the Teapot
by Betty Yurdin, illus. by William Pene duBois
After all the threatening, ordering, bribing, and pleading of the rest of the family has failed to induce an unwelcome tiger to leave their teapot, it is the littlest girl, radiantly gracious and graceful, who finally succeeds in welcoming him forth. So refreshing!
Holt, Rinehart & Winston, paperback, 4 colors, 5¼" x 7¾", 32 pp.

* Toad
by Anne Rockwell, illus. by Harlow Rockwell
A lovely fact-based prose-poem tale of the days and doings of a toad. A generous opportunity to see

beauty and worth where it might otherwise be overlooked.
Doubleday & Co., hardcover, 4 colors, 8″ x 8″, 40 pp.

William's Doll
by Charlotte Zolotow, illus. by William Pene duBois
Everyone says dolls are for girls, but William's grandmother understands that he needs one "to hug, to cradle, and to take to the park so that when he's a father like you he'll know how. . . ."
Harper & Row, board, 4 colors, 5″ x 7″, 32 pp.

So many ways to be a child (*stage four cont'd*)

As much as possible it is good if books about racially, nationally, religiously, culturally, or economically different children are not specifically about the differences. Let there be stories that stand as stories, and in art and text express the universal beauty and worth of life in all forms, with difference being one of the things that's the same about all of us. Some of the hardcover books included below are not necessarily superior stories but they meet some of these qualifications rather better than others. One way to recognize a good book about children of different cultures or races or what-have-you is that it will be as interesting to one group as to another.

Congo Boy
retold by Mollie Clark, illus. by Beatrice Darwin
An African folktale of a boy who eventually got the hunting spear he yearned for by simply being generous. The story and pictures also show beautifully something of what's the same and what's different about a child in an African village.
Scholastic Book Services, paperback, 2 colors, 6″ x 8″, 48 pp.

Down, Down the Mountain
by Ellis Credle
Two spontaneously generous and appreciative Appalachian children give away most of the turnips

they have raised to buy shoes. Though they still wish for the shoes, they do not regret their generosity and when the shoes come through after all, it seems a bonus rather than a necessity. A good glimpse of Appalachian life and the joys of generosity.
Thomas Nelson, hardcover, 2 colors, 8″ x 10″, 56 pp.

In Africa
by Marc and Evelyne Bernheim
Though not a story at all, this book is included here for the effective way it meets the needs of parents who particularly want their children to know about life in Africa. Simple text and many black-and-white photographs show the very different ways and places (savannah, forest, desert, and city) that African children do the same things as children everywhere: grow up and seek to be happy.
Atheneum, hardcover, 1 color, 9¼″ x 9″, 56 pp.,

In My Mother's House
by Ann Nolan Clark, illus. by Valino Herrera
A poetic account of the close-to-earth life style of some American Pueblo Indians. A bit difficult for some preschoolers, but beautifully done for those with special interest.
Viking Press, paperback, 1 and 4 colors, 7½″ x 9″, 64 pp.

Little Wolf
by Ann McGovern, illus. by Nola Langner
To prove himself as a brave, Little Wolf must kill an animal, but he is too fond of the animals for this to be his way. Instead he proves himself as a healer. "He will not kill the deer or the rabbit or the fox. He will see the animals that run through the woods. He will watch them and he will learn . . . And that is Little Wolf's way."
Abelard-Schuman, hardcover, 2 colors, 7″ x 10″, 52 pp.

Milane
by Robert Vavra
After a summer on the road with his family's tiny circus, a boy is grateful for the winter camp and an amazing wildlife adventure. Although this story is not especially well resolved, it is included because of its astonishing full-color photographs of a Hungarian gypsy boy and a fawn. It is a

privilege to see innocence and beauty made so concretely obvious.
Harcourt Brace Jovanovich, board, full color, 8″ x 11½″, 48 pp.

Mr. Moonlight and Omar
by James Holding, illus. by Aliki
Often in Arabian lands it is still possible to see a donkey and a camel pulling a plow together. In a new fable about an intelligent Arabian boy of Old Morocco this picturesque phenomenon is charmingly explained.
Morrow, hardcover, 3 colors, 7½″ x 9″, 40 pp.

Moy Moy
by Leo Politi
Moy Moy is "a very young American girl whose parents came from China" and who has three loving big brothers to guide her through her first real participation in the best holiday of the year—Chinese New Year.
Charles Scribner's Sons, hardcover, 4 colors, 8″ x 10″, 32 pp.

Pizzoro
by Robert Vavra
Pizzoro is overjoyed with the gift of a burro of his own, and he is frantic when for a while the burro is lost. A loosely constructed story of the son of a Mexican sharecropper included mainly for its lovely photos which express once more the beauty, that is to be found in any child growing up somewhere.
Harcourt Brace Jovanovich, board, 4 colors, 8″ x 11½″, 48 pp.

Rosa
by Leo Politi
A rural Mexican girl who is happy in school but lonely in the summer longs for a doll for Christmas. Instead she receives something even better—a baby sister. Along the way we are privileged to see much beauty in the Mexican landscape as well as details of the lives of some Spanish-speaking children.
Charles Scribner's Sons, hardcover, 2 and 4 colors, 8″ x 10″, 40 pp.

Soo Ling Finds a Way
by June Behrens, illus. by Taro Yashima
When a laundromat threatens to close her grandfather's Chinese hand laundry, a little girl is inspired with an idea that enhances everyone's

profit and satisfaction. The old with the new for the better.
Golden Gate, hardcover, 3 colors, 9½″ x 7″, 40 pp.

The Sunshine Family and the Pony
by Sharron Loree
A commune of freedom-seeking families learns that their pony needs freedom to be happy too.
Seabury Press, hardcover, 9″ x 6″, 56 pp.

Stage four—might also enjoy

Adventures of Raggedy Ann
by Johnny Gruelle
Especially for children who are fond of Raggedy Ann and Andy. Five adventures of Raggedy Ann and her doll friends, all of whom come alive when their little-girl mistress isn't around. There are other Raggedy Ann books waiting if this one catches on with your child.
Mulberry, paperback, 1 and 4 colors, 5¼″ x 7¾″, 64 pp.

The Best-Loved Doll
by Rebecca Caudill, illus. by Elliot Gilbert
It is the oldest, raggediest, and kindest of the dolls who is chosen to attend a doll party and who wins the most important prize.
Holt, Rinehart & Winston, paperback, 2 colors, 5¼″ x 7¾″, 64 pp.

Clocks and More Clocks
by Pat Hutchins
Not believing in the accuracy of any clock, a man keeps buying more and more of them to see if the others are correct. Finally he accepts a watchmaker's word for it that they are all keeping perfect time. Requires some awareness of the idea of telling time.
Collier, paperback, 4 colors, 9″ x 7½″, 32 pp.

Curious George
by H. A. Rey
Curious/naughty children love the misadventures of this monkey on his way to the zoo, even though the idea that a zoo is a happy situation for any living thing seems rather misleading.
Houghton Mifflin, paperback, 2 colors, 7½″ x 9″, 48 pp.

Flip the Flying Possum
by Noela Young
A flying possum searches for a safe new home.
Grolier, paperback, 2 colors, 5¼" x 7¾", 64 pp.

Hattie the Backstage Bat
by Don Freeman
The story of how the real bat pet of a friendly old stage doorman turned a mediocre mystery play into a howling success.
Viking Press, paperback, 2 colors, 9" x 7½", 32 pp.

How Big Is a Foot?
by Rolf Myller
A funny story about making a bed measured in feet and why the standardizing of the foot was necessary. Only for children aware of and interested in measurement.
Atheneum, paperback, 2 colors, 7" x 8¼", 36 pp.,

The Hungry Thing
by Jan Slepian and Ann Seidler, illus. by Richard El Martin
A friendly, hungry monster asks for "shmancakes" and "tickles," and it takes an alert child to understand that he wants pancakes and pickles. Entertaining and instructive for the child ready to participate in guessing what the monster wants *this* time. Charming pictures.
Scholastic Book Services, paperback, 4 colors, 7½" x 9¼", 32 pp.

I Wish, I Wish
by Lisl Weil
An Italian girl's wishes for a kitten and a small painting come surprisingly true at the same time.
Houghton Mifflin, paperback, 2 colors, 7" x 9¼", 48 pp.

Journey Cake Ho!
by Ruth Sawyer, illus. by Robert McCloskey
Hard times force an old couple to let their hired boy go. On his way the boy's journey cake runs off and rounds up all the livestock needed to get the farm going again.
Viking Press, paperback, 2 colors, 7½" x 9", 48 pp.

Katy No-Pocket
by Emmy Payne, illus. by H. A. Rey
A pouchless kangaroo mother has a problem until she gets a carpenter's work apron with enough pockets to accommodate her baby and all his friends as well.
Houghton Mifflin, paperback, 4 colors, 7" x 9", 32 pp.

Madeline
by Ludwig Bemelmans
A little girl from a French boarding school has such adventures to tell about her appendectomy that all the other girls would like to have their appendix out too. But their very wonderful directress, Miss Clavel, puts a stop to that. " 'Good night, little girls! Thank the Lord you are well! And now go to sleep!' says Miss Clavel."
Viking Press, paperback, 2 and 4 colors, 7½" x 9", 48 pp.

Madeline's Rescue
by Ludwig Bemelmans
This time Madeline falls into the river and is rescued by a dog, whom the board of directors would like removed, whom Miss Clavel allows to stay, whom the girls quarrelsomely adore, and who obligingly produces a puppy for each. It's the atmosphere more than the stories that is so nice in these Madeline books. Also nice is the motherliness, firm and gentle, of Miss Clavel who without really being a mother (she is a nun) is nevertheless the prototype of a good one.
Viking Press, paperback, 2 and 4 colors, 7½" x 9", 48 pp.

Mr. Brown and Mr. Gray
by William Wondriska
King Horse and some peasant pigs prove that happiness is not to be found in power and riches but in simplicity.
Holt, Rinehart & Winston, paperback, 2 and 4 colors, 7½" x 9", 40 pp.

My Box and String
by Betty Woods
A boy makes something from a box and learns that the real fun is in the making and sharing and not in the having only.
Scholastic Books Services, paperback, 2 colors, 6" x 8", 48 pp.

My Friend Mac
by May McNeer and Lynd Ward
A lonely French-Canadian boy befriends a moose,
an only semi-satisfactory substitute for the
company of other children whom at last he meets
in school.
Houghton Mifflin, paperback, 2 colors, 6¾" x 9¼",
80 pp.

Norman the Doorman
by Don Freeman
How an art museum mouse happened to win first
prize in a museum exhibit.
Viking Press, paperback, 4 colors, 9" x 7½",
64 pp.

The Plantsitter
by Gene Zion, illus. by Margaret Bloy Graham
Things get wonderfully out of hand when a boy
undertakes the job of caring for vacationing
neighbors' plants in his own home.
Scholastic Book Services, paperback, 3 colors,
7¾" x 10¾", 32 pp.

Red Fox and His Canoe
by Nathaniel Benchley, illus. by Arnold Lobel
The funny story of an Indian boy who discovers
that a small canoe just his size is better than a
giant-size one full of uninvited animal hitch-hikers.
Scholastic Book Services, paperback, 2 colors,
6" x 8", 64 pp.

Silly Sam
by Leonore Klein, illus. by Harvey Weiss
Sam trades away his clothes in an effort to get a
good birthday present for his friend. He is duped
into one worthless present after another, and
everyone laughs when he arrives at the party
wearing hardly anything and bringing only an egg.
But out of the egg hatches a golden bird, the best
present of all.
Scholastic Book Services, paperback, 2 colors,
7" x 9", 48 pp.

The Story of Ferdinand
by Munroe Leaf, illus. by Robert Lawson
The modern classic of a peace-loving and happy
young bull who could not be induced to fight. Many
preschoolers do not have enough knowledge of
violence to understand this bullfighting tale, but you
may be glad to know of it for later.
Viking Press, paperback, 1 color, 7½" x 9",
72 pp.

That's What Friends Are For
*by Florence Parry Heide and Sylvia Worth
Van Clief, illus. by Brinton Turkel*
When Theodore elephant has a hurt leg, he and his
jungle friends slowly learn that friendship means
helping and not just giving advice. Very pretty
pictures.
Scholastic Book Services, paperback, 4 colors,
9" x 7½", 40 pp.

Time of Wonder
by Robert McCloskey
A lovely account of summer days and a hurricane
on an island off the coast of Maine. It is very long,
but the drama of the storm sustains the interest of
many children.
Viking Press, paperback, 4 colors, 7½" x 9",
64 pp.

Traditional Tales and Classics

Nursery and fairy tales

The distinction between fairy and nursery
tales is not immediately apparent. Both include a variety of old, untraceable folk tales
plus certain original materials, or at least
canonized retellings of traditional tales by
famous storytellers such as the Brothers
Grimm. For the purposes of this book, nursery tales are considered to be those traditional tales suitable for preschoolers, and
fairy tales those which are for the most part
better appreciated by children of grade-
school age. In general, nursery tales are about
anthropomorphized animals (that is, animals
behaving as people), or people, or both, and
they are usually intended to convey simple
messages or behavioral codes. Fairy tales tend
to include more magic, the changing of things
and people into people and things—giants,
queens, witches, and of course, fairies. They

are also generally longer and more sophisticated, too long to sustain the very young child's interest and a little too fantastic to be sorted out by the untraveled 3 year old. *The Shoemaker and the Elves* is all right, but let *Cinderella* and *Jack and the Beanstalk* wait a minute.

Many of the traditional nursery tales are especially violent and bloodthirsty, and we have to exercise some discretion in the versions we introduce to our children at first. Yet even in some of the most horrendous tales, there are germs of truth to be recognized. And it is surprising how a consciousness of good values on the part of the parent can be transmitted wordlessly to the child with the result that seemingly startling and erroneous values may fail to capture the child's attention. On pondering the story of *The Three Little Pigs*, one 3-year-old said, "The big bad wolf is just people with a mask on. If I made a stick house in the woods, I would leave off the door. Then the wolf and I could be friends." This child is on the way to understanding that the truly strong dwelling place is a consciousness of love and not a house of hay or sticks or even bricks.

The Three Bears expresses the idea that error results in unnecessary fear. (The bears meant no harm, but since Goldilocks was intruding wrongfully, she was terrified to see them.) *Little Red Ridinghood* was meant to teach children to stay on the path and never speak to strangers. But the same story can reassure the child that when help is needed it appears.

Here are a couple of good nursery-tale anthologies plus some good and inexpensive editions of single nursery tales.

*Jack Kent's Book of Nursery Tales
illus. by Jack Kent
The most communicative book of nursery tales we know—definitely best for the very youngest. Every event in each story is illustrated with a picture. Thus in a very little while the child can learn to "read" the pictures and tell himself the familiar story. 7 stories, 157 illus.
Random House, board, 4 colors, 9¼" x 12½", 172 pp., (1–4).

Great Children's Stories
illus. by Frederick Richardson
An especially beautiful collection. The companion reprint to the Richardson Mother Goose book. 17 stories, 125 illus.
Hubbard Press, hardcover, 4 colors, 9" x 12", 160 pp., (2–4).

Favorite Stories for Children
illus. by Frederick Richardson
Four good selections from the big classic Richardson hardcover (*Great Chidren's Stories*). A pleasantly inexpensive way to expose children to these striking old illustrations.
Hubbard Press, paperback, 1 and 4 colors, 8½" x 11", 32 pp.

The Tall Book of Nursery Tales
illus. by Feodor Rôjankovsky
A favorite old collection of 24 nursery favorites, beautifully illustrated.
Harper & Row, board, 1 and 4 colors, 5" x 12", 128 pp., (2–4).

The Elves and the Shoemaker
retold by Vera Southgate, illus. by Robert Lumley
How some tiny elves helped a poor shoemaker, and how the shoemaker and his wife found a way to thank them. An acceptable fairy tale for preschoolers. Informative detail of Renaissance life and dress.
A Ladybird Book. Penguin Books, board, 4 colors, 4½" x 6¾", 56 pp., (4).

The Enormous Turnip
retold by Vera Southgate, illus. by Robert Lumley
The story of how a mouse's strength finally made the decisive difference in tugging up a gigantic turnip. Especially nice about this version are the

Slavic setting, detailed costumes, and family warmth.
A Ladybird Book. Penguin Books, board, 4 colors, 4½" x 6¾", 56 pp., (3–4).

The Gingerbread Boy
retold by Vera Southgate, illus. by Robert Lumley
A good, simple retelling of the runaway gingerbread man and how the fox finally caught him. Lumley's very realistic paintings are just perfect for preschoolers.
A Ladybird Book. Penguin Books, board, 4 colors, 4½" x 6¾", 56 pp., (2–4).

Goldilocks and the Three Bears
retold by Vera Southgate, illus. by Eric Winter
Somewhat saccharine illustrations, but a fine, simple retelling of this old story.
A Ladybird Book. Penguin Books, board, 4 colors, 4½" x 6¾", 56 pp., (2–4).

The Little Red Hen/La Pequena Gallina Roja
adapted by Letty Williams, illus. by Herb Williams
An instructive and delightful, bilingual retelling of this story of the industrious red hen and her lazy friends, this time in a Spanish setting (complete with corn and tortillas).
Prentice-Hall, paperback, 3 colors, 7" x 9", 32 pp., (3–4).

The Little Red Hen and the Grains of Wheat
retold by Vera Southgate, illus. by Robert Lumley
Charmingly realistic (unclad) animals in an informatively detailed, old English farm village.
A Ladybird Book. Penguin Books, board, 4 colors, 4½" x 6¾", 56 pp., (2–4).

The Shoemaker and the Elves
by the Brothers Grimm, illus. by Adrienne Adams
Another lovely edition of this worthwhile tale of the poor shoemaker who wanted to thank the elves who helped him. Especially nice illustrations.
Charles Scribner's Sons, paperback, 4 colors, 7½" x 9", 32 pp., (3–4).

The Three Bears
by Paul Galdone
A truly mischievous Goldilocks and lively bears characterize this version.
Scholastic Book Services, paperback, 4 colors, 8" x 9", 32 pp., (2–4).

The Three Bears
by Feodor Rojankovsky
Rojankovsky's very furry bears and blush-cheeked Goldilocks are perfect.
A Little Golden Book. Golden Press, board, 4 colors, 6½" x 8", 24 pp., (2–4).

Winnie-the-Pooh and Peter Rabbit

The Winnie-the-Pooh stories by A. A. Milne and those of Peter Rabbit and company by Beatrix Potter are, in fact, not that well suited for reading to preschoolers. The Pooh stories, beloved by adults, are largely eventless, loving portrayals of psychologically befoibled people in stuffed animal form. They are very kind and quite funny, and any adult who doesn't recognize himself there in several disguises hasn't looked in the mirror lately. But on a concrete, blow-by-blow level they are dull; very little happens that is appreciable by the young child.

Nevertheless, kindness is the prized value in the Pooh books and Pooh is a literary friend. Thanks to his many faithful adult followers and, like it or not, to Walt Disney studios and Sears Roebuck—he is a very aggressive literary friend who will probably waddle into your child's life whether or not you invite him. Though unfaithfully embellished, the Disney Pooh films (which occasionally appear on TV) are hilariously funny to preschoolers and not harmful. Posters and stuffed animals based on the original art are available, as are Disney-based records, stuffed animals, sheets, pajamas, dishes, bedroom sets, and playclothes (Sears). There is something to be said for having a friend from a book. So you might want a Winnie-the-Pooh or two—just be prepared to abridge or wait a few years for the friendship to mature.

The Beatrix Potter stories are much more eventful and, of course, beautifully illustrated. They are very absorbing to preschoolers who identify almost too easily with the disobedient, naughty animal in awful, repercussive predicaments. And we would rather instill in our children the motive of being good for goodness' sake than for badness' sake. Nevertheless it's a fine thing to have some book-based friendships, and Beatrix Potter's many classic animal children are certainly easy for children to love. Her illustrations are among the first best and she knew so well how to tell a tale to a young child. Like Pooh, Peter Rabbit will very likely hop into your child's life with or without your help. Posters (see pages 159–60), stuffed animals, and dishes are available. But how to choose from among the 23 original Peter Rabbit books? Some are really unsuitable, but below is a list of 10 that seem best suited for reading to preschoolers.

Pooh's Library
by A. A. Milne, illus. by Ernest Shepherd
A boxed set of four volumes: *Winnie-the-Pooh, The House at Pooh Corner, When We Were Very Young* (poems), and *Now We Are Six* (poems).
E. P. Dutton & Co., hardcover, 1 color, (4).

A Treasury of Winnie-the-Pooh
by A. A. Milne, illus. by Ernest Shepherd
The same as the above set, but in paperback instead of hardcover.
Dell Publishing, paperback, 1 color, 4 vols., 5" x 7½", (4).

*The Tale of Peter Rabbit (x)
The Tale of Two Bad Mice
The Tale of Tom Kitten
The Tale of Jemima Puddle Duck
The Tale of Jeremy Fisher (x)
The Tale of Benjamin Bunny (x)

*The Tale of Mrs. Tiggy-Winkle (x)
The Tale of the Flopsy Bunnies
The Tale of Mrs. Tittlemouse
The Tale of Miss Moppet (x)
by Beatrix Potter
All from Frederick Warne, hardcover, 4 colors, approx. 64 pp., 4" x 5¼".
(x)-marked titles are available from Mulberry in paperback, 4 colors, 5¼" x 7¾", (2–4).

Anthologies

Except for the heavily illustrated Mother Goose and nursery tale books, anthologies are not a primary purchase for the preschool years. Preschoolers need pictures to help them understand the stories. Generally speaking, when a child is ready for fewer illustrations, a good collection such as *Little Pear* or *The Poppyseed Cakes* is better than a hodgepodge of pictureless picture-book tales (which are now too young for the child) and nursery tales with which he is already familiar. Most of the illustrated anthologies for preschoolers contain stupid stories by people who must think children are either stupid or already grown up. Nevertheless, there is a place for an anthology on the preschool level, if you wish, as a source of short stories for storytelling by memory or a glove compartment special for long car trips.

The Child Study Association storybooks seem to include the best anthologies specifically designed for young children. They each contain from 20 to 50 stories and poems well suited to the ken of the preschooler. Many are the texts from the best picture books (having the picture books themselves seems better). Most are contemporary stories of "everyday and familiar relevance." It is impossible to say which is best. You could buy any one with confidence in its quality. But go to the library first and see which one you like best.

Read to Me Again
illus. by Garry MacKenzie
T. Y. Crowell, hardcover, 1 color, 6½″ x 9″,
166 pp.

Read Me Another Story
illus. by Barbara Cooney
T. Y. Crowell, hardcover, 1 color, 6″ x 8½″,
184 pp.

Read Me More Stories
illus. by Barbara Cooney
T. Y. Crowell, hardcover, 1 color, 6″ x 8½″,
184 pp.

Read-To-Me Storybook
illus. by Lois Lenski
T. Y. Crowell, hardcover, 1 color, 5¾″ x 8¾″,
168 pp.
(All of the above were compiled by the Child Study Association of America.)

My First Big Storybook
selected by Richard Bamberger, translated from the German by James Thin, illus. by Emanuela Wallenta
A good inexpensive collection of usefully brief European (mostly folk) tales.
Penguin Books, paperback, 1 color, 5″ x 7¾″,
192 pp.

Four-Volume Treasury of Little Golden Books
This does not fit the description of the above anthologies. It includes 58 nearly complete Little Golden Books (full-color pictures included) of which a number are very worth while and not always available as single titles. Also included are some which could certainly be left out of any child's life. They are pleasant to use, and children enjoy choosing a story. But they are definitely an extra purchase—not to be bought instead of others, only along with. Especially valuable in this treasury is the volume called *Our Wonderful World,* which contains a number of the best first earth science books for young children in existence (see page 252 for these individual science titles).
Golden Press, board, 4 colors, 6½″ x 8″, 4 vols. in a cardboard case.

Special Paperback Sources

There are two sources for inexpensive paperback editions of excellent children's books otherwise available only in hardcover editions in American bookstores. One is the Children's Book Centre of London which carries the largest selection of children's books anywhere and publishes a newsletter and the booklet *Reading for Enjoyment with 2–5 Year Olds* listed above. They have many American titles for which paperback rights have been licensed to British publishers. Though some of these are not available for sale in the U.S., books that are available from the Centre are often sufficiently low in price to be less expensive, even with postage charges, than when purchased here. If you send $5.00 to the Children's Book Center Ltd., Mail Order Section, Little Mead, Alfold Road, Cranleigh, Surrey GU6 8NU, you will receive a credit token (toward the purchase of books), 4 issues of *Children's Book Newsletter* (Mar., June, Sept., Nov.), and a number of supplementary lists such as the Centre's *Right-From-the-Start Books, With Under 4s.* To make things easier for the U.S. buyer, order forms on recent publications from the Centre have postage-inclusive prices in dollars and cents.

In this country Scholastic Book Services has the largest list of children's paperbacks. Some are inexpensive editions of recent hardcover books; others are new reprints of old classics. All of the titles (more than 800) in Scholastic's Starline catalog are available to the general public through local bookstores or by direct mail from Scholastic. Besides its many wonderful paperbacks available to the general public, Scholastic also holds institutional (sometimes temporary) paperback rights to a number of the best modern American juveniles in existence. There are various types of purchasing memberships which schools can have with Scholastic. It is sometimes possible for an individual to arrange to buy books through such local school memberships. Scholastic's low prices are often even lower for schools and you may be able to get some excellent books otherwise only available in expensive hardcover editions. Contact your local schools to see what possibilities exist.

Books and Booklets on Books

None of these is more comprehensive than the present book in its listing or treatment of books specifically for children of preschool age, but all are different in premise and/or objectives. They are listed here for people who wish to supplement or seek alternatives to the booknotes herein.

The Black Experience in Children's Books
by Augusta Baker
An excellent, comprehensive, annotated bibliography of hardcover books through 1971 that show "the whole range of black life." 120 pp.
New York Public Library, 8 E. 40th St., New York, N.Y. 10016. 50¢.

A Book List for the Jewish Child
630 annotated books, divided into categories with age levels listed. Through 1972. 57 pp.
Jewish Book Council of the National Jewish Welfare Board, 15 E. 26th St., New York, N.Y. 10010. 75¢.

Books in Pre-School
Choosing and using books for preschoolers. One of the best pamphlets available. See especially the article on integrity in children's books. 48 pp.

National Association for the Education of Young Children, 1834 Connecticut Ave. N.W., Washington, D.C. 20009. $1.75.

Children's Books of the Year
An annually prepared listing of good children's books. 48 pp.
Child Study Association of America, 50 Madison Ave., New York, N.Y. 10010. $2.50.

Good and Inexpensive Books for Children
An annotated bibliography of inexpensive books for children throughout grade school. A most useful aspect of this publication is its bibliography of book-related publications for parents and teachers. 84 pp.
Association for Childhood Education International, 3615 Wisconsin Ave., N.W., Washington, D.C. 20016. $2.

Libros en Espagnol
An annotated bibliography of children's books in Spanish, organized according to age level and including some books for learning Spanish. Through 1971. 52 pp.
New York Public Library, 8 E. 40th St., New York, N.Y. 10016. 50¢.

Reading for Enjoyment with 2–5 Year Olds
by Elaine Moss
An enthusiastic bibliography of books for the youngest. Helpful comments on what is good about each book, and a wholesome emphasis on the importance of sharing books with our children. 32 pp.
Children's Booknews Ltd., 140 Kensington Church Street, London, W.8 4BN England. 50¢ (postage included).

Reading with Your Child Through Age 5
An annotated book list of about 250 books for preschoolers plus some introductory notes on their use. Through 1972. Prepared by the Children's Book Committee of the Child Study Association. 48 pp.
Child Study Press, 50 Madison Ave., New York, N.Y. 10010. $1.50 plus 35¢ for postage and handling.

Just as a blue, red, or white lotus grows in stagnant water, but rises clear and unpolluted out of it, a truth-finder grows up in the world but overcomes it, and is not soiled by it.

–Buddha in *The Dhammapada*, trans. by P. Lal

One word determines the whole world;
One sword pacifies heaven and earth.

–Lao Tzu in *The Gospel According to Zen*, ed. by Sohl and Carr

For the word of God is living and active, sharper than any two-edged sword, piercing to the division of soul and spirit, of joints and marrow, and discerning the thoughts and intentions of the heart.

–Paul, Hebrews 4:12

Truth is always truth
untruth always untruth
this is what matters, this is right desire.

–Buddha in *The Dhammapada*, trans. by P. Lal

You must understand that One exists who is without not only speech but mouth itself, who lacks eyes, the four elements and the six roots of perception [in Buddhism the mind is a sixth sense]. Yet none can call him a void, for it is he alone that brought your body and mind into being.

–Keizan in *Zen: Poems, Prayers, Sermons, Anecdotes, Interviews*, ed. and trans. by Stryk and Ikemoto

For as the rain and the snow come down from heaven, and return not thither but water the earth, making it bring forth and sprout, giving seed to the sower and bread to the eaters, so shall my word be that goes forth from my mouth; it shall not return to me empty, but it shall accomplish that which I purpose, and prosper in the thing for which I sent it.

–Isaiah 55:10, 11

Through faith we understand that the worlds were framed by the word of God, so that things which are seen were not made of the things which do appear.

–Paul, Hebrews 11:3

In the beginning was the word.

–John 1:1

Words do not matter; what matters is Dhamma.
What matters is action rightly performed,
after lust, hate, and folly are abandoned
with true knowledge and serene mind,
and complete detachment from the fruit of action.

–Buddha in *The Dhammapada*, trans. by P. Lal

What? No Books on Child-Rearing?

The best thing to read when trying to raise a child is the child. Maybe it is even more important that we learn to read ourselves. Most of the time when we try to read books that tell us how to deal with problems we get problems. Problems are very contagious. Look how easily our children catch them from us.

The trouble with most problem-solving books for parents is that they start with the idea that the child has a problem. Then they try to tell us how to fix the child, or else, after blaming the parent, they suggest how we can fix ourselves. It is better to think that there are no problems, only ignorant beliefs and their symptoms. We experience problems because we have certain beliefs that don't work. We try to make them work, but they don't because they are false. We are only ignorant. But we are not ignorant because we haven't read the right book; we are ignorant because we haven't discovered the right questions.

In the beginning our children don't have any problems. They simply reflect our ignorance, just as a thermometer registers a fever. There is nothing you can do to the thermometer that will change the illness. You can shake down the thermometer so that the fever doesn't show, but the fever itself is not affected. Likewise even if we can shake the symptoms of error out of our children (and sometimes some of us in frustration do literally shake our children into obedience), nothing will have happened—at least nothing constructive. The problem is not in the child any more than the sickness is in the thermometer.

When a man who has had a fever becomes healthy again, he can put a thermometer in his mouth and it will not register a fever any more, only health. That's how it is with our littlest children. If we become healthy, they will stop registering ill health as symptoms.

Now the interesting thing is that *we* don't *have* problems either. We are only ignorant of truth. Actually ignorance is a positive step for most of us. We have to move from the wrong ideas we are certain of (ignorance of ignorance) to knowing that we don't know (conscious ignorance—receptivity). Once that occurs, understanding comes rapidly, for there is nothing to interfere with it.

But we must not *blame* ourselves for not knowing or for having wrong beliefs which are reflected disharmoniously in our children. If we already knew all that we needed to know to raise our children harmoniously, we probably wouldn't be having children. Perhaps it would even be invalid for us to have children then. Children are children so they can become adults; parents are parents so

they can become understanding (which is the same as loving). Learning seems to be the point of it all.

Likewise we must not fear that we can wreck our children with what we don't know. The thermometer isn't sick just because somebody's fever is registered on it. Neither is the baby. As a matter of fact, until the child is about 2 years old, there seems to be a sort of grace period in which the symptoms of error disappear in the child the very instant the errors are corrected in the parents' thought. All this time the child is becoming more and more self-aware, and sooner or later he begins to take on the parents' errors in the form of his own mistaken beliefs. But even then, perhaps even more then, the crucial progress has to be made in the consciousness of the parent, and it is really a kind of condemnation and trespassing to think that the child must be fixed.

Our children need to be comforted, cared for, encouraged, trained, protected, instructed, reprimanded, forbidden, and prevented. But we must also have regard for them, for their right to be wrong or, more correctly, for their ability to learn to be right. Where their mistakes are not dangerous to themselves and do not impinge radically on the rights of others, we must allow them their freedom. We must respect their privacy as much as we must respect the privacy of a complete stranger, an adult with whom we have no family ties whatever. This isn't just being nice; anything else is a denial of truth and of the child as a truthful, competent being.

Sooner or later he must consciously seek truth as we are doing. When this time comes (rarely before adolescence), he must have confidence that truth is and that he can perceive it. If we are constantly fixing our children (in effect affixing error and lack *to* them), they will not have this confidence. Instead they will only think of themselves as needing to be fixed. Negatively, perhaps this is the meaning of so many young people turning to drugs these days, needing "a fix." More positively, perhaps it is the meaning of the following story:

The kingdom of heaven may be compared to a man who sowed good seed in his field; but while men were sleeping, his enemy came and sowed weeds among the wheat and went away. So when the plants came up and bore grain, then the weeds appeared also. And the servants of the householder came and said to him, "Sir, did you not sow good seed in your field? How then has it weeds?" He said to them, "An enemy has done this." The servants said to him, "Then do you want us to go and gather them?" But he said, "No, lest in gathering the weeds you root up the wheat along with them. Let both grow together until the harvest; and at harvest time I will tell the reapers, Gather the weeds first and bind them in bundles to be burned, but gather the wheat into my barn."

–Matthew 13:24–30

The field is each man's consciousness. The seeds are truthful, fruit-bearing ideas; the weeds false, hindering ones. We are all the sowers striving, servants sleeping, and reapers discerning. The enemy is ignorance passing for knowledge. The farmer is the One Mind. The harvest is the reunion of the individual mind with the One Mind in consciousness. For us "the time for the harvest is now." The time for our children is also always now, but that is their business, theirs and the farmer's. With regard to our children, as parents we must simply tend to the wheat.

Love

Love is not a sentiment or a feeling. It is not something we have to give or get from each other. It is not a fair trade. Love is a way of knowing, a mode of perceiving. Ultimately it is *the* way of knowing. Anything less than love is not knowledge; it is opinion or belief, and it is always mistaken. True love begins with the simple desire to be good. It proceeds with the conscious affirmation and discovery of goodness. It ends or is fulfilled in the realization that there is nothing but goodness and that there never was anything else in the first place. Love is the accurate perception of the truth of being.

Water (its properties of fluidity and buoyancy) is the truth about a wave. Everything else about it—its shape and size, its place in space, its duration in time, its force and speed —have nothing to do with the lasting truth of its being. Wetness (fluidity, buoyancy) is its only lasting characteristic. In its wetness it is one with all water. Dryness or firmness are the truth about an island. In its solidity it is one with all land. The islands appear to be floating but are really one with each other and with the land. On a superficial level the wave is separate and largely surrounded by air. But the underlying truth is that it is entirely supported by the water from which it came, of which it is made, and to which it returns. Even the iceberg, even an isolated drop of water vapor are yet one with the water. Wetness remains the true quality of water no matter what form it takes.

As wetness is to the wave, so consciousness is to man. Consciousness is the truth about man. It is his definitive characteristic to be aware or conscious. In consciousness he is one with all consciousness. Consciousness is awareness, the awareness of that which truly is.

As ideas, *baby, child, teenager* are all limited just as *wave* is a limited representation of the idea of water. They all imply incompleteness, weakness, dependency, *uncon*sciousness. But the truth of the child's being is whole. He cannot be half-true any more than water can be half-wet. Therefore, it can be said that perfect consciousness is the truth of the child's being. Everything else, anything less, no matter how convincing it seems at the moment, is transitory and untrue. Love perceives this distinction between the true and the untrue, thus allowing the untrue to fall away into nothingness.

In life the process of growing from babyhood to maturity is not a matter of acquiring consciousness or changing from baby to man. Rather it is a matter of revelation in which the already existing truth of the child is made manifest. It is a process of realization and revelation, a coming to light of what is already so. It is not a matter of the baby's becoming what she isn't or wasn't, but rather of becoming what she is.

How can this be so? Truth is what is. Is is now. Is is always now. Was isn't. Will be isn't. Only truth always is. Therefore anything that passes away is not truth. Only that which always is, is truth. All the things that define a baby as a baby pass away. Given a wholesome environment, all the weakness and limitation that characterize the baby will fall away. The only quality of the new baby that will remain is consciousness.

It could also be said that consciousness is the actual substance of the baby. Whatever passes away is insubstantial. Only that which endures is ultimately substantial. True substance is that which can be substantiated. Love is the perception of that which is substantial. Love is substantiating.

Often at the time of birth we are so preoccupied with bodies—the mother's big one, the baby's tiny, breathing one—that we do not stop to consider what is the most outstanding characteristic of the newborn baby. Look at his eyes. Evidently they are seeing next to nothing, and yet seeing-ness or alertness is what they express most of all. Clearly he knows next to nothing and yet there he is, *conscious, aware, alert*. He is above all interested in seeing—not judging, not liking or disliking—just seeing what is so.

This consciousness, the desire to be conscious, is his definition. Any mother thinking back to the first moments when she and her baby looked at each other can remember this consciousness. This looking and looking. This wide-awakeness. This quality is most memorable because it more than anything else is the truth of the child. As the wave is to water, the baby is to consciousness. He comes of it (conception), is made of it, and to it he returns. Only insofar as he becomes fully conscious does he become himself. Life, then, for each of us is a process of consciousness seeking to know itself as consciousness.

Of what possible earthly use is this? How does it help us to be good parents? How does it help us and our children to be happy? Isn't it just a speculative and useless philosophical gymnastic to say that the baby is perfect(ly conscious)? No. The full appreciation of this is the secret to beneficial parenthood. There is no more practical definition of love than to say that it is the realization of the truth of

being of the beloved. And this love is as rewarding for the one who loves as it is for the beloved.

There are two ways of seeing that this is so. The first way is the painful discovery that any other definition does not work. Love as an attitude, as a way of treating each other, as a feeling—all such definitions of love are based on an idea of twoness, good/bad, self/other. This puts love on a have and have-not basis, in which the gift of love always amounts to an experience of loss (in fact, theft) on the part of both the loving and the beloved. Between parent and child this kind of love is always tinged with anxiety, worry, frustration, weariness, and resentment on the part of the parent, and with insecurity, dependency, rebelliousness, and depression on the part of the child (just to name a few of the possibilities). For the implication is always that the child is *un*whole, *in*adequate, *un*safe, *in*capable, even bad. In this kind of love the beloved is always the belittled. And life as a context is cast as being equally *in*complete, *un*fulfilling, *im*perfect, and *un*reliable.

The second way to see effective love as the realization of the perfection of the beloved is to try it out. This seems difficult at first since it involves our knowing what we do not know, but it can nevertheless be tested through affirmation. In our thoughts (consciousness) we affirm that, and in life we proceed as if, the child is really perfect (consciousness) and everything else is a passing illusion. Of course we still deal with the signs of immaturity—ministering, caring, correcting, comforting, teaching, serving as needed—but we do not affix them to the child.

We consciously separate him—his true, perfect, conscious, whole self—from everything else that seems to be. Sincere and steadfast practice of this awareness cannot fail to translate what is otherwise a meddlesome, interfering, and trespassing counterfeit of love into an environment of letting be, in which the child is allowed to become what he truly is most effortlessly.

On the human level the benefits of just this little bit of vigilance ease immeasurably the lives of both parent and child. But the true benefit and the real transforming event occurs on a much higher level, and though vast improvements can be made in the meantime, true harmony cannot really come into our experience until it has occurred.

The child, after all, is not the only one who is maturing. We, too, are on the path of becoming what we truly are, that is, consciously conscious. Since consciousness is our true substance it is interesting to note that the word *substance* comes from the Latin meaning *under* and *to stand*, that is, to stand under or *understand*. We have said that love as the perception of that which is substantial is itself substantiating. To be loving is to be understanding. To be understanding is to be conscious. If the truth of the child's being is perfection (perfect consciousness) and we are successful in perceiving that this is so, then we have become conscious. In perceiving the true substance—the consciousness of the child—we become ourselves conscious, and thus realize, or substantiate, our own lives more fully.

This is the most fervently to be desired of all objectives. It is the goal of life. In the instant of perfect consciousness there is one-ness—the realization that there is only one mind, one self, and that it is all good.

Now the question arises as to what is so great about oneness? And how can we know that it will be (is) good? All experiences of evil are based upon some idea of conflict, hence upon some idea of twoness. Badness is thus twoness. Badness is always bad as *opposed to* something. Goodness then is oneness. Therefore, to be rid of badness one must realize oneness. To reach this point an assumption has to be made that this may be the case. We have to make some assumption of basic goodness (for we cannot yet conceive of oneness enough even to desire it) and then set out to validate it before we can see it to be so. This assumption may be made about self or other or life (God). It is not important which, since, in reality, all these are one.

For those with children, children are an easy starting point. For most of us God is altogether too doubtful, too unreal. It is too much to try to assume the goodness of something we doubt the existence of in the first place. And we are too much in hate with ourselves, too busy trying to make up personally for the fact that God probably isn't there, to begin with any right concept of self-goodness. But perhaps even for the wrong reasons it is a little easier to make this assumption of goodness about our children, at least at first. The point is that we want to be loving toward our children all the time, even and maybe especially in those moments when we are called upon to act or speak with authority. But genuine, steadfast, assured love is only possible when based on knowledge of goodness.

The baby is dirty all the time. We are constantly changing his diapers and wiping his bottom. And yet it is so easy to see that he is pure. All that defecating has nothing to do with him; he doesn't even know about it. And all that ignorance of the mess he is making doesn't have anything to do with him either; he will learn. We are not at all deceived by the mess into thinking that he is either impure or stupid. We have never seen such purity! No matter what he does to sheets, diapers, clothes, or our laps, purity remains to us an obvious characteristic of the child's true self.

This purity we see—that's truth! And the distinguishing we do between the purity and the mess, that's love! We deal with the mess twenty-four hours a day, but we do not allow it to become confused in our thoughts with the perfect picture we have of the child, hence, it does not interfere with love. It is very important here not to confuse the love with the diaper changing, just as we do not confuse the baby with the mess. Love is not the diaper changing or the fixing of meals or disciplining or whatever it is that we must do along the way. *Love is the sorting out in thought* of the perfect child from all suggestions to the contrary.

No matter how orderly and clean the parents may be, if they continuously include their child's waste products in their picture of the child, the child may become involved with his excrement too, perhaps smearing it or relieving himself in inappropriate places. Likewise the child who is held in thought to his errors will manifest them steadfastly. He cannot do otherwise. But a clear picture of the perfect child in the parent's consciousness, which sees (unsees) all imperfection as irrelevant to the child's true being, allows the child to develop truthfully with the speediest and most effortless falling away of all irrelevant behavior.

It is fairly easy with diapers because we more or less know what we have to do. But crying? Staying awake late? Hitting? Demanding? Whining? It seems so much harder then as we concern ourselves more and more with what to do instead of what it is that we need to know. But just as we can see purity right in the middle of the diaper mess, so also must we learn to see gentleness in the middle of the violence, innocence in the face of guile, perfection where imperfection seems to be, intelligence where there appears to be stupidity, goodness and the desire to be good right where there seems to be willful badness.

These qualities of purity, innocence, intelligence, gentleness, and goodness are true. Whenever we see them, we see God (good). When we find them in our children, we discover them in ourselves. When we see them clearly and discover them everywhere, we begin to see that they are true—not as personal virtues but as the truth of being. When we see that they are true, we are conscious. Now we are what we are, which is at one with all that truly is. When we are at one, all discord, effort, and conflict drop away, and instead there is only love. This love, this perfect consciousness is now all that we meet and all that we express, just as the water at one with all water expresses fluidity and buoyancy, the essential qualities of water.

There is a Zen story that tells of a student who could not understand Japanese. Therefore, instead of speaking with him, his master gave him a drawing to meditate on, that he might ultimately become enlightened as to the truth of being. The drawing consisted of a simple circle with a dot in the center. After a time the student brought the drawing back to the master. He had erased the dot. The master indicated that this was a good beginning but not enough. The student went away again. After still more time he returned, this time having erased the circle. He had become enlightened as to the truth of being. The dot stood for self. The circle represented others. He had discovered that there was only one mind. He had attained true selfhood.

In the Bible Jesus is quoted as saying, "Hear, O Israel, the Lord our God is one Lord; and thou shalt love the Lord thy God with all thy heart, and with all thy soul, and with all thy mind and with all thy strength. This is the first and great commandment, and the second is like unto it: thou shalt love thy neighbor as thyself." These two commandments are the same. The self that is loved in neighbor or child and the self that loves must ultimately be seen to be the one self. Otherwise love is not possible. There is nothing arbitrary about the first commandment and nothing sentimental about the second. They mean literally that there is one self and that there is no other reality and hence no alternative. It is not even really so much a commandment as it is a statement of what is so.

Of course the two stories are also the same. Both the story of the Zen student and Jesus' two-commandments-that-are-one tell us that to be conscious of one goodness (God, the One Mind) is necessary for man's redemption. These two stories also describe the path that most people take toward this realization. In the early days of parenthood, we try to erase the self to serve the other (the baby). This is good and we can all attest to the benefits of learning in some small measure to put someone else first. But it is not enough and, since it is also not really the truth, ultimately it becomes untenable (we become so tired; it doesn't seem fair). As Jesus' second commandment indicates, the true worth of both self and other has to be clearly seen. Or as the Zen story explains, both self and other as distinct (through imperfection and limitation) from the One Mind have to be erased.

Some people think that the erasing of the dot and the circle, of self and other, leaves nothing. That belief, that fear, is of course what makes it so hard. (Without our separateness—which is to say our limitation, our lack—will we be nothing?) But the erasing of self and other results only in the loss of twoness—that is of conflict, disharmony, lack, anxiety, loneliness, evil. It is not possible to be loving as a separate self any more than one wave can float a boat or, for that matter, even be a wave by itself. As Jesus taught, once self and other are erased (the second commandment), love, that is conscious at-onement with good (God), is left (the first commandment).

In the beginning was the Word, and the Word was with God, and the Word was God. All things were made by him and without him was not anything made that was made. In him was life; and the life was the light of men. And the light shineth in darkness; and the darkness comprehended it not . . . The true Light which lighteth every man cometh into the world. He was in the world, and the world was made by him, and the world knew him not. He came unto his own, and his own received him not. But as many as received him, to them gave he power to become the sons of God, even to them

that believe on his name; which were born not of
blood, nor of the will of the flesh, nor of the will of
man, but of God. And the Word was made flesh
and dwelt among us, and we beheld his glory, the
glory as of the only begotten of the Father, full of
grace and truth.

—John 1:1–14

Awareness of love is what erases the dot and the circle. It is thus important that our children discover love. The child's relationship with the world around her, with plants, animals, friends, siblings, parents is all part of her path toward the discovery of love and true selfhood. These are all aspects of love which serve as channels bringing love into her experience. But it is important to be aware that in none of these instances is relationship the objective. Relationship is two, and what we are after is at*one*ment. It is only in being at one with love that true self-realization, true individuality is attained. Accomplishment, having friends, knowing facts, growing things are nothing except for what they reveal that is of the spirit. As parents we must foster our children's discovery and appreciation of love as it is revealed. We must help them to value it, find it, and to express it everywhere, through qualities of helpfulness, kindness, respect, forgiveness, gratitude, and generosity. Gardening, caring for pets, playing with friends, and exploring the world in general are all activities in which love is the central issue. As outlined more fully on pp. 138–44 under discipline, the three basic ways in which we can help our children come to this realization are: silent knowing, exemplifying, and, least of all, teaching.

In the process of discovering love, our children will almost certainly come to believe in the existence of the dot and the circle. We can scarcely hope to spare them all the painful experiences of loss, argument, unkindness, loneliness, disrespect, and occasionally even injury that come with thus viewing life as a matter of self and other. However, we do not need to encourage falsely a personal, self/other view of life either. If only we remember that the key issue in any situation is truth, the perception and expression of love no matter what, it will be much easier for our children to let go of discordant experiences. If we are successful in seeing through ignorant behavior of our children and other children to the already perfect, idea(1) children, our sons and daughters will be less concerned with *establishing themselves* (in ours or anyone's sight, as equal to or better than others). In this way love unimpeded will more easily and obviously reach through to them as a fact of life rather than a wished-for dream.

To a certain extent we can help our children to consciously see love, rather than persons, as the true issue by simply encouraging them to see the significance of their experiences in the light of love. "Yes, it is happy to be helpful, isn't it! See how your baby sister is smiling now!" And a bad experience rightly understood can sometimes be even more revealing of love as a fact and a necessity than a good one. For example, when a child learns to let go of (forgive) another's unkindness, he may see the unkindness disappear, thus demonstrating that love is powerful. So we can heighten our children's awareness of love by pointing out the need, fact, and the joy of love wherever it is revealed.

Mostly, however, we must concentrate on silent discerning and knowing. For it's weeds and wheat again. Most likely the personal sense will arise along with the discovery of love. We cannot hope to root out the personal sense from these young ones without adding to their growing conviction that life is a matter of persons, a self/other struggle. Any attempts we make to deal directly with illusions of personal sense may foster a sense of personal insecurity in the child and only add to her impressions that reality in general and love in particular are interpersonal; that she is a person in need of persons (us most of all) or freedom from persons (us most of all) or triumph over persons (which is of course the straightforward manufacturing of oneself as an enemy) or a better personality (the mask that hides the perfect child even from herself). So the place to root out the weeds of personal sense is in our own thoughts. With our children we must only and strictly be concerned with sowing and tending the seeds of spiritual love so that at harvest time (maturity) their fruits will be the only obvious thing worth harvesting.

I planted the seed, Apollos watered, but God gave the increase.
I Corinthians 3:6

Oats, Peas, Beans, and Babies

Oats, peas, beans, and barley grows,
Oats, peas, beans, and barley grows.
Nor you, nor I, nor anyone knows
How oats, peas, beans, and barley grows.
–Traditional nursery rhyme

So goes the nursery rhyme and so grow the grains and so, too, grow children. It is written into the very nature of the oat, pea, bean, and barley to grow into fruitful plants. Nobody questions whether they want to do this or can. So why do we question the potential and motivation of our children?

The role of the farmer and the parent are similar. We do not cause seeds or children to grow—it is given to them to do that. We are rather tenders, fosterers of growing. When the farmer sows a nice, round, healthy oat and it doesn't grow well, he doesn't say, "What's the matter with this oat? It must be lazy or sick or emotionally disturbed in some way." He assumes that something is wrong with the environment in which he knows that oat is trying to grow. Then he sets about trying to perceive what is needed.

Parenthood is similar, although in two ways it's harder than farming. First of all, we have a less clear picture of what a healthy man or woman is than we do of a mature crop of oats. Secondly, the growing environment of the young child is not made up of soil and weather conditions; it's us—what we know, our consciousness. On this our perspective is not quite so panoramic and detached as the farmer's. But in one way our task is easier than farming, for, unlike the oat, the child is constantly telling us what he needs.

One of the finest activities we can do with our children is gardening. The activity of growing things is a prayer for the awareness of love that we and our children can participate in together. You begin by kneeling down and soon you will see love sprouting up all over the place. At 1½ or 2 years old a child can already begin to participate in, enjoy, and learn from numerous planting, transplanting, and tending experiments. It is not necessary to have a garden or even a window box. On any spring walk seedlings can be found pushing up last fall's leaves beneath the budding trees. Discovering these beautiful little sprouts under the soggy old brown leaves is a delight. Choose one or two promising ones and dig them up with a good clump of dirt. Take them home in an ice cream cup or a pair of careful, small, bare hands. At home they can be planted in small pots and watered from time to time. Be sure to pot them tightly, pressing down the soil firmly around the roots.

In autumn maple seeds, pine cones, and acorns can be harvested. The seeds can be planted indoors. Our most successful venture was with a seed from the honey locust tree. It grew nicely and each night its leaves folded up, each morning they opened. Such astonishing precision! Even indoors it had its autumn/spring cycle, complete with the falling and returning of leaves.

The important thing with both child and plant is not to insist on anything in particular happening. The object is simply to see what is revealed. Let the child help, but don't insist. It is good to keep in mind that growth of both the child and the plant is what is being fostered. If the plant appears to need water, you will give it water; if it appears too wet, you will refrain from watering it. Likewise, if the child appears interested, encourage him; if he becomes bored, let him move on to the next thing, and you carry on with the plant.

Again, let him help wherever he can and wants to, even if it's only in the finding of the sprout, the holding of it on the way home, the pressing down of the earth in the pot. From doing, his interest is sustained, and he learns a bit more dexterity. From watching the plant and listening to you, he gains botanical information. But he learns most of all from watching you. From this he begins to learn the nurturing point of view—the patient waiting, the faithful caring, the joyful appreciation of growth. The other name for this is love, which is, after all, what we are supposed to be learning, too.

Some Good Growing Projects

• Set an onion pointed side up in the top of a glass or jar of water. The bottom of the onion should just touch the water. In only a few days it will send roots down and soon after leaves up. It grows with almost visible speed!
• Cut the tops off a couple of carrots and beets and put the tops in a flat dish of water. A few pebbles will help to keep them in place. New leaves will grow like crazy. It's an interesting way to demonstrate that different leaves grow from different plants.
• Nasturtiums are very satisfying for little children to cultivate. The seeds are big and obvious for little fingers to push into the soil. They can be grown indoors if placed in a window with lots of sun. They take quite a while to bloom (over a month) but in the meanwhile they produce many pretty leaves. When the flowers do come, they are likely to be abundant. From 4 to 5 seeds you may have as many as 30 blossoms open at one time. Pick them and more will follow. Buy a package and just follow the directions on the package.
• Plant, tend, and harvest something edible

from seed—basil or carrots, for example. Carrots take rather a long time to grow—up to two weeks just for germination. But there is no hurry and as a revelation of the miracle of growth and fruition they are particularly wonderful for children. From the slow-growing seed so tiny and brown come the feathery green leaves up and at last the secret carrot down—to be tugged up all at once, so startlingly orange and crunchy.

For a quicker response, try sprouting alfalfa seeds in a small, covered dish. Soak in lukewarm water overnight in a dark place. Then drain off the water and rinse with fresh, lukewarm water through a tea strainer or piece of cheesecloth stretched over the dish. Continue to keep the dish covered and in a dark place, rinsing this way once or twice a day. In two or three days, when the seeds have sprouted and the seed leaves have opened, place the dish in a light window for a few hours to turn the leaves green. Then harvest —which means eat—raw as a post-nap snack, in a liverwurst sandwich, in a salad or soup. They really are delicious and reputed to be highly nutritious as well. The seeds can be bought in any health food store.

If you learn to appreciate sprouts and develop the habit of keeping some in process, you may want to buy a sprouter. There are many things to be sprouted and many kinds of sprouting devices for a variety of prices. These are also available in most health food stores and now in many department stores.

• Experiment with seeds from your child's plate—watermelon, apple, grapefruit, grape, squash, pear. Beans and corn grow with gratifying speed but must be dried hard first. As for technique, you can either green-thumb

your way hoping or do a little simple research at the library. Some seeds need wintering. A day or two in the freezer should be enough to fool Mother Nature.

• Gift-wrap a little package of ready-to-grow, paper-white narcissus bulbs for your own child or as a birthday gift for a playmate. It may be passed over for the moment but will soon prove itself a wonderful gift. Besides

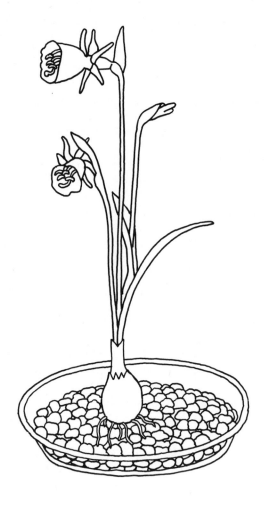

providing more fun, the gift wrapping says the truth so nicely—that the growing of a beautiful flower is a gift.

Place the bulbs on a bed of pebbles in a dish. Keep the pebbles in water up to the bottom of the bulbs. That's all! If possible, when the bulbs flower, keep them near the child's bed so he can enjoy their lovely scent in the darkness and their pure glory in the morning.

Child-size garden tools—If you do a fair amount of gardening yourself, a set of real child-size garden tools such as Creative Playthings offers is worth the investment. Your child will like to work along beside you or, with your help, to have a garden of his own. And the tools themselves will be useful to you from time to time for getting into small places. By teaching and example, help your child to learn the value of orderly maintenance of the tools as well. Give him a hook for his hoe and a hook for his rake and a hook for his spade, just as you have for your tools. □

If you aren't a gardener don't bother with such a costly set, as your child will develop a sustained interest in gardening only if you have one. Basically he still wants to be with you. For sandbox play and now-and-then gardening, lightweight plastic tools can be bought for about $1 in almost any big toy or department store in spring or summer. These generally fall apart after a while, but they are safer in the sandbox than real wood-and-metal ones, and they are fun and educational while they last.

Bamboo leaf rake—If you want to buy just one good yard-helper tool for your preschooler, a sized-down bamboo leaf rake is probably best. And it is certainly a handy auxiliary tool for raking between hedges.

Books to garden by

[*Note:* Numbers in parentheses indicate comprehension levels (not age) as outlined on pp. 7–9, 195, 197, 201, 207. Starred titles are those deemed superior for a preschoolers' home library. See pp. 6–7, 193–94 for additional information regarding book notations and selection.]

Best Word Book Ever
by Richard Scarry
This has a page that can break the ground of the really young preschooler on the subject of gardening and seeds. His *What Do People Do All Day* goes a bit further. See pages 184 and 252 for complete descriptions of these books.

The Carrot Seed
by Ruth Krauss, illus. by Crockett Johnson
A small boy plants a carrot seed. Everyone says it won't come up. But he is steadfast through days of watering and weeding and waiting, and despite all discouraging words, the carrot comes magnificently up. A whole wheelbarrowful of a carrot. It is no more complicated and no less marvelous than that. Scholastic Book Services, paperback, 2 colors, 6″ x 8″, 24 pp., (2).

How a Seed Grows
by Helene J. Jordan, illus. by Joseph Low
Good general background on what seeds are, followed by an interesting, see-for-yourself experiment with planting and studying seeds in an egg carton. Don't buy this book unless you plan to help your child do the experiment, since most of the book is devoted to this project. T. Y. Crowell, paperback, 1 and 3 colors, 8½″ x 8″, 40 pp., (3).

Indoor and Outdoor Gardening for Young People
by Cynthia and Alvin Koehler
Almost every publisher has a gardening book for children of elementary-school age. They are useful sources of interesting experiments, inspiration, and savoir-faire for the parents of preschoolers as well. This is a very helpful and inexpensive one. Grosset & Dunlap, spiral-bound board, 2 colors, 5¼″ x 8″, 64 pp.

The Story of Johnny Appleseed
by Aliki
Apple-appreciating youngsters are interested in this
story of Indians, pioneers, and a man who made a
helpful difference to his fellow men.
Prentice-Hall, paperback, 1 and 4 colors, 7″ x 9″,
32 pp., (4).

Once There Was a Tree
by Phyllis Busch, photos by Arline Strong
Much about trees as the constantly changing homes
of many plants and animals.
Scholastic Book Services, paperback, 1 color,
9¾″ x 8″, 48 pp., (4).

Pebbles and Pods
*by Goldie Taub Chernoff, illus. by Margaret
Hartelius*
Leaf prints, wood rubbings, and other things to
make from the findings of a walk outdoors.
Walker & Co., hardcover, 4 colors, 9″ x 7½″,
32 pp.

A Tree Is Nice
by Janice May Udry
A grateful book on the value of trees (shade,
shelter, beauty, climbing, fruit, etc.).
Harper & Row, hardcover, 1 and 4 colors,
6½″ x 11″ 36 pp., (3).

The Wonder Book of Flowers
by Cynthia Iliff Koehler
A surprising amount of information in a very little
book.
Grosset & Dunlap, board, 4 colors, 6¼″ x 7¾″,
24 pp., (4).

The Wonder Book of Trees
by Cynthia Iliff Koehler and Alvin Koehler
Again, quite a lot of information about trees and
their growth for a bargain price.
Grosset & Dunlap, board, 4 colors, 6¼″ x 7¾″,
24 pp., (4).

These books listed elsewhere in Whole
Child/Whole Parent, also include botanical
activities or information: *The Apple and the
Moth* (p. 239), *Three, Four, Open the Door*
(p. 73), *What Do People Do All Day?* (p.
252), and *What To Do When "There's Nothing to Do"* (p. 74).

Animals

One of the first reasons children are interested in animals is that they make (and make
us make) such interesting sounds. That's why
some very first animal books are listed back on
page 183 as books helpful in teaching children
how to talk. But of course, the child's interest
in animals is much more profound than that.
Some say children identify with animals as
underdogs. They are furry and some are small
and man has dominion over them. In theory at
least, the child has dominion over them, too.
So, the theory goes, the child for once feels
superior.

But there is still more to this matter. The
child seems to identify with the animal as a
fellow aliveness. Watch a baby the first time
he sees an animal—total delight, recognition,
almost a look of *I know you, we are the same.*
Unconsciously children seem to know themselves to be at one with that which is alert and
alive. They are thus existentially interested
in what animals can do, how they live, how
they treat each other. Perhaps the child's first
concern with animals is not so much an interest in others but rather in self-discovery. Can
a deer run so fast? Then to run is a possibility
for me. Can a bird fly? Then flying is a possibility for me. Can a beaver build such a dam?
Then such a dam and such a pond, perhaps
even better ones, can be built.

Love, or one-ness, is assumed until sooner
or later some information to the contrary
breaks in on the child. It may be a frightening
encounter with a big dog or the witnessing of

a fight between two animals. It always comes as news, to the child, and it is always a bit sad. *Can and do they fight and hurt each other? Must I? Would they hurt me? Must I be afraid? Must I hurt them?* Yes, it is sad to see. But it is not the end. *If I love them will they love me? Is love?*

This brings up the biggest issue with regard to man and animals: Which is true— love or fang and claw? the wrathful God or the loving? two or one?

Noah's Ark is often the first and sometimes even the only Bible story and exposure to the idea of God that young children are given. It is an impressive story easily misunderstood and worth giving a little attention to here.

The story of Noah and the flood is usually presented as a fang-and-claw story. Man and the animals were bad; *therefore* God killed most of them off, then felt sorry and started over. Even the people who wrote down the story thought God was wrathful. The God of this story is made in the image of man, just bigger and stronger. It is not possible to maintain such a view of God and transcend the law of fang and claw.

But this story can be viewed another way. In the beginning of the Bible we are told that God made man in his own image, to have dominion over the earth and the creatures of the earth. What is described is a state of harmony—not *dominance,* not man dominating the animals through superior power, but rather a state of being together in which love has *dominion.* In this state love is not the greater power; it is the only power. Man is not even really aware of it (which is perhaps the reason he loses it so easily in this story).

It is only when dualism occurs, when man separates himself from God into two, that the knowledge of good *and* evil and the need of *one* to dominate *the other* occurs. Only at this point does the idea of emnity between man and animals, or, for that matter, between animals and animals, occur. When man decides to be equal to God, to be "like God," he has set himself apart from or against God. Fang and claw, the need to dominate is part and parcel of this idea. It is not a matter of God punishing; it is only karma, the nature and fruit of dualistic belief, the need of one to have power over the other. The flood is simply an example of this universal belief expressed universally.

Noah, however, is depicted as a non-dual man of God—loving man, at-one. He is protected from experiencing the flood and violence through his at-onement with goodness. There is no logical possibility of violence in the idea of one. Instead of personal power (dominance), the power of love (dominion) governs and is expressed through him so that all two-ness is overcome. The animals who come on two by two are able to live peaceably *as one* under his roof, which is his consciousness of love's dominion. This is a perfect example of the power of love as knowledge.

So as our children encounter animals (and people with animals) love must remain the issue. Power is the dangerous, dualistic alternative. They will meet people and animals who reflect love and understanding; and they will see people and animals responding to each other out of fear and the desire to dominate. Love is the mode of being that is based on the idea of one; power is the mode of being based on the idea of two and it is always reflected in the desire to dominate and control and own (or in the fear of being dominated, controlled and owned). This is fang and claw, the hunting and circus motive which we do not hope for our children to learn. We do not hope for them to become interested in being killers; we do not want them to become interested in forcing animals to do stupid, undignified tricks. But we do hope for them to see love where it is revealed, to see the need for love where it is not revealed, to express love where it is welcomed, and to perceive in the long run that it is love, not fang and claw, that is the force which ultimately has dominion over the earth.

It is in this way that the story of Noah's ark can be used to enlighten rather than frighten the young child. Tell him that when people do not know how to be loving they are flooded with troubles. Then show him the power of love in the life of Noah—how all the animals that normally fight and eat each other were able to live together and be safe from the flood.

And the Spirit of the Lord shall rest upon him, the spirit of wisdom and understanding, the spirit of counsel and might, the spirit of knowledge and the fear of the Lord. And shall make him quick of understanding in the fear of the Lord. He shall not judge by what his eyes see, or decide by what his ears hear, but with righteousness shall he judge the poor, and decide with equity for the meek of the earth; and he shall smite the earth with the rod of his mouth, and with the breath of his lips shall he slay the wicked. Righteousness shall be the girdle of his waist, and faithfulness the girdle of his loins.

The wolf shall dwell with the lamb, and the leopard shall lie down with the kid; and the calf and the young lion and the fatling together; and a little child shall lead them. And the cow and the bear shall feed; their young shall lie down together; and the lion shall eat straw like the ox. The sucking child shall play on the hole of the asp, and the weaned child shall put his hand on the adder's den. They shall not hurt nor destroy on all my holy mountain; for the earth shall be full of the knowledge of the Lord, as the waters cover the sea.

–Isaiah 11:2–9

Pets

Oh, a hunting we will go.
And a hunting we will go.
We'll catch a fox
And put him in a box,
And then we'll let him go!

Preschoolers are too young to undertake the full responsibility of owning and caring for a pet alone. Neither is it feasible for any household to maintain on a permanent basis all the catchables and patables that capture the young child's interest. Nor, alas, can many creatures endure for long the tender, loving ignorance we inflict upon them.

But preschoolers are not very possessive. They are simply very interested in understanding and in expressing goodness. Temporary, brief visitations are a happy solution for everyone, and one of the best ways to help youngsters develop a reverence for life that includes both their innate desires to understand and to be good.

Initially, at least, the sometimes cruelty of young children is no more than ignorant interest, the desire to understand without the realization of painful, even fatal consequences for their subjects. However, if children are dominated and tyrannized (how tyrannical we are!) and thus do not perceive the reverent mode of being in the world, they will become interested in dominating and tyrannizing whatever they find that is weaker and smaller than they are. It is not as complicated as ven-

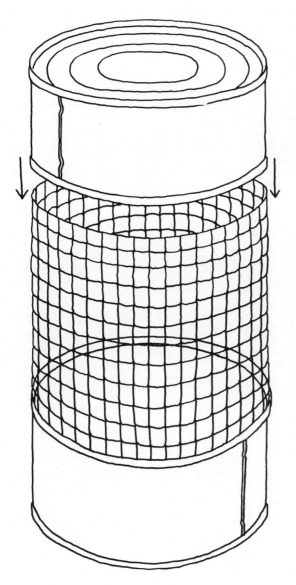

geance; it is simply that, knowing no other way, they will behave as we do. There is no substitute for *our* understanding what reverence is, for *our* knowing the difference between dominion and dominance; but catching, studying, caring for, and above all releasing to freedom various insects and small animals are ideal ways for us to share in discovering the difference between dominion and dominance. We can develop the quality of reverent awareness with our children.

In watching a captive creature, the true object of our attention is not the animal itself but the intelligence reflected in it. Watch the child for this intelligence, too. We perceive that intelligence governs each life, that intelligence has dominion. Likewise, guided by the same governing intelligence, we try to perceive how we can be beneficial, briefly through providing the captive creature with a suitable temporary environment and food, and ultimately through setting it free, releasing it to the care of the governing intelligence at large. A key emphasis should be on letting be. Letting be free, letting be so. Beautifully, the very young child (still so unpossessive of either property or power) will be spontaneously overjoyed with setting free almost more than with capturing. In these moments he, we, and the insect, or whatever it is, unite in relying on the fact of one, all beneficial intelligence. The child's joy is pure gratitude that what is so is so.

Fish tank—A well-balanced fish tank is something even a baby can appreciate. Vinyl ones are available for hanging over cribs, but they seem cruel and the fish do not survive in them for long. A 5- or 10-gallon tank outfitted with a light, air bubbler, and a filter system

Creature	In what?	How long?
caterpillar	in a jar with holes in the top, and inside a twig and fresh greenery sprinkled with water each day until the cocoon is built. Then keep some wet sand in the bottom of the jar for moisture.	until there is a butterfly—if possible release before the butterfly is ready to fly.
frog or fish or insect or any waterborn insects' eggs	gather with a jarful of the water in which you find them. From time to time scoop out a cupful of water and put in a cupful of new water from wherever you found them.	until they hatch—then release or else do a lot of research on what is needed by a growing, captive whatever-you-have.
fishlings	catch in a bath towel and keep in a jarful of their own lake, brook, or sea water. Baby fish are wonderfully transparent; significantly, they are little more than eyes with locomotive ability.	an hour of daylight.
fireflies	in a jar with a little greenery to perch on inside and holes in the top.	an hour of darkness.
ants (about 2 dozen from the same colony) the bigger the better	in a thin plastic box (with tiny holes made with a pin heated red hot on the stove) or a jar with an upside down jar inside (to make a narrow space so you can see tunnels). Fill with sand. Cover side with dark paper when you aren't looking so the ants won't be sneaky. Put in a drop or two of honey or syrup once or twice a week. If ants get through the holes (the advantage of having big ones), stand your ant house in a little bit of water; then they will go back through the holes.	if you don't catch a queen, release in about a week and a half.
any insect or animal you run into	in a jar with holes in the top or in a creature cage (see Steven Caney's *Toy Book,* page 73, illustration on p. 237)	just for a close look—see, she can fly! She needs more space to move around in.
a baby bird that has fallen out of its nest	nothing; just lift it gently off the ground and place it in a nearby tree just out of cat range.	only as long as it takes to put it in a tree. Now be very still and watch its parents come to it.

seems a good investment. It is especially nice if you can have a lighted tank in the child's bedroom where she can watch the fish in the dark at bedtime, free of other distractions. If you buy only goldfish (there are many fancy varieties), you will not need a heater. With gravel for the bottom, two or three weighted plants, a small everlasting supply of fishfood flakes, and a few fish (approximately 3 for a 5-gallon tank; 5 to 7 for a 10-gallon tank) the whole outfit should not cost more than $20. While the preschooler or even the young gradeschooler is not mature enough to be responsible for managing the feeding alone she will benefit most if she is included in the daily feeding (a pinch of about 5 or 6 flakes). Include a catfish among your fish and you will have a built-in sanitation department devouring most of the waste from the other fish. Watch how they swim perpetually, randomly, not in squares or in circles or straight back and forth within the confines of the tank, but as if freely, and never bumping into one another.

In him we live and move and have our being.
–Acts 17:28

Animal books

Some of the books listed below are a little too difficult for most preschoolers to listen to all at once with sustained interest. But when the toad is in the hand or the wog is in the jar— that's when a little extra information will be appreciated. Such books are also very useful for parents who wish to be ready when the questions come.

[*Note:* Numbers in parentheses indicate comprehension levels (not age) as outlined on pp. 7–9, 195, 197, 201, 207. Starred titles are those deemed superior for a preschoolers' home library. See pp. 6–7, 193–94 for additional information regarding book notations and selection.]

*All About Eggs
by Millicent Selsam, illus. by Helen Ludwig
The story of how all animals—chickens, fish, frogs, dogs, cows, *and* people—begin with eggs. On a preschool level this is one of the most helpful books around for answering the question of where did I come from.
Young Scott, hardcover, 1 and 3 colors, 6″ x 7½″, 72 pp., (3).

All Kinds of Babies
by Millicent Selsam, illus. by Symeon Shimin
A very simple, clear presentation of what various babies turn out to be and some of the different ways they grow up. Beautiful, muted pictures. Useful as a what's-the-name-of-this book for the very youngest and a first science book for sentence-comprehending children.
Sholastic Book Services, paperback, 1 and 2 colors, 9″ x 7½″, 40 pp., (2).

*The Apple and the Moth
by Iela and Enzo Mari
Beautifully simple illustrations relate the life cycle of a moth from the time it hatches as a tiny caterpillar in an apple to maturity. A picture book without words.
Pantheon Books, hardcover, 3 colors, 8½″ x 8¼″, 36 pp., (2–4).

American Animals
illus. by James Audubon
Small reproductions of 29 of Audubon's paintings of North American animals. Adequate, spare, factual text. Certainly a bargain opportunity to introduce children to the beautiful work of this artist and to more of the diversity of the animal world.
Grolier, paperback, 4 colors, 5″ x 7½″, 64 pp. (3–4).

Animal Dictionary
by Jane Werner Watson, illus. by Feodor Rojankovsky
Nearly 200 animals or animal details (e.g., horn, hoof, egg). A picture, the name, and a fact about each. Gives a pretty good picture of the vastness of the animal world. One-line captions don't say much, but they're good for starting a conversation.
A Little Golden Book. Golden Press, board, 4 colors, 6½″ x 8″, 24 pp., (3).

Animals Everywhere
by Ingri and Edgar d'Aulaire
Animals environmentally grouped and moodily illustrated—briefly where they live, what they do, and how they sound.
Doubleday & Co., paperback, 1 and 4 colors, 7″ x 9¼″, 32 pp., (3).

Animals in the Zoo
by Feodor Rojankovsky
An alphabet of 26 animals.
Knopf/Pantheon, paperback, 2 and 3 colors, 7″ x 9″, 32 pp., (1).

Animals of Warmer Lands
by Jean Wilson, illus. by Rien Poortvliet
Camel, elephant, giraffe, lion, monkey, tiger—a
small, individual paperback about each. 6 books in
a small slipcase. Very simple information and
dramatic illustrations in a format that is especially
appealing to children. This package is part of a
series of excellent little books imported from
England where they are used in the British infant
schools. (See other books in this series on this page
and on pp. 241 and 262.)
Addison-Wesley, paperback with light cardboard
slipcase, 4 colors, 4¾" x 5¾", 16 pp. ea., 6 books for
(2).

The Baby Animal ABC
by Robert Broomfield
Very charming illustrations of 26 animals and their
young.
Penguin Books, paperback, 4 colors, 7¾" x 5½",
32 pp., (1).

Bees
illus. by Tancy Baran
Some of the best first science lessons and the
pleasantest conversations between parent and child
can begin by speaking of the things on the table and
how they got there. This one is for speaking of
honey. A lot of information simply presented. (See
also *Milk* and *Eggs,* page 57.)
Grosset & Dunlap, board, 4 colors, 6¼" x 7⅞",
32 pp., (3).

Bees and Beelines
by Judy Hawes, illus. by Aliki
More difficult and more thorough than the preceding
book—for the very interested preschooler.
T. Y. Crowell, 1 and 2 colors, 8½" x 8",
40 pp., (4).

The Cat Book
by Jan Pfloog
All about Cindy the cat and how she cares for her
kittens.
A Golden Shape Book. Golden Press, paperback,
4 colors, approx. 8" x 8", 24 pp., (1).

*The Chicken and the Egg
by Iela and Enzo Mari
Beautifully simple illustrations relate the life cycle
of a chicken from the laying of an egg to maturity.
A picture book without words.
Pantheon Books, hardcover, 3 colors, 8¼" x 8¼",
36 pp., (2–4).

Creatures of Colder Lands
by Jean Wilson, illus. by Rien Poortvliet
Arctic fox, husky dog, penguin, polar bear, reindeer,
and seal—a small, individual paperback about each.
6 books in a slipcase. Excellent basic information
and dramatic pictures in a format children love.
A companion set to *Animals of Warmer Lands*
above.
Addison-Wesley, paperback with light cardboard
slipcase, 4 colors, 4¾" x 5¾", 16 pp. ea., (2).

Monsters—If a visit to a natural history
museum is planned, a book about dinosaurs
might prove useful. Perhaps the interesting
fact to be understood by the preschooler is
that these biggest, scariest-looking ones did
not last. The most monsterlike ones died out,
and only the meeker creatures endured. Monsters are interesting. They are big creatures
that are supposed to be able to control and
even possibly destroy us through size and
might and fright. This is clearly as much a
definition of us as struggling parents as of
any imaginary or historical animal. One little
boy even refers to his private monster as a
"mommit." It is an imaginary animal, of
course, for we only behave monstrously when
we imagine that life is a matter of two and
that harmony can only be effected by our
dominating our uncooperative children.

The best antidote to monster fears is the
parents' realization that love is the only power
and that nothing else ever need be "resorted
to." At such a point, of course, the monster is
gone and the monster fears with it. In the
meantime, dinosaurs provide us and our chil-

dren with an interesting illustration of the powerlessness of power.

Dinosaurs
illus. by Laurent Sauveur Sant
A simple introduction to what dinosaurs looked like.
Grosset & Dunlap, board, 4 colors, 6½" x 7⅞", 32 pp., (3).

Dinosaurs
by Jane Werner Watson, illus. by William de J. Rutherford
A little more thorough, and makes the point that dinosaurs are all gone.
A Little Golden Book. Golden Press, board, 4 colors, 6½" x 8", 24 pp., (3).
See also *My Visit to the Dinosaurs* below.

Do Baby Bears Sit in Chairs
by Ethel and Leonard Kessler
A very little bit for the very young child about what's the same and what's different in the lives of baby animals and children.
Doubleday & Co., paperback, 2 colors, 7" x 9¼", 32 pp., (2).

The Dog Book
by Jan Pfloog
Simply, there are many kinds of dogs (big, small, long-haired, short-haired, etc.).
A Golden Shape Book. Golden Press, 4 colors, approx. 8" x 8", 24 pp., (2).

Dolphins
by Mickie Compere, illus. by Irma Wilde
A bit more information than many preschoolers want, but all of it fascinating. For the interested, older preschooler.
Scholastic Book Services, paperback, 2 colors, 6" x 8", 48 pp., (4).

The Farm
by M. E. Gagg, illus. by C. F. Tunnicliffe
A lovely, small book about a beautiful farm-complex and all the animals there. Just right for beginners with books.
Penguin Books, board, 4½" x 6¾", 56 pp., (1).

Farmyard Animals
by Jean Wilson, illus. by Rien Poortvliet
Cow, cock and hen, goat, horse, pig, sheep—a small, individual paperback book about each. 6 books in a slipcase. Excellent basic information in a format children love. Another in the same series as *Animals of Warmer Lands* (see page 240).
Addison-Wesley, paperback with light cardboard slipcase, 4 colors, 4¾" x 5¾", 16 pp. ea., (2).

Five Hundred Animals from A to Z
by Joseph Davis, illus. by Tibor Gergely
500 animals are pictured in full color, each with an accompanying brief note describing some distinctive characteristic of the animal. Quite fascinating.
American Heritage, board, 4 colors, 9¼" x 11¾", 96 pp., (3).

How Animals Sleep
by Millicent Selsam, illus. by Ezra Jack Keats
For comfortably verbal preschoolers, this is a pleasant factual survey of the very different sleeping habits of 24 animals. You could read about one animal each night as a bonus on top of a bedtime story.
Scholastic Book Services, paperback, 2 colors, 6" x 8", 64 pp., (4).

How to Be an Animal Detective
by Millicent Selsam, illus. by Ezra Jack Keats
If circumstances provide your child with a lot of animal tracks to be curious about, this well-written book can help to heighten interest and awareness.
Scholastic Book Services, paperback, 2 colors, 7½" x 9", 48 pp., (4).

It's Nesting Time
by Roma Gans, illus. by Kazue Mizumura
Another useful book for the child whose interest in the subject is already awakened. Did she find a nest in the bush by the kitchen door? What nests are for, how and where they're made and by whom —so many kinds.
T. Y. Crowell, paperback, 1 and 4 colors, 8½" x 8", 40 pp., (4).

Jennifer's Walk
by Anne Carriere, illus. by Arthur Getz
A little girl takes a walk alone through the fields behind her home. She sees and hears and smells a

great many things and meets a number of animals. Though there is not much plot, children really listen to this simple tale of a child's awakening to the wonders of nature.
Golden Press, board, 4 colors, 9¼" x 12½", 32 pp., (3).

Koalas
by Bernice Kohn, illus. by Gail Haley
The story of koala bears, how they eat, sleep, and grow.
Prentice-Hall, paperback, 2 and 3 colors, 7" x 9", 32 pp., (4).

My Sea
by Hermann Fay
Lovely, full-color painting of individual marine animals. One to a page against a white background, each with a simple color frame around it and its name below in large letters.
Hubbard Press, board, 4 colors, 8¼" x 10¾", 40 pp.

My Visit to the Dinosaurs
by Aliki
A boy describes his visit to the dinosaur exhibit in a natural history museum. A good presentation of dinosaurs—what kinds there were, how they lived, and that they disappeared.
T. Y. Crowell, paperback, 2 and 3 colors, 8½" x 8", 40 pp., (3).

*My Zoo
by Hermann Fay
Beautiful full-color paintings of individual wild animals (one to a page) against a white background, each with a simple color frame around it and its name below in large letters. Reverent simplicity.
Hubbard Press, board, 4 colors, 8¼" x 10¾", 40 pp., (0–4).

Only One Ant
by Leonore Klein, illus. by Charles Robinson
If you saw an ant fall on its back and it couldn't turn over, what would you do? Well, what if it was a spider instead of an ant? Four children tell what they would do in a variety of circumstances and invite the listening child to speak up, too.
Scholastic Book Services, paperback, 2 colors, 8" x 9", 40 pp., (3).

*Our Animal Friends at Maple Hill Farm
by Alice and Martin Provensen
In this unique animal book the Provensen's own real farm animals come wonderfully alive as comic and lovable individuals.
Random House, board, 4 colors, 9¼" x 12½", 64 pp., (3, 4).

The Puppy Book
by Jan Pfloog
How puppies look and the ways they play.
A Golden Shape Book. Golden Press, board, 4 colors, approx. 8" x 8", 24 pp., (1).

Raccoons
by Bernice Kohn, illus. by John Hamberger
A pleasantly readable and informative book about raccoons.
Prentice-Hall, paperback, 1 and 4 colors, 7" x 9", 32 pp., (4).

Some of Us Walk, Some Fly, Some Swim
by Michael Frith
Though designed for beginning readers, this is perhaps even more useful with the beginning talker. (Readers, it would seem, are ready for more information). 246 weird and familiar animals, half-rhymed, pictured, and loosely classified according to what they do. Kooky. One child knew the names of all the animals in this book before the age of 2 just because they were so pleasant to say in rhyme. The book's biggest contribution to the preschooler is its presentation of the infinitely diverse ways there are to be a creature.
Random House, board, 4 colors, 8" x 11", 72 pp., (2).

What I Like about Toads
by Judy Hawes, illus. by James and Ruth McCrea
Fascinating and very thorough, for the very verbal child who just caught one. (See also *Toad*, by Anne Rockwell, page 209.)
T. Y. Crowell, paperback, 1 and 3 colors, 8½" x 8", 40 pp., (4).

What's Inside?
by May Garelick, photos by Rena Jakobsen
Tap by tap, the hatching out of a—could it be a chicken? Then maybe a . . . ? (It's a gosling.)
Scholastic Book Services, paperback, 2 colors, 9" x 7½", 40 pp., (2).

Wild Animals and Their Babies
by Jan Pfloog
Lovely, big paintings of 32 wild animals and their
young in their natural surroundings.
Golden Press, board, 4 colors, 10¼" x 11¾",
72 pp., (1–3).

Wild Animals from Alligator to Zebra
by Arthur Singer
Detailed colored pencil drawings of about 75
animals. Brief, factual captions with about a third
of the pictures.
Random House, paperback, 4 colors, 8" x 8",
32 pp., (2–3).

The Zoo
by M. E. Gagg, illus. by Barry Driscoll
Realistic paintings of animals in the zoo with an
excellent, simple question/answer text for the very
youngest children.
A Ladybird Book. Penguin Books, board,
4 colors, 4½" x 6¾", 56 pp., (1).

So many of these animal habit and habitat
books, especially when boiled down to such
simple presentations, are startling revelations
of the fact of intelligence at large. It is wonderful to notice and so good to point out to
the child that (and how meticulously) it is
given to these animals to know what marvel-
ously to do. Don't belittle this intelligence by
calling it instinct; we do not need to conde-
scend. Don't attribute it to the hidden genius
of the creatures themselves; that is not only
a fantasy, it also conceals its relevance to the
child's existence. The intelligence is there
providing the needed idea and the needed
skill at the right moment. Share in the marvel
of it and let its significance live in the child
as a sense of security and confidence and sufficiency.

A little light is going by,
Is going up to see the sky,
A little light with wings.

I never could have thought of it,
To have a little bug all lit
And made to go on wings.
–Elizabeth Madox Roberts, *Firefly*

Exploring the World

If it is remembered that love and the knowledge of goodness are inseparable, it is easy to
see that the child's interest in science is one
more aspect of his quest for love, not love as
a feeling or a commodity or an attitude, but
as a discernible and reliable fact of life. He is
supremely interested in how it all is—this life
around him and all these goings on. He would
like to know that life is a loving circumstance
in which to be. The evidence, as everyone is
eager to point out, is conflicting and even
contrary. So you can't just jump in and say
that life is filled with love. That would certainly be misleading, and someone might even
question your sanity if you said it too loudly.
But it is equally false to stop with the evidence to the contrary. What we can do is to
foster our children's natural interest in truth
along with their desire for love. The two mo-
tivate each other just as love and truth are
aspects of one reality.

So our first concern in the study of the
world around us is not the gaining of information, but rather the discovering that truth is,
and that it is perceivable. And that, hence, we
are perceiving, truthful beings—of truth and
not apart from it. The important thing to see
is that there is order and intelligence and that
every event or phenomenon and even the self
itself signifies or expresses some aspect of

this intelligence when perceived aright. This is the one sure premise upon which the discovery of love can be based.

O Shiva, what is your reality?
What is this wonder-filled universe?
What constitutes seed?
Who centers the universal wheel?
What is this life beyond form pervading forms?
How may we enter it fully, above space and time,
    names, and descriptions?
Let my doubts be cleared!

–*Zen Flesh, Zen Bones,* compiled by Paul Reps

In fostering the child's scientific awareness, we are not only helping him to become equipped with skills and knowledge for living in the world. More importantly we are helping him to develop his sense that truth is and that he, as an understanding being, is part of it. This realization, more than anything else, can help him to transcend the troubles of this world. As with anything else, the child's initial interest is spontaneous and existentially valid. His unconscious but rightful motive for wanting to know what is so is the desire to be reunited—with the One Mind through awareness; with goodness through the awareness of good; with love—the awareness that love is. It is his nature (and ours) to be drawn toward this reunion. Each revelation that truth is pleases him because it underscores his secret yearning and hunch that he belongs or is at one with what is.

The details of how things work are not so important as the revelation of the fact that they do work according to certain laws, that is, according to what is so, this One Mind. The so-called facts of how things work are constantly being proved wrong and revised in the light of new understandings. Facts are replaced by physical principles, physical principles are replaced by spiritual ones. Insofar as we foster the valuing of facts, of acquired information or knowing a lot, we are chaining our children to the idea of having a personal mind and thus driving them apart from the one mind. If knowing a lot is important, learning becomes impossible; what is already known must be clung to even if it is erroneous. In this way understanding cannot occur since the child is placed constantly in the position of having to prove himself as a knower, knowing more or better than others. In the end this renders the experience of love and true friendliness impossible since the child is constantly pitting himself against those who would otherwise be his friends.

On the other hand, if we foster the valuing of truth as the central concern, we make it easier for our children to remain open to new understanding. On a worldly plane this improves their effectiveness as performers or scientists or whatever they attempt, since new discoveries can be made only by those whose appreciation of the value and possibility of truth allows them to relinquish old facts in the light of new revelation. At the same time their position in life is secured; their selfhood is defined in the light of truth instead of in contrast to others whom they must constantly best to feel secure.

But most important of all, by maintaining truth as the central concern we leave open the possibility of our children continuing to assume and ultimately discover for certain that life is harmoniously ordered in favor of good. Only when life is thus discerned as being basically intelligent, is it possible to discover that love, love-intelligence, is its underlying force and nature.

Our main parental role in our children's explorations is simply not interfering. We must provide them with materials for learning and opportunities that inspire, but more often than not our prime task is to get out of the way and allow the learning to take place. This letting be is the best testimony we can offer to the fact that truth is and that the child as an understander is part of it. In thought and, *when called for,* also in word and action we must continue to perceive our children as beholding and understanding individuals rather than as doers and knowers. If we realize that the most important objective for our children is not to know things, but rather to develop their faculties of perceiving, we will be better guided in what to say, do, and provide that will foster learning. We will be less inclined to correct wrong answers and to interfere, or to do over what the child's unskilled hands can do only awkwardly. And we will be able to appreciate with genuine joy the discovery of principle, rather than the acquisition of fact.

Along the way it is more than likely that our children will become concerned with possessing information, doing better or worse than others, and being right rather than understanding more clearly. They cannot live in this world and go through our schools, play with neighboring children, and have us for parents without being touched to some extent by these values and experiencing the accompanying disappointments, frustrations, and discouragements. We cannot entirely prevent this, nor should we try too hard to correct it, but neither must we abandon our children there. Most attempts to contradict or root out these concerns only exaggerate their importance and make our children insecure. Such efforts belie our conviction that truth and our children are one.

Instead of	*It will occur to us to say*
That is very good (or bad).	It doesn't work very well that way.
You are very good (very bad).	Now you can see that thus and such is so. (E.g., Glasses break when they fall on the hard floor.)
Oh, what a stupid (smart) child you are.	You have discovered . . . or, Isn't it wonderful, this shows us . . . or, What good pouring! or, That pouring was a little unsteady; perhaps it would be easier with two hands.
Don't (do) you know how to do that yet (already)?	You are learning. That was only a mistake. (See how smoothly it goes!)
Oh, what a lot you know! (You can say the whole alphabet!)	How wonderful! (The whole alphabet! That is the beginning of learning to read!) I see that you are finding out . . .
You can't (can) do that very well.	It is still a little difficult to manage such a . . . It's getting easier and easier to . . .
What a lucky girl you are!	Isn't it wonderful to see that such a thing can happen!

By offering comforting dismissals, we can help our children to let go of their disappointments and false concerns to a certain extent. But mostly our help is a matter of standing by, sowing and watering the good seed, revealing with our every breath that truth is all that is important. As our children grow and the good seed bears fruit, everything else will be exposed as valueless weeds. Secure in their ability to perceive, our children, once grown, will distinguish easily between the weeds to be burned and the fruitful harvest.

In allowing this process to occur without interference from us, we will see for ourselves that it works. This way we come nearer and nearer to the realization that what we are staking our lives and the lives of our children on is indeed so. In the meantime if it seems hard at any point, just consider what the alternatives are. In truth this is the only easy way.

A child less than 2 years old went for a winter walk in a carrier on his father's back. Somewhere along the way the father made for the child his first snowball. So beautiful it was, scooped clean and white from beneath the surface and molded gently into a perfectly round, firm ball that just fit into the child's cupped and mittened hands. On the way home he fell asleep on his father's back and still clinging to the snowball. The father tried to remove the snowball, but the child woke up and cried. So they brought the snowball inside, put it in the freezer, and the child finished his nap. That evening, when the child was having his bath, the parents brought him his snowball. "It will melt," they explained. "Put it in the water and watch it melt. Snow is made of water. In the warm water the snow will become water again." He was not sad when his snowball went away. He was amazed.

It's hard to say what's science and what's not for preschool children. If nothing else, preschoolers are certainly physical scientists. How does it feel? How does it taste? What does it smell like and sound like and do? Where did it come from? Where will it go? How did it happen? How does it work and what happens next? Everything they do, every mess they make, every toy they break, every tumble and every stumble is for science' sake. So the question isn't what's a good scientific toy or activity for a preschooler. What isn't? What is needed is just a certain amount of scientific license and some enlightened appreciation on the part of the parent that science is what's going on. The cracking of an egg, the peeling of an apple are scientific revelations! Let the child play once with the peels, crack one egg and then crumble the shells, and squash a few round green peas with a fingertip. It is a little hard to get started because we don't remember so well that we once *learned* what we now know. But in the moments when we realize that science is what is happening, it is a happy and easy thing to jump in and find out more with our children.

A Hodgepodge of Science Activities

Science-related toys and activities have already been listed under other headings, but here are a few more for inspiration.

Magnets—Try all the experiments in *Mickey's Magnet* (see below for a full description of this book). Tie a small magnet to a piece of thread and the thread to a stick. With your child cut out some fish from colored paper and draw eyes on them (or stripes, or anything). While he colors in a paper-plate pond, put a small paper clip on the nose of each fish. Put the fish in the pond on the floor and let the child fish from the bridge (on her knees, over the back of a chair). If the magnet is too strong, all the fish will jump up out of the "water" all at once—no fun. A small magnet, such as one pried out of a magnetic letter, is much more challenging.

Buy a good strong horseshoe magnet and let her experiment with it. Set up a tray with three dishes on it: one containing a mixture of magnetic and unmagnetic things, two empty ones for sorting the magnetic from the unmagnetic. Show her the "magic" trick of driving some magnetic object all around a metal tray or piece of paper by moving it with a hidden magnet below. □

Sparkler—A mechanical sparkler is one of the best cheap toys around. The friction-produced sparks are fascinating and so is the mechanism that makes the wheel go around to make the sparks. If you look at the sparks

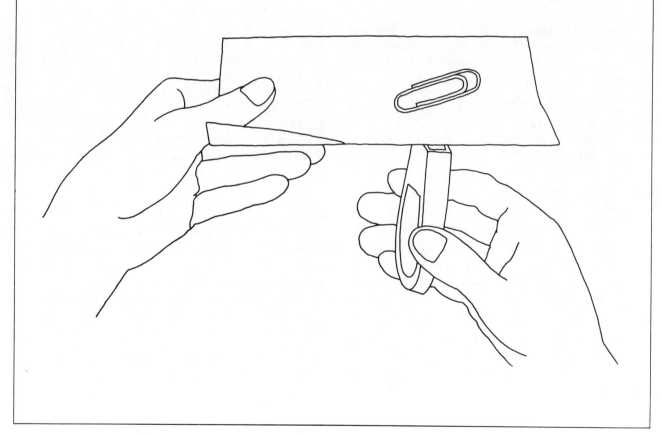

through the red and blue transparent windows on the wheel they appear to be violet, but if you look behind they are still yellow. Less than $1 in almost any novelty or toy store.

Measuring—In the kitchen or bath, experiment with pouring water or rice into different sizes of containers. Just pouring is a pleasing activity to the very young child (a year or more), and if the containers are transparent, you can help your child make interesting observations about how the same amount of water looks different in different containers.

Pulley—If she doesn't discover it herself, she will be fascinated at some point by the fact that a heavy object tied to a string can go up easily when she pulls down on the string if the string goes over something (e.g., a doorknob) on the way.

Mixing paints—Blue and yellow make green. Red and yellow make orange. Red and blue make violet. Everything makes mud.

Cooking—He can do some stirring, pouring, and kneading while learning that some things thicken, some rise, some jell, and some melt. Within the limits of your understanding, explain what he can understand.

Rock candy—Follow the recipe for rock sugar crystals in the revised edition of *The Joy of Cooking*, using disposable cake or loaf pans to make them in. For a quicker crystal experiment using a variety of household chemicals see *Three, Four, Open the Door* (page 73). This book has an excellent section on simple science.

Freezing and melting—Make juice or Koolade pops in an ice-cube tray (stick toothpicks in when the freezing has begun). Drop an ice cube in warm water. Put a warm hand on a frosty window.

Balancing scales—Hours of pleasure with weight and measure. Take a straight dowel or stick and put eye hooks at either end and one as close to the center as you can determine (balance the stick on the edge of a knife blade and mark it). Suspend a margarine cup from the eye hooks at each end. Fold the tips of a sturdy, wire coat hanger toward each other to make a V-shaped base. Pull the center of the coat hanger up to a good height and angle, and bend the hook back. Slide the center eye hook of the scale over the coat-hanger hook.

Magnifying—A small pocket magnifying glass or a glass of water or a big, standing magnifying lens. □

Candle—Don't touch, but see—the flame goes up no matter what; it needs air. (Water douses it, a snuffer suffocates it, you can blow it out.) Fire can melt some things, burn some things, give warmth and light, cook, hurt, change colors.

Electricity—Wire and tape the exposed end of a piece of insulated copper wire to a flashlight bulb. Tape the exposed tip of the other end of the wire to the base of the battery. When the child touches the bottom of the bulb to the tip of the battery, it will light. Just a simple rig like this can be given as a gift, a wonderful gift, to a small child. More elaborately you can make a switchboard. Purchase 3 different switches (e.g., toggle, turning and pushbutton), 2 or more D-cell flashlight batteries and battery mounts. Mount on any suitable piece of wood in any desired arrangement using lightweight, insulated single-strand wire. Wire the board in circuits, as shown, starting at one end of the battery

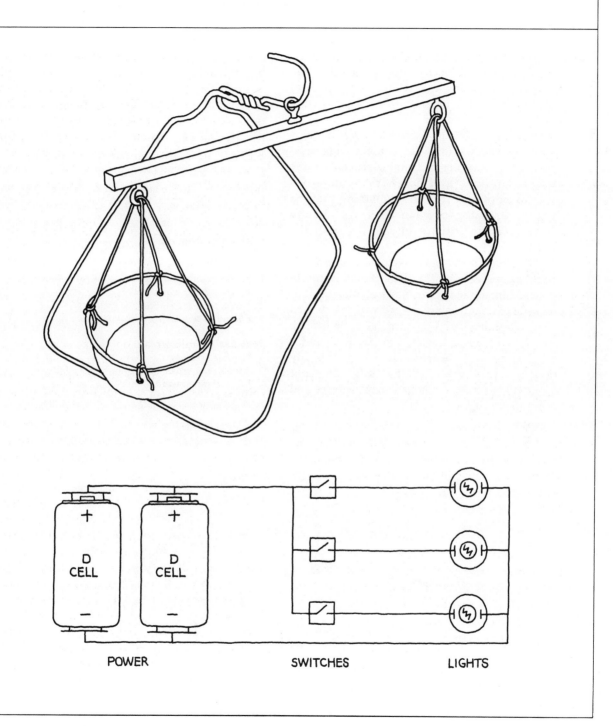

POWER   SWITCHES   LIGHTS

mounts and, after running through the switches and bulbs, returning to the other end of the battery mounts. Place the batteries parallel in the mounts so that like ends are connected to each other.

Telephone—From Steven Caney's *Toy Book* comes this idea for a homemade telephone of 4-inch plastic funnels stuck into the ends of any length of hose. It's an improvement over the old tin-can-and-string method because the hose can touch things and go around corners without interfering with the sound.

Play-Doh Fun Factory—As an art toy this seems offensively mechanical, but it is really an excellent science toy. Made of plastic, it is a simple extruder, a press with various-shaped holes through which play dough can be forced. Useful starting somewhere between 2 and 3 years of age. Do restrict the use of this toy intelligently so that the play dough does not get stuck on shoes, tracked everywhere, and ground into rugs. □

Air isn't nothing—You can blow up a paper bag with it, or a balloon. Put out a candle by depriving it of air. Try to hold your breath. Blow bubbles under water. Moving air cools things, and dries things, and moves things and can help things to fly. Fly a kite. Sail a boat. Blow up a bunch of balloons (long ones for bats, short ones for balls) and see how light and easy to keep aloft they are. (And by the way if you want to help your child learn to catch a ball have her practice with a balloon.) □

Who has seen the wind?
  Neither I nor you;
But when the leaves hang trembling,
  The wind is passing through.

Who has seen the wind?
  Neither you nor I;
But when the trees bow down their heads,
  The wind is passing by.

–Christina Rossetti, *Who Has Seen the Wind?*

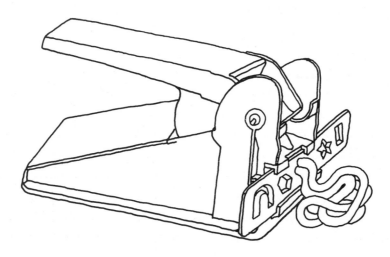

When helping our children with their scientific discoveries, we are often asked the question of why? It is fine to answer these questions, and we must, but they are not of ultimate importance. While answering why, ask what the meaning is. What does it mean that we can see the work of the wind but never the wind at all?

The wind bloweth where it listeth, and thou hearest the sound thereof, but canst not tell whence it cometh, and whither it goeth; so is everyone that is born of the Spirit.

–John 3:8

Ball—Certainly somewhere in this book there ought to be mention of this most basic of all toys for all ages of children. This is as good a place as any. The rolling, the bouncing, the arcing, and the weight-bearing capabilities of a rubber ball—they are all fascinating to children. Then there's the ball bearing!

Flashlight—Would you like to see a child's face light up? Give him a flashlight. A 2-year-old was "helping" by holding a flashlight while his father did some work on a semi-dark corner of the house. "Okay," the father called, "would you please come back and give me a little light now?" The child ran happily to his father's side, shook the flashlight like a salt shaker or a watering can over the corner and then ran off to play, clearly believing that the light he had sprinkled would continue to enable his father to see. On a spiritual level, how like the child we are, flicking little bits of love, little partial understandings, at dark corners and then being bewildered and disappointed at the lingering darkness. Will the child learn about light? Then surely we can learn to see the light, to be enlightened.

Science books

[*Note:* Numbers in parentheses indicate comprehension levels (not age) as outlined on pp. 7–9, 195, 197, 201, 207. Starred titles are those deemed superior for a preschoolers' home library. See pp. 6–7, 193–94 for additional information regarding book notations and selection.]

ABC Science Experiments
by Harry Milgrom, illus. by Donald Crews
26 very easy science experiments that are also very easy to set up. "Put an ice cube in a dish. Let it stand for a while. What happens to the ice?" Perhaps the best thing this little book does is to enhance the awareness of both children and parents of the scientific possibilities of almost everything. Short additional remarks at the back of the book help the parents to gain a fuller understanding of the significance of each experiment to be shared with the child in response to his questions.
Collier, paperback, 3 colors, 7½" x 9", 32 pp., 95¢

* The Brook
by Carol and Donald Carrick
The story of a brook from mountain spring to lake. Meticulous, beautiful, poetic word choice and impressionistic watercolors.
Macmillan, hardcover, 3 colors, 7¾" x 10", 40 pp., (3–4).

Gravity and the Astronauts
by Mae Freeman, illus. by Beatrice Darwin
Explains what gravity is by contrasting the astronauts' experience of weightlessness in space with what happens to "you" on earth. Clear and interesting.
Scholastic Book Services, paperback, 9" x 7½", 32 pp., (4).

Mickey's Magnet
by Franklyn M. Branley and Eleanor K. Vaughan, illus. by Crockett Johnson
The story of a small boy's discoveries with a magnet, including how to make one. A small magnet is included with the book.
Scholastic Book Services, paperback, 2 colors, 6" x 8", 48 pp., (3).

* The Pond
by Carol and Donald Carrick
A day in the life of a pond—many of its creatures and moods. The haiku-like text is not easy but so beautiful and precise as to inspire attentiveness. Gentle, dramatic, and appreciative.
Macmillan, hardcover, 3 colors, 7¾" x 10", 40 pp., (3–4).

Rain
illus. by Michael Ricketts
A wonderfully simple survey of the subject of rain for very young children— drops, drains, umbrellas, rainbows, plants, brooks, deserts, clouds, thunder and lightning.
Grosset & Dunlap, board, 4 colors, 6¼" x 7¾", 32 pp., (2).

Richard Scarry's Great Big Air Book
by Richard Scarry
Many silly stories on the subject of air and what it is and does in the lives of Scarry's busy animal people. A bit up in the air itself, this book is nevertheless a useful and pleasant introduction to a vast subject.
Random House, board, 4 colors, 9¼" x 12½", 72 pp., (3).

The Sunlit Sea
by Augusta Goldin, illus. by Paul Galdone
A sound introduction to the vastly busy life beneath the seemingly tranquil sea.
T. Y. Crowell, paperback, 1 and 3 colors, 8½" x 8", 40 pp., (3).

* Swamp Spring
by Carol and Donald Carrick
The coming of spring to a swamp. Beautifully distilled in vivid haiku-like poetic text and lovely watercolors. Appreciative and reverent.
Macmillan, hardcover, 3 colors, 7¾" x 10", 40 pp., (3–4).

Telephones
illus. by Christine Sharr
Another suitably simple introduction to a subject of great interest to young children. Just a little bit about wires, cables, and exotic phones such as video and deep-sea telephones. Ends with instructions for making a tin-can telephone.
Grosset & Dunlap, board, 4 colors, 6¼" x 7¾", 32 pp., (3).

What Makes a Shadow?
by Clyde Robert Bulla, illus. by Adrienne Adams
A quite thorough elementary exploration of the idea of light through the subject of shadows. Includes some shadow plays and a good explanation of day and night.
Scholastic Book Service, paperback, 3 colors, 8½" x 8", 40 pp., (4).

*What Do People Do All Day
by Richard Scarry
As usual for Scarry this book is brimful of hundreds of little animals in people guise. But it is less useful as a book about people (alas, Scarry's women never do anything but clean house and help doctors) than as a scientific book about the world. For this it is unmatched. Its coverage of such topics as coal mining, wood, waterworks, electricity, how and where clothes come from makes it invaluable and totally fascinating to preschoolers. Work around the sexism; every child should have a book like this to grow on.
Random House, board, 4 colors, 9¼" x 12½", 96 pp., (2 up).

* Where Everyday Things Come From
by Aldren Watson
Besides such things as cotton and bread, this excellent book includes some of the really hard ones such as plastic, chocolate, and paint. Like Scarry, Watson employs animal "people," but his illustrations are bigger and fewer, and the text more concise and to the point. Each approach has its own advantages.
Platt and Munk, board, 4 colors, 10" x 12", 96 pp., (3).

The Wonderful Looking-through Glass
by Mae Freeman
Experiments with a magnifying glass. A small, plastic magnifying glass is included with the book.
Scholastic Book Service, paperback, 1 color, 6" x 8", 32 pp., (3).

Golden Press has the best collection of suitable books on physical science for children under three. We didn't see anything at any price as good for 2- and 3-year-olds as the three books starred below. The fact that they are in full color makes a tremendous difference. Unfortunately, at this writing none of these Little Golden Books is in print. Perhaps they will become individually available again. Otherwise, you might consider purchasing the *Four Volume Treasury of Little Golden Books* (see p. 217) which includes them all.

*The Deep Blue Sea
by Bertha Morris Parker and Kathleen Daly, illus. by Tibor Gergely
Superb summary of the depth and width and busyness of the sea—everything from plankton to whales, from deep-sea mountains to sailing and gathering salt.
A Little Golden Book. Golden Press, 4 colors, 6½″ x 8″, 24 pp., (3).

*The First Golden Geography
by Jane Werner Watson, illus. by William Sayles
An invaluable introduction to the idea of what the earth is; that it is round and in space, and vast, and beautiful, and has mountains, seas, continents, islands, and deserts. A bargain necessity.
A Little Golden Book. Golden Press, board, 4 colors, 6½″ x 9″, 24 pp., (3).

*My Little Golden Book about the Sky
by Kathleen Daly, illus. by Tibor Gergely
A brilliant introduction to the difficult, but to preschoolers so attractive, subjects of air, weather, seasons, day, night, sun, moon, and stars. Beautifully compact.
A Little Golden Book. Golden Press, board, 4 colors, 6½″ x 8″, 24 pp., (3).

The Seashore
by Kathleen Daly, illus. by Tibor Gergely
Another book about our world by this author. Perfectly tailored to the preschooler's level of comprehension. Get it for sure if you're going to the seashore.
A Little Golden Book. Golden Press, board, 4 colors, 6½″ x 8″, 24 pp., (3).

Self and Other

There was once a puppet show which delighted many children from the ages of 6 to 10, but from which many of the younger children recoiled in fear. A 3-year-old who had left the show was overheard relating the episode to his spellbound companions in the nursery school carpool.

"It was very scary," he concluded. "But grownups aren't scared. When we grow up, then we'll be happy, right?"

"Right!" cried all four of the other children at once.

Another small child tried to help his mother by carrying the vacuum cleaner back to the closet. It was too heavy for him and after struggling a moment unhappily he asked his mother to help. Some time later he said to his mother. "When will I grow up?"

"Do you mean when will you be strong enough to carry the vacuum cleaner?" she asked.

"Oh yes!" sighed the child.

Concurrent with the child's growing awareness of himself is the growth of wishfulness —the desire to be as intelligent as intelligence, as powerful as all power, as good as goodness, as whole as holy. While for many years he will act out this wishfulness in terms of self-confirmation and self-betterment, the ultimate yearning is really for the conquering of the sense of separate selfhood altogether. What the separate self yearns for is reunion with all infinite goodness, or, in other words, love. Awareness of love as truth is the only power that can overcome the lonely sense of separation that our usual concept of self carries with it. All human efforts at self-confirmation are really at heart the yearning for love. As the child self goes forth into the world to meet other selves, forward in time toward mature selfhood, what he hopes to meet is goodness, himself and others as lovable and loving. If we are to be helpful as parents, it is well for us to keep this real objective of the life quest in mind.

In an ideal sense there is no quest. The child who journeys toward love is in essence already one with love. The journey is not from separate, incomplete, lonely selfhood to more together, greater, or merged selfhood as we suppose along the way. For the idea(l), real, essential individual is already at one with the infinite. The separate, lacking, limited self-thing (id entity) is only a belief—albeit a universal belief—in separation, lack, and limitation.

We are not journeying anywhere or acquiring anything; we are only ceasing from a dream, relinquishing our conflict with what is already true. We have seen how this works with the law of gravity which is already so and already applies to us even while we are yet in ignorant conflict with it. Our experience of conflict with it falls away simply through our alignment with it.

It is the same love; it is the same with ourselves as expressions of love. When we become aware that we are expressions of love, we become what we already are, at one with love, in it and of it. The only difference is our awareness of it and, hence, oh hallelujah!, our experience of it. The fact is that even when we behave hatefully love is still being expressed, just as the unsteady toddler expresses the law of gravity by falling down when he cannot find his balance. When we violate love in deed or thought, violence occurs, which only goes to prove that love is inviolably so.

These ideas can only be mentioned whisperingly. They are as yet unthinkable and thinking about them either positively or negatively or analytically is almost as irrelevant as thinking about the law of gravity is to the child who is learning to walk. You can't think about the law of gravity until you have validated its existence at least to some extent in your experience. What *is* worthwhile is to consider our experiences and our children in the light of these ideas. For although they are not thinkable, they are realizable and, as we move toward realization we can harmonize our entire human experience and to a large extent the experience of our children through aligning ourselves with them.

The practical implications of these unthinkable thoughts are tremendous. If we are at one with love, we can only be loving. If we are expressions of infinite goodness, we can only be good. If this is true of our children and "other people's children," then we can meet only love and goodness in them. If we behold ourselves and our children as inadequate or immature and try to force ourselves to be good or mature, we always fail. Every day we resolve to be better parents and every day we fail because it is not possible to express two ideas at once; you cannot keep your claim to being an inferior parent and be a superior parent at the same time.

So if we want our children to experience the harmony of being in alignment with love as they grow toward realization of love, there are two things to keep in mind. The first is to behold everyone in the light of infinite love. Acknowledge that each individual, particularly oneself, is an expression of infinite love and that anything else is only part of the dream and not worthy of consideration. The second both follows from and verifies the first. It is the expressing of this affirmation in our daily lives—in all our responses to our children and others, and even in any passing references we may make to ourselves. Both of these steps comprise one twofold prayer—contemplative and expressive—which can transform us as parents, provide our children with loving models of being, and weaken their bondage to the self-confirmatory mode of being.

It is a funny thing that in reality our efforts to be more loving are really a pretense that we are not loving. The child's so-called pretend play on the other hand may be practice of reality. We call it pretending because of the imaginative ways it is carried out. At play with others or by himself the child acts out his current concepts of himself and life. Most often the child's pretend play is role playing. He casts himself in one or another adult form and proceeds to try on various mature selfhoods. He is practicing maturity, seeking his true, whole, unique selfhood. Ultimately, of course, this is not a matter of becoming somebody else or even of becoming his own separate self; it is a matter of discovering his unique individuality as an aspect of the One self or as an expression of infinite love.

You could say that if the concept being acted out in the child's play is truthful, the play is healthy practice, whereas if it is basically erroneous, it is pretense. In healthy play the child is aligned with the reality of love and thus will have harmonious experiences of love. In unhealthy or error-based play, the child experiences the disharmony of love violated. The difference is in the underlying concept of what is or isn't and whether the ultimate objective is healthy (that is true) or unhealthy (false). The child is not aware of such distinctions and the surface content of the play may be the same in both. But while both begin with the premise that experience is not as good as it might be, the unhealthy pretense is only escape and the healthy really a form of transcendence. One child fantasizes that he has wings so that he can get away from his home full of monsters; another pretends wings because flying is beautiful and freedom desirable.

The littlest ones' version of pretense is simply to be themselves grown up, in short to be like mommy and daddy doing what we do. They want to develop all the skills and freedoms we seem to have, to be of some "use," to help, accomplish, etc. The child wants to grow up or at least to learn what grown up is. Grown up is what he thinks we are. Even when he tries on other roles and pretends to be somebody else he will still act like mommy and daddy. He may pretend to be an astronaut, but he will be an astronaut our way. The concept of reality that the little child acts out is a crude, but accurate mini version of the parents' concept of reality. The concepts of self and other that the child acts out will likewise be direct copies in rough material terms of our own self concept. The priorities, approaches, *and the consequences* are essentially the same, because the underlying premise is for sure the same.

This fact of the faithfulness with which the child models himself according to our life view has several implications. First is the obvious imperative that if we want to be helpful as parents we must become ourselves healthy models of the love-intelligent mode of being. Second, if we accept the principle that the only thing standing between us and love is our erroneous beliefs in something else, then we can perceive through our child's play whatever it is that is standing between us and greater happiness or love-fullness. What may be subtle and serpentine in our secret thoughts becomes concrete and clear in the child's play, along with its consequences, making it easier for us to discern and let go of the love-violating beliefs we hold.

Each child is thus a sort of hand mirror in which we can perceive and improve our mental image of ourselves and life. Through proper use of this hand mirror it is possible for us to come to a greater realization of love on a conscious plane and, through providing our children with loving models of being, afford them the harmonious experiences of love that accompany the loving mode of being.

For this to happen it is necessary to know how to look into the hand mirror and to understand clearly its significance. The secret is to look into it as a mirror of our thoughts. The image itself cannot be faulted or corrected, nor can we even fault or correct ourselves as causes of the image. In this mirror we do not see either our true (ideally perfect) selves nor the true self of the child, nothing real at all in fact, but rather only the reflections of our beliefs about reality. So we must not view what we see with fear or blame or desire or any thought that gives reality to the image. The image has value only for its significance of what we do not know about reality. Otherwise both image and imagery are of no consequence. To try to correct the child is like putting a lipstick smile on the reflection of an unhappy face in a mirror. To correct or try to change ourselves is like putting a lipstick smile on the unhappy face itself. Both of these actions are absurd; only the knowledge of something truly happy can transform the face and the face's reflection with a genuine smile. The following story can be used as an illustration.

Whenever visitors came to his home, one 2-year-old boy would constantly interrupt by pretending to offer his parents and their guests imaginary good things to eat. He would touch an imaginary refrigerator on the wall and then run to an adult with an offer of an ice cream cone or a piece of candy. His constant demands for attention disrupted every visit.

Instead of trying to do something about the child, the parents asked what the significance of the game might be when considered in the light of love. They discerned that while there was nothing good or bad about the pretense itself, the underlying ideas expressed in it were not healthy, that is, not wholesome. Evidently the child believed that happiness required his receiving constant attention, and that the way to get that attention (his idea of love) was through giving good things to eat (his idea of being loving). He further believed that the best he had to offer was something to eat. On either a childish level or translated to an adult level, the idea of constantly needing personal attention and trying to get it through offering goodies would never bring forth the desired and needed love. To be lovable and loving and loved, a better underlying concept of love was needed. The parents then recognized that their own view of love, including their love for the child (a goodie in their lives) was both materialistic and dualistic. They sought a higher concept of love as the knowledge of infinite goodness (of goodness as the knowledge of infinite love), and the child soon gave up his annoying habit.

It is important to understand that it is the idea underlying the fantasy in this story that was unhealthy, not the child and not the parents. The belief that both child and parent held in common was unhealthy because it would not result in wholeness; it could never bring the desired and needed love into expression or experience. However, it is a sign of health in the child that he sought a positive solution to his problem, and it was good that he was able to act out his concern so that his parents could perceive his need and improve the mental climate of their home.

But it is crucial to understand that while the pretense had significance, it had no value per se, good or bad. No matter how many times the child might go through his pretend game, the game itself would not solve his problem, nor would playing it louder or more intensly help. In this pretense both the need and the answer to the need are based on a misconception. Likewise on the parents' part no response to the pretense itself will be of any help. Forbidding the child to interrupt the adult conversation or giving him more attention or something to eat as a distraction

would have been equally ineffective in producing health or answering the child's valid need for love. Both approaches would have reinforced the child's erroneous concept that love was a matter of the personal give and take of goodies.

In some way life has become estranged from reality, and this estrangement precludes real happiness until it be overcome.
–Huston Smith, *The Religions of Man*

All children do both kinds of play, healthy and unhealthy, fantasy and transcendence, escape and practice. They do this alone and as they come into contact with others. All accordingly experience the reality of love as discord when in violation of it and as infinite joy when in alignment with it. Likewise as adults we find that love seems to come and go in our lives as we, unawares, step in and out of alignment with it. The important thing in all our experiences as adults and in our observations of our children's play and behavior is not to deal with them as if they had any reality but rather for what they signify in the light of reality. Shakespeare wrote:

Life's but a walking shadow, a poor player That struts and frets his hour upon the stage And then is heard no more: it is a tale Told by an idiot, full of sound and fury, Signifying nothing.

By themselves our experiences do indeed signify nothing, for it is nothingness that our strivings are based on—nothingness which we are trying to turn into something, nobody which we are trying to turn into somebody, nowhere that we are trying to turn into somewhere. Yet there isn't any body we could become or any thing we could have or any where we could go that could answer our need to know love. But if we start with the premise of love and view our experiences in its light as a present reality, we can learn to align ourselves with it and thereby validate it in our experience. In the end, it is possible to become so completely aware of love that it is impossible any longer for us to slip out of alignment with it. Then do we realize that while no body has love, love is the everyone we each are; and that while no where is love, it is already now here.

Row, row, row your boat
Gently down the stream.
Merrily, merrily, merrily, merrily—
Life is but a dream.
–Traditional nursery rhyme

Blind, blind is the world; only a handful can see.
Only a handful escape, like birds from a net.
–Buddha in *The Dhammapada*, trans. by P. Lal

In his later years, when India had become electric with his message and kings themselves were bowing before him, people came to him even as they were to come to Jesus asking what he was. How many people have provoked this question: not "Who are you?" with respect to name, origin, or ancestry, but "What are you?—what order of being do you belong to, what species do you represent?" Not Caesar, certainly. Not Napoleon, nor even Socrates. Only two, Jesus and Buddha. When the people carried their puzzlement to the Buddha himself, the answer he gave provided a handle for his entire message.

"Are you a god?" they asked. "No." "An angel?" "No." "A saint?" "No." "Then what are you?"

Buddha answered, "I am awake." His answer became his title, for this is what Buddha means. In the Sanskrit root budh *denotes both to wake up and to know. Buddha, then, means the "Enlightened One" or the "Awakened One." While the rest of the*

world was wrapped in the womb of sleep, dreaming a dream known as the waking life of mortal men, one man roused himself. Buddhism begins with a man who shook off the daze, the doze, the dreamlike inchoateness of ordinary awareness. It begins with a man who woke up.

–Huston Smith, *The Religions of Man*

Like the moon slipping from behind a cloud and shining on the earth
is the man who, once foolish, has determined to be wise.
–Buddha in *The Dhammapada*, trans. by P. Lal

Playthings

Our active role as parents in the pretending play of our children or even in their general behavior is peripheral. We need neither encourage nor discourage such play. We must not interfere overly much and we should stand apart unless invited. When invited, we can participate cheerfully and with generosity. We can provide materials when called for and play roles when asked, but never with fear or judgment or any strongly positive or negative involvement with the fantasy itself.

Not much is needed for pretend play, since most of the joy of it involves setting the scene: building a house with a blanket over a chair, making a bed for a doll from a tray on some blocks, painting a mask on a paper bag. Often the arrival of fancy equipment marks the end of a period of enthusiastic play. Since the first purpose of pretend play seems to be growing up, perhaps the best first toys are "real" grownup tools that really work, sized down so that the child can actually develop the skill for using them. A simple push broom is a perfect example. After that you can pretty much just follow the child's own direction. A doll? Some play animals? A doll house? A fireman's hat? These things can be found anywhere as the interest arises. The world is full of things for playing at life. The question is not where to find them but whether or not it is something your child will really use? Usually the answer is no. The things listed below have been chosen either because many people would not have thought of them as serving the purpose or because they seem rather better than other similar things available.

Housework

Push broom—The best broom for a toddler is a push broom. That's what he will do with a broom anyway, a process that just makes hay of a normal broom. With a push broom he can actually learn to do some effective sweeping. And even before that the newly walking child will enjoy simply driving a push broom around. □

Carpet sweeper—Probably the best push toy around—not just aimless entertainment. Also, it's handy for the parent for quick nursery rug sweep-ups. A carpet sweeper with a see-through top would be ideal, but we couldn't find one. □

Housekeeping set—For most children, the carpet sweeper and push broom are more than sufficient for sized-down housekeeping equipment. If you prefer to buy a set, try to find one that includes a push broom. Also with all of these things make sure that there is a specific place, preferably a hook, for the orderly storage of each thing.

Tea and luncheon sets—One of those rare junky things that turns out to be a real bargain is a cheap set of tiny teacups, teapot, sugar bowl, creamer, and spoons. It will be used most often in the bathtub for serving dozens of soapsuds soufflées and watery cups of tea at dozens of poolside tea parties. But it will also be pleasant in the kitchen on occasion with real tea or juice, sugar, and milk.

As the child grows, a set of bigger dishes becomes increasingly useful. You can compile one yourself (in fact, normal-size cups are better than child-size ones) or purchase ready-made ones in stores. They are available in all sizes and materials (plastic and china breakable, melmac and metal durable) for all prices. Even disposable paper cups and plates are fine. The important thing is some independent practice in serving and socializing.

As a matter of fact, from about age 2 on, it's a nice idea from time to time to let children pour their own milk at the table. They can use the practice, relish the responsibility, and are likely to drink milk more enthusiastically. Just put a small pitcher of milk on the table beside the empty glass. □

Pots and pans—Your own are perfectly adequate, but perhaps you don't want them traveling to the sandbox, garden hose, and bathtub. If not, buy a set of children's pots and pans—a set of really sturdy ones is worth the extra money.

Housepainting—with a bucket of water and a good-size paintbrush is "work" almost any preschooler will do by the hour with relish. For even more enjoyment add a small stepladder, a painter's hat, a roller and roller pan, another child, and a wagon to haul the equipment in. Super paint buckets to hook on fences can be made from the top part of a wire coat hanger (simply cut off the cross bar) hooked through two holes near the top of a coffee can.

Dolls and miniatures

Dolls—These never appeal to some children, while others become quite interested in practicing parenthood with them. There is probably no difference on the preschool level between the numbers of boys and girls who would or would not be interested in playing with dolls if they were not specifically taught that boys build roads and girls keep house. When women's lib is over, it's going to be discovered that the boys were the ones who were really gypped all along by not being allowed to do any of the "girls' stuff" they loved their mothers for so much. It is almost frightening to see in nursery school how sharply the lines have already been drawn.

Most preschoolers are not yet interested in systematically playing house or caring for a doll, but if yours is, you may have difficulty locating a simple washable, inexpensive doll that doesn't do anything much but blink. Wetting, crying, talking dolls miss the point—they are so biological, and evoke such a materialistic concept of love.

Dollhouses—Again, the few children who genuinely play with these are mostly beyond preschool. For most children the real run of a dollhouse is making and furnishing it. Try stacking cardboard boxes and getting right down to interior decorating. Cardboard cartons are wonderful for all kinds of play buildings; just cut out doors and windows wherever she wants them, get out the paints, and scraps of cloth, and let her go to town. You can build a disposable garage or farm the same way tomorrow. For the handy carpentering parent a nice idea might be a wall-mounted dollhouse—partitioned storage shelves with stairs and doorways and windows.

Miniature people—The best feature of the big Fisher Price sets (farm, airport, garage, castle, etc.) is the sturdy little cylindrical people which really fit into the cars and chairs and which can also be used in improvised play setups. Other positive features of these sets are their extraordinary sturdiness and the fact that the people from one set fit well into others. In general we think these are too permanent and too specific to encourage creative play, but there are a number of youngsters for whom they are just perfect. And they are certainly better for preschoolers than more fragile affairs.

Miniature animals—A small treasure chest of unbreakable, detailed, and accurately scaled miniature animals is useful in a variety of ways. They are informative and can be used as the cargo or inhabitants of almost anything a child might build with blocks or crystal climbers or dirt or stones. □

Playboards—A very pleasant activity for preschool children is making landscapes for small toy animals. Paint a barn floor brown and pastures green and ponds blue on a stiff piece of cardboard. Even better, make a landscape collage with sand or gravel roads, bark bridges, pebbly stone walls, twig fences, etc. Then turn the animals loose. "Now what would make a frisky long-legged colt happy? Or a duck, web-footed for swimming?" It can be a loving and totally enjoyable time for these little ones, who like gluing and learning and working together with us best of all.

1. CUT 3 PIECES OF RED FELT OR USE
   CONTRASTING COLORS (EG. RED FOR
   CAPE & BLUE FOR BAND & SHIELD.)

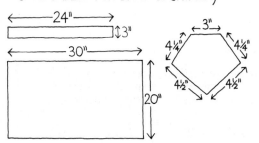

← 24" →
↕ 3"

← 30" →
20"

← 3" →
4¼" 4¼"
4½" 4½"

2. PIN TUCKS IN CAPE PIECE.

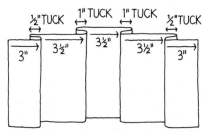

½"TUCK 1"TUCK 1"TUCK ½"TUCK
3" 3½" 3½" 3½" 3"

3. FOLD BAND IN HALF & IRON FLAT.
4. PIN EVERYTHING TOGETHER AS
   SHOWN TOP RIGHT. START WITH
   SHIELD & THEN ADD CAPE.
5. SEW ALONG DOTTED LINES.
6. CUT OUT 2 SUPER S IN GOLD
   FELT. YOU MAY USE CHILD'S OWN
   INITIAL(S) INSTEAD OF S.
7. SEW OR GLUE SUPER LETTERS
   TO FRONT & BACK OF CAPE.

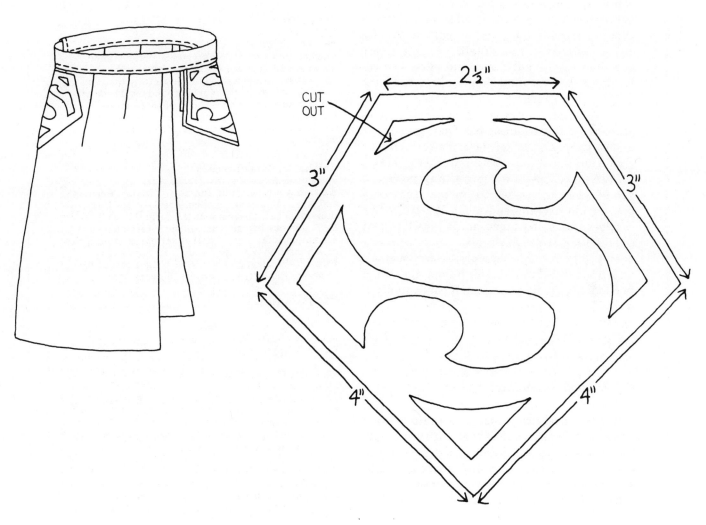

CUT
OUT

2½"
3"   3"
4"   4"

Dressing up

Dressing up is one of the first "pretending" activities children enjoy, so, as you think of it, set aside bits of clothing, costume jewelry, purses, briefcases, that might be donned on a rainy afternoon or slow morning. A cape (even if it's only a towel or scrap of cloth) that floats behind a flying or galloping child is perfect. And best of all, of course, are grownup things, such as an old purse or wallet stocked with photos and papers and pennies in all the pockets.

Hats—Especially pleasing to the little ones are an old, felt business hat from grandpa, a baseball cap, a kerchief, or made-for-children version of a real construction worker's helmet.

Penny pocket—Sew a big penny pocket, a good-size kangaroo pouch on the front of a pair of bib overalls and stock it with a few jingly coins or an apple and a small box of raisins for a walk. It's a place to collect outdoor things for a collage or to carry a small treasure. Much more useful than the small pockets that come on the small pants children wear.

Cape— Make the wonderful cape on p. 261 — the youngest super-kids can put it on and off by themselves.

Books about becoming

[*Note:* Numbers in parentheses indicate comprehension levels (not age) as outlined on pp. 7–9, 195, 197, 201, 207. Starred titles are those deemed superior for a preschoolers' home library. See pp. 6–7, 193–94 for additional information regarding book notations and selection.]

Busy Day, Busy People
by Tibor Gergely
What people do on construction sites, farms, and streets; at fires, post offices, and airports; in stores, hospitals, circuses, garages, restaurants, and TV studios.
Random House, paperback, 4 colors, 8" x 8", 32 pp., (2–3).

*Busy People
by Joe Kaufman
A good, big book about 8 vocations (fireman, teacher, policeman, doctor, zookeeper, postman, clown, and telephone installer). Big, bright, unconfusing pictures and much usefully distilled information about the world around us. Three of the people are women and one of those is the telephone installer!
Golden Press, board, 4 colors, 10¼" x 11¾", 96 pp., (2).

Children of Many Lands
by Jean Wilson, illus. by Mance Post
Eskimo, Chinese, Zulu, Indian (of India), Peruvian, and Australian aboriginal children—a small, individual paperback about the daily life styles of each. 6 books in a slipcase. Basic information in a format children love. Another set in the same series as *Animals of Warmer Lands* (see page 240).
Addison-Wesley, paperback with light cardboard slipcase, 4 colors, 4¾" x 5¾", 16 pp. ea., (3).

The Farm Book
by Jan Pfloog
The daily routine on a farm.
A Golden Shape Book. Golden Press, paperback, 4 colors, approx. 8" x 8", 24 pp.

The Fire House Book
by Colin Bailey
A quick little account of the life of a fireman. Where he sleeps and eats, what he must do to take care of the fire truck, etc.
A Golden Shape Book. Golden Press, paperback, 4 colors, approx. 8" x 8", 24 pp., (2).

A House for Everyone
by Betty Miles, illus. by Jo Lowry
All kinds of houses for all kinds of people. Peaceful.
Knopf/Pantheon, paperback, 1 and 4 colors, 7" x 9", 32 pp., (2).

Just Suppose
by May Garelick, illus. by Brinton Turkel
Simple text and pictures suggest how children can look like the animals they pretend to be.
Scholastic Book Services, paperback, 2 colors, 7½" x 9", 32 pp., (3).

*A Little House of Your Own
by Beatrice Schenk de Regniers, illus. by Irene Haas
A poetic account of the many ways of having a secret house or hiding place. Inspires and values a sense of privacy.
Harcourt Brace Jovanovich, hardcover, 1 color, 4¼" x 8¾", 48 pp., (3).

The Little Airplane, *The Little Auto, *The Little Farm, The Little Fire Engine, *The Little Train, The Little Sailboat, and Cowboy Small and Policeman Small.
Lois Lenski's classic books about Mr. Small are perfect vehicles for helping children to imagine themselves as all kinds of different grownups (alas, all male). They are not quite up to date, but no one has done better yet than she has with her little man who looks like a child. They are all informative books with simple story lines. Paperback editions of the two most useful (*The Little Farm* and *The Little Train*) are available for $1.50 ea., see pages 196 and 199. The rest: Henry Z. Walck Inc., hardcover, 1 and 2 colors, 7" x 7" or 8¼" x 7", 48 pp.

My Doctor
by Harlow Rockwell
A good, straightforward presentation of what to expect in a doctor's office. Shows all the equipment clearly, as tools (not weapons) of a helpful individual.
Macmillan, hardcover, 4 colors, 9½" x 8¾", 32 pp., (2).

My House Book
by John Miller
The rooms and familiar things in a house.
A Golden Shape Book. Golden Press, paperback, 4 colors, approx. 8" x 8", 24 pp., (1).

Puppet Party
by Goldie Taub Chernoff, illus. by Margaret Hartelius
How to make puppets out of paperbacks, socks, and any old thing. This book is so nicely done that some small children like to hear the large-type parts of the text read aloud.
Scholastic Book Services, paperback, 4 colors, 9" x 7½", 24 pp., (4).

Seven Little Postmen
by Margaret Wise Brown and Edith Thacher Hurd, illus. by Tibor Gergely
A storybook account of the postal system.
A Little Golden Book. Golden Press, board, 4 colors, 6½" x 8", 24 pp., (3).

What's in Mommy's Pocketbook?
by Georgess McHargue, illus. by Jean Simpson
For as long as it lasts, this is an absorbing gimmick book. Cardboard versions of everything in mommy's purse, and a separate slot for each to go in.
Golden Press, board, 4 colors, 5¾" x 6", 16 pp., (2).

Letting Go

Behold what love the Father hath given us, that we should be called children of God; and so we are. Therefore the world knoweth us not, because it knew him not. Beloved, we are God's children now; it doth not yet appear what we shall be, but we know that when he shall appear we shall be like him, for we shall see him as he is. And every man that hath this hope in him purifieth himself even as he is pure.

—I John 3:1–3

And joy follows a pure thought,
like a shadow faithfully tailing a man.
We are what we think,
having become what we thought.

—Buddha in *The Dhammapada*, trans. by P. Lal

As soon as we have conceived, we have to start letting go of our children. In fact, for some people letting go of the idea of *having* children is a prerequisite to conception. So often when couples who have had difficulty conceiving finally give up and turn to adoption, they suddenly discover that the pregnancy they sought so long to achieve is under way. There are various interpretations of this phenomenon, most of them referring vaguely to the idea of uptightness. But perhaps it is possible to be more specific. Maybe the moment of conception coincides with a shift in the parents' motivation from the desire simply to "have a child of their own" to the desire to become parents regardless. Maybe it is when the parental motive slightly edges out the purely possessive one that the idea of a child (which is conceptually dependent on the idea of a parent) can occur. The child is conceived as the parent is conceived.

But of course this is barely a beginning. We must keep on and on letting go—letting our children be born, letting them sleep, letting them mature. We have to let go of the diapers, let go of the mistakes, and sooner or later we have to let go of them altogether, let them walk right out of our lives to the care of a sitter, to a first overnight at grandma's, to nursery school for half a day, to grade school, to college, to marry, to live in another part of the world. It can all be very painful, very hard, and very sad if we do not understand what all this letting go is for.

Having struggled so hard to learn to love them, why must we let them go? What is the good of the love if the beloved goes away? Some people deal with this by not "getting involved" whether or not they have any children. Some people deal with it by having a lot of babies, one right after the other. Intervals of two and a half years are supposed to be ideal—each time one child shoves off, another comes along to take its place. Perhaps the parents get over the loss of all these beloveds by getting sick and tired of them. On the other hand, there are all those grandchildren coming along by then. So they are never totally at a loss, they are always maternal or paternal grandparents. The only thing wrong with this solution is that the number of losses is increased to at least the intensity of the one possible, original loss. There is no judgment implied here, only the effort to show that having or not having is the same—both are sooner or later lonely, both amount to loss.

But the fact of the matter is that, just as with the nearly adoptive parents, the true love, the truth that love is, does not come to us until we let go of our beloveds (beloved self, beloved beloved). The real loss in letting go is the loss of two, the two that is you and me, lover and beloved revolving around each other in the nothingness, protecting each other from the nothingness, exchanging our nothingness for nothingness. If we have each other we lose each other, an event so painful that we wonder how we ever could have thought the having would be worthwhile. If we do good to each other, we also do bad to each other; if we help, we also hinder. So what is it all worth? Nothing. As two (not only separate from each other, but separate, two, from everything) it is all a fifty/fifty proposition—fifty percent of the time you win, fifty percent of the time you lose. It all averages out to nothing. Two cannot become one.

So losing this twoness is no loss at all. We already talked about that. But what *is* it for then? When Abraham and Sarah were old and childless, they had to surrender or let go of their belief that they were old (persons) and childless (persons) who could not *have* (by personal means) a baby (person). But that wasn't all. Letting go of their sense of personal adequacy/inadequacy (it's the same, of course), they also acknowledged that there was One who could and would fulfill them. Two(ness) could not produce a baby, but the One could. One did. Sarah conceived and bore a son. When they let go of their sense of personal impotency/potency (the same again), they discovered power. When they let go of wanting/having a child, they *became* parents. And although they were old before they started, they lived to be—how old? Well, they remained young a long time after they had grown old. So, by giving up a little of their twoness, they discovered that God is creative power.

Then they went about the same sublime/ridiculous business of parenting that we are involved in, for of course they were as young as parents as Isaac was young as a child, newborn in the first, most ignorant sense of the word. Isaac must have slept and cried, pleased, perturbed them, worried, and made them proud. They must have struggled to learn to love just as much as we struggle. You just aren't having children any more after you've learned what love is. Just like us they must have loved their boy—cherished him, wanted to protect him, and hold him close, and dreaded the inevitable, that he must (for his good if not for theirs) move away from them to become a man instead of a child!

And he said, Take now thy son, thine only son Isaac, whom thou lovest, and 'get thee into the land of Moriah, and offer him there for a burnt offering upon one of the mountains which I will tell thee of.
–Genesis 22:2

Give up what is before, what is behind,
Give up what is now, and cross the stream.
Then will your mind be free,
then will you cross birth and old age.
–Buddha in The Dhammapada, trans. by P. Lal

And so it happened that Abraham was called upon to sacrifice Isaac. He loaded Isaac up with the kindling wood for his own sacrificial fire and, knife in hand, climbed the mountain with his son—his cherished, precious, dearest son—prepared to kill him in obedience to God. This time he was prepared to slaughter the two for the One. In his consenting thought he had already done so. So, of course, such a thing was not necessary. God did not want him to kill his son, only his *own* son, his having of a son. But Abraham didn't know that until the last minute.

This time in sacrificing the twoness—his role as a lover (the father person) of the beloved (the son person)—he discovered another aspect of the One. As long as he knew God only as the creator, he was able to imagine (unable not to imagine) God the destroyer. But in surrendering once again his attachment to twoness he discovered this aspect of the One—that God is Love. In the slaughtering of both father and son, neither father nor son is lost, except as insufficient, slaughterable persons. Instead there is revealed infinite love which is no less available to one than to the other. Both father and son are revealed to be *in* love, both are seen to be children of God. Sacrificing *his* child, Abraham discovers that Isaac is God's well-protected child. Sacrificing himself as father (the desire to protect and defend), he discovers that God is father. It is no little thing, but it is no big deal either. The experience of sacrifice may be enormous, but the revelation of truth is that there was never anything to sacrifice, no sacrifice at all, in the first place. There is only love sustaining the only loving.

We all go through the same thing. Each letting go is experienced as a sacrifice—first of ourselves to the child, then the child to sitter, to other children, to teacher, to the freedom to make mistakes and be terribly wrong and unhappy. We are even called upon to supply our children with errors. Having learned to behold the eternally perfect qualities in our children, we have to teach them the finite. We must teach them worldly, material concepts in what we finally begin to see is a spiritual universe. In the very process of learning ourselves to see with a single inner eye, we teach our son/daughter that he/she has two outer ones. Quantity, time, space, corporeality—all these are ultimately false. But they are necessary for living in the world and they are required as the kindling for the fire at which the grown child will ultimately have to sacrifice his own material sense.

And Abraham took the wood of the burnt offering, and laid it on Isaac his son; and he took in his hand the fire and the knife. So they went both of them together. And Isaac said to his father Abraham, "My father!" And he said, "Here am I, my son." He said, "Behold, the fire and the wood; but where is the lamb for a burnt offering?" Abraham said, "God will provide himself the lamb for a burnt offering, my son." So they went both of them together.

—Genesis 22:6–8

Existence having born them
And fitness bred them,
While matter varied their forms
And breath empowered them,
All created things render, to the existence and
*   fitness they depend on,*
An obedience
Not commanded but of course.
And since this is the way existence bears issue
And fitness raises, attends,
Shelters, feeds, and protects,
Do you likewise:
Be parent, not possessor,
Attendant, not master,
Be concerned not with obedience but with benefit,
And you are at the core of living.

—*The Way of Life According to Lao Tzu,* trans. by Witter Bynner

This is such a beautiful detail of the story. Abraham does what he has to do (the laying of the kindling on his son's back), but he *speaks* to him only of God (the spiritual, the true). While doing *as if* for a God who takes away (demands this sacrifice), he speaks of God as the provider. He does not try to carry either his son or his son's burden up the mountain. The son must climb for himself, bearing his own burden of error to the summit. But he walks beside him, keeping silent about the sacrifice, the evil, and the error, teaching only that God is good (an idea he is not even sure of himself). At the same time that he supplies his son with the material kindling for material sacrifice, he endeavors wholeheartedly to kindle his son's interest in spiritual reality.

As the son climbs the material mountain, the father ascends the spiritual one. Both the child and the man are sacrificed upon the mountain. As the child is sacrificed, the man is born; Abraham relinquishes his mental holding of Isaac to childhood. As the man is sacrificed, the child is born; in giving up his aggressive, protective, defensive selfhood, Abraham becomes as innocent, as trusting and pure as his son. For Isaac to be born a child, Abraham had to conceive of parenthood. For Isaac to be born a man, Abraham must become a child again.

What really happens in this second birth of Abraham is that, through the loss of both (two) material father and son, the spiritual fatherly/sonly, loving/humble One is born (realized in Abraham's consciousness). There is no loss of individuality, but rather only the fulfillment of individuality. Abraham and Isaac do not become one with each other, but rather each is seen to be individually one with the father.

Thus it can be seen that in losing there is no loss. In sacrificing the material son, Abraham gains and sets free the spiritual one. This son, the perfect, spiritual child of God, eternally in the care of infinite, fathering love can never be lost to him. Now he and his son share sonship. Having seen the unslaughterable, perfect spiritual identity of his son, Abraham can see it in everyone. And sacrificing his material fatherhood to see the unslaughtering, perfect spiritual identity of the father, he becomes truly fatherly. Thus it is that Abraham sires more children than the stars in the sky. He becomes at one with the father of the eternally eternal, spiritual children of God. He is fatherly with the father and a son with the sons. The twoness of loss is erased when thus the father and son are one. "Son, all that I have is thine."

So it is with us and our children. On the one hand, we *do* for them, and teach them how to get along in the material world, but at the very same time we have to sacrifice our notion of them as material selves, our notions of our *own* personal responsibilities, and our own personal *having/needing* selves. At the same time that we deal with and seem to be material selves, we behold the spiritual, relinquishing errors, lacks, and problems as nothing (fasting, forgiveness) and maintaining in consciousness the spiritually perfect (prayer, atonement). At the same time that we let our children go from us forth into the world, we acknowledge that there is only one father/mother/parent—infinite, omnipresent love never withheld, only to awaken in.

The secret in letting go of our children is to know that, although we are releasing them into the world, we are not turning them over to the world. This realization can be attained by constantly, consciously turning them over to the one loving father: ("not I, but the father in me," "I and my father are one," "in him we live and move and have our being"). This is both the secret of our redemption and a vital protection of our children from worldly harm.

There is nothing to be lost but loss. Our loss of a sense of finitude yields awareness of eternity; loss of the sense of impotence, creative power; loss of the material, awareness of the spiritual; loss of the beloved, awareness of Love; loss of personhood, awareness of full selfhood. In becoming at one with the father instead of striving to become one with each other, both we and our children become channels for and recipients of the infinitely various spiritual qualities of beauty, truth, creativity, and love.

The man Jesus had no children, yet in recorded history there is no man who ever saw more clearly that each of us is a child of love, born of love, and in essence and consciousness at one with love. At the end of his life he prayed and left for his brothers/sisters/children the following most supremely parently prayer:

I have manifested thy name to the men [children] whom thou gavest me out of the world; thine they were, and thou gavest them to me, and they have kept thy word. Now they know that everything thou hast given me is from thee for I have given them the words which thou gavest me, and they have received them and know in truth that I came from thee; and they have believed that thou didst send me. I am praying for them; I am not praying for the world but for those whom thou hast given me, for they are thine; all mine are thine, and thine are mine, and I am glorified in them. And now I am no more in the world, but they are in the world, and I am coming to thee. Holy Father, keep them in thy name which thou hast given me, that they may be one, even as we are one. While I was with them, I kept them in thy name, which thou hast given me; I have guarded them, and none of them is lost but the son of perdition . . . But now I am coming to thee; and these things I speak in the world that they may have my joy fulfilled in themselves. I have given them thy word; and the world has hated them because they are not of the world, even as I am not of the world. I do not pray that thou shouldst take them out of the world, but that thou shouldst keep them from evil. They are not of the world, even as I am not of the world. Sanctify them in the truth; thy word is truth. As thou didst send me into the world, so I have sent them into the world. And for their sake I consecrate myself, that they also may be consecrated in truth . . .

–John 17:6–19

Additional Information*

[18] *Baby seat.* There are many adequate baby seats available. Although much more expensive than the lightweight ones, the General Motors Infant Safety Carrier, specifically designed as a safe car seat, is a good buy if you drive a car. Though rather heavy to carry around, it is sturdier and less tippy as a baby seat than the lightweight ones, which are not safe as car seats. Useful from birth to 20 lbs. Available from General Motors dealers.

[20] *Baby bath.* The only bath arrangement we located that appeared worthwhile is a combination plastic tub and tubular metal stand that can be set up in or near the regular bath, where it can be easily filled and dumped. The same base also serves as a stand for Mothercare's Carry Cot, which becomes a carriage when set on a wheel base. Tub and stand could be used later as a sand or water table. We didn't see this item, but it might be good. Mothercare, Ltd.

[20] *Babycare mat* (as illustrated). By Velbex. From Mothercare Ltd.

[21] *Double-locking pins* (as illustrated). From W. T. Grant stores.

[28] *Standard crib* (as illustrated). One good example is the Childcraft standard crib with a single, two-position drop side. From Childcraft.

[28] *Crib/settee* (as illustrated on p. 29). From the Children's Workbench, 47 Park Ave. South, New York, N.Y. 10001.

[46] *Glow-in-the-dark stars* (as illustrated). "Universe" of 137 stars, planets, comets, and moons. From Childcraft for about $2.00.

[52] *Mini Jars.* Oster manufactures small jars which fit all their blenders and are reputed to be useful for preparing baby food. The jars cost about $1.00 each.

[53] *Training cup* (as illustrated). By Tommee Tippee. Generally available.

[54] *Highchair* (as illustrated). Peterson manufactures a very satisfactory highchair. It has a large fiberglass tray (less noisy than metal) and nylon web safety belt. Footrest, arms and tray are removable to convert the highchair to a youth or utility chair. Space between the backrest and seat makes cleaning a breeze. Easily collapsible for storage. Department stores and infant supply stores.

[68] *The Open Home.* The only thing you might want along the lines of a home learning program is a subscription to this monthly 6-page foldout full of good insights and practical suggestions to help parents of preschoolers understand what is happening to their growing babies and to become themselves effectively responsive teachers. One mother who reviewed all the issues published so far wrote: "I only wish I could have had them sooner." Alas, *The Open Home* has a reputation for being not quite punctual in its mailings, and it sometimes happens that four tardy, eagerly-awaited issues get mailed out at once. So, order early. $5.95 yearly. The Open Home, 159 W. 53rd St., New York, N.Y. 10019.

[69] *The Surprise Box.* One of the good exceptions among gimmicky "busy" toys is this plastic box with five different switches that make five different figures pop up. It's not the prettiest thing around, but it will keep a more-or-less one year old educationally busy off and on for quite a while. By Kohner. Generally available.

[81] *Step stool* (as illustrated). The Tri-chair is one of the best buys we found in toddler furniture, especially if space is any problem. It is a combination rocker, chair, and two-step stair that will prove its worth in many circumstances. From Childcraft.

[90] *Carriages.* In the category of good moderately priced carriages are the Marmets (as illustrated) imported from England by many American infant supply stores. Although we have not seen them, other apparently intelligent carriage setups are the Carry-cot and Carry-cot Transporter combinations from Mothercare. The Carry-cot serves as a car bed and can also be set on the Carry-cot/Bath Stand (see baby bath, above).

[91] *Carriage accessories.* All items mentioned can be ordered from Mothercare Ltd., but many are available in the U.S. as well.

[91] *Umbrella strollers.* Cross River and Gerry run neck and neck. Both are excellent. A carrying pouch is the only extra you might want to watch for. Compare styles and prices, then take your pick.

[91] *Moderately priced, sturdy folding strollers.* In this category Morris recommended Headstrom's #8378 and Strollee's #216. See page 105 for Morris' credentials.

[92] *Baby carriers.* Gerry Cuddler, Happy Baby Carrier, or Snugli. Take your pick. The Cuddler is least expensive and lightest but will not support

---

* As indicated by □ in the rest of the book. Except for a few addresses given here, the addresses and catalog descriptions of all mail order sources mentioned can be found on pp. 75–77.

Numbers in brackets refer to the page in the book where products are discussed.

as heavy a baby as comfortably as the others. The Happy Baby carrier is the Japanese model and is probably best all around for sturdiness and simplicity (illustrated on p. 93). The corduroy Snugli made by a cottage industry of Dunkard farm wives in Ohio, is cozy, adaptable, but expensive and too warm in summer. Dolly snuglis are also available. Snuglis can be ordered from Snugli, Rte. 1, Box 685, Evergreen, Colorado 80439. Happy Baby Carriers and Gerry Cuddlers are available in infant supply stores and departments.

[93] *Frame-type back carriers.* Again, take your pick. Gerry and Cross River are about the best-known manufacturers. Models vary: nylon web or canvas fabric, with and without carrying pouch, with and without stand. We found the pouch indispensable for sandwiches and diapers, the stand only temporarily and marginally useful. Generally available.

[95] *Car seat for babies.* See GM Infant Safety Carrier under *baby seat,* above. Also worth looking into may be the Peterson Safety Shell which combines many features of both the GM Infant Safety Carrier and the Ford Tot Guard, and can be converted for use with both infants and toddlers.

[99] *Crib gym* (as illustrated). The Activator is a crib gym that really does something. You pull on it here and something moves or rings there. Easy to put on and take off. Remains interesting to the child for quite a while. From Creative Playthings.

[99] *Jumper* (as illustrated on p. 100). There are a number of models available varying largely in the "saddle" or harness for the baby. Some of those that hold the infant most firmly in position are the hardest when it comes to saddling up, and vice versa. Mostly it's a matter of individual preference. Jumpers are generally available. The illustrated model is from Creative Playthings.

[100] *Walker.* The Century Hoola Coop seems to be one of the best designed (simple, circular, with tray, light, and untippable) and reasonably priced walkers around. Generally available or by mail from Constructive Playthings.

[101] *Doorway swing mounts.* Either the Doorway Expansion Hanger or the Doorway Clamp from Child Life are good, or you can purchase an expandable gym bar for doorways from many sporting goods and toy departments.

[101] *Doorway gym* (as illustrated). This wonderful swing-plus includes a rubber belt swing, trapeze bar and rings, and blocked climbing rope. Beautifully made with all parts adjustable by children, for whom rearranging the parts is half the fun. Rope, bar, and rings provide a lot of extra activity even at the toddler level. Can be suspended from a wooden doorframe with eye hooks. For metal doorframes Child Life offers the above alternative mounts, though it would be less expensive and conceivably even more secure to simply bore through the wall just above the doorframe and hang the swing from the frame itself. Of course, an available rafter with more space below for hanging around in is even nicer than a doorway.

[100–03] *Indoor gyms.* Some good ones are: *Kinder Climber* from Child Life (as illustrated, p. 102, top left); Variplay House-Gym and Slide from Community Playthings; or, if the lid is off on cost, the Climbing House from Childcraft, Constructive Playthings, or Novo.

Simpler ladder-type climbers. Some good ones are: A-Frame Climber and Slide from Community Playthings (as illustrated, p. 102, bottom); Horizontal Ladder from Child Life; Folding Ladder Climber from Child Life.

Small combination piece. The Quad Unit (as illustrated, p. 102, top right) is a combination desk/rocking boat/playhouse/perch—a rare multipurpose item in which no aspect seems trivial, tacked-on, or compromised for the sake of the combination. Each Quad is made of two sides of rounded particle board, one with a 12" hole for crawling through, the other side to be used as a desk or table. The sides are held together by four 1-inch threaded and capped dowels, three of which slip through heavy duck to form the seat/walls/roof/floor. The manufacturer recommends them for children from two to six, but we found that children less than a year old safely enjoyed standing on the canvas floor and rocking the boat. On top of everything else, it is nice-looking cheerful furniture for a child's room. Make a slide from a sanded, heavily waxed 54" x 11" x ¾" board glued and bolted at one end to an 11" x 1" x ¾" stick hooked over one of the dowels. One Quad is fun, two are ideal for sharing (each child with his own house, or, when pushed together, a sort of 2-door igloo). By Gerico. By direct mail from Mead.

[103–04] *Outdoor climbing gyms.* Two good ones are the Fireman's Gym and the Playhouse Gym (same as Fireman's Gym plus tent top), from

Child Life. Less elaborate and less expensive is the Kinder Climber recommended above for indoor use. Also from Child Life.

[104] *Swing parts.* Got a single tree with no reachable sturdy branches? See Child Life's fine assortment of swing mounts, hangers, and seats to suit all circumstances and ages.

[105] *Sled.* For winter mobility the Coleco Sno Jet is an ideal sled for a preschooler at an ideally low price (less than $5.00). Made of strong plastic, it is light enough for even a two year old to tug up a hill and yet big enough to seat a parent and two small children. Because of its tub-like shape the children will not easily fall out of it or run over their fingers, and being nearly flat-bottomed it glides over anything—even patches of bare grass. Coleco also makes a saucer out of the same material for coasting. From toy stores, or you might try writing Coleco Industries, Inc., Gloversville, N.Y. to find the name of the nearest dealer.

[109] *Porta-Yard.* A marginal purchase, at best, for temporary emergencies. As with play-pens the best use of this expandable pen is probably to fence children out rather than in. Fence in a charcoal grill to free your cookout from tiresome "no, no"s and the danger of burns. As a place for a toddler a pen with a gate would be nicer because it could be set up around a tree or some-thing interesting instead of only in open places. From infant supply departments or by direct mail from Childcraft.

[109] *Child-Guard Saf-T Latch* (as illustrated). From Shur-Lock Manufacturing. Inc., Hutchins, Texas.

[109] *Socket caps* (as illustrated). From hardware and houseware departments.

[118–19] *Infant hand toys.* Some good ones are: *Beaded stick rattle* (as illustrated, p. 118, bottom right). A smooth wooden shaft with inset bright-colored sliding beads. From Creative Playthings. *Fingers Full* (as illustrated, p. 118, left). Among the best bargains we saw was this package of two. The bright yellow giraffe of hard, slightly flexible plastic is a particular favorite. His long neck and legs are just right for gnawing and grabbing. Also an appealing flexible tubular ring with sliding rubber shapes. By Hasbro. From toy stores. *Five-Finger Exerciser* (as illustrated, p. 118, top right). A silly name for a mysteriously long-lasting toy. Red, orange, yellow, blue, and green

wooden balls suspended from a 5¾″ wooden bar. From Creative Playthings. *Plastic discs* or keys on a chain—just nothing, but just perfect. From many drug, dime, and toy stores. *Hedgehog*—a flexible, yellow plastic creature that is interesting to touch or chew. Usually prepackaged in twos or threes, which is silly since one is all you need. Share with someone else if you can't find a place that sells them singly. Creative Playthings, Childcraft, or toy and novelty stores.

[119] *Pole and rings* (as illustrated, p. 120, left). Playskool's #170 is good. Toy stores or by direct mail from Mead, Novo, Constructive Playthings, and Childcraft.

[120] *Stacking/nesting cups* (as illustrated, right). Playskool's #1039 is good. Toy stores.

[121] *Shape sorter.* Playskool's #506 is nice. Toy stores or by direct mail from Mead or Constructive Playthings.

[122] *Pegboard and pegs.* By direct mail from Childcraft, Constructive Playthings, DLM, Mead, and Novo. *Landscape peg set*—For two years and older a peg town is available and fun. Colored wooden blocks, balls, and cones fit over the pegs to make houses, trees, and flowers. Good for story telling. By Playskool. Toy stores and by direct mail through many of the educational toy catalogs.

[122–23] *Knobbed wooden puzzles.* About the best and most abundant in the U.S. are the Simplex puzzles imported from Holland. Look especially for the farm animal puzzle (as illustrated, p. 123) available from toy stores or by direct mail from Constructive Playthings and Childcraft). Also uniquely ideal at first is Galt's geometric-form puzzle (as illustrated, p. 122) offered in the U.S. through direct mail by ETA ("Geometric Shape Inset Board").

[123] *First Picture Puzzles.* As usual Childcraft has an excellent assortment. See especially the puzzles from Abbat of England, Didago of Belgium. Also excellent are Playskool's fish (#135–2), butterfly (#135–5), and frog (#135–6) puzzles. From toy stores or by direct mail from Childcraft, Mead, and Constructive Playthings.

[124–25] *Parquetry* (as illustrated, p. 125, top left). Probably the nicest sets of parquetry are those from DLM with which it is also possible to purchase various sets of colored design cards for the older preschooler to follow. These cards augment considerably the value and length of early use of the tiles. (DLM's tiles appear to be identical to those from Milton Bradley, which are generally available, but the design cards seem to be an exclusive offering of DLM).

[125] *Math materials.* The colored wooden Cuisenaire rods (as illustrated, bottom right), imported from France, are perfectly lovely materials that look, feel, and when hit together even sound nice. On the preschool level, we found that the rods and sorting tray themselves were inspiring enough, and that the teaching materials (cards, book, and record) were rather expensive for the use we got from them. In the long run, perhaps the whole kit ($17.95) is worthwhile, but we were glad to learn that the rods and tray could be purchased separately ($7.95 for this "Supplementary Kit"). From Learning Games, Inc.

[128] *Colored Inch Cubes.* By Milton Bradley. By direct mail from Novo, Mead, Childcraft, and ETA, or from DLM, where you can purchase companion sets of design cards as well.

[128] *Wooden block sets.* Two ideal sets for the preschooler's home are the Intermediate Set from Childcraft, and the Five-Year-Old Set from Community Playthings. Large cylinders and arches can be bought individually as extra gifts.

[129–30] *Non-block construction sets.* Some good or promising ones are:

Peg and hole block set. Blocks with built-in pegs and holes. We haven't seen it, but it might be wonderful for children about one year old. The only potential problem we can see is humidity, which could make the pieces fit too tightly or loosely. From Vermont Wooden Toys.

Giant Tinker Toys—large scale, bright-colored plastic version of the old standby wooden ones. Costly, but remarkably inspiring for young preschoolers from about two years and up who will build spectacular free constructions with them if left alone. Most mileage is to be had from this set if it is introduced early enough. A wonderful "major" present for a preschooler. From toy stores or by direct mail from a number of the educational toy catalogs.

Make-A-Toy. Playskool #803. Refreshingly few pieces from which a surprising variety of cheerful-looking wheeled things can be made. There are Make-A-Toy sets with more pieces, but, at least on the preschool level, this small set is plenty.

Build-O-Fun. Sets of plastic panels and corner posts for building houses and free constructs. From Tupperware.

Crystal Climbers (left-hand illustration, p. 130). Rigid plastic squares, rounds, rectangles, and cylinders interlock to form fascinating and colorful constructs. The shapes are most effective when used in combination with each other, so either buy one set of each kind or a mixed set. From toy stores or by direct mail from Constructive Playthings you can buy a 62-piece mixed set for $6.00.

Free-form posts (middle illustration, p. 130). One of the best non-block sets around for very young children. The 8″ blue and yellow pieces fit together easily, stay together well, and yet can be pulled apart easily. The structures are quickly rewarding and easy to stabilize, and best of all they can be carried about without immediately falling to pieces. By Pressman. From toys stores.

Multi-Fit (right-hand illustration, p. 130). So far the easiest set for real "thing" construction. Bespindled flexible, plastic pieces stick firmly when pressed together. Parts include real turning wheels, beams, windows, triangles, squares, rectangles, and circles of red, blue, yellow and green. Has the widest age range of any set. One year olds can stick pieces together; three year olds can build vehicles that really roll; grade schoolers can do quite sophisticated, precise building. Multi-Fit is disappointingly expensive, but it may be cheaper if you order individual assortments of pieces directly from Hasbro. Write Hasbro Multi-Fit, P.O. Box 90, Longueuil, Quebec, Canada, for an order form. Or order whole sets from Childcraft.

[131] *Pounding Bench.* Playskool's #125 was the best one we saw. It can be adjusted to make the pegs loose enough for the just-learned-to-sit child to move back and forth by hand, or tight enough to require a skillful hammer blow. Toy stores or by mail from Childcraft, Novo, or Constructive Playthings.

[131] *Workhorse.* The advantage of this modified sawhorse as a workbench for a preschooler is its compactness and reasonable price. From Community Playthings.

[132] *Bags of wood.* Good for: shapes for a homemade sorting box, parts for a cribmobile, stringing as a toddler activity, gluing into constructs, decorative touches for block buildings, shapes for a baby to play with. Some sources for

these wood parts are: Weston Bowl Mill, Vermont 05161 (25¢ for a 40-page catalog); Blotner Woodcraft, Lawrence, Mass; or Novo.

[132] *Vise* (as illustrated). A woodworking vise (don't confuse this with the jaw-type machinist's vise) may be purchased along with some workbenches from good hardware stores, Childcraft, or Community Playthings.

[135] *Wooden boats that float.* See, e.g., the Lake Steamer from Vermont Wooden Toys or the Tug from Montgomery Schoolhouse.

[137] *Busy Bath.* Among the "busy" contraption toys this one is quite entertaining and educational. Its main feature is a pump. Pumped water spouts out of a fish's mouth to power either a water wheel or a merry-go-round. Provides good demonstrations of water power. By Kohner. From toy stores.

Pump bucket (as illustrated, p. 137). A plastic pail with a hand pump that really works. Not very sturdy but worth every one of the less than two hundred pennies it costs. Found seasonally in toy and drug stores.

Water Wheels. Several kinds of plastic water wheel machines exist to delight children. Water poured into the top makes numerous wheels spin or see-saw parts flip back and forth. Also not very sturdy, but also less than $2.00 and worth it. Also found seasonally in toy stores.

Tonka snorkel truck. A fancy fire engine. Its real fire hydrant with adjustable pressure attaches to a regular garden hose. Water flows through the truck's own smaller hose to the top of an extendible cherry picker affair. It can shoot a stream more than 10 ft. (greater pressure sometimes causes the hose to pop free). For extra enjoyment set it up a few feet away from a small splash pool and add a sponge, strainer, cups, coffee pot, etc. Toy stores.

Vinyl fish. Not a water machine, but not to be overlooked either, these bright-colored vinyl fish adhere when wet to tub and tiles. Children enjoy sticking them on and peeling them off. They make pretty designs and can be fit together to form larger fish. From Creative Playthings.

[151] *Music Box.* Creative Playthings offers an especially nice and reasonably priced hand-operated version of a music box. It is a see-through music box of wood, metal and plastic that plays a pretty bar from Swan Lake. A good present for the parents of a new baby or for a newborn to "give" to an older sibling as an ice breaker. The tone can be surprisingly amplified by holding the wooden case against a wooden chest or table.

[151] *Records.* Write to Folkway Records, 701 Seventh Avenue, N.Y. 10026, for a listing of their fine children's records.

[151] *Rhythm Instruments.* The greatest variety at reasonable prices can be found at Rhythm Band, Inc., Fort Worth, Texas 76101. Write for a free catalog. DLM has a nice smaller selection and you can buy sets or individual instruments from Mead, Novo, Constructive Playthings, or Childcraft.

[152] *Xylophone.* You can look a long time for a straightforward xylophone that doesn't play by itself (thus defeating the purpose), double as a pull toy, come apart, or sound awful. Simple, clear-toned eight-note xylophones with colored bells on a wooden base are available from DLM, Rhythm Band, Inc., Novo, and Constructive Playthings.

[159] *Lucite frames.* Many similar kinds at a variety of prices. From art supply, framing, and variety stores.

Bracket-type wall mounts. E.g., braquettes. From art and picture-framing stores.

Sectional frames. From variety and art supply stores.

[160] *Chubbi Stump crayons.* From Childcraft, DLM, and ETA.

[161] *Felt-tip pens.* Any will do, fine line and stubby, but a particularly nice set of lovely, long-lasting markers is available from Creative Playthings.

[162] *Paint pan* (as illustrated). A very useful type of paint pan. From almost any art store.

[162] *Free-standing easel.* All educational supply catalogs have a variety of easels, but among the best is the Double Adjustable Chalkboard Easel for two. Plastic paint trays are easily removed for washing. From Childcraft.

Wall easel. Better suited to the space and budget requirements of many homes. Good ones are available from both Community Playthings and Childcraft.

[163] *Clay.* For the child who is beginning to really model shapes a small Caran D'Ache set is an ideal gift. Included are 3 tools and 10 small blocks of non-hardening "Modelling Material" in beautiful colors, all in a permanent storage tray. The clay is just enough stiffer than dough to hold its shape, but soft enough to be modeled by a young child. It is not a bad idea to reserve this

costly set for special, careful modeling times as the colors are especially nice. Play dough is still best for just mushing together. From art supply and toy stores.

[164] *Brayer* (as illustrated, p. 165). A 4″ rubber brayer (roller) is about right. Art supply stores.

[164] *Stamp pad kit.* 24 plastic cube stamps with felt shapes and 4 colored ink pads. Children love stamping and this set offers endless possibilities. Encourage the children (three years and up) to stamp each stamp clean on an extra piece of paper before switching to another color. From Childcraft.

[167] *Lefty scissors.* From Childcraft, Mead, Constructive Playthings.

[168] *Bag of wood.* See note above for page 132.

[168] *Etch-a-Sketch.* By turning the two knobs at the sides of a box-like frame the child can make a fine line appear and grow in any direction on the plastic window. Shake the box and the picture disappears. By Ohio Art. Generally available in toy stores.

Colorforms. There exist many sets and kits of these colorful vinyl shapes that adhere and readhere to smooth surfaces. Nicest and least adulterated is the one offered by Creative Playthings. A perfect gift for the beginning of a long car trip. (see p. 96).

[233] *Child-size garden tools.* Sturdy ones. Hoe, spade, and garden rake. Metal with hardwood handles. From Creative Playthings.

Plastic garden tools. Cheap ones. Available seasonally in toy stores.

[247] *Magnets.* An enormous assortment of magnets is available through the Edmund catalog. And any older preschooler would love a set of Magniks—6 strong magnets (2 rings, 4 cylindrical rods) that attract and repel each other. Fascinating. And remember those little magnetized black and white Scottie dogs that jumped together when moved close to each other? Rumor has it that they are still available in some parts of the country.

[248] *Standing magnifying lens.* Large magnifiers on legs are available through most educational toy catalogs. Edmund has an extensive selection of lenses of all types as well as a great variety of prisms.

[250] *Play Doh Fun Factory.* Generally available.

[250] *Balloons.* There's nothing like a bagful of balloons for a rainy afternoon, and nothing so nice as a little cardboard hand pump for inflating them. They do exist and are very useful if you can find them. The Edmund catalog offers small balloons by the gross and wonderful 8 ft. (fragile) and 3 ft. (sturdier) balloons as well as small cans of helium. Consult *balloons* in the classified pages of your telephone directory. For super-big birthday parties it is sometimes possible to rent larger tanks of helium (that have to be returned).

[259] *Push broom.* From Childcraft.

[259] *Carpet sweeper.* "Little Helper"—a child-size sweeper by Bissell. From toy stores or by mail from Childcraft.

[259] *Aluminum luncheon, pot and pan, and baking sets.* The advantage of the more expensive ones is that they are heavy enough to do real cooking in as the child gets older, and they will last at least until the grandchildren. Available for around $10.00 per set from Creative Playthings and by mail from Mead, ETA, Novo, Childcraft, and Constructive Playthings.

[260] *Miniature toy animals.* Britain's model animals are by far the best and most diverse available. They can be bought individually from selected toy stores across the country or in sets by mail from Reiss Brothers, 54 East 59th St., New York, N.Y. 10022. Reiss will mail you Britain's and other miniature brochures upon specific written request.

Book Title Index

Index